# Contents

# access to history

# The Early Stuarts and the English Revolution

## 1603–60

KATHERINE BRICE AND MICHAEL LYNCH

SECOND EDITION

**HODDER**
EDUCATION
AN HACHETTE UK COMPANY

The Publishers would like to thank the following for permission to reproduce copyright material.

**Photo credits: p3** AF Fotografie/Alamy Stock Photo; **p13** Library of Congress LC-USZ62-104640; **p20** Courtesy National Gallery of Art, Washington; **p43** Wellcome Library, London (Creative Commons Attribution only licence CC BY 4.0 http://creativecommons.org/licenses/by/4.0/); **p54** incamerastock/Alamy Stock Photo; **pp80, 87** Wellcome Library, London (Creative Commons Attribution only licence CC BY 4.0 http://creativecommons.org/licenses/by/4.0/detail); **p89** Trustees of the British Museum; **p94** Classic Image/Alamy Stock Photo; **p117** Wellcome Library, London (Creative Commons Attribution only licence CC BY 4.0 http://creativecommons.org/licenses/by/4.0/detail; **p135** Heritage Image Partnership Ltd/Alamy Stock Photo; **p139** Wikimedia Commons; **p142** Hathi Trust/University of Missouri-Columbia; **p155** Bridgeman Images; **p178** Album/Alamy Stock Photo; **p193** Courtesy of the Cromwell Museum, Huntingdon; **p208** Flickr Commons.

**Acknowledgements:** Arnold, *Cromwell* by J.C. Davis, 2001. Blackwell, *A Companion to Stuart Britain* by Barry Coward, 2003. Cambridge University Press, *Oliver Cromwell* by David L. Smith, 1992; *The Stuart Constitution* by John P. Kenyon, 1966, 1986, 1989. Chapman & Hall, *Oliver Cromwell's Letters and Speeches with Elucidations* edited by Thomas Carlyle, 1857. Clarendon Press, *Select Statutes and Other Constitutional Documents Illustrative of the Reigns of Elizabeth and James I* by G.W. Prothero, 1898. Collins & Brown, *Revolution and Restoration* by John Morrill, 1992. Fontana, *Politics and the Nation 1450–1660* by David Loades, 1986. Funk & Wagnalls, *The World's Famous Orations* edited by William Jennings Bryan, 1906. H. Colburn, *Diary of Thomas Burton Esq* edited by John Towill Rutt, 1828. Harvard University Press, *Fleeting Things: English Poets and Poems 1616–1660* by Gerald Hammond, 1990; *The Writings and Speeches of Oliver Cromwell* edited by W.C. Abbott, 1937–47. Head of Zeus, *Providence Lost: The Rise and Fall of Cromwell's Protectorate* by Paul Lay, 2020. J.M. Dent, *Speeches of Oliver Cromwell* edited by Ivan Roots, 1989. John Murray, *The English Revolution*, edkited by Barry Coward, 1997. Jonathan Cape, *King James VI and I* by D.H. Willson, 1956. Little, Brown, *Civil War* by Trevor Royle, 2004. Longman, *Oliver Cromwell* by Barry Coward, 2000; *The Clarke Papers* edited by C.H. Firth, 1901; *Calendar of State Papers, Domestic Series 1659–60* edited by Mary Ann Everett Green, 1886; *Memoirs of the Life of Colonel Hutchinson* edited by Julius Hutchinson, 1808; *James VI & I* by Roger Lockyer, 1998; *The Revolt of the Provinces* edited by John Morrill, 1976. Macmillan, *The British Republic 1649–1660* by Ronald Hutton, 2000. Methuen, *England Without a King* by Austin Woolrych, 1983; *The Letters and Speeches of Oliver Cromwell* edited by S.C. Lomas, 1904. Oxford University Press, *Rebellion or Revolution?* by G.E. Aylmer, 1986; *Historical Research*, volume 68 by Pauline Croft, 1995; *The Memoirs of Edmund Ludlow* edited by S.H. Firth, 1894; *The Constitutional Documents of the Puritan Revolution 1625–1660* edited by S.R. Gardiner, 1906; *Rebellion: Britain's First Stuart Kings* by Tim Harris, 2014; *The Crisis of Parliaments* by Conrad Russell, 1971. Palgrave, *The Causes of the English Civil War* by Ann Hughes, 1998. Phoenix, *Cromwell: An Honourable Enemy* by Tom Reilly, 1999. Routledge, *The Stuart Age* by Barry Coward, 1980, 2014. Weidenfeld & Nicolson, *The Noble Revolt* by John Adamson, 2007; *The English Civil Wars 1640–1660* by Blair Worden, 2009.

Every effort has been made to trace all copyright holders, but if any have been inadvertently overlooked, the Publishers will be pleased to make the necessary arrangements at the first opportunity.

Although every effort has been made to ensure that website addresses are correct at time of going to press, Hodder Education cannot be held responsible for the content of any website mentioned in this book. It is sometimes possible to find a relocated web page by typing in the address of the home page for a website in the URL window of your browser.

Hachette UK's policy is to use papers that are natural, renewable and recyclable products and made from wood grown in well-managed forests and other controlled sources. The logging and manufacturing processes are expected to conform to the environmental regulations of the country of origin.

Orders: please contact Hachette UK Distribution, Hely Hutchinson Centre, Milton Road, Didcot, Oxfordshire, OX11 7HH. Telephone: +44(0)1235 827827. Email: education@hachette.co.uk Lines are open from 9a.m. to 5p.m., Monday to Friday. You can also order through our website: www.hoddereducation.co.uk

ISBN: 978 1 5104 5978 6

© Katherine Brice and Michael Lynch 2021

First published in 2015

This second edition published in 2021 by
Hodder Education,
An Hachette UK Company
Carmelite House
50 Victoria Embankment
London EC4Y 0DZ

www.hoddereducation.co.uk

Impression number   10  9  8  7  6  5  4  3  2  1
Year                      2025  2024  2023  2022  2021

Cover photo © Glasshouse Images/Alamy Stock Photo
Typeset by Gray Publishing, Tunbridge Wells, Kent
Printed in the UK by CPI Group Ltd

A catalogue record for this title is available from the British Library.

# Introduction: about this book

This book has been written primarily to support the study of the following courses:

- AQA 1D: Stuart Britain and the Crisis of Monarchy, 1603–1702 (AS/Part 1 content only, Paper 1)
- OCR: Unit Y108/Y138: The Early Stuarts and the Origins of the Civil War 1603–1660 (Paper 1).

The specification grid on pages vii–viii will help you understand how this book's content relates to the course that you are studying.

The writers hope that student readers will regard the book not simply as an aid to better exam results, but as a study which is enjoyable in itself as an analysis of a very important theme in history.

The following explains the different features of this book and how they will help your study of the course.

## Beginning of the book

### Context

Starting a new course can be daunting if you are not familiar with the period or topic. This section outlines what you need to know about the beginning of the period and will set up some of the key themes. Reading this section will help you get up to speed on the content of the course.

## Throughout the book

### Key terms

You need to know these to gain an understanding of the period. The appropriate use of specific historical language in your essays will also help you improve the quality of your writing. Key terms are in boldface type the first time they appear in the book. They are defined in the margin and appear in the glossary.

### Profiles

Some chapters contain profiles of important individuals. These include a brief biography and information about the importance and impact of the individual. This information can be very useful in understanding certain events and providing supporting evidence to your arguments.

### Sources

Historical sources are important in understanding why specific decisions were taken or on what contemporary writers and politicians based their actions. The questions accompanying each source will help you to understand and analyse the source.

### Key debates

The key debates between historians will help you think about historical interpretations and understand the different points of view for a given historiographical debate.

### Chapter summaries

These written summaries are intended to help you revise and consolidate your knowledge and understanding of the content.

### Summary diagrams

These visual summaries at the end of each section are useful for revision.

### Refresher questions

The refresher questions are quick knowledge checks to make sure you have understood and remembered the material that is covered in the chapter.

### Question practice

There are opportunities at the end of each chapter to practise exam-style questions, arranged by exam board so you can practise the questions relevant for your course. The exam hint below each question will help you if you get stuck.

## End of the book

### Timeline

Understanding chronology (the order in which events took place) is an essential part of history.

Knowing the order of events is one thing, but it is also important to know how events relate to each other. This timeline will help you put events into context and will be helpful for quick reference or as a revision tool.

## Exam focus

This section gives advice on how to answer questions in your exam, focusing on the different requirements of your exam paper. The guidance in this book has been based on detailed examiner reports since 2017. It models best practice in terms of answering exam questions and shows the most common pitfalls to help ensure you get the best grade possible.

## Glossary

All key terms in the book are defined in the glossary.

## Further reading

To achieve top marks in history, you will need to read beyond this textbook. This section contains a list of books and articles for you to explore. The list may also be helpful for an extended essay or piece of coursework.

# Online extras

This new edition is accompanied by online material to support you in your study. Throughout the book you will find the online extras icon to prompt you to make use of the relevant online resources for your course. By going to www.hoddereducation.co.uk/accesstohistory/extras you will find the following:

## Activity worksheets

These activities will help you develop the skills you need for the exam. The thinking that you do to complete the activities, and the notes you make from answering the questions, will prove valuable in your learning journey and helping you get the best grade possible. Your teacher may decide to print the entire series of worksheets to create an activity booklet to accompany the course. Alternatively they may be used as standalone activities for class work or homework. However, don't hesitate to go online and print off a worksheet yourself to get the most from this book.

## Who's who

A level History covers a lot of key figures so it's perfectly understandable if you find yourself confused by all the different names. This document organises the individuals mentioned throughout the book by categories so you know your Diggers from your Levellers!

## Extended research

While further reading of books and articles is helpful to achieve your best, there's a wealth of material online, including useful websites, digital archives, and documentaries on YouTube. This page lists resources that may help further your understanding of the topic. It may also prove a valuable reference for research if you decide to choose this period for the coursework element of your course.

## Dedication

### Keith Randell (1943–2002)

The *Access to History* series was conceived and developed by Keith, who created a series to 'cater for students as they are, not as we might wish them to be'. He leaves a living legacy of a series that for over 20 years has provided a trusted, stimulating and well-loved accompaniment to post-16 study. Our aim with these new editions is to continue to offer students the best possible support for their studies.

# Specification grid

| Chapter | AQA | OCR |
|---|:---:|:---:|
| **Chapter 1 Context: The kingdoms of Britain in 1603** | | |
| 1 English society in 1603 | ✓ | ✓ |
| 2 The political system in England | ✓ | |
| 3 Scotland and Ireland | ✓ | ✓ |
| 4 Implications of the accession of James I | | |
| **Chapter 2 James I: Consensus under strain 1603–25** | ✓ | ✓ |
| 1 The new king of England | ✓ | ✓ |
| 2 Problems with the financial system in the early seventeenth century | ✓ | ✓ |
| 3 Religion | ✓ | ✓ |
| 4 Foreign policy | ✓ | ✓ |
| 5 Relations with Parliament | ✓ | ✓ |
| 6 Key debate: Wise or foolish: which is the more accurate description of James I? | ✓ | ✓ |
| **Chapter 3 The reign of Charles I: 1625–38** | ✓ | ✓ |
| 1 Charles became king | ✓ | ✓ |
| 2 Foreign policy in the 1620s | ✓ | ✓ |
| 3 The rise of Arminianism 1625–30 | ✓ | ✓ |
| 4 Relations with Parliament 1625–9 | ✓ | ✓ |
| 5 The Personal Rule 1629–40: economic policy | ✓ | ✓ |
| 6 The Personal Rule 1629–40: religious policy | ✓ | ✓ |
| **Chapter 4 The collapse of the Personal Rule and the approach of civil war 1638–42** | ✓ | ✓ |
| 1 The end of Personal Rule | ✓ | ✓ |
| 2 Attacks on Charles's government | ✓ | ✓ |
| 3 The emergence of a royalist party | ✓ | ✓ |
| 4 The move towards civil war | ✓ | ✓ |
| 5 Key debate: How have historians interpreted the causes of the English civil war? | ✓ | |
| **Chapter 5 The civil wars and their aftermath 1642–9** | ✓ | ✓ |
| 1 The first civil war 1642–6 | ✓ | ✓ |
| 2 Analysing the first civil war | ✓ | ✓ |
| 3 The failure to reach a settlement 1646–9 | ✓ | ✓ |
| 4 The trial and execution of the king 1649 | ✓ | ✓ |
| 5 The growth of political radicalism: the Levellers | ✓ | ✓ |
| **Chapter 6 The Commonwealth 1649–53: an experiment in republicanism** | | ✓ |
| 1 The Rump and the establishment of the Commonwealth | | ✓ |
| 2 The radical sects | | ✓ |
| 3 The third civil war 1649–52: Cromwell in Ireland and Scotland | | ✓ |
| 4 The achievements of the Rump | | ✓ |
| 5 The dissolution of the Rump, April 1653 | | ✓ |
| 6 Key debate: How repressive was Cromwell's military policy in Ireland? | | ✓ |

| Chapter | AQA | OCR |
|---|---|---|
| **Chapter 7 The search for a settlement 1653–8** | | ✓ |
| 1 The Nominated Assembly 1653 | | ✓ |
| 2 The early Protectorate 1654–5 | | ✓ |
| 3 Cromwell and the sects | | ✓ |
| 4 Royalist resistance 1652–9 | | ✓ |
| 5 The Major-Generals 1655–7 | | ✓ |
| 6 The later Protectorate 1656–8 | | ✓ |
| **Chapter 8 From Protectorate to Restoration 1658–60** | | ✓ |
| 1 Richard Cromwell's Protectorate, September 1658 to April 1659 | | ✓ |
| 2 The restored Commonwealth, May to December 1659 | | ✓ |
| 3 The path to the Restoration, December 1659 to May 1660 | | ✓ |
| 4 Reasons for the failure of the republic by 1660 | | ✓ |
| 5 Key debate: What was the legacy of the English Revolution of 1640–60? | ✓ | |

# CHAPTER 1

# Context: The kingdoms of Britain in 1603

The death of Elizabeth I in 1603 brought the Tudor dynasty to an end and the ruler of a foreign country (albeit one with close ties to England) became king. This was to cause difficulties for James I. An established and successful king in Scotland, his transition to England (which looked similar but had very different traditions) was to be less straightforward than he hoped or expected. This chapter looks at the situation in Britain under the following headings:

◆ English society in 1603

◆ The political system in England

◆ Scotland and Ireland

◆ Implications of the accession of James I

## 1 English society in 1603

■ *How was order maintained in seventeenth-century England?*

On a chilly morning in January 1649, Charles I, the anointed king of England, Wales, Ireland and Scotland, and God's representative on earth, was executed at Whitehall in London. Kings had been deposed, murdered, forced to abdicate or killed in battle but never before or since has a British monarch been tried in court and condemned to death. This event, the civil war which preceded it for seven bitter years, and the attempts to forge a new political system after it, have preoccupied historians from that time onwards. This book looks at the 57 years from the accession of James I in 1603, which began the **Stuart Age**, up to the restoration of his grandson, Charles II, in 1660. This chapter begins with an exploration of the England that James I now ruled in 1603.

### England in 1603

James had high expectations of his new territories: he described himself as being 'like a poor man wandering about 40 years in a wilderness and barren soil, and now arrived at the land of promise'. However, England was not quite as rich as James believed. Its population approximately doubled between 1500 and 1650, to about 5 million (probably because plague was no longer as deadly as it had been), but agricultural production and industry were not able to increase at the same rate. This led to **inflation**, unemployment, and, for the first time in England, a large subclass which neither rented nor owned land. These people existed on the margins of society, scraping a living from whatever occasional

> **KEY TERMS**
>
> **Stuart Age** The period 1603–49 and 1660–1714 when the Stuart monarchs were on the throne.
>
> **Inflation** A sustained price increase with a fall in the value of money.

work could be found. In times of harvest failure, this group was especially vulnerable and, in the 1620s, there were deaths from famine. This background of increased pressure on resources should be borne in mind when looking at the tax demands made by the early Stuart kings.

As the poor were getting poorer, the rich were getting richer. The increased population meant that landlords could charge higher rents. For example, the rents of the manor at Stoneleigh in Warwickshire increased from £418 in 1599 to £1440 in 1640. Landowners could also benefit from the higher market price their products would command. With the rich gaining at the expense of the poor and with no police force or army to enforce order, what kept society from falling apart?

## Currency conversion

Until 1971, sterling was divided into pounds, shillings and pence, also referred to as £, *s.* and *d.* There were twelve pennies (*d.*) in a shilling and twenty shillings (*s.*) in a pound.

Converting amounts from the past into their equivalents today is a very imprecise art as we are much richer now. An easy calculation which splits the difference is to multiply seventeenth-century amounts by 1000 to get an approximate idea of cost and value.

## KEY TERMS

**Gentry** The class of landowners ranking just below the nobility.

**Justices of the peace (JPs)** Unpaid members of the gentry who enforced government decisions and acted as judges to lesser crimes.

**Tithe** One-tenth of a farmer's produce which was due to the Church to pay the priest and so he could give assistance to people in need. The produce was stored in a tithe barn.

## Justices of the peace

Government directives were enforced by members of the **gentry** called **justices of the peace (JPs)**. In turn, they relied on a network of local officials to act as, for example, parish constables and overseers of the poor. As these positions were held usually only for a year or two, many men had a role in governing their own communities and this acted as a break on how far central government could impose unpopular policies. Rioting was the means by which common people drew attention to a grievance, such as food needing to be available and at a reasonable cost in times of scarcity. It was their only means of attracting attention and it usually followed a specific pattern. The rioters rarely attacked people and a specific target was usually the focus of attack, such as a **tithe** barn in times of scarcity, or enclosure fences when unemployment was high. The authorities recognised that rioters were not rebels and they were seldom severely punished – fining or whipping were the most common sanctions – but more importantly, the government, if it was wise, would listen to the rioters and take action to satisfy their legitimate grievances. The only food rioters to be executed under the Stuarts were three men and a woman who were hanged at the start of the Personal Rule in 1629 at a time when the government did seem to have lost touch with the mood of the country.

## The 'Great Chain of Being'

English society was seen as a single unit with interdependent parts and this encouraged a sense of order and authority. For example, the king was the head on the body of the country, or the **commonwealth** was described as a tree.

**KEY TERM**

**Commonwealth** Often used to describe England and its people. It links back to the idea of the 'common weal' or public good.

SOURCE A

The Great Chain of Being. A late fifteenth-century illustration showing animals and plants at the bottom, topped by God and the angels. The people in the middle represent the various social classes.

**SOURCE QUESTION**

What does Source A suggest about social mobility?

There was a 'Great Chain of Being' stretching from God to the lowest forms of non-human life in which each creature had its appointed place.

Just as each person's place in society was divinely ordained, so each had duties which it was his or her responsibility to God and his or her neighbour to discharge. Thus, the nobility and gentry could expect service from their tenants but they were expected in return to provide protection, employment and sometimes promotion. The upper classes in their turn were in a position of dependence on the monarch. The whole of society was linked in a series of relationships and the role of the king was compared to that of the father in a family. As a contemporary (Sir Robert Filmer) put it: 'As the father over one family, so the King as father over many families, extends his care to preserve, feed, clothe, instruct and defend the whole commonwealth.'

The most dangerous person was the 'masterless man', one who was not bound into the system of allegiance and service. For this reason, vagrants, or those with no settled home, were regarded with great suspicion and were often savagely punished for no apparent crime other than their poverty. In the seventeenth century, the existence of such people seemed to strike at the very foundations of order and threaten the social structure.

However, it must not be forgotten that the 'Great Chain of Being' was an abstract ideal rather than an accurate description of reality. Society was not, in fact, static: it was possible to move up, or down, and people did not always honour their obligations. In particular, life in the towns did not necessarily conform to the ideal. It was possible for an enterprising and hard-working young man (and it was always men) to raise himself by some astute trading: buying cheap and selling at a profit. Trading was the way to make wealth. Agriculture did not yet produce the surpluses for there to be a mass market for new products. Instead, men could get rich through investing in new cloths to replace the heavy **broadcloth** which was going out of fashion. This was also the period when English merchants sought to extend their reach overseas with a series of new trading companies. The Levant and Barbary companies were established in the 1580s to trade in the Mediterranean and in 1600 the English East India Company was founded. These had varying fortunes in their early years but they do illustrate how some men became rich by becoming merchants.

The urban wealth of the country was overwhelmingly concentrated in London, which grew in population from 200,000 in 1600 to 400,000 in 1650 to become the largest city in Europe. London was the centre of the country's trade and there were many rich merchants who built fine houses in the area to the west of the city walls. These men often had ready money at their disposal and they were an important source of finance when the king needed a loan (see page 75).

**KEY TERM**

**Broadcloth** A type of heavy, dense cloth which was shrunk after weaving to make it thicker.

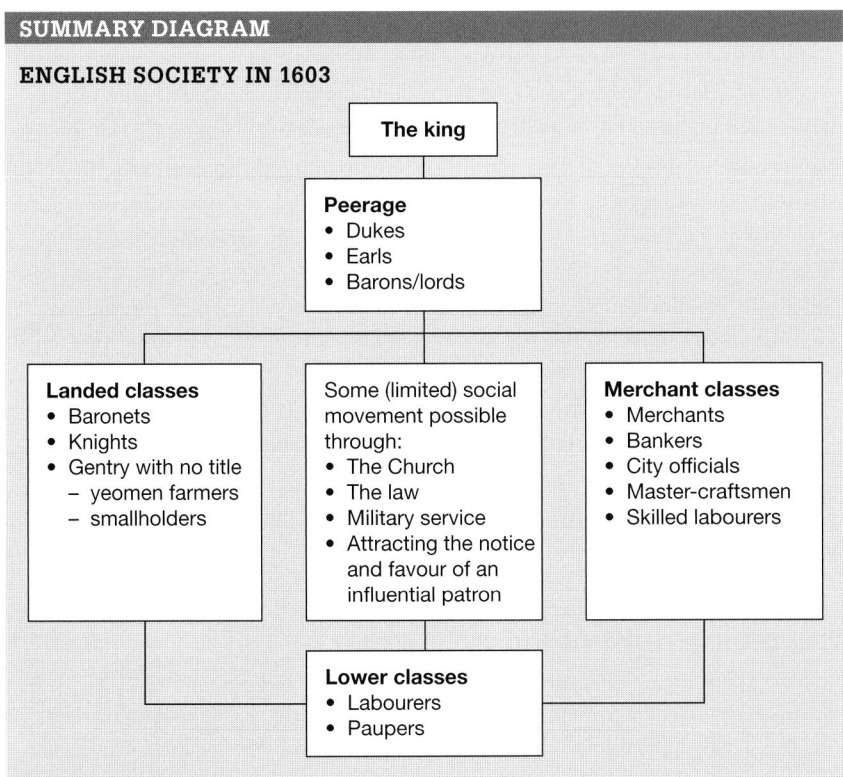

**SUMMARY DIAGRAM**

**ENGLISH SOCIETY IN 1603**

# 2 The political system in England

■ *How did the key parts of the political system operate?*

The political system in England in 1600 was still heavily dependent on the monarchs: their personality and the court that they created around them. Increasingly, however, Parliament was coming to play an indispensable role and one that would increase in significance as the Crown's wealth diminished.

## The king of England

The king was the undisputed head of the political system (this applied to reigning queens as well). He determined policy and controlled the distribution of offices (government posts) and gifts such as money or land. By long custom there were things which the king could do under the **royal prerogative**, while other matters required the consent of Parliament or of the judges. Since the establishment of a **Protestant** Church of England, the sovereign had been head of the Church and had the power to alter radically religious practice if he or she

**KEY TERMS**

**Royal prerogative**
The king's power to act on his own authority without reference to others. It included control of foreign policy, war and peace, the regulation of overseas trade and of the coinage, and the pardoning of criminals.

**Protestant**
The Churches that had broken away from the Catholic Church in the sixteenth century.

## KEY TERMS

**Common law**
Law established by long custom through the decisions of courts.

**Statute** A law passed by Parliament.

**Proclamation** A public statement of the king's wishes, which had less force than a statute.

**Crown** Used throughout the book as another term for monarch.

**Privy councillors**
Members of the Privy Council who were both advisers and administrators.

**Gentlemen of the chamber**
(Or bedchamber), the personal attendants on the king who performed apparently menial tasks, such as helping the king to dress, yet had great influence.

so chose. The highest form of law was enforceable in the **common law** courts. To change these laws required a **statute**. The king could issue **proclamations** which were intended to remedy defects in statutes, but only the king-in-parliament (when the king used Parliament to achieve his objectives) could pass statute law.

The theoretical powers of the king did not create much dispute, although when it came to applying them, there were often grey areas when **Crown** and Parliament could each make a reasonable case for their own viewpoint. In these circumstances, conflicting theories developed to justify each position. The divine right of kings was the name given to the theory which promoted the king's power (see the box below), while those who wished to limit royal actions put their faith in 'the ancient constitution'. They argued that the common law had been established over the centuries and so it could not be changed by an individual even if he was the king. They also believed that the king's prerogative should not be used to undermine the liberty of the subject. These two contrasting views of the way the king should act caused increasing conflict before the civil war.

## The divine right of kings

This was the principle that monarchs derived their power from God and were accountable only to Him. Representative institutions, such as Parliament, existed only at the king's pleasure. As the king alone possessed political power, he alone was the lawmaker. There was no safeguard against a tyrannical ruler, only the belief that God would punish him.

## The court

The court was the centre of power and the hub of the political system, although it was not a specific place. It revolved around the king and the great officers of state who attended him. The king was expected to listen to the advice of his **privy councillors**, although he was not bound to act on it. In an age of personal rule, access to the king was all-important: if one had the king's ear things would get done.

The court was divided into the public outer chambers, and the privy (private) lodgings which were starting to be known as the bedchamber (see Figure 1.1, page 7). This was where the king enjoyed some privacy and to which access was strictly controlled:

- The Privy Council was the formal organ of advice and administration, although this was sometimes bypassed.
- The **gentlemen of the chamber** consisted of those personal attendants whom the king appointed to wait on him.

The gentlemen of the chamber passed freely into the inner world of the private lodgings and accompanied the king on his frequent trips out of London. This meant that they saw considerably more of the monarch than ordinary courtiers.

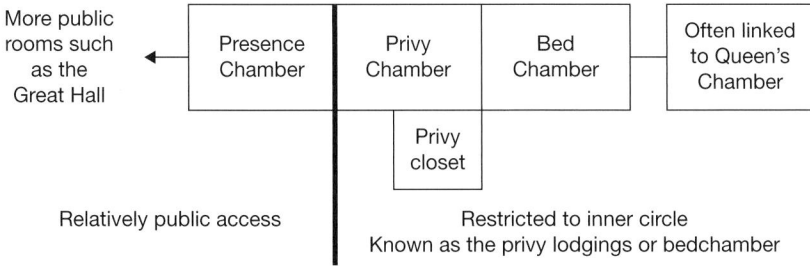

**Figure 1.1** Typical arrangement of the privy lodgings in royal palaces.

The gentlemen of the chamber had no formal role in the government but their proximity to the king meant that inevitably he was aware of their concerns and needs, and those of their clients.

An example of this was Lord Hay, who was showered with gifts, pensions and land by James, good fortune which was entirely owing to his position in the bedchamber. James created resentment because appointments to his bedchamber were primarily given to Scotsmen. The first appointment of an Englishman was not until 1615. This meant that the English felt excluded from real power and patronage even though they held all the major offices of state.

It was at court that the major issues were debated and where holders of opposing views sought to win the king's support. In these struggles, each side would try to use its connections to gain advantage. Marriage was an important tool used to create a network of links with powerful families. It was also used to neutralise an opponent or seal a friendship. Few people married for love; marriages were arranged or were 'marriages of convenience'.

## Patronage

Patronage was an important part of the political system and could lead to the growth of factions. A young man who was anxious to succeed in life needed to acquire a patron, whom he supported and served in whatever way was required. He might also make financial gifts to his patron; in return, the patron advanced his client's interests and looked for a favourable position for him. (Women did not have the same opportunities and the only way for them to advance significantly was through one, or preferably several, shrewd marriages.)

It was a mark of political power to have a large number of clients, as this gave a man considerable influence. It also attracted men who were eager for office or favours. The patronage system was never static. It was necessary for an ambitious noble to always strive to improve his position. In the 1620s, the Duke of Buckingham (see page 43) monopolised the lion's share of the available patronage and was overwhelmed with requests for help from would-be clients, yet even he believed it was worth his while to win over the Earl of Pembroke, head of an opposing faction, by arranging a marriage alliance between the two families.

# Parliament

Parliament was the meeting place of the king and his representatives in the localities. Here, policies were explained and approval was sought; serious disquiet was expressed if necessary and policies were modified. In Parliament, members were always extremely polite when they addressed or talked about the king. This initially misled James I into thinking that Parliament would defer to him unconditionally. He was used to the plain-speaking Scottish Parliament, where members spoke their minds although their power was limited. The English Parliament might be polite but it was also outspoken when the situation demanded it. English Members of Parliament (MPs) knew their rights and did not let any challenge to their liberties pass unnoticed. Inflation was increasing the number of **forty-shilling freeholders** who elected the House of Commons. It has been estimated that by 1640 as many as 40 per cent of the adult male population had the right to vote.

James I had conflicts with his Parliaments from the start. It is, therefore, easy to see the king and Parliament as opponents, each seeking to undermine the other and win a tactical advantage. Nothing could be further from the truth. The traditional view was that the king was at his most powerful when Parliament was in session because the king-in-parliament could enact statute laws and obtain additional taxes (or **subsidies**) from his subjects. Parliament had no independent right of assembly. One of the monarch's most powerful weapons was his ability to dismiss Parliament at will.

In previous centuries, MPs had won the right to freedom of speech, which was intended to provide the sovereign with good advice unhindered by fear of reprisals. If the king chose to ignore their advice as he had the right to do, Parliament could register a protest by refusing to grant subsidies. Increasingly, this was a course MPs chose to take. The long years of war (1588–1604) at the end of Elizabeth's reign and the consequent heavy financial demands made on the country through Parliament had produced the conditions in which Crown decisions were questioned. Frequent requests for money meant MPs expected their views to be considered by the monarch.

The king's ordinary revenue was intended to be sufficient for his usual needs, with Parliament granting extraordinary taxation (known as **supply**) in times of emergency. As inflation reduced the Crown's real income, this control over extraordinary supply gave Parliament a valuable bargaining point which began to affect the balance of power between it and the king. Harmony remained the ideal to which everyone paid lip service, but as it became increasingly difficult to reconcile the wishes of both sides, Parliament was ready to exploit its new position.

## The role of Parliament

Parliament was a national institution that spent much of its time dealing with local grievances. When enough of these grievances coalesced, the sovereign and his advisers took note, if they were wise, and sought to deal with the problem.

**KEY TERMS**

**Forty-shilling freeholders** The right to vote in the counties was based on owning land worth forty shillings (£2) a year.

**Subsidy** The main form of taxation, based on a fixed system of assessments. Over time, the value of the subsidy decreased.

**Supply** Taxation granted on an occasional basis to supply the monarch's needs.

National and local concerns overlapped. The MPs who passed laws and voted for subsidies were often the same men who had the responsibility of enforcing or collecting them, since many MPs also acted as JPs (see page 2).

Parliaments were an important part of government but they met irregularly and the timing and length of sessions were entirely at the king's discretion. Members did not expect to be summoned for more than a few months at a time; the ideal was to hear the king's needs, respond in an appropriate way with counsel, and financial supply if necessary, express the concerns of their constituencies, and then return to their localities. Some Parliaments passed no legislation and most laws were about relatively minor matters. The two main functions of Parliament were expressed by Lord Chancellor Bacon in 1621: 'the one for the supplying of your estates; the other for the better knitting of the hearts of your subjects unto your Majesty'. In an age which did not have newspapers, the importance of Parliament as propaganda should not be underestimated. It was a useful forum for informing the country about the direction of royal policy and explaining unpopular policies.

## The structure of Parliament

Parliament was made up of the House of Commons and the House of Lords (see Table 1.1, below).

**Table 1.1** The English Parliament

| House of Commons | House of Lords |
|---|---|
| Members of the Commons were elected by 40s. freeholders (those who owned land worth at least 40s.) in the counties, and by a more varied system in towns. The majority of elections were not contested. | The Lords were made up of peers of the realm and also bishops. They were not elected and took their seats because of their position in society. |
| Most MPs came from the ranks of the wealthy gentry and they would often agree amongst themselves who should stand for Parliament. This meant that the electorate had merely to confirm the candidate who had come forward. | |
| The Commons were responsible for voting subsidies but in other respects they were far less important than the House of Lords. | The Lords were the most important part of Parliament in 1600 but this was to change over the Stuart period. |

Most of the king's advisers were members of either the Commons or the Lords and they would explain the Crown's position and outline its needs. Parliament was not part of the government. There was no equivalent of the modern prime minister and cabinet: their functions were exercised by the king and his ministers. Nor were there any political parties in the House of Commons, not even in the sense of a 'king's party' and an 'opposition'. MPs might oppose some strands of government policy but they were likely to agree with other aspects of policy. Few MPs maintained a consistent role in opposition. As a result, groupings in the Commons were fluid, as members agreed on some issues then diverged on others. Some MPs sought to use their opposition to force the king to take notice of them and bring them into government. Sir Thomas Wentworth, who became one of Charles I's chief ministers, had been an outspoken parliamentary critic in the 1620s.

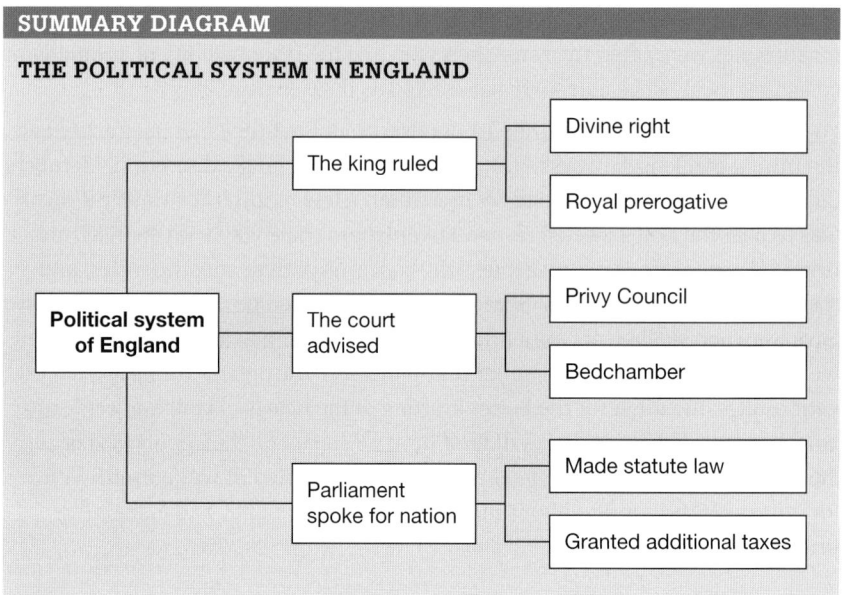

**SUMMARY DIAGRAM**

**THE POLITICAL SYSTEM IN ENGLAND**

- Political system of England
  - The king ruled
    - Divine right
    - Royal prerogative
  - The court advised
    - Privy Council
    - Bedchamber
  - Parliament spoke for nation
    - Made statute law
    - Granted additional taxes

# 3 Scotland and Ireland

■ *How did the political system in Scotland and Ireland differ from the system in England?*

## KEY TERMS

**Early modern age**
The period between the medieval and modern ages, approximately 1485–1789.

**Kirk** The Scottish Church.

**Presbyterianism**
A system of Church government without bishops, which gave considerable responsibility to individual congregations who chose their own ministers and elders. It was a strict form of Protestantism which placed great emphasis on the Bible and less on tradition.

In the **early modern age**, monarchy was still personal and proximity to the king carried the possibility of advancement (see pages 6–7). James, by becoming the ruler of three kingdoms, created tensions. Monarchs tended to prefer the richer and more powerful part of their territories but this could leave the outer kingdoms feeling ignored. The situation in Britain was compounded by the fact that Ireland was a separate island.

## Scotland

James, as the ruler of England, was a force to be reckoned with on the European stage and could make a plausible claim to being the leader of the European Protestants. By contrast, Scotland was relatively poor, weak and backward. Scotland's population was twenty per cent of England's but it provided the king with less than five per cent of his revenue. The nobility and **Kirk** wielded much of the effective power and a strict **Presbyterianism** had been introduced against royal wishes.

Having survived a number of plots against him, James spent much of his adult life undermining the position of the Scottish nobility and manipulating factions to his advantage. By the time he left Scotland, he had redressed the balance of power and successfully subdued the nobility. He recognised the strength of the Kirk and had been careful not to alienate it. In comparison to England, the

Scottish government was underdeveloped. There were weaker links between the centre and the localities, and there was less taxation because the government played a smaller part in people's lives. The king was entitled to sit and vote in Parliament, which had a long tradition of advising and criticising the king. Religious matters were dealt with by the General Assembly, which provided a meeting place where decisions could be taken at a national level. James took great care to manage the debates of the General Assembly by appearing in person so that decisions did not go against his interests.

One of James's most cherished projects was a union between England and Scotland, but the English were unwilling to admit the Scots as citizens of England just because they shared the same ruler. 'The air might be wholesome but for the stinking people that inhabit it' (Sir Anthony Weldon) was a typical English comment on the Scots. (Weldon was a courtier who lost his job because he was abusive towards the Scots. He became very embittered and took his revenge after James's death, see page 19.) Scotland remained an independent state with its own Parliament, religion, legal system and local government.

From 1603, Scotland had to endure an absentee monarch with all that implied for reduced favour and positions and unresolved grievances. It is a tribute to James's reign that Scotland was to cause no trouble in his lifetime. Unfortunately, his son, the future king Charles I, did not display the same tact and sensitivity (see pages 80–1) and, in 1638, Scotland was the first of the three kingdoms to rebel (see page 82).

## Ireland

Ireland was the most problematic of James's three kingdoms. It was not an independent kingdom as Scotland was, but was more similar to a colony, in that its government was subordinate to the English one and had to conform to English demands, at least in theory:

- The Dublin administration was headed by a **Lord Lieutenant** or Lord Deputy, the Irish Parliament had to implement the laws made in England and the English Privy Council was fully entitled to discuss and direct Irish affairs.
- A Protestant Church of Ireland had been established on a similar basis to the Church of England. This was imposed on the country and the vast majority of the inhabitants remained **Roman Catholic**.
- English politicians tended to ignore the reality that Ireland was a foreign country with its own language (Gaelic) and culture.

There were three different groups in Ireland:

- The 'mere' or native peasant Irish, who were Catholic. They comprised the vast majority of the population. With a few exceptions, they were excluded from taking part in political life.
- The 'Old English' were the descendants of pre-Reformation English settlers. They were usually Catholic. As owners of one-third of the profitable land in Ireland, they were accustomed to thinking of themselves as the island's

**KEY TERMS**

**Lord Lieutenant**
The monarch's representative and head of the government.

**Roman Catholic**
The only accepted form of Christianity in western Europe for the 1000 years before the Reformation of the early sixteenth century which brought in Protestantism. Catholics and Protestants tended to regard each other with deep suspicion or even hatred.

natural rulers. They felt increasingly threatened by the third group, the 'New English'.

- The 'New English' were Protestants who had arrived since the Reformation in the 1540s and who controlled the government in Dublin. In general, they favoured a policy of **plantation** to introduce more Protestant settlers, often at the expense of the 'mere' Irish. Ireland was usually a drain on the English **exchequer** and English authority was precarious enough to require an army to maintain it. In the 1590s, there had been an uprising in **Ulster** led by the **Earl of Tyrone**, which finally collapsed in 1603, although his position was not destroyed. An uneasy truce developed which would not be sustained for long (see page 32).

Ireland was often ignored by politicians in England. Once the Ulster rising had been dealt with, the reign of James I was no different. It was the more intrusive policies during the reign of his son, Charles I, that were to lead to serious discontent in Ireland once more.

# 4 Implications of the accession of James I

■ *What problems faced James on his accession to the English throne?*

The end of one dynasty and the establishment of a new one was bound to cause some problems. The new king needed to create a sense of loyalty, which could be engendered by some well-judged generosity. The ease with which James VI of Scotland became James I of England surprised many onlookers. In large part this was because James had developed close links with Elizabeth's chief minister, Robert Cecil (see page 23). It was in both their interests for James's accession to be as trouble-free as possible and there was no hesitation in proclaiming James as the new king. He assumed the role as soon as the news reached him of Elizabeth's death. The nation was relieved to have an active male on the throne again after half a century of being ruled by women.

## Politics

In the sixteenth and seventeenth centuries, official salaries were so low as to be almost worthless. To have a reasonable income, courtiers and office holders relied on the Crown to make grants of many different kinds.

Elizabeth I gave away very few pensions, offices, titles or gifts, especially in the final years of her reign. By the time of James I's accession, there was enormous pent-up demand from unsatisfied courtiers. It was, therefore, inevitable that James would dispense more patronage than Elizabeth had. In addition, James had a wife and children who all needed their own households, which were expensive. Unfortunately, James was generous to a fault. He was incapable of

# James I

**1566** Born to Mary, Queen of Scots, and Henry, Lord Darnley

**1567** Became king of Scotland on the abdication of his mother

**1583** Took over the government of Scotland

**1589** Married Anne of Denmark, daughter of the Danish king

**1594** Oldest son, Henry, born

**1600** Second son, Charles, born

**1603** Became king of England and moved to London

**1612** Henry died

**1616** George Villiers (see page 43) became James's favourite

**1625** Died and was succeeded by Charles

James's early life was troubled. He was born to parents who were already estranged from each other after Darnley's murder of Mary's secretary, David Riccio. Darnley was himself murdered when James was only six months old. Mary's ill-advised marriage to the Earl of Bothwell, who was widely credited with Darnley's murder, ensured that she was imprisoned and forced to abdicate when James was only thirteen months old. James was brought up in a loveless environment by a succession of Scots nobles who were vying for power, backed by the Church. James's first two **regents** were assassinated and there were many other incidents which threatened the young king's life; for example in

1583, he was imprisoned by some nobles who wished to control the king. On his release, James imposed his authority on Scotland by limiting the power of the nobles and the Church.

This early insecurity led to James's dislike of violence, his suspicion of a Church without a hierarchy, such as existed in Scotland, and his reliance on **favourites** who would give him the affection he craved. It also made him much more conscious of slights to his authority. In Scotland, James became a strong and effective ruler, but his early experiences were not a good preparation for ruling England and this was to lead to problems (see pages 40–1).

James married Anne of Denmark in 1589. They had seven children although only three survived childhood. However, the marriage was not a success and James and Anne were living very separate lives by the time he became king of England.

James inherited the English throne through his great grandmother, Margaret, the older daughter of Henry VII. He became king at a time when the existing system of government and finance was coming under strain. James had disputes with Parliament but he retained its respect and juggled the competing demands made on him with some skill (see page 48).

saying no to any request from a favourite and he loved to shower rewards on those around him. He pointed out in 1610 that 'a king's liberality must never be dried up altogether, for then he can never maintain nor oblige his servants and well deserving subjects'. But James's liberality knew no bounds. In one famous incident on his journey south from Scotland, he created 46 knights before breakfast. This was designed to win over the English but its scale was counter-productive because it devalued the gifts and encouraged further demands.

## Finance

The scale of James's giving had serious implications for finance, as did his general extravagance. Elizabeth had been very careful to restrain her expenditure so that she would not be dependent on Parliament for her ordinary revenue. At her death she had left a surplus of £90,000 in the Treasury and a debt of £400,000. This debt was covered by money owed by France and the Dutch, and by an uncollected subsidy voted in 1603. This was an impressive achievement, given that England had been at war for fifteen years. It contrasted

**KEY TERMS**

**Regent** A person appointed to run the State when the monarch cannot do so because of either youth or illness.

**Favourite** A young man with a close relationship to the king who received many gifts of land, titles or money.

very sharply with James's financial position within three years of coming to the throne, by which time there was already a debt of £816,000, despite making peace with the Spanish in 1604. He had been king for less than a year when the Archbishop of York warned him that 'he would exhaust the treasure of the kingdom and bring many inconveniences'. James himself acknowledged in 1610 that he had been too lax with money when he promised that 'the vastness of my expenditure is past which I used in the first two or three years after my coming hither'.

## Elizabeth I's financial legacy

Although Elizabeth managed her own finances remarkably successfully, she often did so at the cost of her successors. The only long-term solution to the problem of finance was to increase royal revenue so that it went up in line with inflation. Elizabeth did not do this. Her policy had been to cut expenditure and, if all else failed, to sell Crown lands, which eventually led to an impoverished Crown. This meant that in Elizabeth's reign there was no increase in customs duties in the **Book of Rates** and there was no attempt to exploit the Crown lands effectively. In 1587, a 50-year lease on some Crown property in Bermondsey was agreed at a rent of £68 a year. In 1636, when the lease was due for renewal, it was found to be worth £1071 a year.

The Stuarts were also hit by a fall in the value of the parliamentary subsidy because the local elites responsible for land valuations (on which the subsidy was based) tended to under-assess themselves and their neighbours considerably. Thus, the yield of each subsidy fell from about £130,000 in the mid-sixteenth century to £55,000 by 1628. This was at a time of inflation, so the real value had gone down even more. The Commons failed to appreciate this fully and were reluctant to vote additional sums to make up the deficit. MPs could not understand why the Crown made such poor use of their generosity.

# Religion

Under Elizabeth, the Church of England had become firmly established in the country. Few people retained a memory of Catholicism under Mary and the number of practising Catholics was dwindling. It was a commonly held idea in this period that religious dissent equalled political dissent, and that for a country to harbour members of another creed was to invite political subversion or rebellion. This had been true often enough to give real substance to the belief. In England, the plots surrounding Mary, Queen of Scots, and the plans to assassinate Elizabeth had made all Catholics seem potential traitors. The **papal bull** which **excommunicated** Elizabeth in 1570 released her subjects from allegiance to her and excommunicated any that obeyed her orders. English Catholics were put in the unhappy position of obeying their ruler by remaining loyal, or of obeying their spiritual leader. War with Spain had brought the prospect of Catholic domination once more.

## KEY TERMS

**Book of Rates** Listed the customs duty payable on specific items. It was periodically revised. The last revision had been in 1558, carried out by officials in Mary I's reign.

**Papal bull** A formal proclamation issued by the pope.

**Excommunication** Being excluded from the services and membership of the Church. Catholics believed that excommunicants would go to hell, if they did not reconcile themselves to the Church first.

Although most English Catholics were peaceful and law-abiding, they wanted an opportunity to worship in private. They also wanted an end to the **recusancy fines**, which, if strictly enforced, could ruin a family. In 1603, Thomas Tresham, who had paid out more than £2000 in recusancy fines, presented a petition for more lenient treatment of Catholics. James had a reputation as a tolerant man who liked to follow a middle way. Catholics hoped that in the new reign they would be freed from the fear of practising their faith.

At the opposite end of the religious spectrum were the **Puritans** who put much greater stress on the preaching of 'the word' (the Bible) and the individual's response to the message of God. They attached far less importance to the power of the sacraments (**baptism** and **communion**) or to the role of worship. In the 1580s, there had been an upsurge in Puritanism, with some people advocating a Presbyterian system which would have swept away the bishops. This had been suppressed by Elizabeth and the Archbishop of Canterbury. By the end of James's reign there was little trouble from the Puritans. However, their hopes of reform had merely been deferred, and the arrival of a king from Presbyterian Scotland inevitably created new expectations.

# Foreign policy

As king of Scotland, James VI had been on the periphery of European affairs. It was a very different matter when he became James I. As king of England, he was ruler of the most powerful Protestant state in Europe and if he so wished, he could assume leadership of the European Protestants.

James inherited a war with Spain and an alliance with the Dutch, who were fighting to win their independence. His wife, Queen Anne, was Danish so there were strong connections with Denmark, an important Protestant power. The German Protestant princes wanted a more active role from England, but James had no desire to place himself at the head of a Protestant crusade. War was repugnant to him and he spent his life trying to avoid being dragged into conflicts.

James desired to act as a mediator and peacemaker. This involved being on good terms with all sides, yet this policy – which had worked when he was king of Scotland – was more difficult in England. A neutral policy was often impossible without favouring one side in a conflict at the expense of the other.

An active foreign policy was also extremely expensive, especially as military costs rose faster than general inflation and could not be financed out of ordinary expenditure for long. A war would place the monarch in a position of much greater dependence on Parliament. The king had sole responsibility for the direction of foreign policy but, if Parliament disliked the policy, it could refuse to grant taxes to finance it. This was to lead to major problems in the 1620s, with repercussions not only for foreign affairs but also for the conduct of domestic policy.

**KEY TERMS**

**Recusancy fines** Payable by people who did not regularly attend the Sunday services in their local parish church. In practice this was a fine for being Catholic.

**Puritans** Members of the Anglican Church who wished to 'purify' it of the last vestiges of Catholic worship. These included an end to the ring in marriage, signing with the cross at baptism, bowing at the name of Jesus and wearing vestments (clergymen's robes).

**Baptism** The service by which babies became members of the Church, as symbolised by being sprinkled with water.

**Communion** Service of the Church at which members received bread and wine to represent Christ's body and blood. For Catholics, this was the most important service because of their belief in transubstantiation. Protestants, especially Puritans, gave it less importance.

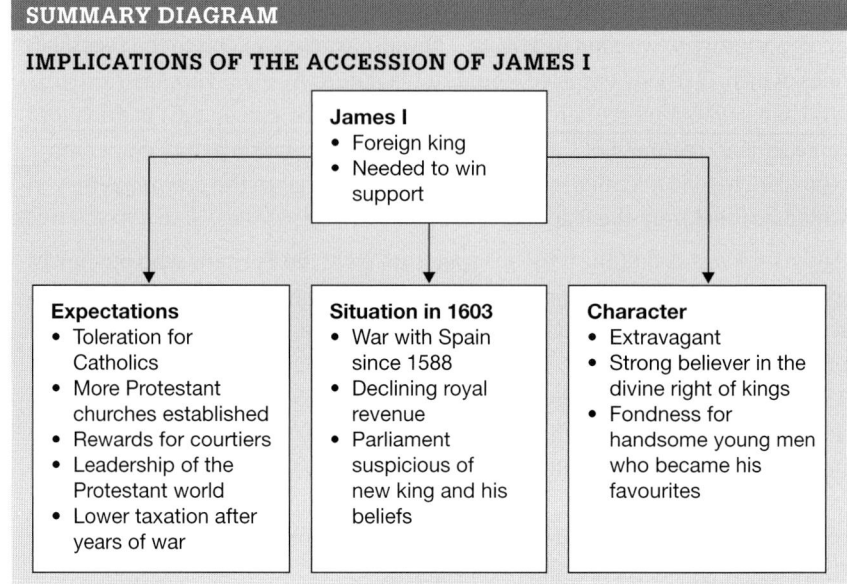

**SUMMARY DIAGRAM**

## IMPLICATIONS OF THE ACCESSION OF JAMES I

**James I**
- Foreign king
- Needed to win support

**Expectations**
- Toleration for Catholics
- More Protestant churches established
- Rewards for courtiers
- Leadership of the Protestant world
- Lower taxation after years of war

**Situation in 1603**
- War with Spain since 1588
- Declining royal revenue
- Parliament suspicious of new king and his beliefs

**Character**
- Extravagant
- Strong believer in the divine right of kings
- Fondness for handsome young men who became his favourites

**ONLINE EXTRAS**
OCR  WWW

Get to grips with selecting evidence by completing Worksheet 1 at **www. hoddereducation.co.uk/ accesstohistory/extras**

# CHAPTER SUMMARY

England in 1603 was pleased to welcome its new king. There were many expectations of the new reign. Courtiers were eager for more rewards, and both Catholics and Puritans had high hopes of change under James, although their desires were mutually incompatible. In foreign policy there was war-weariness but also a desire for England to play a role as the leader of the Protestant states. It would be difficult for the king to satisfy everyone.

England's political and financial system appeared to have functioned well enough under his predecessors, but there were already strains.

These had been partly masked by Elizabeth's policy of selling lands and deferring expectations of reward. James was to make the problem worse with his extravagance and failure to understand how best to manage Parliament, but the fault was not all his.

In addition, James was now ruler of three kingdoms rather than one and this was to add to the challenges he faced. The skilful and successful king of Scotland found that becoming king of England raised challenges that were not easy to overcome.

## Refresher questions

Use these questions to remind yourself of the key material covered in this chapter.

1 How was order maintained in the absence of a police force or army?

2 What was the role of Parliament?

3 What were the differences between the two views (the divine right of kings and the ancient constitution) of the role of the king?

4 What was the political significance of the bedchamber?

5 Why was the financial system for raising taxes coming under strain?

6 Why was James's experience as king of Scotland not necessarily an advantage as king of England?

7 What were the problems of being a ruler of multiple kingdoms?

8 What hopes did the Puritans and Catholics have of James?

9 What were James's priorities in foreign policy?

10 Why would it be difficult for James to meet all the expectations placed on him?

# CHAPTER 2

# James I: consensus under strain 1603–25

This chapter examines the start of the Stuart era, which began with high hopes of the new monarch. James's extravagance, laziness and tendency to lecture Parliament caused these hopes slowly to fade. In addition, the long-standing mechanisms for raising money were becoming increasingly inadequate, causing further tension. The outbreak of the Thirty Years' War in Europe and James's pursuit of a Spanish marriage for Charles added further to distrust of the monarchy. The stages in this disillusion can be traced through the following events:

◆ The new king of England

◆ Problems with the financial system in the early seventeenth century

◆ Religion

◆ Foreign policy

◆ Relations with Parliament

The key debate on page 47 of this chapter asks the question: Wise or foolish: which is the more accurate description of James I?

## KEY DATES

| | | |
|---|---|---|
| **1603** | **March** | James VI of Scotland became James I of England |
| **1604** | | Hampton Court conference |
| **1605** | **Nov.** | Gunpowder Plot |
| **1606** | | Bate's case |
| **1610** | | Failed negotiations over the Great Contract |
| **1612** | | Death of Prince Henry. Charles now heir to the throne |
| **1613** | | Marriage of Princess Elizabeth to Frederick, Elector of the Palatinate |
| **1614** | | The Addled Parliament |
| **1616** | | George Villiers replaced Robert Carr as favourite |
| **1619** | | Elector Frederick accepted the offer of the Bohemian throne |
| **1621** | | Third Parliament: debates over monopolies, the Protestation |
| **1623** | | Charles and Buckingham's trip to Madrid |
| **1624** | | Fourth Parliament, impeachment of Cranfield |
| **1625** | **Jan.** | Failure of Mansfeld's expedition |
| | **March** | Death of James, accession of Charles I |

# 1 The new king of England

■ *How far did James I's character fit him to be king of England?*

Many of James's personality traits can be traced back to his childhood. Deprived of both his parents as a baby, he grew up as a lonely boy who was to crave affection throughout his life. His marriage to Anne of Denmark, after a successful start, became loveless. James turned to a series of young men, who supplied the sense of family that James had never known as a child and was unable to create successfully as an adult, despite having two sons, Henry and Charles, and one daughter, Elizabeth. It is striking that James's relations with George Villiers, later Duke of Buckingham (see page 43), were more cordial than with his own son, Charles. James signed his letters to Buckingham 'your darling Dad' and addressed him as 'sweet child and wife'. It is uncertain whether James was a practising homosexual, although contemporaries were scandalised by the way he caressed his favourites in public, and resentful of the honours he heaped on them.

James disliked the public attention which he received as king and, unlike the previous monarch, Elizabeth I, he did not try to cultivate a positive image of himself or his court. He disliked formality, often dressing casually himself and encouraging a relaxed and even dissolute atmosphere at court, which scandalised contemporaries. This allowed unfavourable assessments to go unchallenged, such as that by Sir Anthony Weldon: 'his eyes large, ever rolling after any stranger that came in his presence … He was very liberal of what he had not in his own grip, and would rather part with £100 he never had in his keeping than one twenty shilling piece within his own custody.'

James had no one on whom to model himself as king. It is unfortunate that his manners, which were extremely coarse, had not been corrected as a child. The harsh treatment he received at the hands of the Scottish nobility as he was growing up, and a number of assassination attempts in Scotland, instilled a strong belief in hierarchy and the importance of order. Members of Parliament (MPs) resented the king's anger if they disagreed with him and did not enjoy James haranguing them for hours at a time. He went so far as to apologise for this in 1621: 'I never meant to weary myself or you with such tedious discourses as I have done heretofore.' James was extremely fond of hunting and it has been calculated that he spent half his reign away from London on the chase. This meant he did not always pay close attention to government and allowed others to dictate events.

A more positive side of James's character was his love of learning. He was genuinely interested in philosophy and theology, and wrote a number of books (see page 39). James was unusually tolerant for the early seventeenth century. The execution of Catholic priests virtually ended in his reign. He also sought to be a peacemaker and tried to keep England out of war. These attributes are considered praiseworthy now, but they were regarded with suspicion at the time.

**ONLINE EXTRAS** **WWW**
AQA
Practise writing essay titles by completing Worksheet 1 at **www.hoddereducation. co.uk/accesstohistory/extras**

**ONLINE EXTRAS** **WWW**
OCR
Practise creating essay plans by completing Worksheet 2 at **www.hoddereducation. co.uk/accesstohistory/extras**

The family tree of James I. An engraving by Benjamin Wright, 1619.

**SOURCE QUESTION**

In Source A, why did James I want his family tree to show that he was descended from Henry VII?

**SUMMARY DIAGRAM**

**THE NEW KING OF ENGLAND**

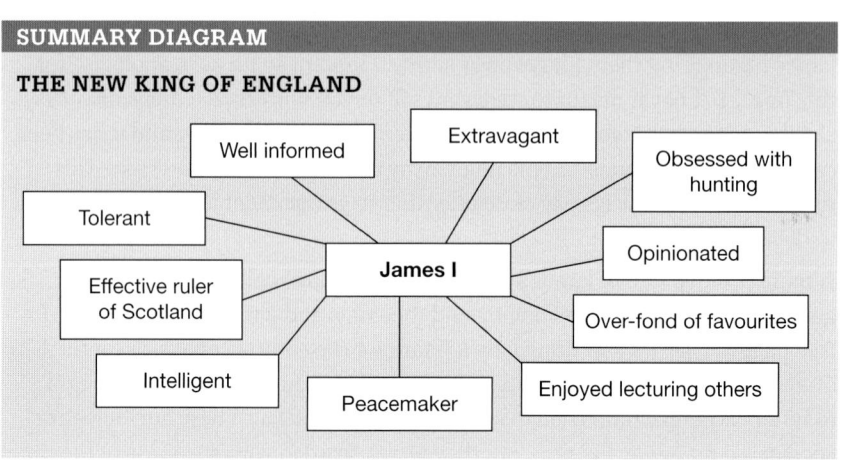

# 2 Problems with the financial system in the early seventeenth century

■ *How far was James I responsible for his financial problems?*

The side to James's personality that was to cause him the greatest political problems was undoubtedly his extravagance. He did not appreciate that, although England was much richer than Scotland, the mechanisms for tapping that wealth effectively in the Crown's interest did not exist. Instead, he marvelled at the wealth displayed by the nobility in England and embarked on a colossal spending spree, doubling expenditure on the royal household from 1603 to 1610 and spending an enormous £185,000 on jewels by 1612. James's spendthrift attitude meant he could not live on his ordinary revenue alone.

## Ordinary revenue

Ordinary revenue was the income that the monarch received each year. It was not dependent on parliamentary grants, unlike extraordinary revenue, or taxes, which were granted in times of emergency (for example, war, or a special occasion such as a coronation). This ordinary revenue came from a number of sources.

## Crown lands

At the beginning of James's reign the most important source of revenue was still the Crown lands, even though Elizabeth had sold over £800,000 worth of estates. It was difficult for the king to maximise his income from land because extracting economic rents was unpopular, and the Crown lands were a convenient form of patronage (see page 23). Leases on favourable terms were a way of rewarding courtiers and officials without direct cost to the exchequer. The Crown lands diminished in importance throughout the reigns of James and Charles (see page 66) because, as one financial crisis gave way to another, successive lord treasurers saw the sale of land as being the quickest and easiest way to raise money, despite the reduction in future income.

## Customs revenue

Customs revenue, or **tonnage and poundage**, was the second major source of ordinary revenue. There was considerable scope for improvement in the revenue from customs. By 1621, customs revenue brought in nearly three times as much as the revenue from Crown lands.

In 1604, direct collection of the customs was abandoned and it was **farmed out** to a syndicate of merchants. In return for an annual rent, the **customs farmers**

**ONLINE EXTRAS**
AQA **WWW**
Get to grips with breaking down factors by completing Worksheet 2 at **www. hoddereducation.co.uk/ accesstohistory/extras**

**KEY TERMS**

**Tonnage and poundage** Taxes on imports and exports.

**Farming out** Leasing out the administration of customs in return for an annual rent.

**Customs farmers** Merchants who would pay the Crown for the right to collect customs revenue.

were able to collect and keep the customs revenue, which had the following advantages:

- The king received a regular income and an additional source of patronage. This also created a group closely linked to the Crown, who would probably be willing to make loans when the king was in financial difficulty.
- For the farmer, the system brought considerable rewards because the Crown never demanded a price for the customs that reflected their true worth. The king believed it was more important to have supporters in the merchant community than to gain the maximum in income.

The farmers had an interest in collecting the maximum from the customs which, in effect, meant a new indirect tax had been created. This caused great unease in Parliament, which saw its control of taxation being undermined.

### Bate's case

This fear was dramatically increased after 1606 when a merchant, John Bate, was taken to court for refusing to pay a duty on currants. Bate claimed that the duty had not been sanctioned by Parliament. The judges decided the case in the king's favour because the monarch had the right to regulate trade for the security of the realm. Bate's case opened the way to vastly increasing the scope of the customs. In 1608, new duties known as **impositions** were levied on 1400 items with no real pretence that it was in the interest of trade. These brought in an additional £70,000 a year to the exchequer. By the end of the 1630s, the Crown was dependent for half of its income on customs.

## Wardship

The third strand in Crown finances was made up of feudal tenures and wardship, which dated from the Middle Ages. They had largely lost their justification by the seventeenth century, although not their financial usefulness to the Crown:

- Feudal tenures originated in the period when major landowners owed a duty of military service to the king, who was entitled to take over their property if they died and left a minor or a woman as heir.
- Wardship was the name given to the system whereby an estate was managed after the death of its owner until the heir came of age or, in the case of a woman, was married. It was a useful tool for rewarding courtiers. For a family, two or more wardships in rapid succession could bring ruin. There were many calls for an end to this system, which brought about £65,000 to the Crown in 1610.

### Purveyance

Purveyance was another medieval relic. It was the right of the court to buy provisions at fixed prices which were well below market rates. It was established at a time when the court moved frequently around the country, thus ensuring that the burden of its expense did not fall only on one area.

This system was open to gross abuse by corrupt officials who could buy excess provisions and then sell them at a profit. The burden fell heavily on a small section of the people since the court no longer spent most of its time travelling around the country. It was worth about £40,000 to the court and Parliament was anxious to put an end to it, but MPs could not agree on how to compensate the king.

## James's extravagance

By 1603, the Crown's ordinary revenue was ceasing to meet the actual cost of running the country. But James's extravagance concealed this fact. Queen Elizabeth had spent less than £300,000 a year in peacetime. Under James, this figure rose almost immediately to £400,000 and reached a peak of £522,000 in 1614.

Contemporaries would have minded less about the scale of James's extravagance if it had not gone so largely on conspicuous consumption, or into the pockets of the hated Scottish foreigners. One of these was Lord Hay. On one occasion he gave a banquet for the French ambassador which occupied 30 cooks for twelve days. The food alone cost £2200 (£480,000 in today's prices). With the knowledge that the king had paid Lord Hay's debts, it is scarcely surprising that the Commons believed James should be able to live comfortably on the Crown's traditional sources of revenue if he practised a bit more economy.

> **SOURCE B**
>
> An anonymous rhyme quoted in Pauline Croft, Libels, popular literacy and public opinion in early modern England, *Historical Research*, volume 68, 1995, p. 277.
>
> *The Scotchmen are but beggars yet,*
> *Although their begging was not small.*
> *But now a Parliament doth sit,*
> *A subsidy shall pay for all.*

**Robert Cecil**, Earl of Salisbury, tried to restrain James's extravagance by issuing the *Book of Bounty* in 1608. This prohibited the Crown giving away major items such as lands, customs or impositions. However:

- It did not succeed in its intention of lowering the expectations of courtiers because James gave cash instead. In the last four months of 1610 alone, he was persuaded to give away over £36,000.

- The other reason for its failure was that no one could afford to oppose the king's wishes for long if he valued his position.

Even Salisbury found himself suggesting the transfer of Sir Walter Raleigh's manor at Sherborne to Robert Carr, the new favourite, as a way of bypassing the rules. (Sir Walter Raleigh's estates had been forfeited to the Crown when he was found guilty of high treason in 1604.) For this, he earned the gratitude of both the king and Carr, which was worth more to Salisbury than the long-term

**SOURCE QUESTION**

What does the rhyme in Source B show about contemporary views of James's need for money and the Scots?

**KEY FIGURE**

**Robert Cecil (1563–1612)**

Earl of Salisbury 1605, lord treasurer 1608. Cecil was chief minister to both Elizabeth I and James. He did much to smooth the succession of James by establishing contact with him while Elizabeth was alive. He was an effective minister on whom James could rely.

financial viability of the Crown. This is one example of how James's ministers 'bent the rules' for him and helped to enable his extravagance.

# Structural weaknesses

The financial problems encountered by James were not all of his own making. Even though peace had been made with Spain in 1604, military expenditure (where costs rose much faster than for other items) did not come to an end.

In Ireland, between 1603 and 1608, £600,000 was spent on the army. In addition, there was expenditure to maintain English garrisons in the **Netherlands**. These factors tended to be overlooked by Parliament, which did not understand why the Crown made such poor use of the funds it granted. MPs looked back to Elizabeth and what she had achieved and, ignoring both inflation and the falling value of the subsidy (see page 14), attributed the Stuarts' repeated requests for money to incompetence or extravagance. Finally, the system by which the Crown received revenue was riddled with corruption, as royal officials siphoned off money for themselves which was intended for the king.

## Official self-interest

A good example of people seeking to enrich themselves at royal expense is the Earl of Salisbury, even though he was a loyal and dedicated servant of the king:

- In 1609, as master of the court of wards, Salisbury gained £1400 from a wardship that earned the Crown £370.
- More spectacularly, in 1610 as lord treasurer, he negotiated the renewal of the silk duties to himself on the original terms even though the trade had greatly expanded. Instead of the modest profit of £434 which he had originally enjoyed, he was now gaining £7000 a year.

This unscrupulous stealing from the Crown coincided with Salisbury's efforts to strengthen royal finances by negotiating the Great Contract with Parliament. It illustrates the problem that too many people had a vested interest in the system remaining unreformed.

## Taxation

Self-interest also affected parliamentary taxation, known as supply (see page 8). Those who were liable to pay the subsidy, which excluded the poorest, had to declare what they were worth, yet these assessments were usually hugely underestimated. **Lionel Cranfield** (lord treasurer 1621–4) privately estimated his total wealth at £90,000 but was taxed on only £150, while Buckingham, the richest man in the kingdom after the king, was apparently worth a mere £400. Death caused the **subsidy rolls** to shrink and new families did not make up the numbers. In Suffolk, 66 people had been assessed in 1557 on land and goods worth £521; by 1628, only 37 people were assessed on £77. With major landowners refusing to take a responsible share of the costs of running the kingdom, it is small wonder that the Crown found itself in trouble. However, the

---

**KEY TERMS**

**Netherlands** England's biggest trading partner. In the late sixteenth century, the northern Netherlands had waged a protracted campaign to win their freedom from Spain. Elizabeth I had assisted this struggle and had been given the right to hold some towns in return.

**Subsidy rolls** Records of taxation which were used to determine how much each area should pay.

**KEY FIGURE**

**Lionel Cranfield (1575–1645)**

A London businessman and lord treasurer 1621–4. He successfully reduced Crown expenditure but was less successful at making structural reforms, as these attacked the vested interests of Crown officials and politically this was very difficult to achieve.

glaring fact of James's extravagance enabled the Commons to ignore that their subsidies were worth less and less. Both Crown and Commons could view the actions of the other as unreasonable, with some justification. The 1624 Subsidy Act granted James £300,000, which was totally inadequate for his needs but the Commons believed they were being exceptionally generous.

As the record of James's reign illustrates, the Crown could not rely on Parliament granting sufficient taxation. James's first Parliament (1604–10) showed itself to be wary about making grants, although it was not uncooperative. The first session gave no supply because a large grant made at the end of Elizabeth's reign was still being collected. The second session met in 1606 in the aftermath of the Gunpowder Plot (see page 29) and made the unusually large and unexpected grant of £400,000. This helped to mislead James into believing that Parliament would always pay his debts. In fact, the subsidy reflected the relief that king and Parliament had not been blown up. The grant was passed with the slimmest of majorities (one vote) and this, rather than the king's optimistic view, gave a more realistic picture of the difficulty which James would henceforth experience when trying to raise money from Parliament. Between 1606 and 1621, James received only one grant of under £100,000. By the 1620s, disillusion with the Crown's handling of its finances made obtaining adequate parliamentary funds an increasing problem. A new financial system was needed and an attempt to achieve this was made in the Great Contract of 1610.

# The Great Contract

In 1610, an imaginative scheme was suggested by Salisbury. In return for an annual grant of £200,000 from Parliament and a one-off payment of £600,000 to clear the Crown's debts, Salisbury proposed to abolish wardship, purveyance and the feudal tenures (see page 22).

After months of negotiations, the Commons had agreed to the annual grant, although MPs would only give £100,000 from a subsidy that had already been voted towards discharge of the debt. For his part, James had agreed to a bill that would legalise the impositions already granted but would prevent him issuing new ones without parliamentary sanction. This was a neat way of preserving everybody's interests: the king did not lose out because he kept his impositions and Parliament maintained its control over taxation. All that remained was for both bills to be enacted when Parliament reassembled in November 1610.

## Failure of the Great Contract

However, over the summer, doubts surfaced on both sides. The Commons could not be certain that the king would not accept their grant and continue to pocket the feudal revenues. Many MPs disliked the idea of funding the king's extravagance and feared that the Scots would be the major beneficiaries. As one member put it: 'to what purpose to draw a silver stream into the royal cistern if it shall daily run out thence by private [stop] cocks?' There was also uncertainty about how the money to compensate the king would be raised.

The court was also having second thoughts:

- It was calculated that the revenues the king would lose were about £115,000 a year, giving the king a net gain of some £85,000 a year. This was unlikely to be increased to take account of inflation. On the other hand, these revenues could be exploited more efficiently to make them very profitable (see page 72).

- The success of the Great Contract would also mean that James would accept the bill on impositions, preventing him from expanding his revenue from customs. Since customs was the only part of Crown revenue capable of increasing significantly, this might seriously impede the king's freedom of action.

- The surrender of wardship would remove a useful source of patronage from the monarch. Granting a rich manor to a courtier was an easy and cheap way of paying a political debt and the financial compensation might not equal the loss.

With hindsight, the failure of the Great Contract was unfortunate for both the Stuart dynasty and the country. The existing system continued to cause strain and it was eventually replaced after the civil war. If it had been passed, Parliament would have taken more responsibility for financing the government, and it might have understood the problems of government finance more clearly. This may have helped to minimise the conflict between the House of Commons and the Crown from the 1620s to the civil war. However, the scheme came to nothing.

## Years of drift 1612–18

Both James's eldest son Henry, and his treasurer, Salisbury, died in 1612, one from fever, the other from old age. Crown finances were in a sorry state, and declined further as the years went on. Initially, James did not replace Salisbury as treasurer and instead a committee took over. James did not want to have a chief minister who would control the government. However, he lacked the application to fill Salisbury's roles as treasurer and secretary of state himself. The years 1612–14 saw the government drifting with no sense of purpose.

The Parliament of 1614 failed to grant any money so James was reduced to selling titles. He even created the new title of 'baronet' just so it could be sold. Even this was unsuccessful, as the market was soon saturated and the price of a barony fell from £1095 to £220 by 1622. Selling earldoms at £10,000 was more successful: the number of earls increased dramatically from 28 in 1615 to 65 in 1628, although many were appalled that a title which should have been bestowed because of merit was being sold to anyone who had enough money. More damagingly, James was persuaded to give government agreement to an ill-considered scheme involving the cloth trade.

## Cockayne's scheme

William Cockayne, a London merchant and alderman, wanted to break into the monopoly held by the **Merchant Adventurers** for the sale of unfinished cloth to the Netherlands, England's biggest export market (see page 24). In 1614, he persuaded the king to prohibit the export of unfinished cloth on the grounds that this would generate employment in the finishing of the cloth, and increase customs revenue by increasing the value of the product. In fact, the opposite happened for the following reasons:

- The Dutch reacted to the attempted attack on their industry by finding new sources of unfinished cloth.
- Unlike the Merchant Adventurers, Cockayne and his backers did not have the resources to purchase all the cloth produced, and unemployment soared in the clothing districts.

In two years, exports sent through London went down by a third and customs revenue fell accordingly. At this point the Merchant Adventurers were allowed to resume their control of the cloth trade, which gradually recovered but never again reached the high point of 1614.

## A new treasurer

In 1614, the Earl of Suffolk, a member of the Howard family, became lord treasurer. Unfortunately, his corruption surpassed anything yet seen. In his four years as treasurer, Suffolk built the manor Audley End, which was said to have cost at least £80,000. James said that it was too big for a king but fit for a lord treasurer. While Suffolk was in control, the Crown's debt nearly doubled from £500,000 to £900,000. At last, his actions were too much even for James. Suffolk was dismissed in 1618 and convicted of **embezzlement**.

# Cranfield and the king's finances 1618–24

The appointment of Lionel Cranfield as **master of the wardrobe** in 1618 brought some improvement to James's finances. It was agreed that if costs fell from the existing £42,000 to £20,000, Cranfield could keep any additional savings. He soon made a profit of over £7000 a year. Cranfield achieved similar success in other departments such as the ordnance (supply of weapons) and the navy, where costs fell respectively from £34,000 to £14,000 and £53,000 to £30,000. He achieved this by attacking waste (such as insisting that candles were used more than once), by accurate budgeting and accounting, and by eliminating corrupt and unnecessary officials.

In 1621, Cranfield was created lord treasurer and the Earl of Middlesex. He attempted to control the flow of royal generosity by demanding an immediate stop to the payment of pensions and insisting that he screen all new grants. This system could only have worked with the full cooperation of the king, but James found it impossible to resist the greed of his courtiers. He once burst out to them,

**KEY TERMS**

**Merchant Adventurers**
A group of merchants who were the only people allowed to export cloth.

**Embezzlement**
Fraudulently taking money entrusted to an individual because of his position.

**Master of the wardrobe** The official in charge of a department in the royal household.

'You will never let me alone. I would to God you had, first my doublet, and then my shirt; and when I were naked, I think you would give me leave to be quiet.'

## Cranfield's fall

Cranfield survived as lord treasurer for only two and a half years. He fell from power because he made a very ill-judged attempt to promote his nephew Arthur Brett as a new favourite, when Buckingham was absent in Madrid (see page 36), and he opposed the war with Spain which would be difficult to finance (see page 37). At Charles and Buckingham's insistence he was impeached for corruption.

Cranfield achieved some impressive savings and he increased royal income by about £80,000. However, ultimately he made no lasting difference because the king could not restrain his extravagance. In addition, even Cranfield, the would-be agent of reform, took the opportunity to become one of the richest men in the country at royal expense.

**ONLINE EXTRAS**
**OCR**　**WWW**

Develop your essay-writing by completing Worksheets 3 and 4 at **www. hoddereducation.co.uk/ accesstohistory/extras**

### SUMMARY DIAGRAM

**PROBLEMS WITH THE FINANCIAL SYSTEM IN THE EARLY SEVENTEENTH CENTURY**

| The king's needs | Parliament's perceptions |
|---|---|
| • Costs of government increasing, especially war<br>• The king's needs were greater because his wife and children needed households<br>• Amount received from taxation declining and was also worth less because of inflation<br>• Crown lands no longer contributing meaningful amounts<br>• Vested interests of courtiers made reform difficult | • James was too extravagant<br>• In the 1620s, MPs felt that they were being very generous<br>• If the court made economies there would be no problem<br>• Too much money was going to individuals like Buckingham<br>• Allowing the king to raise money from customs would undermine the role of Parliament |

# 3 Religion

■ *How successfully did James manage religious differences?*

## James I and the Catholics

Persecution of Catholics in England had become more severe after the outbreak of war with Spain in the 1580s. Catholics were seen as potential traitors, which a handful had confirmed by their involvement in plots revolving around Mary,

Queen of Scots. Recusancy fines (see page 15) were increased and 146 Catholics were executed in England between 1586 and 1603, either for being, or for sheltering, priests.

At first, James seemed to be tolerant towards Catholics. He promised that he would not 'persecute any that will be quiet and give an outward obedience to the law'. He ordered the recusancy fines to be reduced and they fell to less than a quarter of their level before 1603. This leniency was to be short lived. In 1604, all priests and Jesuits were ordered out of the kingdom and, in November, recusancy fines were ordered to be collected in full. The reason for this abrupt change of policy was almost certainly the adverse reaction his tolerance provoked among James's Protestant subjects. The 1604 Parliament passed an act calling for 'due execution of the statutes' against 'any manner of recusants'. The king did not want to antagonise Parliament when he was trying to promote his cherished dream of union between England and Scotland (see page 40). He hoped that if he agreed to the request for harsher measures against Catholics, Parliament would make concessions over the terms of union.

## The Gunpowder Plot 1605

The blow to the Catholic community was severe and encouraged a few to seek a more extreme remedy for their troubles. England's peace with Spain in 1604 (see page 33) had deprived the Catholics of the hope of foreign intervention to promote their cause. In desperation, a plot was hatched to remove the king and his entire government. This was the Gunpowder Plot. Its failure is still commemorated every 5 November: Guy Fawkes or Bonfire Night.

The conspiracy involved digging a tunnel under the Houses of Parliament with the intention of setting off an explosion to kill both the king and MPs with one stroke. The plot was led by **Robert Catesby** and the main plotters came from gentry families which had suffered most from recusancy fines. The plot was revealed when one conspirator sent a warning to a relative to keep away from Parliament.

James was upset by the plot. The Venetian ambassador reported that 'the king is in terror. He does not appear nor does he take his meals in public as usual. He lives in the innermost rooms with only Scotsmen about him.' Recusancy fines were increased and Catholics were forbidden to live in or near London, or to hold public office (known as the penal laws). They were also required to take a new oath of allegiance which denied the pope's authority to depose kings. The pope opposed the oath but most Catholics were happy to demonstrate their political loyalty by taking it.

After the plot, the Catholics gave James no further trouble. They were allowed to practise their religion, albeit at a financial cost. The penal laws were often ordered to be enforced more strictly when a Parliament was due to meet, as a concession to the violently anti-Catholic Commons. However, Catholicism did not become a major political issue until after the outbreak of the Thirty Years'

**KEY FIGURE**

**Robert Catesby (1572–1605)**

Came from a prominent recusant family and was involved in the Essex rebellion of 1601 against Elizabeth I. After the discovery of the Gunpowder Plot, Catesby fled north but he was shot and killed in Staffordshire.

War in 1618, when a number of events then combined to increase fears about **popery** and the Crown's commitment to Protestantism. These included:

- James's attempts to secure a Spanish bride for his son, Charles
- the failure to support the Protestant cause on the Continent
- the relaxation of the recusancy laws in 1622–3 as part of the negotiations with Spain.

## James I and the Puritans

Despite his Presbyterian upbringing, James did not favour the Scottish Kirk. He preferred the more ordered worship of the Church of England and its hierarchical government by bishops. His instinctive reaction to the demands of the **Millenary Petition**, handed to him as he travelled south in 1603, was to regard it with suspicion. However, the vast majority of English Puritans wanted moderate, piecemeal reforms to cleanse the Church of the last remains of **popish** practice.

James announced that he would hold a conference at **Hampton Court** in January 1604 at which bishops and Puritans could debate the issues raised by the Millenary Petition and would also look at wider Church issues including **pluralism** and the endowment of a preaching ministry. There was a general desire to see the quality of the clergy improved. Because **stipends** were so low, many clergymen were forced to hold more than one **living** just to survive, but this left many parishes with inadequate pastoral care.

## The Hampton Court conference 1604

The conference was a disputation (formal debate) between several bishops and four or five moderate Puritans. In general, the discussions were harmonious and there was much agreement. A new version of the Bible was decided on which appeared in 1611 as the Authorised or **King James Bible**. However, the conference was a failure for the Puritans because they failed to win any of their demands. Among the reasons for this were:

- If they suggested any major alteration of Church government, such as the removal of bishops, they would be branded as extremists. Therefore, they pursued the opposite line, but their demands, such as not having to wear a **surplice**, were so moderate that James dismissed their grievances as trivial and unworthy of note.

- The Puritans also wished to impress the king with the strength of their following and a petitioning campaign was organised in many areas of the country. This backfired because James disliked being subjected to what he saw as undue pressure. The last thing James wanted was a Presbyterian Church based on the Scottish model, in which ministers asserted that he was subject to Church discipline like any other member. Therefore, when the word Presbytery was mentioned, James burst out with 'No bishop, no king.'

# The outcome of the conference

The Puritans were not granted any changes in Church organisation or practice, although there was agreement between them and the bishops on the poverty of the Church. Since the dissolution of the monasteries in the mid-sixteenth century, vast amounts of Church lands had passed into lay hands and, more significantly, so had the tithes from many parishes, leaving insufficient money to support a minister. Parliament made sympathetic noises about the poverty of the Church but ultimately was unwilling to act because its members were often the ones who had benefited. They also considered any reform as an attack on their property rights.

The Hampton Court conference brought little consolation to those Puritans who had looked to James for reform. In addition, James now regarded the Puritans with some suspicion. However, in 1610 James appointed the Puritan George Abbot as Archbishop of Canterbury. Under him, those who wished for more preaching or fewer popish ceremonies were appointed to Church posts. The Puritans would cause no further trouble until the end of the reign.

# Religious divisions reappear 1618–25

The outbreak of the Thirty Years' War (see page 34) increased religious polarisation. Fears about the international spread of Catholicism were heightened by the Spanish marriage negotiations (see page 34) which, if an agreement was reached, would mean a Catholic queen and Catholic worship in London. An apparent change in James's attitude to religion increased the worries of many.

## Arminians

James had always been **Calvinist** in his theology even if he disliked the Calvinist method of Church organisation. This meant that he believed in **predestination**, the standard orthodoxy of most of the Church of England. This view was challenged by a Dutch theologian, **Jacob Arminius**, and his followers, who were known as **Arminians**. As well as free will, Arminians believed in more ceremonial services and put more stress on the sacraments. Unlike most Protestants, they regarded the Catholic Church as a true Church although they thought that aspects of Catholic belief, such as acceptance of papal authority, were wrong. Arminians also put a high value on the power of the Crown.

James was at first an opponent of Arminius, but, towards the end of his reign, he became more sympathetic to the Arminian cause because of the practical support it gave him. The 1620s saw mounting protests against Catholicism and his negotiations with Spain (see page 35). There were questions about the Crown's handling of foreign policy, but the Arminians upheld royal authority and did not share the irrational hatred of popery. It was natural, therefore, for James to promote Arminians, which made many in the Commons suspicious,

## KEY TERMS

**Calvinist** Follower of the teachings of John Calvin, who set up a strict Church in Geneva which was non-hierarchical. Calvin believed that preaching was the most important part of the service and he emphasised predestination.

**Predestination** The belief that God had already decided who would go to heaven and who to hell.

**Arminians** Protestants who believed in free will and a ceremonial form of religion which resembled Catholic practices.

## KEY FIGURE

### Jacob Arminius (1560–1609)

A Dutch theologian who asserted that the Calvinist doctrine of predestination was wrong and that people had free will to decide their own fate, because God willed the salvation of all who believed. His views were very controversial at the time.

as they regarded Arminians as little better than **papists**. Under James, religious tensions never became severe, but they were to be a major factor in the problems his son, the future King Charles I, was to face with his Parliaments.

**SOURCE QUESTION**

How does Source C justify James's reputation as a peacemaker?

**ONLINE EXTRAS**
**OCR** WWW

Get to grips with supporting judgements by completing Worksheet 5 at **www. hoddereducation.co.uk/ accesstohistory/extras**

---

### SOURCE C

King James's directions to preachers 1622, quoted in Roger Lockyer, *James VI & I*, Longman, 1998, pp. 121–2.

*[No one under the degree of bishop or dean should discuss] the power, prerogative, and jurisdiction, authority or duty of sovereign princes, or otherwise meddle with … matters of state and the differences betwixt princes and the people … Preachers should not fall into bitter invectives and indecent railing speeches against the persons of either papists or puritans, but modestly and gravely … free both the doctrine and discipline of the Church of England from the aspersions of either adversary, especially where the auditory [audience] is suspected to be tainted with the one or the other infection [that is, to be Catholic or Puritan].*

## Religion in Scotland 1603–25

James wanted to bring the Scottish Church into conformity with the Church of England. He knew that there could not be complete harmony but he was determined to introduce bishops into Scotland. He succeeded in winning the nobles away from their former alliance with the Kirk (see page 10), which enabled him to impose bishops in 1618, although the underlying Presbyterian structure remained. James also forced a number of liturgical reforms – the 'Articles of Perth' – through the general (Church) assembly. These were deeply unpopular, especially the one that prescribed kneeling to receive communion, which implied a more **Catholic interpretation** of the service. James realised he had gone too far. The Articles were not strictly enforced and a new prayer book, which had been prepared in 1619, was not introduced. In this way, James avoided open religious conflict, a sensitivity which Charles was not to share (see page 81).

## Religion in Ireland 1603–25

The situation in Ireland was more complicated. In 1607, the two Earls of Ulster fled into exile following the failure of an earlier rebellion. Their lands were confiscated and given to Calvinist Scots and English settlers in what is known as the plantation of Ulster. This meant that there were three faiths in Ireland: the Catholic majority; the established Church of Ireland, which was much more uniformly Calvinist than its English counterpart; and a smaller group of newly arrived Presbyterians. In an age which believed that religious differences led to political dissent, it was natural for the ruler to seek uniformity throughout his territories. In Ireland this would be a difficult and potentially dangerous task. It was one that James, wisely, did not undertake.

**KEY TERMS**

**Papist**
An uncomplimentary name given to Catholics.

**Catholic interpretation**
Catholics believed that in the communion service or mass, the bread and wine were transformed by a miracle at the moment of consecration into the actual body and blood of Jesus, although their outward form remained the same. This is known as transubstantiation.

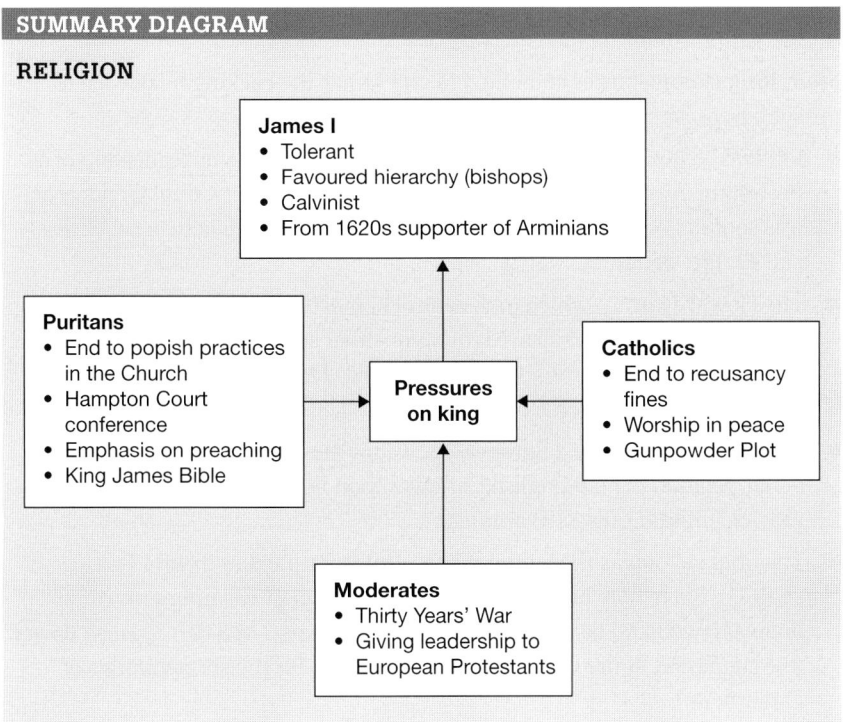

**SUMMARY DIAGRAM**

**RELIGION**

**James I**
- Tolerant
- Favoured hierarchy (bishops)
- Calvinist
- From 1620s supporter of Arminians

**Puritans**
- End to popish practices in the Church
- Hampton Court conference
- Emphasis on preaching
- King James Bible

**Pressures on king**

**Catholics**
- End to recusancy fines
- Worship in peace
- Gunpowder Plot

**Moderates**
- Thirty Years' War
- Giving leadership to European Protestants

# 4 Foreign policy

▪ *Why did foreign policy become a source of tension between king and Parliament?*

By the beginning of James's reign, war with Spain had already been dragging on for fifteen years. Both sides were anxious for peace, which was agreed in the Treaty of London in 1604. This gave English merchants the right to trade in Spain and the Spanish Netherlands (see page 24). The war had achieved very little for either side. Now that it was over, trade could be built up again. For the next five years, James concentrated on securing his position in England and there was little participation in foreign affairs. The proposal that James should take up the leadership of a Protestant alliance, suggested in 1603, was turned down. England's only role on the Continent was a limited involvement in the **United Provinces**' continuing struggle for independence from Spain.

James wanted to use the marriages of his children to further his aim to be the peacemaker of Europe. In 1613, his daughter Elizabeth was married to Frederick, **Elector Palatine**, whose family was already connected to many of the leading Protestant figures. To balance this, James sought to promote a Catholic marriage for his remaining son, Charles, despite knowing how unpopular this would be in England.

**KEY TERMS**

**United Provinces**
The seven northern provinces of the Netherlands that won their independence from Spain.

**Elector Palatine**
The prince of a Rhineland province in the Holy Roman Empire.

**ONLINE EXTRAS**
AQA | www

Get to grips with assessing individuals by completing Worksheet 3 at **www. hoddereducation.co.uk/ accesstohistory/extras**

## The Spanish marriage

From 1613, circumstances combined to give James the backing he needed to pursue a Spanish marriage and a pro-Spanish foreign policy:

- Philip III of Spain was anxious that England might take up leadership of a Protestant coalition. To prevent this, a new ambassador, Count Gondomar, was sent to London to offer the possibility of a marriage between Charles and Philip's daughter, Maria.

- The Howard family, which took control of most major offices in 1614 (see page 27), were pro-Spanish. Many were either still Catholic or merely nominal members of the Church of England. They encouraged James to pursue a Spanish match for Charles.

- Spain was the strongest European power of the day and was, therefore, in a better position to help English Catholics than France, which had a twelve-year-old child (Louis XIII) as king.

- The final factor was the failure of the Addled Parliament in 1614 (see page 41). No money had been forthcoming to satisfy the king's severe financial needs, so he turned instead to the prospect of a rich Spanish **dowry** (the suggested figure was £600,000) to make up for the shortcomings of Parliament.

Sir John Digby was sent to Madrid to pursue negotiations, although there was no immediate urgency because Charles was only fourteen, and the *infanta* (princess) Maria four years younger.

The Spanish marriage highlighted divisions in the Privy Council. The Howard family opposed summoning Parliament and encouraged the king to act on his prerogative, while a rival Protestant faction (led by the Earl of Southampton) wanted frequent parliaments and a display of unity between king and country. This division hampered the pursuit of clear objectives and was ultimately to lead those who were unhappy to seek allies in the Commons. This challenged the king's right to be solely responsible for the direction of foreign policy.

## KEY TERMS

**Dowry** Payment in money, goods or land made by the family of a bride to her new husband and his family.

**Bohemia** A region in the modern-day Czech Republic.

**Habsburg** The family that ruled both in the Holy Roman Empire and in Spain.

**Holy Roman Emperor** Ruled over the Holy Roman Empire, which covered a large area of central Europe centred on Germany. It was an elective title, although in practice the position was held by the Habsburg family for centuries.

## Outbreak of the Thirty Years' War

Philip III had no real desire to marry his daughter to Charles but it suited him to keep negotiations dragging on. This stalemate came to an abrupt end as a result of events in Prague, the capital of **Bohemia**. The **Habsburg** Archduke Ferdinand had been elected king of Bohemia in 1618. As his anti-Protestant attitude became apparent, fear grew, and in May the nobles revoked their allegiance to him. In 1619, they offered the crown to Frederick of the Palatinate.

Frederick was one of the seven electors who chose the **Holy Roman Emperor**. If he accepted the Bohemian crown he would gain another vote and the Protestants would be in a majority in the electoral college, instead of the Catholics. This was a threat that the Habsburgs could not afford to ignore. It would alter the balance of power in central Europe and the Catholics might lose their political control of the region.

Without waiting for James's advice, who was strongly against it, Frederick accepted the throne of Bohemia. He and Elizabeth took up residence in Prague but Ferdinand, who was by now emperor, immediately moved against them. Frederick and Elizabeth became known as the winter king and queen because their brief reign was brought to an end at the **Battle of the White Mountain** in November 1620. Worse was to follow when the Palatinate was occupied by Spanish and Bavarian troops, and its elector and his family were forced into exile in the Netherlands.

## Impact on England

These dramatic events had major repercussions in England. The fate of Frederick would have caused concern in any case, but that he was James's son-in-law intensified the pressure for England to act decisively on his behalf. James himself was very concerned. He thought Frederick had been extremely foolish to accept the Bohemian crown and would not help him to regain it. He considered the Palatinate to be a very different matter. It was Frederick's hereditary land and James would make every effort to ensure that Frederick was restored as its ruler, although preferably without the use of force if possible, after a report put the cost of sending an army to the Continent at £800,000 a year.

James pinned his hopes on the Spanish and sought to persuade them to use their influence to ensure the return of the Palatinate. James believed a settlement could be reached if the marriage treaty was achieved and the Spanish accepted his mediation. In this he was sadly mistaken. The Spanish had been fighting the Dutch since 1621 and they wanted to avoid England joining the war. They, therefore, held out the promise of a marriage, while they hoped that events on the battlefield would move in their favour. From 1618 to 1623, James's policy consisted of negotiations with Spain that proved fruitless. However, James was a realist and knew that the negotiations might fail to achieve their aim. To ensure that he had funds ready to meet an emergency, Parliament was summoned in 1621.

> **KEY TERM**
>
> **Battle of the White Mountain** Destroyed the Bohemian army and left Frederick and Elizabeth with no option but to flee.

### SOURCE D

Archbishop Abbot quoted in John Rushworth, *Historical Collections of Private Passages of State: Volume 1, 1618–29*, London, 1721, p. 11.

*God had set up this prince [Frederick] as a mark of honour throughout all Christendom, to propagate the gospel and to protect the oppressed … Therefore let not a noble son be forsaken for their sakes who regard nothing but their own ends … The Parliament is the old and honourable way for raising of Money, and all that may be spared is to be turned this way … Certainly, if countenance be given to this action, many brave Spirits will offer themselves: Therefore let all our spirits be gathered up to animate this business, that the world may take notice that we are awake when God calls.*

> **SOURCE QUESTION**
>
> What does Source D reveal about opinion in the country?

# Foreign policy and Parliament 1621

The king took the unusual step of inviting MPs to discuss foreign policy, even though this lay outside their jurisdiction. He hoped that an aggressive display of hostility would put pressure on Spain to make concessions to avoid the likelihood of war.

The Commons was asked for a speedy vote of taxation but it was not clear what the money would be used for. Parliament wanted an alliance with the Dutch and a naval war against Spain. This was a less foolish option than it seemed. Spanish gold helped to pay for soldiers in Germany and its troops occupied the Palatinate. If Spain and the Spanish Netherlands came under threat, Spanish pressure might force Emperor Ferdinand into a settlement.

James had a very different strategy. He wanted to use Parliament to push Spain into concessions, but if this failed, he was prepared to mount an expedition to try and win back the Palatinate directly, in alliance with the Dutch and the German princes. He did not want to break his ties with Spain because that would put an end to his hopes of negotiating a marriage treaty for his son.

## The outcome of the Parliament of 1621

Having invited MPs to discuss foreign policy, James made the mistake of not informing them fully of his intentions:

- He wanted an anti-Habsburg rather than an anti-Catholic league because he hoped for French involvement, and so he avoided mentioning religion.
- He was also reluctant to name the enemy as this would restrict his freedom of action.

This meant that the Commons was left uncertain about the king's real intentions. In a petition, MPs urged James 'to pursue and more publicly avow the aiding of those of our religion in foreign parts'. They wanted all negotiations with Spain to be ended, but rather than consider this, James dissolved Parliament.

This abrupt termination of Parliament marks the beginning of the Commons' active dislike of the Crown's foreign policy, which was to intensify in Charles's reign. James's behaviour seemed inexplicable. The country could not understand why a Protestant monarch should seek to marry his son to a Catholic princess, whose fellow countrymen were fighting his own son-in-law's troops. They were to be even more appalled by the foolish trip to Madrid.

# The trip to Madrid

In February 1623, two young Englishmen with the unlikely names of Jack and Tom Smith set off for the Continent. When they were arrested for suspicious behaviour in Canterbury and to secure their release, Tom Smith had to remove his false beard to reveal that he was the lord admiral, the Marquess of Buckingham (see page 43). His 'brother' was the heir to the throne, Prince Charles. They were on their way to Spain on a foolhardy journey that took them through France, where they visited the court in Paris. James had been very reluctant to allow them to go, but he found it hard to resist the pleas of both his son and his favourite.

The purpose of the journey was to demonstrate the depth of Charles's commitment to the *infanta*. At 23, Charles was eager to marry. By appearing in such dramatic fashion on the Spaniards' own doorstep, he hoped to push the negotiations to a conclusion. The Spanish were understandably amazed when Charles presented himself in their midst, although they treated him with the utmost courtesy. However, he was not allowed to see the object of his affections, which frustrated the young prince so much that he climbed a garden wall to try and catch a glimpse of her. Nor did the presence of Charles soften the Spanish line in negotiations. If anything, the reverse was true, as Charles became effectively a prisoner. The Spanish insisted on firm guarantees about tolerance for Catholics and would give no guarantees about the restoration of the Palatinate.

As negotiations dragged on, James became anxious to get Charles and Buckingham back on any conditions. The outline of a marriage treaty was agreed on but, once Charles and Buckingham were safely away from Spanish shores, it was not marriage they were thinking of. Instead, they wanted war, in revenge for their humiliation.

## Moves towards war

When Charles and Buckingham returned home from Spain in October 1623 they were met with scenes of tumultuous rejoicing, 'the loudest and most universal of the whole kingdom that the nation had ever been acquainted with'. The people felt that their prince had been restored to them. He was alive, and still a Protestant. In the polarised conditions of the 1620s it was difficult for an important power such as England to maintain a neutral stance for long. To avoid war, which had been James's policy up to 1623, was, in effect, to help the Catholic side. When Charles and Buckingham returned, eager for revenge on Spain, the only way this vengeance could be adequately expressed was by declaring war – an enormously popular notion for the country which had been waiting in vain for a distinctly Protestant lead from James. Less thought was given to the question of how such a war would be paid for.

One person who did consider this was the treasurer, Cranfield, Earl of Middlesex, who opposed the war because of its damaging effect on the Crown finances. Buckingham wanted to remove Cranfield and he used Parliament to have him accused of corruption and impeached (see page 45). Parliament then proceeded to vote £300,000 for the war.

This show of solidarity between Crown and Commons was deceptive: the Commons was clear that it wanted a sea 'war of diversion' against Spain which would be partly self-financing through the capture of Spanish prizes. MPs did not want the uncertainty and expense of a Continental war and the subsidy was, therefore, voted in on the specific understanding that it would be used for the navy and to subsidise the Dutch, and not to mount an expedition to the Palatinate.

## The French marriage alliance 1624

Buckingham wanted a grand anti-Habsburg alliance. To be successful, this would require the cooperation of France, which could also provide a wife of sufficient status for Charles. It was also only in alliance with France that James would contemplate military action. This would send confusing messages to the country about the depth of commitment to the Protestant cause. But, if the strategy of encircling the Habsburgs was successful, Buckingham would be vindicated.

Negotiations were begun for a marriage treaty and also for a joint Anglo-French expedition from French territory to the Palatinate to restore Frederick. In expectation of French military assistance, Buckingham was prepared to make concessions to the French over religion that he had considered unacceptable the previous year in Spain.

In the marriage treaty, signed in November 1624, it was agreed that:

- Henrietta Maria, the French princess, her children and servants would be allowed to practise their religion freely and to have a chapel in London, open to the public, served by 28 priests and one bishop.
- Her children were to be educated as Catholics until they were thirteen.
- Catholics were to be granted toleration.

The treaty did not mention a military alliance.

These extraordinary terms were extracted from Buckingham by Louis XIII's new chief minister, Cardinal Richelieu, who had no intention of making war on the Habsburgs until it suited his own purposes. Buckingham had made all the concessions and had gained nothing in return. He had become too heavily committed to withdraw from negotiations and had therefore accepted a treaty that he knew would cause outrage in England. The Crown again appeared less than committed to the Protestant cause.

## Mansfeld's expedition 1625

All might have been forgiven if the Anglo-French expedition had been a success. However, at the last moment, Louis (who had nothing to gain) refused to send any troops or to allow the expedition to cross French territory. The expedition set off under its leader, an experienced German mercenary, Count Mansfeld, in January 1625, but it immediately met with disaster. The troops were poorly equipped and the Dutch countryside where they landed had already been stripped bare by a previous army. Many soldiers died of disease and the rest melted away through desertion. The expedition achieved nothing, but over £60,000 of the Commons subsidy had been wasted in express defiance of their instructions.

## Protestant allies

Another part of Buckingham's strategy was to gain Protestant allies in northern Europe. In 1624, James agreed to finance 6000 English troops for two years to fight in the Netherlands' war of independence. In February 1625, England committed to paying for 7000 troops, at a cost of £30,000 a month, in return for a Danish campaign in Germany. This was a way of helping the Protestant cause while avoiding war, yet it required considerable finance, which would have to come from Parliament. The Commons had already made clear that it did not want to subsidise foreign allies and it disliked this use of parliamentary funds. The conduct of the war was proving controversial. This would cause problems for Charles, who succeeded to the throne on James's death in March 1625.

**ONLINE EXTRAS** OCR **WWW**

Practise assessing impacts by completing Worksheet 6 at **www.hoddereducation. co.uk/accesstohistory/extras**

**ONLINE EXTRAS** OCR **WWW**

Practise developing an argument by completing Worksheet 7 at **www. hoddereducation.co.uk/ accesstohistory/extras**

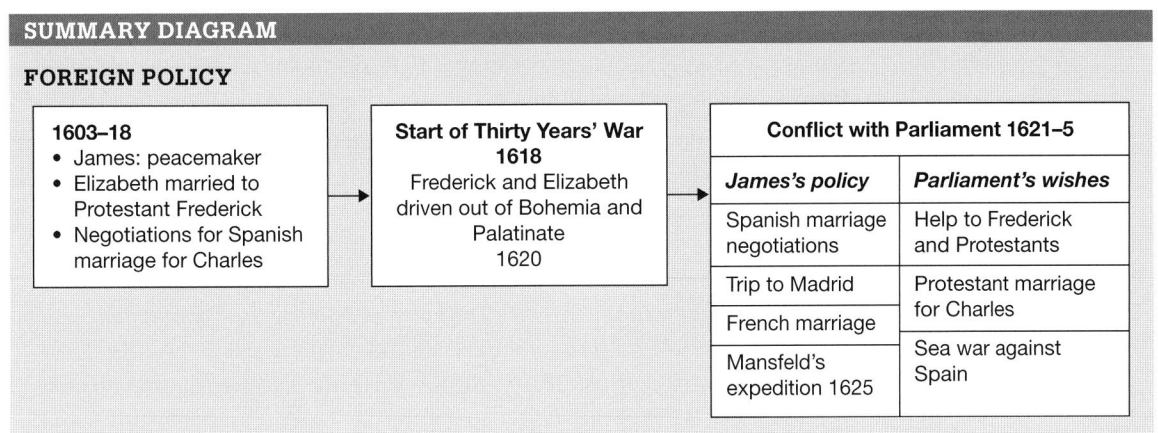

**SUMMARY DIAGRAM**

**FOREIGN POLICY**

**1603–18**
- James: peacemaker
- Elizabeth married to Protestant Frederick
- Negotiations for Spanish marriage for Charles

→ **Start of Thirty Years' War 1618**
Frederick and Elizabeth driven out of Bohemia and Palatinate
1620

→ **Conflict with Parliament 1621–5**

| *James's policy* | *Parliament's wishes* |
| --- | --- |
| Spanish marriage negotiations | Help to Frederick and Protestants |
| Trip to Madrid | Protestant marriage for Charles |
| French marriage | |
| Mansfeld's expedition 1625 | Sea war against Spain |

# 5 Relations with Parliament

■ *Why did the relationship between James and Parliament deteriorate so rapidly?*

Despite the general goodwill that had surrounded James's accession, there had been some apprehension about his intentions. His reputation had preceded him as the author of *The Trew Law of Free Monarchies* (1598) with its emphasis on the divine right of kings: 'Kings were the authors and makers of the law, and not the laws of the king' and 'the king is above the law, as both the author and giver of strength thereto'. In the early seventeenth century, representative institutions were under threat all over Europe as several monarchs sought to end their effectiveness. For this reason, MPs were very sensitive to any apparent attack on their privileges and were liable to see a challenge to their status where none was intended.

# The Parliament of 1604

The first Parliament, which met in March 1604, started badly when there was a dispute over the Buckinghamshire election. This led to angry speeches by both James and MPs. Although both sides backed down from a confrontation, it was not a promising beginning.

The atmosphere did not improve when James emphasised his wish for a full union between his two kingdoms: 'I am assured that no honest subject of whatsoever degree within my whole dominions is less glad of this joyful union than I am.' He could hardly have been more wrong.

The English cordially detested their northern neighbours in Scotland, and regarded the Scots' presence at court with deep suspicion and loathing. The Commons therefore created as many delays as they could to all of James's requests. When they refused to change the country's name to 'Great Britain', James issued a proclamation in October 1604 to announce that he would take the title of 'King of Great Britain'.

The failure of the Union, which James continued to seek up to 1610, was a bitter disappointment to him and caused him to lose faith in the Commons. The Commons became increasingly anxious about the king's absolutist tendencies and feared it was being misrepresented to the king so that he looked more harshly on it. At the end of the 1604 session, the Commons produced a statement of its position. This was **The Form of Apology and Satisfaction**, which was entered into its journal, although MPs did not present it to the king. Their fears were summed up as: 'The prerogatives of princes may easily and do daily grow; the privileges of the subject are for the most part at an everlasting stand.' It was easy for the MPs to believe that the king intended to increase his power at the expense of their own.

**KEY TERM**

**The Form of Apology and Satisfaction**
A method for the Commons to show its feelings about royal action or its own privileges in a way that was not confrontational was to write it in a journal, which was a record of all that happened in the Commons.

## The second session

The second session of the first Parliament was due to meet on 5 November 1605, although this was adjourned on the discovery of the Gunpowder Plot (see page 29). An atmosphere of patriotic thankfulness filled the session when it did resume in January 1606. Doubts about the king's extravagance were overcome in a desire to show him how relieved members were that the Gunpowder Plot had failed: James was given the largest peacetime supply that had been known, over £400,000. However, by the time the third session began, in the winter of 1606, the Commons had resumed its suspicious attitude. MPs spent months discussing the Union but failed to arrive at a satisfactory conclusion.

## The end of the first Parliament

The final session of the first Parliament was largely taken up with negotiations over the Great Contract. Underlying all the reasons for the breakdown in negotiations (see page 25) was the lack of trust between king and Parliament. Neither side felt the other could be relied on to keep its side of the unspoken agreement between them: that the king would rule in the best interests of the country, supported by Parliament with any necessary money and legislation. Instead, both sides insisted that they were in the right.

James lectured about his prerogative; the Commons made statements about its rights and privileges:

■  It was unhelpful of MPs to write in the apology of 1604 that their privileges had been 'more universally and dangerously impugned than ever (as we suppose) since the beginnings of parliaments', because it was a gross exaggeration.

■  Similarly, it was tactless of James to make a speech of two hours to Parliament full of sentiments such as 'Kings are justly called gods for that they exercise a manner or resemblance of divine power upon earth … They make and unmake their subjects, they have power of raising and casting down, of life and death, judges over all their subjects in all causes, and yet accountable to none but God only.'

In his actions, James had been careful not to attack the privileges of the Commons directly. He had shown great skill in managing his Scottish Parliaments but he made some elementary mistakes in dealing with his English subjects. One such mistake was to fail to explain Crown policies clearly. In part, this stemmed from another mistake, which was the failure to ensure sufficient representation for privy councillors in the Commons. Lacking adequate information, MPs were often ready to suspect the Crown of sinister intentions and were, therefore, uncooperative. James became frustrated and angry.

## Addled Parliament 1614

In 1614, James called a Parliament. There was no agenda and, in the absence of clear leadership from the court, the Commons turned to a discussion on impositions (see page 22). There seemed no prospect of agreement on taxation. When one MP demanded that the Scottish members of the bedchamber should be sent home, James dissolved Parliament after a session lasting only a few weeks. Because it passed no legislation and made no supply, this is known as the Addled Parliament. An addled egg was one which went rotten and did not produce a chick.

## Robert Carr and George Villiers (Duke of Buckingham)

The period between the parliamentary sessions of 1610 and 1621 was dominated by the rise of two favourites: Robert Carr and George Villiers. Their connections and influence determined the policy of the court.

### Robert Carr

Robert Carr, a young French-educated Scot, had come to James's attention in 1607. Salisbury's death left a power vacuum at court which was filled by Carr. He became Earl of Somerset and was showered with money, offices and titles.

In 1613, after a scandalous divorce case (in which it was alleged that the Earl of Essex was impotent – a charge he strongly denied), Carr married Frances Howard, Countess of Essex, the daughter of the Earl of Suffolk. The Howards favoured a pro-Spanish foreign policy (see page 34).

The anti-Spanish faction, led by the Earl of Pembroke and the Archbishop of Canterbury, decided to try to entice James's favour away from Carr by introducing a new young man to court in 1615. The choice fell on George Villiers, a member of the Leicestershire gentry. James was captivated by him but the appearance of an additional favourite did not result in the immediate fall of Carr. It took the scandal of the Overbury affair to remove him from court.

### The Overbury affair

**KEY TERM**

**Tower of London** A royal residence, but increasingly it was used more as a secure place to keep influential wrongdoers in relative comfort.

Sir Thomas Overbury was a close friend and mentor of Carr but he had opposed Carr's marriage to the Countess of Essex. As a result, he was put in the **Tower of London** on an invented charge, but the countess, eager to have him out of the way completely, arranged to have him poisoned in 1613. News of the murder was kept secret for two years. When the scandal broke, both the countess and her husband were found guilty of the murder, although Carr's involvement is less certain. James reduced their sentence of execution to imprisonment and after a few years gave them a full pardon. This created suspicions that James knew of the plot and contributed to a disenchantment with the court. Carr's fall led to Buckingham's rise.

## George Villiers, Duke of Buckingham

Buckingham was only 22 when he came to the king's notice in 1614. Initially, he seems to have impressed everyone he met. Bishop Goodman described him as 'the handsomest-bodied man of England; his limbs so well-compacted and his conversation so pleasing and of so sweet a disposition'. However, this admiration soon turned to envy at the unprecedented way that Buckingham accumulated offices. One contemporary noted sourly, 'No man danced, no man runs or jumps better, indeed he jumped higher than any Englishman did in so short a time from private gentleman to dukedom.'

The fall of the Howards in 1618, following the Overbury scandal and the dismissal of Suffolk as lord treasurer, left the field open to Buckingham. James lavished gifts on him and gradually allowed Buckingham, who also developed a close relationship with his son Charles, to take over much of the direction of affairs.

## The Parliament of 1621

By 1621, there had been no effective meeting of the nation's representatives since 1610. James was worried about the news from the Palatinate (see page 35) and wanted a parliamentary grant.

# George Villiers, Duke of Buckingham

| | |
|---|---|
| **1592** | Born in Brooksby, Leicestershire |
| **1615** | Appointed gentleman of the bedchamber |
| **1618** | Became Earl of Buckingham |
| **1623** | Trip to Spain with Charles. Made a duke, the first non-royal duke for over a century |
| **1625** | Became chief adviser to King Charles |
| **1625–8** | Led war against both Spain and France as lord admiral and captain general |
| **1626** | The Commons attempted impeachment; Charles dissolved Parliament to save him |
| **1628** | Murdered at Portsmouth |

As the eighth child of a minor member of the Leicestershire gentry, his prospects would normally have been very limited, but Buckingham became the dominant figure at court between 1618 and 1628 because of his close relationship with both James and Charles. In James's reign, his influence was limited and other points of view could still get a hearing at court. Yet by 1625, Buckingham had a monopoly of patronage. By excluding other counsels from the king's consideration, he distorted the system of government. The Privy Council lost its importance and those who could not make their voices heard turned to Parliament, especially the Commons, to get their message across.

Buckingham had a damaging effect on Charles's relations with Parliament (see page 64). Charles disliked administration and he left the direction of business to Buckingham. The favour shown to Arminians (see page 60), lax enforcement of the laws against Catholics and his command of the armed forces prompted fears that Buckingham was intending to seize control of the government and establish a Catholic State. The Commons refused to work with Charles while Buckingham was in office and they would not vote the finances needed to protect the country from invasion. Charles raised money instead through non-parliamentary taxation, which confirmed the suspicions of the Commons that they were to be superseded.

Buckingham's death did not solve any problems. Charles became even more remote from his people and followed increasingly unpopular policies without the shield of a chief minister who could be blamed.

## The first session

The country was experiencing the worst depression of the century and so the Commons felt able to grant only two subsidies (about £140,000), which was far short of what was required. The Commons then turned to domestic grievances and, particularly, **monopolies**. These were unpopular as they caused inflation. On the other hand, they were an easy source of revenue for the Crown, which by 1621 had sold over 100 monopolies.

For once, king and Commons were in harmony in agreeing that monopolies were harmful. A bill restricting monopolies failed only because of rejection by the Lords, who might perhaps have lost by it. More ominous for Crown servants was the revival of the medieval practice of impeachment when officials were tried by the Lords. Cranfield joined with the lord chief justice, Sir Edward Coke, to remove a rival of his, the lord chancellor, Sir Francis Bacon, on a charge of corruption. It was an act that Cranfield would shortly come to regret.

## The second session

The most pressing problem was the Palatinate and the best means of securing it for Frederick (see pages 35–6). The Commons were eager to see England take

> **KEY TERM**
>
> **Monopolies** These gave groups or individuals the right to be the sole supplier of a product or service.

a lead in the Protestant cause and petitioned that James's son Charles 'may be timely and happily married to one of our own religion'. James reacted angrily to this clear infringement of his prerogative, which led to a series of sharp exchanges:

- James told the Commons not 'to meddle with anything concerning our government or deep matters of state' and that he felt 'very free and able to punish any man's misdemeanours in Parliament, as well during their sitting as after it'.

- The Commons replied, 'Your Majesty doth seem to abridge us of the ancient liberty of Parliament for freedom of speech.'

- James then warned MPs 'that your privileges were derived from the grace and permission of our ancestors and us', they should 'beware to trench [encroach] upon the prerogative of the Crown, which would enforce us, or any just king, to retrench [remove] them of their privileges.'

- MPs then decided to enter a formal account of their privileges into their journal in a document known as the 'Protestation'.

**SOURCE QUESTION**

What does Source E suggest about the feelings of the Commons?

### SOURCE E

From the Commons' Protestation 1621, quoted in John Rushworth, *Historical Collections of Private Passages of State: Volume 1, 1618–29*, London, 1721.

*The liberties … of parliament are the ancient and undoubted birthright [of the English] … urgent affairs concerning the king, state and defence of the realm and of the Church of England and the maintenance and making of laws and redress of mischiefs and grievances … are proper subjects and matters of counsel and debate in parliament and that in the handling and proceeding of those businesses, every member of the House of Parliament hath, and of right ought to have, freedom of speech to propound, treat, reason, and bring to conclusion the same, and… that every member of the said house hath like freedom from all impeachment, imprisonment, and molestation.*

When he learnt about the Protestation, James sent for the Commons' journal and ripped the page out. This was not a childish tantrum. The Commons' claim that it had the right to discuss the 'defence of the realm', that is foreign policy, would in effect give MPs a voice in the making of policy. The Crown's freedom of action would be severely curtailed. The 1621 Parliament was abruptly dissolved. It had passed a subsidy bill but no legislation. Religion and foreign affairs had raised the stakes and tensions would escalate in the following years.

## The Parliament of 1624

Trouble had flared in the 1621 Parliament when the Commons discussed foreign policy, yet in 1624 they were invited to do so again. This time conditions were very different. Charles and Buckingham had returned from Madrid bent on a war of revenge, which suited the popular mood (see page 37). Only the reluctant James and some of the council stood in the way of war, but pressure from Parliament could sweep objections aside. Charles regularly attended debates in the House of Lords and was pleased at the anti-Spanish sentiment he found there. This made him ready to accept a number of potentially disturbing developments. The three most important of these were the Subsidy Act, the statute of monopolies and the impeachment of Cranfield.

## The Subsidy Act

The Commons approved the idea of a war but was less happy about the huge sums that would be needed, especially after bad harvests in both 1622 and 1623. To ensure a grant, Buckingham and Charles were prepared to accept restrictions on the use to which the money could be put. In return for under £300,000, the Crown agreed that the money:

- would be used only for specific aspects of the war: the defence of the realm, Ireland, aid to the United Provinces and the navy
- would be spent under the supervision of officials appointed by Parliament. This did not indicate any great trust in the king.

The idea of a Continental expedition to the Palatinate was deliberately excluded.

This was a dangerous precedent because it was a short step from specifying how money was to be spent to the formulation of policy. Parliament was unlikely to remain content for long with the former role.

## The statute of monopolies

The second attack on the king's prerogative was not intended as such, but was a constitutional landmark as the first statutory limitation of the royal prerogative. The statute of monopolies was a restatement of the 1621 bill which had failed. The king's right to make grants to individuals was severely limited. No longer could patents of monopolies be issued except for new inventions, in which case they were limited to fourteen years. However, the statute left a large loophole which was exploited by Charles's lord treasurers in the 1630s: patents of monopoly could still be issued to chartered companies and corporations, so that anyone who wanted a monopoly had only to form themselves into a company and a patent could be issued legally. Thus, for example, in 1632, a very unpopular monopoly on soap manufacture was granted to a Catholic company of soap makers.

## The impeachment of Cranfield

The third action of the Commons which undermined royal authority, but was encouraged by Charles and Buckingham, was the impeachment of Cranfield. The lord treasurer was a strong supporter of Spain because he hoped that a Spanish dowry would cover most of the king's debts while he knew that war would undo all his attempts to improve the Crown's financial position. The prince and the duke were determined to remove him, but Cranfield still had the king's support. James knew that he was an efficient and reliable treasurer even if he had made a large fortune for himself as well. Therefore, it was decided to use again the parliamentary weapon of impeachment. Cranfield was found guilty of corruption, fined and sent to the Tower. James, who had felt unable to resist the demands of his son and favourite, nevertheless delivered a stern rebuke to each which was to be extraordinarily prophetic.

**SOURCE QUESTION**

According to Source F, why did James foresee problems in the actions of Charles and Buckingham?

### SOURCE F

Correspondence from James to Buckingham and Charles in Edward Hyde, Earl of Clarendon, *History of the Rebellion and Civil Wars* (written in the 1660s).

*[To Buckingham] 'You are a fool and will shortly repent this folly, and will find that in this fit of popularity you are making a rod with which you will be scourged yourself.' And, turning in some anger to the prince, told him, 'That he would live to have his bellyful of parliaments, and that when [James] should be dead, he would have too much cause to remember how much he had contributed to the weakening of the Crown by this precedent he was now so fond of [meaning] as well the engaging the parliament in the war as the prosecution of the Earl of Middlesex [Cranfield].*

## The situation at the end of James's reign

The Commons had been given some useful lessons in how to strengthen its position. Members could restrict the way money was spent, unpopular ministers could be impeached, and aspects of the king's prerogative could be curbed by legislation.

It was not long before the Commons found it necessary to remember these lessons because almost immediately the Crown swung away from its stated intentions. Charles and Buckingham had promised informally that there would be a war at sea. Instead, there was no naval war nor even a breach with Spain, but against the express intentions of the Commons, Mansfeld's expedition (see page 38) was sent to the Continent.

Worse still, Charles had promised Parliament that no religious concessions would be made in the negotiations over a marriage treaty with France. This promise was broken when the recusancy laws (see page 15) were suspended and Henrietta Maria was allowed to worship freely in her chapel, which was open to the public. Thus, the position when James died, in March 1625, was that the new king and his subjects were apparently united in a common purpose. In practice, royal actions had aroused deep suspicion about Charles's ultimate intentions, suspicion which would surface with unexpected rapidity.

**SUMMARY DIAGRAM**

## RELATIONS WITH PARLIAMENT

| Money | | Power | |
|---|---|---|---|
| **Parliament** <br> • James extravagant <br> • Parliament being more generous than before <br> • Impositions were attack on Parliament's right to grant taxation <br> • Corruption in office holders | **James** <br> • Greater need for money <br> • Subsidy worth less <br> • Inflation eroding value of grants <br> • Need to find new sources of revenue – Book of Rates and impositions <br> • Reform of system was very difficult | **Parliament** <br> • Worried that James did not support Parliament <br> • Suspicion led to 1604 conflict over election <br> • 1610 failure of Great Contract <br> • 1614 Addled Parliament <br> • 1621 Protestation | **James** <br> • Believed in the divine right of kings <br> • Failed to understand English Parliament <br> • Frustrated by Parliament but committed to it |
| Patronage | | Foreign policy | |
| **Parliament** <br> • Disliked rewards going to Scots <br> • Suspicious and resentful of James's favourites, Carr and especially Buckingham | **James** <br> • Wanted to reward those he felt close to <br> • King's prerogative to dispense patronage in way he chose | **Parliament** <br> • Wanted explicitly Protestant foreign policy and sea war against Spain which would be partly self-financing | **James** <br> • Keen to be mediator and peacemaker in Europe <br> • Increasingly lost control of policy in the 1620s as Charles and Buckingham took over |

# 6 Key debate

■ *Wise or foolish: which is the more accurate description of James I?*

James VI was one of the most successful Scottish kings. His reputation as king of England is much lower. This is partly because historians have looked back from the viewpoint of the English civil war, which began in 1642, to see the tensions beginning in James's reign. It is also because of the very unflattering account given of James by Sir Anthony Weldon (see page 19). The historian D.H. Willson was a key exponent of the idea that James was a disaster as king of England.

**ONLINE EXTRAS**
**AQA** | **WWW**

Practise ranking factors by completing Worksheet 4 at **www.hoddereducation. co.uk/accesstohistory/extras**

**ONLINE EXTRAS**
**OCR** | **WWW**

Develop your analysis of factors by completing Worksheets 8 and 9 at **www. hoddereducation.co.uk/ accesstohistory/extras**

**INTERPRETATION QUESTION**

How far do Extracts 1–3 see James as a successful king of England?

---

**EXTRACT 1**

From D.H. Willson, *King James VI and I*, Jonathan Cape, 1956, p. 174.

*To the problems of [England] James gave no serious study. No doubt in any case he would have lacked the patience and humility to do so, but in his present exalted state of mind application became superfluous. Hence he arrived at his decisions far too quickly and in too offhand a manner. They were based upon preconceived ideas and principles forged in the melee of Scottish politics and now applied uncritically to England. They were founded upon emotion and self-interest. His approach to government was personal, and much of his policy was a mere projection of plans for his own advantage.*

**KEY TERMS**

**Revisionists** Historians who challenge the prevailing historical interpretations.

**Post-revisionists** Historians who modify the stance of revisionist historians without totally discrediting it.

## Revisionism

The **revisionists** sought to rehabilitate James and look at his reign in its own light, rather than with the shadow of the civil war looming over it. They were also more critical of the inheritance James had received from Elizabeth. This view is summed up by historian Barry Coward.

---

**EXTRACT 2**

From Barry Coward, *The Stuart Age*, Routledge, 1980, pp. 98–9.

*The political tensions of the reign were not caused solely, or indeed mainly, by James I. Elizabeth's legacy to the new king in 1603 was not a good one: a country at war, dissatisfaction in many quarters with the condition of the Church [and] a royal revenue system in need of radical reform. … It is now clear that James carried out the daunting task of governing Britain with much more success than he has often been given credit for, using the political skills of flexibility and compromise that he had long deployed in Scotland to defuse some of the fears of his new English subjects. James saw himself as a peacemaker king in foreign affairs. He also displayed the same qualities in domestic affairs. James's court might have lacked the formal decorum of the courts of Elizabeth I but its informality allowed a wide variety of views to be openly expressed. James's experience in coping with the factional jungle of Scottish politics made him adept at balancing faction in the English court; and also at acting as an arbitrator, defusing the factional tensions within the English Church.*

**ONLINE EXTRAS**
**AQA** WWW

Develop your analysis of interpretations by completing Worksheet 5 at **www. hoddereducation.co.uk/ accesstohistory/extras**

# Post-revisionism

As is often the case, the favourable assessments of James were felt by many to have gone too far. **Post-revisionists** such as historian Tim Harris acknowledge the positive achievements of James but also hold him responsible for poor judgement and over-confidence.

---

**EXTRACT 3**

From Tim Harris, *Rebellion: Britain's First Stuart Kings*, Oxford University Press, 2014, pp. 501–2.

*Certainly, in terms of the goals James set himself one could argue that James failed on virtually all accounts: he failed to achieve his much-desired union between England and Scotland, he failed to put the monarchy on a firmer financial footing, he failed to heal his kingdoms' religious divisions, and he failed in his foreign policy ambition to be the peacemaker of Europe. We should also question the assumption that there was a fundamental discontinuity between the reigns of James and Charles. In many respects, Charles saw himself as continuing policies which had been begun by his father. In continuing and bringing to fruition what he thought were his father's policies, Charles inevitably went further than his father had done and did things James might never have done. We have noted already James's tactical acumen. It has also been said that although the early James was not a particularly good politician, he improved with time. He learned from his mistakes. Perhaps above all, he knew or learned how to back down graciously, rather than force the issue when things were not going his way.*

---

**ONLINE EXTRAS** WWW
**AQA**

Test the strength of your own knowledge by completing Worksheet 6 at **www.hoddereducation.co.uk/accesstohistory/extras**

**ONLINE EXTRAS** WWW
**OCR**

Get to grips with arguments and counter-arguments by completing Worksheet 10 at **www.hoddereducation.co.uk/accesstohistory/extras**

# CHAPTER SUMMARY

James was greeted with high hopes on his accession, but within ten years, there was conflict. This was, in part, because he was a Scottish monarch who relied too heavily on the Scots he brought with him. It was also because James's extravagance masked the very real structural problems in the system for financing government. James's lack of attention to government and his poor choice of advisers after the death of Salisbury undoubtedly made things worse and have led to historians making unfavourable assessments of him as king of England.

However, James's reign should not be judged in the light of the civil war to come: that was much more the product of mistakes made by Charles. James did not push too far. He knew when to compromise and make concessions, such as those over religion in Scotland and Ireland.

He was also aware of his own faults and often apologised for them. His reputation would be higher if his reign had not coincided with the outbreak of the Thirty Years' War, when to be tolerant and accepting of others' beliefs was seen as a serious weakness. The last years of the reign saw religion and foreign policy becoming the focus of attention. Fears about the success of the Catholics on the Continent led to intolerance in England and difficult relations with Parliament, as the king did not seem to be following a Protestant foreign policy but instead was in negotiation with the most stridently Catholic country, Spain. The fact that Parliament would not provide the funding necessary for a successful war was conveniently forgotten by his critics but not by James himself who was realistic about the limits of his power in effecting change on the Continent.

## Refresher questions

Use these questions to remind yourself of the key material covered in this chapter.

1 How far did James I have the right qualities to be a successful ruler of England?

2 What were the main sources of Crown revenue?

3 How far was the financial system able to meet the needs of the Crown in the reign of James?

4 What were the barriers to reforming the system?

5 How far was James's own extravagance to blame for the financial problems that he faced?

6 Why did the Great Contract fail?

7 Why did relations with Parliament deteriorate so rapidly?

8 How did the rise of Buckingham affect the relationship of king and Parliament?

9 How far were the problems with Parliament the result of misunderstandings rather than fundamental disagreements?

10 How successful was James's religious policy?

11 Why did foreign policy become a source of conflict?

12 How far would you judge James I to have been a successful king of England?

# Question practice: AQA

## Essay questions

**1** 'James I's difficulties with Parliament during his reign, 1603–25, were caused by his reliance on favourites.' Explain why you agree or disagree with this view. [AS level]

**EXAM HINT** You should argue both for and against the proposition. This will mean analysing two or so factors in addition to the stated one.

**2** 'James I was responsible for the disputes over religion in his reign between 1603 and 1625.' Assess the validity of this view. [A level]

**EXAM HINT** You should analyse the reasons for disputes over religion by considering about three factors (including the given one). You need to reach a clear conclusion, which you may be able to anticipate in your introductory paragraph and develop the whole essay from that point onwards.

## Interpretation questions

**1** With reference to Extracts 2 (page 48) and 3 (page 49) and your understanding of the historical context, which of the two extracts provides the more convincing interpretation of James I's successes and failures as king? [AS level]

**EXAM HINT** Analyse the content of each of the two interpretations using your contextual knowledge. It is important to reach a detailed judgement on which is the more convincing, either as you progress through your answer, or in a detailed paragraph at the end.

**2** Using your understanding of the historical context, assess how convincing the arguments in Extracts 1 (page 48), 2 (page 48) and 3 (page 49) are in relation to James I's performance as king 1603–25. [A level]

**EXAM HINT** Analyse the content of each of the three interpretations, reaching a judgement on each one separately. Pick out specific arguments from the text and use your contextual knowledge to analyse how convincing you find them.

# Question practice: OCR

## Essay questions

**1** How successfully did James I manage the financial problems which he faced? [AS level]

**EXAM HINT** Responses should consider a range of financial problems faced by James, such as the relative decline in income, his extravagance and his difficulties in securing parliamentary subsidies. For each problem responses should reach a judgement as to how successful James was in managing them and then use the interim judgements to reach an overall judgement as to his management.

**2** 'James I was a successful king of England.' How far do you agree? [A level]

**EXAM HINT** Responses should establish a set of criteria against which to judge success and then consider a range of issues, such as finance, relations with Parliament and religion. For each issue, answers should reach a judgement as to the relative success and use these interim judgements to reach an overall judgement as to how far he was successful.

# CHAPTER 3

# The reign of Charles I: 1625–38

This chapter looks at the early years of Charles I's reign, his quarrels with Parliament and his decision to rule without Parliament in 1629. The following eleven years became known as the Personal Rule. Outwardly, there was calm, but tensions were building below the surface as long-cherished parliamentary liberties such as the right to agree to taxation were whittled away. The alteration in the established religion of the country to Arminianism, with its support for the royal prerogative, made religion a source of political unrest and disquiet. This disquiet was first to be openly expressed in Scotland when Charles attempted to bring the Scottish Church more in line with its English counterpart. The stages in this process can be seen in the following events:

◆ Charles became king

◆ Foreign policy in the 1620s

◆ The rise of Arminianism 1625–30

◆ Relations with Parliament 1625–9

◆ The Personal Rule 1629–40: economic policy

◆ The Personal Rule 1629–40: religious policy

## KEY DATES

| | | |
|---|---|---|
| 1625 | March | Charles I became king |
| | May | Marriage of Charles and Henrietta Maria |
| | Sept. | Failure of the trip to Cádiz |
| 1626 | Sept. | Forced loan imposed |
| 1627 | Oct. | Failure of expedition to Rhé |
| 1628 | June | Charles accepted the Petition of Right |
| | Aug. | Buckingham assassinated |
| 1629 | March | Dissolution of third Parliament |
| 1632 | | Wentworth became Lord Deputy of Ireland |
| 1633 | June | Charles visited Scotland, crowned in Edinburgh |
| | Aug. | Laud became Archbishop of Canterbury |
| 1635 | | Ship money levied on the whole country |
| 1637 | July | Riot in Edinburgh at the new Scottish prayer book |
| | Nov. | Hampden's trial for refusing to pay ship money |
| 1638 | | Covenant drawn up in Scotland which led to war |
| 1639 | | First Bishops' War |

## 1 Charles became king

■ *How did Charles's character affect the governing of the country?*

The accession of Charles I in May 1625 seemed to make little difference to England and Scotland. However, the huge differences between the ways James ruled compared to his son would become apparent very quickly.

# The legacy of James I

Table 3.1 (see below) shows the legacy that James left in his relationship with Parliament.

**Table 3.1** James's legacy to Charles

| Relations with foreign powers | Religious issues and divisions | Relations between Crown and Parliament |
|---|---|---|
| England had not yet declared war on Spain but it had financed Mansfeld's expedition and was subsidising the armies of Denmark and the United Provinces | Arminians were being promoted but there was still a voice at court for other more Puritan views<br><br>There was increasing concern about the success of Catholic armies in Europe and their potential influence in England | James had been clumsy in his handling of Parliament and his policies did not always meet with approval<br><br>He often did not appreciate Parliament but James accepted it as a necessary part of the political system<br><br>Crown and Parliament generally worked together despite the tensions |

Within the first few months of Charles's reign, this would change. He did not see the need to consult widely and for advice, he relied exclusively at first on Buckingham and then on a small inner circle of advisers. He intensely disliked the negotiations that were part of maintaining good relations with Parliament. In addition, he followed policies (especially in religion and foreign affairs) which caused alarm as they suggested the king was wholeheartedly committed neither to the Protestant Church nor to the maintenance of parliamentary liberties.

# The character of Charles I

Charles I was very different from his father. He was an intensely private man and this led to misunderstandings.

## SOURCE A

Adapted from *A sermon preached before the Honourable House of Commons* by Thomas Sprat, 1678.

*Even his virtues were misinterpreted and scandalously reviled. His gentleness was miscalled defect of wisdom; his firmness, obstinacy; his regular devotion, popery; his decent worship, superstition; his opposing of schism, hatred of the power of godliness.*

**SOURCE QUESTION**

What can you learn from Source A about contemporary views of Charles I?

Charles believed strongly that he had been given his position by God and he took his responsibilities seriously. He did not believe it was necessary to explain his actions, which often caused confusion such as in many of his dealings with Parliament. Charles had been impressed by the decorum which he had observed at the Spanish court and which contrasted strongly with the relaxed and even scandalous nature of James's court. Charles insisted on strictly enforced directives about who was allowed access to the privy chamber and bedchamber

**ONLINE EXTRAS**
**OCR** **WWW**

Develop your analysis of evidence to support or challenge by completing Worksheet 11 at **www. hoddereducation.co.uk/ accesstohistory/extras**

(see page 6). The royal family's public acts, such as eating, were governed by rigid rules of etiquette, laying down, for example, the distance to be kept by onlookers from the royal family and the necessity of serving the king on bended knee.

Charles had a speech impediment which caused him to stammer. In addition, he was very shy and avoided contact with his subjects as far as possible. He was, however, devoted to his own family. After a difficult start, his marriage to Henrietta Maria of France (see page 38) turned into a warm and loving relationship, and the birth of his children undoubtedly gave Charles deep satisfaction. His eldest son, also named Charles, was born in 1630 and six other children followed in the years to 1644.

**SOURCE QUESTION**

What message is the painter seeking to convey in Source B?

**SOURCE B**

Charles I with Henrietta Maria and Prince Charles and Princess Mary. Painted by Anthony van Dyck, 1632.

## Charles's patronage of the arts

The other consuming interest of Charles's life was patronage of the visual arts. He spent more time and energy in the 1630s developing an impressive art collection than on any other activity. Once, when engaged in critical and delicate negotiations over support for the Palatinate (see page 35), Viscount Dorchester found him rearranging his busts of Roman emperors.

Unfortunately, this apparently harmless, if expensive, activity was seen by many in a more sinister light. Charles's patronage of Catholic artists such as Peter Paul Rubens, who painted the ceilings of the Banqueting House in Whitehall, and Gian Lorenzo Bernini, who made a bust of the king, aroused deep suspicion. **William Prynne** saw the negotiations with Bernini, which were assisted by the pope's nephew, as part of a plot 'to seduce the king with pictures, antiquities, images and other vanities bought from Rome'. Even the patronage of the architect Inigo Jones could be regarded with distrust because his **Palladian** style was regarded as profoundly un-English. The purposes to which his buildings were put were also a cause for disapproval. For example, his Banqueting House, which was added to Whitehall Palace, was used for **masques**, which were seen as expensive and immoral imports from France and Italy.

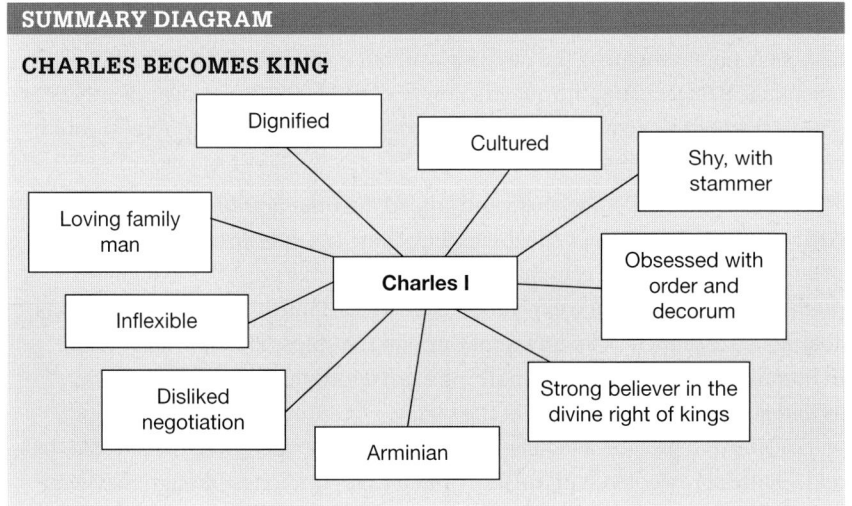

**SUMMARY DIAGRAM**

**CHARLES BECOMES KING**

- Dignified
- Cultured
- Shy, with stammer
- Loving family man
- Charles I
- Obsessed with order and decorum
- Inflexible
- Strong believer in the divine right of kings
- Disliked negotiation
- Arminian

**KEY FIGURE**

**William Prynne (1600–69)**

Prynne was a Puritan who fearlessly challenged the actions of Charles throughout his reign. He wrote attacks on the direction of Church policy and twice he had parts of his ears cut off.

**KEY TERMS**

**Palladian** A style of architecture popularised by the Italian architect Palladio which imitated the classical features of Greek and Roman temples.

**Masques** Elaborate plays full of symbolism, which were performed at court at enormous cost.

# 2 Foreign policy in the 1620s

■ *Why did Charles's foreign policy cause problems with Parliament?*

Charles was anxious to play a full part in the struggle against the Habsburgs, and to secure the restoration of his brother-in-law, Frederick of the Palatinate. All that was needed was money. However, the policy that had been followed was not the one that the Commons had agreed to pay for (see pages 38–9).

## The Commons vs Charles

It was with some justification that the Commons wondered who exactly the enemy was. Members of Parliament (MPs) doubted the king's commitment to the Protestant cause and they wanted firm guarantees about how any war would be conducted. All that the Commons would offer was two subsidies worth £140,000. This decision was justified on the grounds that no war had been declared and there had been no account given of the money voted in 1624.

## War with Spain 1625

Charles was left in a difficult position but decided to press ahead with an attack on Spain, even though he lacked the money for it. Altogether, about £500,000 had been spent preparing the navy for war, but it was still short of many essentials, despite using the queen's dowry of £120,000. It was over twenty years since a fleet of this size had been needed and the administrative system could not cope with the complexity of the task.

The fleet set sail in October 1625 and landed near the port of Cádiz. As the soldiers advanced to attack the town, they came across a farm full of barrels of wine. The expedition was short of water, the soldiers drank the wine with predictable results and the expedition degenerated into a farce. The attack was abandoned and then sickness swept through the ships. The fleet crept home in humiliation; it had achieved nothing at an enormous cost. Buckingham, as lord admiral, received much of the blame, not entirely fairly since he had worked hard to provide adequate provisions for the expedition. Undeterred, he and Charles pressed on with further military preparations although they were already committed to providing the Danish king with £30,000 a month for his army, which was bearing the brunt of the Catholic attack.

In October 1626, another fleet set sail for Spain because it could not be maintained over the winter. The supplies that had been assembled with such difficulty would rot and it would be impossible to prevent large numbers of the sailors from deserting. This time, the expedition failed even to reach the coast of Spain. It was struck by violent storms in the Bay of Biscay and had to return home. It seemed that England was incapable of mounting a successful attack against even one country, yet the Duke of Buckingham was also preparing to go to war with France.

# The beginning of the Anglo–French War 1626

Relations with France had deteriorated steadily from the beginning of 1626. Buckingham was completely outmanoeuvred in his dealings with France by Cardinal Richelieu, Louis XIII's chief minister. Richelieu used English ships on loan to France to defeat a **Huguenot** force in 1625, which caused outrage in England, and then made a separate peace with Spain. Buckingham was furious and decided that he must engineer the removal of Richelieu before there could be any hope of changing French policy. He made contact with the Dukes of Lorraine and Savoy, who ruled territories on the eastern borders of France. They also wished to be rid of the cardinal and determined on a three-pronged attack. An English fleet would be sent to La Rochelle, the Huguenot stronghold, to begin the uprising, to be followed by attacks from Lorraine and Savoy.

**KEY TERM**

**Huguenot** The name given to Protestants in France.

## Buckingham's expedition to Rhé 1627

Buckingham himself led the expedition, which set out in June 1627 with the objective of capturing the island of Rhé, which guarded the approach to La Rochelle. At first, troops were landed on the island and its citadel was besieged: all was going well. Although Buckingham showed great courage and determination, he was inexperienced in military affairs. He did not receive adequate backing from England, with the result that necessary supplies and reinforcements, which had been promised, failed to arrive. The final disaster occurred when the scaling ladders for capturing the citadel were found to be too short. The expedition returned to England in November, having achieved nothing.

Buckingham should not be blamed for the failure of the attack itself, although he bore the major responsibility for the policy which had led to it. The English administration had proved incapable of sustaining a war effort. New systems of credit were needed if military operations were not to be continually halted by a shortage of cash. As armies became larger and more sophisticated in their equipment, more effort and new systems were needed to fit out an expedition. It seemed that one disaster followed another throughout the 1620s, and the English were in no doubt about who should be blamed. One contemporary noted that Buckingham's 'coming safe home occasioned almost as much sorrow as the slaughter and perishing of all the rest'.

## The effect of Charles's foreign policy on Parliament

Foreign policy poisoned Charles's relations with his first three Parliaments, as his lack of direction at the start of the reign was compounded by bungled military expeditions at appalling expense:

- Parliament was unwilling to vote large sums of money only to see them frittered away without anything being achieved.
- In turn, the inadequacy of the sums voted made defeat much more likely.

As Count Mansfeld (see page 38) complained: 'unless I have the full amount I shall be unable to do anything worthwhile. Past experience has shown that the furnishing of money in driblets [small drops] and at long intervals is the surest way to lose and waste it to no purpose.' The lack of adequate finance drove the king to find money by whatever means he could, even if this created further conflict with Parliament. Insufficient funds had an inevitable effect on the success of foreign enterprises.

## England, France and Spain in the Thirty Years' War

France and Spain agreed in principle on a combined attack on England, which came to nothing, but it did necessitate further military preparations to defend the country. In Germany, the Danes, let down by the failure of England to fulfil its promise of money, were beaten by German forces, and King Christian IV was forced to retreat back into Denmark and to withdraw from the war. The Huguenots were requesting aid and the forces of Protestantism were in retreat across the Continent.

### Expedition to La Rochelle 1628

An English expedition to relieve La Rochelle, under siege by Louis's troops, was sent out in the spring of 1628. This was led by Buckingham's brother-in-law, the Earl of Denbigh, and was an even more miserable failure than previous undertakings. Parliament was in session when the expedition returned and its failure fuelled a parliamentary crisis which led to the Petition of Right (see page 66).

## Buckingham's assassination 1628

By 1628, public opinion against Buckingham had reached new heights of disgust. Two former officers on the Cádiz expedition came to exemplify the hate and anger towards Buckingham.

### John Eliot

One, Sir John Eliot, had been a client of Buckingham's but declared in 1626 that 'Our honour is ruined, our ships are sunk; our men perished; not by the sword, not by the enemy, not by chance, but, as the strongest predictions had discerned and made it appeared beforehand, by those we trust.' He became one of the most vocal critics of Buckingham's foreign policy and did much to turn the Commons against the Crown.

### John Felton

The other man disillusioned by the Cádiz expedition was Lieutenant John Felton. He stabbed Buckingham to death in 1628 while the duke was supervising the preparation of a third expedition to La Rochelle. Felton said he had been inspired by the remonstrance which named Buckingham as the cause of the nation's ills (see page 67). He was hanged in November 1628, although many celebrated his action.

---

**SOURCE C**

From an anonymous poem about the murder of Buckingham, 1628, quoted in Gerald Hammond, *Fleeting Things: English Poets and Poems 1616–1660*, Harvard University Press, 1990, p. 61.

*The duke is dead and we are rid of strife*
*By Felton's hand, that took away his life …*
*Though the duke were one whom all did hate,*
*Being supposed a grievance to the state,*
*Yet he a subject was; he ought to die by law …*
*A rotten member, that can have no cure,*
*Must be cut off to save the body sure …*
*Thinking all means too weak to cast him down,*
*Being held up by him who wears a crown;*
*Even then, when least he did expect or know,*
*By Felton's hand God wrought his overthrow …*
*But when his sin was ripe then it must down:*
*God's sickle spares not either king or crown.*

---

**SOURCE QUESTION**

What aspects of the poem in Source C might cause concern to Charles I?

**ONLINE EXTRAS AQA** **WWW**

Develop your comparative skills by completing Worksheet 7 at **www. hoddereducation.co.uk/ accesstohistory/extras**

There were only 100 mourners at Buckingham's funeral and the coffin was empty because the duke had been buried secretly the night before in case hostile crowds tried to attack his body. As one man wrote:

*Here lies the best and worst of fate,*
*Two kings' delight, the people's hate.*

## The effect of Buckingham's death on the public and the king

Over the next decade, the public came to realise that Charles himself, rather than 'evil' counsellors, was responsible for his policies.

The scenes of public rejoicing at his friend's death seem to have scarred Charles and to have played a part in distancing him from his people. He blamed Parliament for Buckingham's death. In terms of foreign policy, initially Charles was determined to carry on with Buckingham's plans. The fleet set out in the autumn with the same sorry results as before. La Rochelle eventually fell to the forces of the French king in October 1628.

## Peace

After this last failure, there seemed little point in pursuing the war. An additional impetus towards peace came from Charles's decision to rule without Parliament in 1629 (see page 68). Peace was made with France in the Treaty of Souza in April 1629, a tacit agreement to bury the past. Peace with Spain took longer to achieve but in November 1630 the Treaty of Madrid was signed. This was essentially a repeat of the 1604 Treaty of London (see page 33) but Philip IV gave a written promise that he would agree to the restoration of the Palatinate as part of a general settlement.

Who was to blame for the failures of the foreign policy of the 1620s? Parliament thought it was Buckingham's fault and Charles condemned the Commons for not providing finance. The wars were poorly planned, financed and executed, which meant they never stood a chance of success.

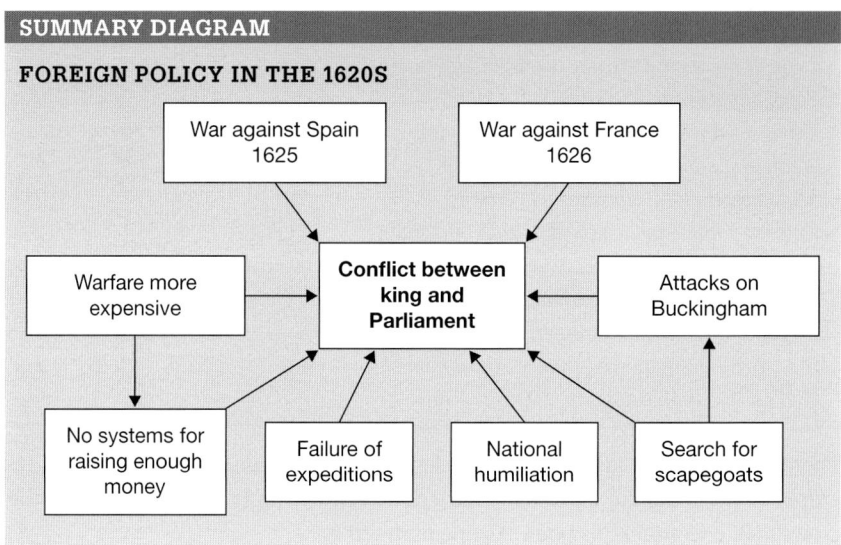

**SUMMARY DIAGRAM**

**FOREIGN POLICY IN THE 1620S**

# 3 The rise of Arminianism 1625–30

■ *Why did Arminianism arouse such strong opposition?*

**KEY FIGURE**

**William Laud (1573–1645)**

The most influential Arminian. After he became Archbishop of Canterbury in 1633 he imposed sweeping reforms on the Church, often called Laudianism. These aroused strong opposition and he was executed in 1645.

A change in religious tone was evident within a few weeks of Charles I's accession as the Arminians (see page 31) steadily gained ground. After **William Laud** became Bishop of London in 1628, second in influence within the Church to the Archbishop of Canterbury, all leading Church posts were filled by Arminians. Calvinists (see page 31) were progressively excluded from the king's counsels.

## Arminianism

Arminians wished to worship 'in the beauty of holiness', in buildings which were dedicated solely to sacred use and where services were conducted in a reverent and dignified manner.

There was much in the existing Church of England to cause them distress: many churches were in a serious state of disrepair, while in others, animals such as dogs were allowed to wander freely. There was also considerable variation in the conduct of services between Puritan or **low church** parishes, which disliked ritual, and **high church** parishes, which were closer to the Roman Catholic Church in their practices (see Table 3.2, below).

**Table 3.2** The Church of England in early seventeenth century

| Puritan/low church parishes | High church parishes |
|---|---|
| No decoration or music in church. Services would include some spontaneous prayers | Highly decorated churches, music and stylised services following the liturgy |
| The minister would wear ordinary clothes or a simple black robe | The minister would wear special vestments, in bright colours |
| Communion table in the centre | Communion table railed in at the east end of the church to indicate respect |
| Long sermons formed the centre of the service, explaining the meaning of the Bible | Short homilies (talks with a religious theme) on how to behave, especially focusing on obedience |
| Infrequent communion service, seen as a service of remembrance only | Communion was the heart of the service, showing great reverence to the bread and wine |

Arminians tended not to enquire too deeply into people's beliefs but did insist on uniformity of worship in accordance with the prescribed **liturgy** of the Church of England. They wanted this uniformity to be maintained through the authority of the bishops and clergy. Because of their stress on obedience to authority, Arminians tended to support the royal prerogative. The appeal of Arminianism to Charles was clear: it mirrored his own concern with order, obedience and hierarchy. Personally and politically, Arminianism fulfilled his needs.

## Religious divisions and clashes with Parliament 1625–9

The House of Commons saw things rather differently. Broadly speaking, the majority of MPs were low church, Calvinist, fiercely anti-Catholic and in favour of an actively interventionist Protestant foreign policy. In all except the last they were at odds with the Crown, and even the war against Spain was not carried out to their liking. There was, therefore, great scope for conflict. Religious divisions gave the disputes between king and Commons a greater depth and a new bitterness.

The promotion of Arminians to positions of influence in the Church led to parliamentary attacks on those who were most outspoken in support of the royal prerogative. Sibthorpe's defence of the forced loan in Source D, which many MPs regarded as illegal (see page 65), was not well received in the Commons, nor was the work of Roger Mainwaring (who supported taxation which had not been approved by Parliament). Mainwaring was impeached, fined, imprisoned and barred from office, but after only a few weeks Charles pardoned him and gave him a new living. Such actions undermined Parliament's trust in Charles as protector of their rights.

**KEY TERMS**

**Low church** Those who wanted simple unadorned churches and services with a minimum of ritual.

**High church** Those who favoured beautiful churches, the use of vestments and formal services which followed the pattern of worship in the prayer book.

**Liturgy** The form of services laid down in the prayer book which all churches were required to follow.

**SOURCE QUESTION**

How does Source D conflict with the views of most MPs about the role of Parliament?

**SOURCE D**

Sermon preached by Robert Sibthorpe in 1627, quoted in G.W. Prothero, *Select Statutes and Other Constitutional Documents Illustrative of the Reigns of Elizabeth and James I*, Clarendon Press, 1898, p. 437.

*If princes command anything which subjects may not perform, because it is against the laws of God or of nature, yet subjects are bound to undergo the punishment without either resistance or railing or reviling, and so to yield a passive obedience, … Tribute, being due to princes by a triple obligation, … by the law of God, as the sign of our subjection; by the law of nature, as the reward of their pains and protection; by the law of nations, as the sinews of the state's preservation … if a prince impose an immoderate, yea an unjust tax, yet the subject may not thereupon withdraw his obedience and duty; nay he is bound in conscience to submit.*

An attempt to heal religious divisions by holding a conference of Arminians and Puritans at York House in 1626 served merely to confirm that the Arminians had the backing of Buckingham and, by implication, of Charles. The Commons could protest at the direction of religious affairs but could do little to change it.

By the beginning of 1629, religion was taking precedence over all other business in the House of Commons. The Commons could see that mass was being openly celebrated at court and it seemed only logical that Arminianism was but the first step on the road to tyrannical Catholicism. Charges of **heterodoxy** were made against Laud and a fellow Arminian, Bishop Neile. One MP, Francis Rous, made a speech linking Arminianism with Catholicism and Spanish tyranny: 'I desire that we may look into the very belly and bowels of this Trojan horse to see if there not be men in it, ready to open the gates to Romish tyranny and Spanish monarchy; for an Arminian is the spawn of a papist.' In fact, Charles was never attracted by Catholicism and enforced the penal laws against Catholics who refused to conform more consistently than either Elizabeth or James, but this was not acknowledged by his opponents.

**KEY TERM**

**Heterodoxy** Heretical opinions.

**SUMMARY DIAGRAM**

**THE RISE OF ARMINIANISM 1625–30**

| Mainstream attitudes | Arminian views |
|---|---|
| • Calvinist<br>• Accepted wide variety of Church practices and beliefs as long as they did not contravene the prayer book<br>• Plain, unadorned churches | • Believed in free will<br>• Emphasis on ordered form of worship with decorated churches<br>• Railed-in altar at the east end of church |
| From 1625 only Arminians were promoted. They came to dominate the Church by 1630. Religion became an additional source of conflict between king and Parliament | |

# 4 Relations with Parliament 1625–9

■ *How far was Charles to blame for the breakdown in the relationship of king and Parliament?*

Charles began his reign with high hopes that he would work harmoniously with Parliament. This proved to be mistaken from the start. Parliament did not like the direction of foreign or religious policy and was not afraid to say so. In return, Charles refused to work with it in the accepted way and by 1629 there had been a total breakdown in their relationship.

## The Parliament of 1625

As soon as Charles became king in March 1625, he called a new Parliament in order to obtain money for the war against Spain. However, there was no royal attempt to woo MPs behind the scenes and nor were MPs given a clear indication of the amount required. Charles seems to have believed that the new Parliament would be as cooperative as the previous one. The Commons were anxious to demonstrate loyalty to Charles and, therefore, voted two subsidies (about £140,000). This was totally inadequate and, against precedent, the Commons was asked for more. (It was accepted that no more money would be voted until the previous grant had been collected.) This gave an opportunity for the doubts which had arisen about the French marriage, Mansfeld's expedition and the lack of a defined enemy (see page 46) to surface.

### Tonnage and poundage

The Commons had not yet voted tonnage and poundage (see page 21) but only about a quarter of MPs were present because of the plague. It was decided that a temporary grant of one year only would be made to give time for a full discussion of reform, including the issue of impositions (see page 22).

The Commons did not intend any personal slight to Charles, but the king was nevertheless deeply offended, especially as the Lords refused to pass the bill granting tonnage and poundage because they disliked innovation. Charles continued to collect customs duties without parliamentary sanction on a plea of necessity, because he could not give up nearly half of his ordinary income when faced with a major war.

Parliament was adjourned, but was ordered to reassemble in Oxford only three weeks later. This turned out to be a mistake. MPs, who had already made clear their unwillingness to grant more money, were not sympathetic to a demand for a speedy supply. They turned their attention to Buckingham, whom they blamed for mishandling the king's affairs. Charles saw this as an attack on his authority and he dissolved Parliament.

**ONLINE EXTRAS AQA** WWW
Practise ranking factors by completing Worksheet 8 at **www.hoddereducation. co.uk/accesstohistory/extras**

**ONLINE EXTRAS OCR** WWW
Practise making a judgement by completing Worksheet 12 at **www.hoddereducation. co.uk/accesstohistory/extras**

## Outcome of the Parliament of 1625

The first Parliament of the reign was not a success. Both king and Commons lost trust in each other:

- Charles felt betrayed. He did not understand how the Commons could fail to finance a war of which it had approved, and he bitterly resented the attacks on Buckingham and the failure to grant tonnage and poundage. He believed that the Commons was being led astray by a small group of conspirators who wished to undermine royal authority. If they could be removed, harmony would be restored.

- MPs were bewildered by the king's refusal to negotiate with them in the usual way. Charles felt it was the Commons' duty to supply his needs first and then to trust him to attend to their problems. Already the Commons had found cause to doubt his word in his breaking of promises about the war and the marriage negotiations.

Another worrying development for Parliament was the favour shown to Arminians who preached in favour of royal power. The stage was set for more conflict in future.

# The Parliament of 1626

The autumn of 1625 saw the failure of the expedition to Cádiz (see page 56). Undaunted, Charles and Buckingham pressed on with more military preparations. In a desperate search for funds, Charles had even secured a loan against the **crown jewels**, but only taxation could produce the necessary money. In February 1626, he summoned another Parliament. To try to ensure a more successful session, Charles selected the most prominent opponents from 1625 as **sheriffs** for their counties. The sheriff was responsible for organising the polls and could not stand for election himself. By this means, Charles removed key figures such as Sir Thomas Wentworth (see page 80) and **Sir Edward Coke** from the Commons. However, his hope that this would transform the lower House was misplaced. It merely gave an opportunity for others to show their dissatisfaction.

## Outcome of the Parliament of 1626

The Parliament went badly. The Commons discussed subsidies but did not pass them. The York House conference, which showed that Buckingham favoured the Arminians, coupled with the failure of the expedition to Cádiz, led to criticism of Crown policy. The Commons wanted a scapegoat and was in no doubt as to who was responsible. As one MP said: 'We must of necessity lay the fault upon somebody. Upon the king we cannot, seeing his care and great wisdom. And upon the Council we cannot. But on nobody but the Lord Admiral [Buckingham].'

The Commons prepared articles of impeachment against Buckingham, ignoring a threat from Charles that 'Parliaments are altogether in my power

**KEY TERMS**

**Crown jewels**
The formal, very precious objects used in the coronation and at other state occasions. They included the crowns and symbols of state such as the orb and mace. These were not the personal property of the king.

**Sheriff** The chief agent of royal authority in each of the shires, responsible for overseeing elections and later ship money.

**KEY FIGURE**

**Sir Edward Coke (1552–1634)**

An influential judge who was outspoken in his defence of the liberties of Parliament. He was instrumental in passing the statute of monopolies and the Petition of Right.

for their calling, sitting and dissolution. Therefore, as I find the fruits of them good or evil, they are to continue or not to be.' To avert the threat to his friend, Charles dissolved Parliament. This left the war effort in a desperate financial predicament. Charles put his loyalty to Buckingham above good relations with his Parliament. This created a situation where Parliament would not give him the funds he needed to be successful at home or abroad.

# The forced loan

The dissolution of Parliament left the government with enormous outgoings on the war and no additional income, other than captured French ships, which brought in £50,000 in 1626. This was trivial when the Crown had undertakings of about £1 million. In 1625, a forced loan worth two subsidies had been levied on Charles's richer subjects. In 1626, it was decided, against some opposition in the Council, to levy another forced loan worth five subsidies but this time on all subsidy payers. This was, in effect, parliamentary taxation that had not been agreed to by Parliament and caused considerable ill-feeling. As the Commons later told Charles, 'there were never any monies demanded and paid with greater grief and general dislike of all your faithful subjects'. However, the method of collection discouraged most from refusing. All subsidy payers were summoned to meetings where they were pressed individually to pay. In an unusually short time (by the end of 1627), over £260,000 had been raised, which removed the threat of immediate bankruptcy from the Crown. However, this financial advantage had been brought at a heavy political cost.

## The five knights' case

The loan was seen as attacking the fundamental right that taxation had to be agreed by Parliament, which also acted as the defender of liberties. If the king could raise money without Parliament, then all other liberties were at risk. Charles's subsequent actions made fears about the imposition of **absolutism** much more acute. Seventy-six people, including prominent MPs such as Sir Thomas Wentworth, were imprisoned for refusing to pay the loan. When the judges would not pronounce that the loan was legal, Charles dismissed the chief justice of the king's bench, Sir Ranulph Crewe. Five knights then challenged for **habeas corpus**. It was too risky for the Crown to allow the case to come to court as the judges might release the knights, so the council stated that they had been imprisoned 'by special command of our lord the king'. The king was now not only taxing without consent but also imprisoning at his pleasure. Southern counties, near where expeditions against France and Spain were being fitted out, had the additional menace of **billeting** and **martial law** to contend with. Liberties of all kinds seemed to be under attack. This was at the same time as practices were being brought into the Church which appeared to be popish. It raised fears, however groundless in fact, that Charles's ultimate aim was the imposition of a Catholic despotism.

Charles did not understand the effect of his actions. He believed the nation should trust him to act in its best interests because his power derived from God.

> **KEY TERMS**
>
> **Absolutism** A system of government where power is concentrated in the hands of one ruler.
>
> **Habeas corpus** Fundamental right in English law whereby if due cause cannot be shown for imprisonment, a prisoner has to be released after 24 hours.
>
> **Billeting** Compelling householders to provide soldiers with shelter and food.
>
> **Martial law** The suspension of civil law and its replacement by army rules. This would often include restrictions on movement such as night-time curfews.

He needed money for the war and, therefore, it was legitimate for him to raise it in any way that could be seen as legal, whatever the political cost.

By 1627, the situation was again desperate. Charles raised a loan from the **City of London** but only by giving it the last major body of Crown lands, worth £350,000. This ended the role of land as a major source of royal revenue and meant the City was unwilling to lend in the future. As foreign policy costs continued to mount, Charles had no alternative but to call another Parliament.

## The Parliament of 1628–9

Both king and Commons realised that they needed to make concessions if Parliament was to be effective. One MP declared, 'This is the crisis of parliaments. By this we shall know whether parliaments will live or die.' He went on to urge the Commons to be conciliatory to Charles 'by trusting the king, thereby to breed a trust in him towards us, for without a mutual confidence a good success is not to be expected'. The Commons quickly offered the king five subsidies, which was unusually generous, and agreed to grant him tonnage and poundage.

### The Petition of Right 1628

Having demonstrated their loyalty, MPs wanted to safeguard their liberties. They decided to present a joint petition with the Lords to the king which, if he accepted it, would have the force of law. The Petition of Right asked for an end to:

- non-parliamentary taxation
- imprisonment without cause
- billeting
- martial law.

It is important to remember that the Commons did not believe it was acting in an innovative manner. Its intention was to confirm what it regarded as being its traditional liberties. The Lords expressed some reservation about the petition but eventually decided to join with the Commons.

Charles viewed the debates on the Petition of Right with deep disfavour. He wanted expressions of absolute trust and loyalty, not restrictions on his freedom of action. He believed that MPs had brought the forced loan on themselves by their actions in refusing him money and that by the Petition of Right they were alienating his affections further. He accepted the petition but only with reluctance. His first reply did not use the traditional form of assent to bills (see box, page 67), which denied the petition the force of law. The Commons insisted on the correct response and, as Charles was still waiting for MPs to pass the five subsidies they had agreed to, he gave the conventional assent. This did not help to build trust in the king.

## Traditional form of assent

The normal way for monarchs to show their acceptance of a parliamentary bill was to say *'soit droit fait comme il est desiré'* ('Let it be done as it is desired'). Charles initially gave a much vaguer answer in English: 'The King willeth that right be done according to the laws and customs of the realm.'

## The Commons' remonstrance

The debates over the Petition of Right had shown deep alienation from the court. It was extraordinary that Charles could not rely on the House of Lords to protect his prerogative and that the Commons were reluctant to trust his word. Parliament was united in its belief that 'the Duke of Buckingham is the cause of all our miseries'. The Commons drew up a **remonstrance** identifying the threats which it faced:

> **KEY TERM**
>
> **Remonstrance** A formal statement of grievances.

- Innovations in religion, including lax enforcement of the laws against Catholics.
- Innovation in government, including total reliance on Buckingham.
- Disasters and dangers at home and abroad.
- The judgement of God on the government, which had turned away from the true light of Protestantism towards the false lure of Rome, as shown by the failures of Buckingham's foreign policy.

When the Commons began work on a second remonstrance, which denounced the unparliamentary collection of tonnage and poundage as contrary to the Petition of Right, Charles adjourned Parliament in June. He had obtained the five subsidies but not confirmation of the customs. He continued to collect tonnage and poundage out of necessity. When this was challenged by merchants who refused to pay, the courts supported the king and said that the Petition of Right was too general to be used against its collection.

## The death of Buckingham

In August 1628, Buckingham was assassinated by Lieutenant John Felton, to the intense joy of the nation and sorrow of the king (see page 58).

The death of Buckingham was a turning point in the reign. There was no longer an obvious target for those who disliked royal policies. Rather, the public came to realise that the real driver of policy was the king.

# The dissolution of the Parliament of 1629

The second parliamentary session, which began in January 1629, was dominated by two issues: Arminianism and tonnage and poundage. Charles had made a number of concessions over religion. The recusancy laws were enforced again and Abbot, the Puritan Archbishop of Canterbury, was readmitted to the Privy

Council, but this was not enough to reassure the Commons. Arminians had been steadily increasing in influence. The Commons resolved unanimously that religion should take precedence over all business and MPs wanted to bargain with the customs duties to obtain religious concessions. They were concerned about the seizure of goods from merchants who had refused to pay tonnage and poundage. The Commons was also troubled that the printed version of the Petition of Right contained Charles's initial, unsatisfactory answer, which had the effect of weakening the petition's impact. This contributed to the growth of distrust in the king's sense of honour.

It became obvious that the Commons was not going to make Charles a grant of the customs without major concessions by the court. He decided on an adjournment but when the speaker informed the Commons of this and attempted to rise from his chair to end the session, he was forcibly held down by two MPs while Sir John Eliot (see page 58) called out three resolutions. These condemned anyone who:

- promoted innovation in religion, popery or Arminianism as 'a capital enemy to the king and commonwealth'
- counselled the collection of tonnage and poundage without parliamentary consent
- voluntarily paid the duties.

**KEY TERM**

**Black Rod** A senior official in Parliament who would convey the king's command for the ending of sessions.

The resolutions were passed with shouts of acclamation and then the House voted to adjourn itself. It was an extraordinary scene, with **Black Rod** hammering on the door for admittance and the speaker struggling to free himself. It came as no surprise that Charles then dissolved Parliament and imprisoned those involved in the demonstration. Their appeals for freedom, based on the Petition of Right, were ignored, showing that the petition had little effect in safeguarding liberties when the king chose to ignore it. Charles's third Parliament, like its two predecessors, had come to an unhappy end. He resolved to do without them in future.

## Why did relations between Crown and Parliament break down?

In four years, the nation's initial approval of Charles had been transformed into serious misgivings about his intentions in religion and whether he would respect the liberties of his subjects.

The House of Commons saw the king pursuing unpopular policies in religion, foreign affairs and finance. Charles did not fully explain these policies, and thus never commanded widespread support for them. Great tact was needed in the presentation of these policies, but there was no effective management of parliamentary debates provided by the court. Money was requested, but the reasons for the Crown's pressing financial requirements were not spelt out.

**SOURCE E**

From Alvise Contarini, the Venetian ambassador writing in March 1629, quoted in *Calendar of State Papers Relating To English Affairs in the Archives of Venice, Volume 21, 1628–1629*, London, 1916.

*Parliament is dissolved in anger, and without deciding anything. The courtiers are very disconsolate, foreseeing that they will remain a long time in need, without money, as they have been for many months. The kingdom is furious against the Treasurer, and bears the king very little love ... What matters is that Parliament has retained the full possession of its privileges without yielding a jot, for on the last two occasions the king has always yielded something. If he returns again he will have to do the same, and if he does not, which many believe to be his determination in order not to lose his crown, it will be a difficult matter to find money.*

**SOURCE QUESTION**

In Source E, what were the two main points of dispute identified by Contarini?

## The changing role of Parliament

Buckingham's domination had suppressed effective discussion in the Privy Council, which was the arena where policy was normally debated. This distorted the traditional system and meant that Parliament became the only place for expressing dissent.

Lesser men found their route to advancement blocked by Buckingham's control of patronage and were driven into opposition. MPs who wished to enter royal service, including Sir Thomas Wentworth and Sir Edward Coke, vented their frustration and bitterness in the Commons and directed debates in the House in a manner that was often hostile to the Crown.

This new opposition role came at a time when the Crown was introducing unpopular changes in religion and pursuing an unsuccessful foreign policy. When this was combined with a long-term financial crisis the results were explosive. No longer did Charles feel at his most powerful in Parliament. The House of Commons had become a severe critic of the government and the king no longer considered it worth the struggle to win its approval.

## Strained relations between Crown and Commons

Lack of royal leadership, coupled with innovatory policies, strained relations between king and Commons. The latter began to adopt procedures which Charles could justifiably regard as going beyond the bounds of tradition. Parliament had agreed to the war against Spain and could therefore have been expected to provide sufficient finance to wage it successfully. However, the Commons refused to do this because of its uncertainty about what the money would be used for and because the need for the huge sums requested was not adequately explained. Charles responded by raising money in whatever way he could – by the forced loan and by continuing to collect tonnage and poundage after the period agreed by Parliament.

When the Commons again refused, in 1629, to grant him tonnage and poundage for life, Charles was persuaded that he could dispense with Parliament. Eliot's outburst in 1629 provided the perfect justification for Charles to put the blame on a few ill-disposed malcontents for the breakdown in relations between himself and the Commons. Eliot died, unrepentant, in the Tower in 1632. Both king and Commons could claim with some justification that their behaviour was in accordance with tradition, and that it was the other who was responsible for the end of the relationship.

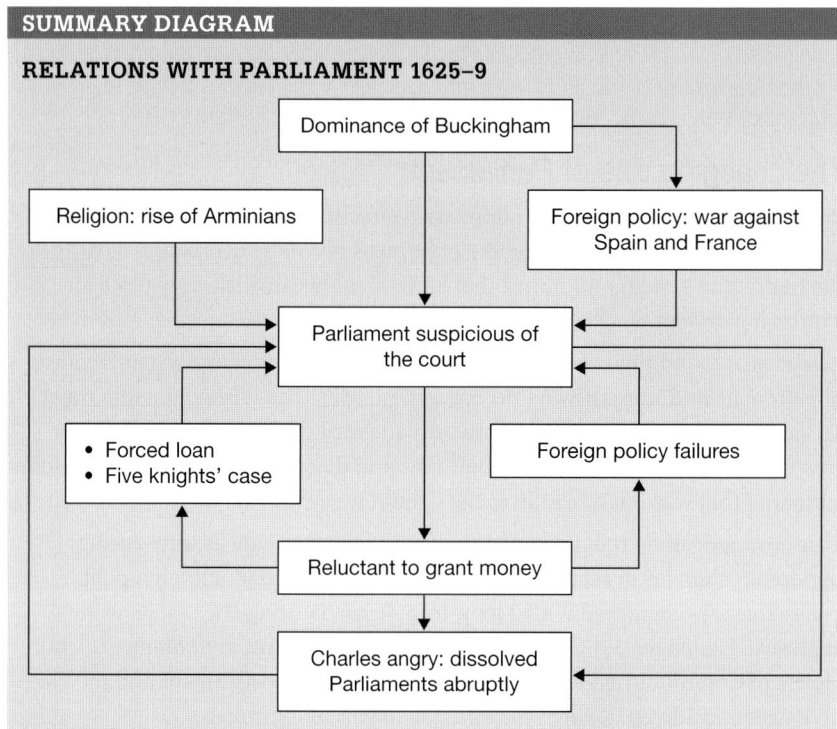

**SUMMARY DIAGRAM**

**RELATIONS WITH PARLIAMENT 1625–9**

**ONLINE EXTRAS**
**OCR**     **WWW**

Develop your analysis of successes and failures by completing Worksheet 13 at **www.hoddereducation. co.uk/accesstohistory/extras**

# 5 The Personal Rule 1629–40: economic policy

◼ *How successfully did Charles I raise money in the absence of Parliament?*

The Personal Rule was the period of eleven years when Charles I governed the country without Parliament. It was not uncommon to have long intervals between Parliaments. However, historians have seen the 1630s as a distinct period because, as the decade progressed, Charles resolved to do without Parliament altogether.

Charles said that he would call another Parliament, 'when such as have bred this interruption shall have received their condign [deserved] punishment, and those who are misled by them … shall come to a better understanding of us and themselves.' However, there was widespread apprehension about the bad feeling between king and Commons. One observer wrote that 'not only all mouths are stopped, but the Parliament doors sealed for many years'. Indeed, the king's attitude hardened over the next decade. It was only a grave national emergency, caused by the folly of his policy in Scotland (see page 81), which prompted Charles to recall Parliament in 1640.

# Economic policy during the Personal Rule

The most pressing problem during the Personal Rule was raising money. It was important to avoid policies which could be seen as illegal, or contrary to custom, because the king could not afford to jeopardise the support of the justices of the peace (JPs) (see page 2) and other local officials, on whom his government depended. The first priority of **Lord Treasurer Weston** was to try to curb royal expenditure.

## Reducing expenditure

The royal household accounted for £260,000 a year, which was about 40 per cent of the king's income. This was partly because of its sheer size. It employed between 1800 and 2600 people. In addition, there was appalling waste. The king had 24 meat dishes from which to choose twice daily. Each day's ration allowance of £25 5s. 4d. would have been enough to feed 1962 people for a whole year. Clearly, there was considerable scope for cost cutting: restricting the diet for the household to what the royal family and their immediate attendants could actually eat would have released £80,000–90,000 a year for other purposes.

Yet, reform was too expensive politically and Weston could not risk alienating royal servants. He managed to halt the upward curve of expenditure, but there were few significant economies, and no structural reform of the king's finances was undertaken. That the Crown was nearly solvent at Weston's death in 1635 owes more to increasing customs revenue and to money from prerogative rights than it does to any success in tackling waste.

## Customs

The Thirty Years' War was still in progress in Europe, but England's involvement had ceased in 1630 (see page 59). Peacetime brought great commercial opportunities and English merchants lost no time in seizing them. They traded in arms, foodstuffs, and military and naval supplies. These were particularly important for the Spanish war effort because its land routes to northern Europe had been blocked by the war, and the sea route or 'English road' became vital. With the Dutch excluded, England obtained a near monopoly of the **Iberian** trade as well as continuing to trade with the Baltic. English overseas trade reached unprecedented heights of prosperity in the 1630s. There was a corresponding increase in Crown revenue, two-thirds of which was accounted

**KEY FIGURE**

**Richard Weston (1577–1635)**

Became lord treasurer in 1628. He was an unpopular figure not only because he devised various ways for Charles to raise money without Parliament but also because he was a Catholic.

**KEY TERM**

**Iberia** Spain and Portugal.

for by customs. This increase meant that by the end of the 1630s Charles was effectively solvent – provided he avoided war.

## Prerogative rights

To be able to dispense with Parliament permanently would have required a radical overhaul of royal finance. However, any attack on corrupt practices would have involved a dangerous erosion of support among the very people on whom the king depended to carry out his instructions. Instead, Weston adopted a series of fundraising measures using prerogative rights which had fallen into disuse. These are collectively known as 'fiscal feudalism'.

### Fiscal feudalism

- One of the most successful moneymaking schemes was distraint of knighthood. In theory, every man with an income of more than £40 a year was supposed to be knighted at the coronation. This practice had gradually fallen out of use. Therefore, the many eligible men who had not been knighted could be summoned and fined for failing to show their support for the king. They were not allowed to choose to be knighted instead, which showed that Charles was only interested in raising money. By the end of the 1630s, this method raised a total of about £170,000, the equivalent of three parliamentary subsidies. Despite its success for the Crown, distraint of knighthood was very unpopular and alienated potential supporters from the king.

- Another scheme, regarding changes to forest law, was much more dubious. The boundaries of the royal forests were declared to be those of the time of Henry II, 450 years earlier, when they had reached their maximum extent. Suddenly, large numbers of people found that they were technically living in a royal forest, and could now be fined for various offences such as engaging in agriculture.

- Wardship (see page 22) also brought in an extra £50,000 compared to earlier in the century. This was done at the expense of those unfortunate enough to be caught in wardship by the untimely death of the estate holder. Two wardships in quick succession could ruin a family.

- Other methods of raising money were less important financially but caused considerable irritation to those affected. They included a proclamation against remaining in London without permission. The justification for this was that the gentry were needed in their localities to preserve order and to keep local government functioning efficiently. One man was fined £1000 for ignoring the proclamation. Men could also be fined for building property too near the capital, and for eating meat during Lent.

What rankled in all these cases was the unfairness of the demands and their arbitrary nature. They affected the political classes most severely – the very group whose support was vital to the king. Sir Arthur Haselrig (who would later fight for Parliament) described these years as a time when two or three gentlemen could not go out together without being charged with a riot. Another problem with such sources of finance was that they provided no permanent solution to the king's need for adequate supply. As the Venetian ambassador put it: 'All these may be called false mines for obtaining money, because they are good for once only and states are not maintained by such devices.'

## Monopolies and grants

Other means of raising money were more permanent, but equally unpopular. Charles broke the spirit of the 1624 statute of monopolies by exploiting a loophole that enabled him to grant monopolies to companies, rather than to individuals. It has been estimated that for every £100,000 raised for the king, £750,000 went into the pockets of the patent holders. The monopoly on the production and sale of soap was especially unpopular. Not only did prices rise, but the new company included a number of Catholics and the soap was apparently of inferior quality. For the Crown, the 'popish soap' brought in £29,000 a year by 1636.

## Ship money

The most profitable of the new ways of raising money was ship money. This was traditionally levied on coastal counties for defence. In 1634, it was levied to build up the fleet to guard against the activities of pirates, who regularly raided the south coast and trafficked young people into slavery. In 1635, against all precedent, it was extended to cover the whole country. The tax was demanded each year until 1640, which was exceptional. The 'emergency' had become permanent and Charles had introduced a national system of taxation by the back door. In 1638, a Somerset grand jury complained of 'the great and heavy taxations, by new invented ways upon the country'. The key word was 'new'. Like many of Charles's other policies, ship money was innovatory and against tradition even if it was technically legal.

### The impact of ship money

Initially, the tax was extremely successful. It raised £190,000 a year and the rate of non-payment was very low, 2.5 per cent in the first three years.

New ratings systems were introduced in many areas to spread the burden of taxation and also to widen its scope. In Essex in 1640, there were 3200 on the roll for parliamentary subsidies, but 14,500 were assessed for ship money. This meant more people were affected by it, which led to a greater degree of political awareness (this greater awareness would become significant when Parliament reassembled in 1640).

However, the methods of assessing and collecting the tax gave rise to much opposition. The sheriff was made personally responsible for collecting the sum decided for his county and this placed a heavy burden on him, both financially and in terms of time. Some sheriffs were still trying to collect arrears and satisfy the Privy Council long after their terms of office were over. The unpleasantness of collecting the tax weakened support for the government.

Nevertheless, despite the grumbles and dissatisfaction, up to 1637 ship money was the most profitable tax ever recorded in peacetime. In October 1637, one observer wrote: 'I think that great tax of the ship money is so well digested … I suppose [it] will become perpetual ... time can season and form minds to comply with public necessities.'

## Hampden's case

This forecast was to prove hopelessly wrong. The following month, John Hampden, a member of the Buckinghamshire gentry, was brought to trial for refusal to pay. Charles was keen to have the judges pronounce on ship money because it would strengthen his claim to collect it. The case aroused enormous interest nationally and when five of the twelve judges refused to find for the king, it was a moral victory for Hampden. In 1638, the amount collected fell by twenty per cent.

Hampden's case might have proved less significant if it had not coincided with the attempt to impose a new prayer book on the Scots. There was increased suspicion about what the money was intended for, even though it was all spent on building up the navy, which was a passion of Charles's. More importantly, the level of government financial demands became excessive. By 1639, the king was seeking money for the militia in the Bishops' Wars (see page 86) and payment fell to twenty per cent. The provinces were being squeezed twice and there were fears of riots if ship money was pressed too far. Ship money could be sustained only when the local elites gave it their cooperation. Once that broke down, as men put the interests of their localities above those of the government, ship money collection collapsed as well.

# Opposition

In 1637, there seemed scarcely a ripple on the calm surface of politics. One observer commented to a friend, 'our times here are so quiet that they yield no occurrence worth the relation'. **Clarendon** looked back on the 1630s as a time when the kingdom enjoyed, 'the greatest calm and the fullest measure of felicity that any people in any age, for so long time together, have been blessed with, to the wonder and envy of all':

- The monarchy, for the first time in decades, was solvent.
- The country was at peace and there were no enemies posing a serious threat to security.
- The king was in excellent health, with five children, so there were no fears about the succession.
- It appeared that Charles could go on governing without a Parliament, and long usage would probably have resigned the majority to his most contentious reforms in the Church.

In the absence of Parliament, there was very little opportunity to express any disagreement with royal policies, and thus no real opportunity for the king to

**KEY FIGURE**

**Edward Hyde, Earl of Clarendon (1609–74)**

A staunch royalist who fought for the king and later wrote an influential history of the civil war. He was, however, quite ready to criticise the actions of Charles I when he felt it to be appropriate.

consider changing or explaining his policies to mollify any discontented citizens. The government clamped down hard on any open opposition, as the fate of Prynne, Bastwick and Burton (see page 78) showed. However, lack of expression did not mean that discontent was not growing.

Significantly, there was an upsurge in emigration. In 1630, for example, eleven ships with a total of about 700 passengers left for America, many seeking the godly commonwealth they could not establish at home. A few of the most active Puritan opponents of the king joined together in the **Providence Island Company** and encouraged each other to maintain an opposition. Those who remained in England had to express their dissatisfaction obliquely. By 1636, when it appeared that ship money had ceased to be an occasional emergency levy and had become an annual tax, disputes over assessments increased markedly in a way that reveals the popular discontent. It was by such indirect means that people could indicate their unhappiness at events. A Parliament would have warned the king about the depth of dissatisfaction in the country. As it was, Charles did not call Parliament until he was so deeply committed to unpopular policies in Scotland (see page 82) that no easy retreat was possible.

# The law

Hampden's case showed how Charles could not rely on the common law courts to produce judgments in his favour. The prerogative courts of the **Star Chamber** and **High Commission** were much more reliable politically. They continued to exercise their function of providing justice to the poor but were also used to attack those who refused to conform to government orders or to raise money, and were used when the common law did not allow for harsh enough penalties. The enormous fines were seldom collected in full, but their purpose was to act as a deterrent to others. Great resentment was generated among those, like the Earl of Clare, who were called before the court.

By 1640, justice seemed to take second place to money. The provision of justice was one of the monarch's most important functions. Allowing the courts to be debased into mere collectors of money did much to undermine trust in Charles's government. The Star Chamber also lost respect because Archbishop Laud used it and the Court of High Commission to enforce his extremely unpopular reforms in the Church (see page 77).

## The City of London

The City and the king had interests in common. He promoted trade and could dispense valuable patronage in the form of customs farms or monopolies. In return, the City was the first place to which the king would look when he wanted a generous loan.

It is a measure of Charles's ineptitude to have so alienated the City in 1635 (see the box) that when he asked for a loan to fight the Scots in 1639 they first granted him a paltry £5000 and thereafter refused any more support.

**KEY TERMS**

**Providence Island Company** Set up in 1630s to establish godly commonwealths in the Caribbean which would make money from tobacco and cotton. It provided an opportunity for like-minded Puritans to meet legitimately.

**Star Chamber** A body made up of members of the Privy Council, formed as needed. It was used to attack those who disagreed with government policy. It was particularly useful as a means of raising revenue because it was speedy and efficient in its dealings and it was able to impose huge fines.

**Court of High Commission** A court created by Henry VIII to exercise control over the Church and enforce ecclesiastical decrees.

**The trial of the City of London**

In 1635, the City of London was put on trial for failing to find enough people to settle in Londonderry, Ireland (which it had been given by the Crown). The City lost its Irish lands, incurred a fine of £70,000 (later reduced) and was publicly humiliated.

**THE PERSONAL RULE 1629–40: ECONOMIC POLICY**

| Source of finance | Reaction |
|---|---|
| Revenue from customs | Resentment at collection of customs not agreed by Parliament and increasing use of impositions |
| Ship money | Hampden's case led to collapse in receipts |
| • Distraint of knighthood<br>• Forest law<br>• Wardship<br>• Monopolies | Seen as unfair and of dubious legality |

**ONLINE EXTRAS**
**AQA**          **WWW**

Develop your analysis of consequences by completing Worksheet 9 at **www. hoddereducation.co.uk/ accesstohistory/extras**

# 6 The Personal Rule 1629–40: religious policy

◼ *Why did Laud's reforms cause so much concern?*

As Archbishop of Canterbury (see page 60) and with the full support of the king, Laud introduced a series of reforms which are known collectively as Laudianism. The changes were of two kinds: the suppression of preaching and changes to the conduct of services. Together, these affected every parish in the country.

## Attacks on preaching

Many Puritan parishes held lectures on Sunday afternoons. These were little more than lengthy sermons, but if they were held after the regular morning service they did not need to conform to the established pattern of worship. Charles and Laud disliked preaching because it was difficult to control the content of sermons, which might pose a threat to the authority of bishops.

The attack on preaching began immediately. In 1629, Charles ordered that catechising (set question-and-answer sessions) replace sermons in parishes. Then it was ordered that each lecturer 'read divine service according to the liturgy printed by authority, in his surplice and hood before the congregation'. In the late 1620s, a group of professional men in London had formed an association known as the '**feoffees for impropriations**' with the aim of using charitable donations to buy up impropriations so that they could endow godly preaching. Laud suppressed the feoffees, whom he feared might stir up unrest, although

**KEY TERM**

**Feoffees for impropriations**
The feoffees were a group of Puritans who appointed their nominees to ministerial and lecturing positions. An impropriation was the right of a layman to collect tithes and to appoint a deputy (or vicar) to take the actual services.

there is no evidence that the preachers were not solely concerned with the spiritual life of their congregations.

# Conduct of services

Services were made more uniform by insisting on a strict adherence to the prayer book, bowing by the congregation when the name of Jesus was spoken, and the wearing of a surplice by the minister. These had all been elements of the Elizabethan settlement, but had been ignored in many parishes. However, the most visible sign of the new beliefs was that the altar was to be railed in at the east end of the church.

## The altar table

The Elizabethan prayer book stated that the altar table was to be kept at the east end and brought into the body of the church during services. In practice, this was too inconvenient and each parish left the altar in its preferred position:

■ Laud not only wanted it permanently at the east end, but also ordered it to be railed off, further creating the impression that the minister was a separate being cut off from his flock with the status to mediate between them and God.

■ This implied that the communion was a sacrificial service, not merely a commemorative one, and was therefore like the Catholic mass.

All of this was anathema to the Puritans, as was the reissue of the **Book of Sports** with its implicit attack upon respect for the **sabbath**. Stained glass, which epitomised the worship of images, was installed in some churches, and organs and choir-stalls were established wherever possible.

# 'Thorough'

Laud brought his motto of 'Thorough' (a determination to see that reforms were properly carried through and efficiently administered) to the enforcement of his ecclesiastical changes. All bishops were ordered to live in their diocese (the area of the country controlled by a bishop) and to make regular visitations of their parishes. Clergy who were found to be infringing Church laws were summoned before a Church court or the Court of High Commission, which developed a fearsome reputation. Some clergy even fled abroad rather than appear before the court.

# Opposition to Laudianism

It is difficult to be certain how unpopular the religious changes were. There was no universal dissatisfaction. Some liked the new ritual of their services and the Book of Sports was welcomed by many because it provided a chance to relax on the one non-working day of the week. Puritans were not popular. As one anonymous pamphlet put it, 'A Puritan is an imperfect kind of a Christian. Hypocrisy is his best tutor … he makes [his religion] wholly to consist in long prayers to little sense [and] long sermons to little profit.' However, Laud's

**KEY TERMS**

**Book of Sports** A list of activities which were pronounced to be lawful on Sundays, including archery and dancing. The declaration had originally been issued in 1618 but James I had pulled back from insisting that it was read out in churches because Puritans were offended by it. Laud insisted that the declaration be read out.

**Sabbath** Another word for Sunday used by Puritans who believed that the instruction in the Ten Commandments to 'keep the Sabbath day holy' prohibited any form of recreational activity.

reforms clearly offended and alienated large sections of the population who were profoundly uneasy at their implications.

In part, this was a product of the feeling that the established Church they had grown up in was changing, and forcing those who had not altered their own beliefs into the position of nonconformists. The Bishop of Salisbury voiced the bewilderment of many: 'Why that should now be esteemed Puritan doctrine, which those held who have done our Church the greatest service in beating down Puritanism, or why men should be restrained from teaching that doctrine hereafter, which hitherto has been generally and publicly maintained … I cannot understand.'

For some, emigration seemed the only answer in an England which was moving in a popish direction. Some who resisted wrote pamphlets in which bishops were described as 'tigers', 'vipers', 'bloodsuckers' and 'cruel stepfathers of the church', but detection of the author could result in severe punishment. The most notorious case was that of William Prynne, a lawyer; Henry Burton, a clergyman; and John Bastwick, a doctor. They had all published attacks on the Church and in 1637 were tried in the Star Chamber, found guilty and condemned to a gruesome punishment: their ears were cut off in the **pillory**, they had to pay a heavy fine and were sentenced to life imprisonment.

**KEY TERM**

**Pillory** A device with holes for securing the head and hands used for punishment and public humiliation.

## Gentry opposition

Much of the outrage at the punishment of Prynne, Burton and Bastwick was caused because they were gentlemen who ought not to have received such a degrading punishment. Laud was seen to be attacking the position and property rights of the gentry, an attack which was felt all the more keenly because Laud's father had been in trade. Prynne called him 'a little, low, red-faced man'.

Laud was anxious to restore the wealth of the Church in order to improve the status of the clergy. Restrictions were put on the terms which ecclesiastical landlords could offer to their tenants. This was designed to stop the practice whereby bishops would offer a long lease on a low rent in return for a high entry fine, thus impoverishing future clergy for their own gain. The tenants who lost out were usually from the gentry. Laud also made unsuccessful attempts to recover impropriations to provide more money for clergy stipends. This could only be done at the expense of the gentry.

Another reason for the gentry to dislike Laudianism was that it blurred social distinctions:

- For example, in Norwich, diocese pews were ordered to be of uniform size so as not to block the view of the altar. This offended the leaders of local communities who sought to underline their importance by having elaborate pews.
- It was the gentry who were so opposed to the reissue of the Book of Sports because it threatened their law enforcement role as JPs by potentially encouraging disorder (through the sanction it gave to such supposedly immoral pursuits as dancing).

However, Laudianism provoked the greatest opposition because it appeared to lead to popery. The attempt to impose religious uniformity on Charles's three kingdoms was to lead to the end of the Personal Rule.

# Ireland: religious and economic policy during the Personal Rule

Ireland was potentially the most troublesome of Charles's kingdoms. This Catholic country had had an alien Protestant ruling class imposed on it and then, in the wake of the rebellion at the start of the century, a series of plantations were created. Land was taken from its original holders if they could not prove a valid title to it and was given to Protestant settlers. This policy affected not only the native Irish but also the Catholic 'Old English' (see page 12). Charles used their insecurity to extract money for his wars in the 1620s by promising to make concessions known as **'the Graces'** which confirmed their right to hold land. These Graces were not confirmed and their implementation became a major objective of the Catholics.

## Wentworth in Ireland

In 1632, when Sir Thomas Wentworth was appointed Lord Deputy, Ireland was a financial liability to England. There was an annual deficit of £20,000. Wentworth brought the Irish Parliament into a position of subservience by exerting great pressure in the choice of parliamentary candidates, and by refusing to allow any debate until the Crown's financial needs had been dealt with. He skilfully exploited the divisions in Irish society to gain more money. For example, in 1634, he promised to implement the Graces in return for additional subsidies from Parliament. Then he broke his word and forged an alliance with the Protestant 'New English'. This was short lived because of Wentworth's religious policy and a campaign to win back Church lands.

The Irish Church was led by Archbishop Ussher of Armagh, who had strongly Calvinist beliefs. He opposed both the appointment of Arminians to vacant bishoprics and the imposition of Arminian ceremonialism, but the Church had no means of making an effective protest. Puritan opposition was crushed by the Court of High Commission, which was set up in 1634. Those who refused to conform lost their livings.

Others who might have supported the reforms were alienated by Wentworth's campaign to win back Church lands, which was intended to alleviate the poverty of the clergy. Since the Reformation most of the Church's wealth had fallen into the hands of laymen. The attack on their property rights made Wentworth influential enemies such as the Earl of Cork. Church reform united many different groups against the government.

## Wentworth's impact on Ireland

Initially, Wentworth was very successful in Ireland:

- He ended the deficit and Ireland began to contribute to the English Treasury.

**ONLINE EXTRAS** AQA **WWW**

Practise writing introductions by completing Worksheet 10 at **www.hoddereducation. co.uk/accesstohistory/extras**

**KEY TERM**

**The Graces** Allowed Catholics to take a full part in political life in Ireland and confirmed their titles to land.

- He extended the powers of the prerogative courts and claimed royal title to huge tracts of land.
- Large fines were imposed on those who opposed his measures.
- The administration of customs was made more efficient and smuggling was attacked.

His policies brought in increased revenue, a more efficient administration and a reformed Church, but these were bought at enormous cost. He alienated every section of society. Within two years of his departure in 1639, royal authority had collapsed as rebellion swept the country. Trouble was to surface even sooner in Scotland.

## Scotland: religious and economic policy during the Personal Rule

Charles showed little enthusiasm for his birthplace. His coronation in Edinburgh was not held until 1633. Then he stayed for only two weeks. In an era of personal monarchy it was important that the king be seen regularly since he was the

# Sir Thomas Wentworth, Earl of Strafford

| | |
|---|---|
| **1593** | Born in London |
| **1614** | Became an MP |
| **1626** | Excluded from the 1626 Parliament |
| **1627** | Imprisoned for opposing the forced loan |
| **1628** | Entered royal service, becoming president of the Council of the North |
| **1632** | Appointed Lord Deputy of Ireland |
| **1639** | Returned to London to assist Charles with the crisis over Scotland Made Earl of Strafford |
| **1641** | Executed after being declared guilty of treason in an act of attainder |

Wentworth was the son of a substantial Yorkshire landowner. He became an MP and was very critical of Charles I's foreign policy. He was typical of a number of people in the 1620s who wished to serve the king but were blocked from doing so by Buckingham's control of patronage. Denied a voice at court, Wentworth expressed his opposition to the direction of Crown policy in Parliament, leading the debates over the Petition of Right (see page 66). After Buckingham's death, the way was open for him to be given office and he became president of the Council of the North and a member of the Privy Council.

Wentworth was one of the most energetic and efficient members of the Privy Council but he also had a genius for alienating people. He was arrogant and insensitive. Charles never liked him or admitted him to his inner circle of advisers. Sending him to Ireland was a good way of securing Wentworth's services while keeping him distant from the real sources of power. His one ally at court was William Laud. Together they conceived a style of government known as 'Thorough'. The attempt to develop 'Thorough' as a method of government in England had limited success, but in Ireland, Wentworth was able to impose much stricter control and to achieve apparent acquiescence to royal commands. For this reason, Wentworth came to symbolise the hated aspects of the Personal Rule.

Parliament was determined to punish Wentworth, by now Earl of Strafford, for what had been done in the 1630s (see page 93). It proved impossible to find him guilty of treason when he so clearly had been acting with the king's knowledge and consent. Instead, he was declared to be guilty in an act of attainder (which removed the need for a trial). Charles was pressured into signing this and therefore agreeing to Strafford's execution. It was something he always regretted.

source of patronage and power. All monarchs experienced problems in ruling their kingdoms unless they went out of their way to ensure that all parts of their dominions received equal attention. The Scots felt slighted by Charles's neglect of them, especially as Charles was the first king to be regarded as foreign. It was the English who received the bulk of royal patronage and the Scots were excluded from England's growing overseas trade.

Charles showed a lack of sensitivity in dealing with the Scots. His first act in 1625 had been to revoke all grants of land made by the Crown since 1540. This included the Church lands given to the nobility as a result of the Reformation. It affected almost all families of substance and was an extraordinarily tactless move. This was later changed so that men could retain their lands on Crown leases with the income going to subsidise the stipends of Church ministers.

This was a generally successful scheme but, like so much else that Charles did, the political price was very high. The nobility, already excluded from power, felt alienated from the Crown. However, opposition remained passive while the nobility was at odds with the Presbyterian ministers, who exerted great influence on political life. An attempt to introduce a new prayer book united the two strands into a fervent nationalist uprising which proved very difficult to contain.

## The imposition of a new prayer book

Scotland was unusual in that the majority of its population supported a version of Protestantism (Presbyterianism, see page 10) that was not acceptable to the king. On instructions from Charles in 1635:

- The Scottish bishops drew up a Book of Common Prayer based on the English version but with changes to make the book more acceptable to the Scots. For example, the word 'priest' was deleted.

- They produced canons 'for the uniformity of … discipline' which stipulated east-end altar tables, kneeling and the practice of confession, which caused much offence.

- There was no consultation with the clergy and the canons were imposed by royal decree.

- The canons required obedience on pain of excommunication to a prayer book that no one had seen because it was not yet completed. There were grave fears about what the book would contain and rumours were widespread that it was full of 'popish rites'.

The biggest mistake came in the manner of the prayer book's imposition. It was introduced by royal proclamation, abandoning all pretence of government by consent. When the new prayer book was used at St Giles's Cathedral, Edinburgh, in July 1637, there was a riot. A woman (Jenny Geddes) who threw a stool at the minister and called out 'the mass is entered upon us!' expressed the opinion of the vast majority of the Scottish people. Protestantism and patriotism combined in a powerful mood of resistance. Charles ignored the frantic warnings from his Scottish ministers about the gravity of the situation and believed that firmness would end the problem, a view shared by Laud, who advised the king to 'risk everything rather than yield a jot'.

In February 1638, Charles issued a proclamation making protests against the new prayer book an act of treason. The Scots now had to choose between loyalty to the king and loyalty to the Presbyterian Church. A **Covenant** was drawn up to which hundreds of thousands of Scots subscribed. Charles refused to back down. He sent the Marquess of Hamilton to negotiate but had no intention of making any concessions, as he made clear: 'I expect not anything can reduce that people to obedience but force only … In the meantime your care must be to dissolve the multitude, and … to possess yourselves in Edinburgh and Stirling … and, to this end, I give you leave to flatter them.' Charles was authorising Hamilton to make promises he had no intention of keeping.

## KEY TERM

**Covenant** A document to which men subscribed, swearing to resist to the death the innovations in religion. They were known as 'Covenanters'.

## SOURCE QUESTION

How does Source F reveal the gulf between Charles and his subjects?

### SOURCE F

**Charles writing to the Earl of Suffolk, February 1639.**

*The great and considerable forces lately raised in Scotland, without order or warrant from us, by the instigation of some factious persons ill affected to monarchical government, who seek to cloak their too apparent rebellious designs under pretence of religion, albeit we have often given them good assurance of our resolution constantly to maintain the religion established by the laws of that kingdom, have moved us to take into our royal care to provide for the preservation and safety of this our kingdom of England, which is by the tumultuous proceedings of those factious spirits in apparent danger to be annoyed and invaded.*

Charles showed little understanding of the motivation of his opponents and the strength of their feeling. His determination to use force was to lead to war with the Scots and an end to the Personal Rule.

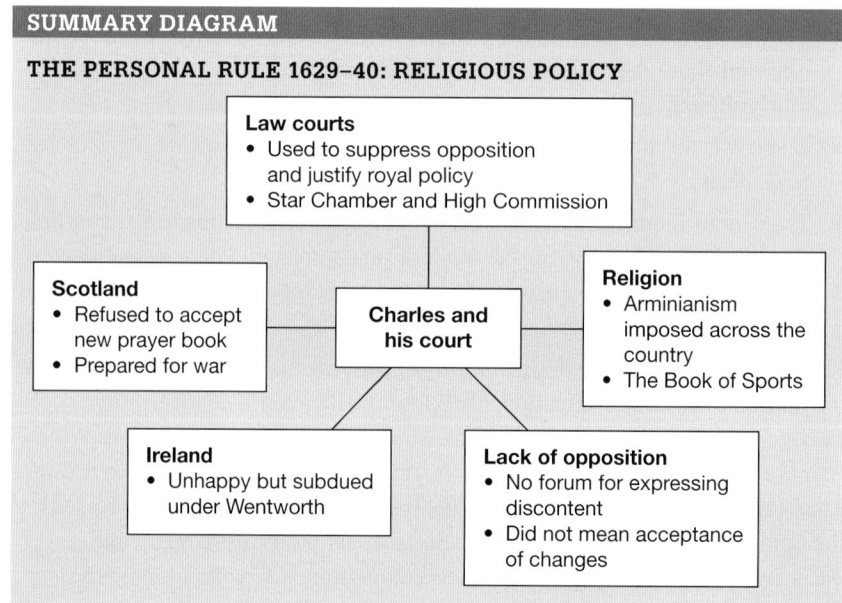

### SUMMARY DIAGRAM

**THE PERSONAL RULE 1629–40: RELIGIOUS POLICY**

**Law courts**
- Used to suppress opposition and justify royal policy
- Star Chamber and High Commission

**Scotland**
- Refused to accept new prayer book
- Prepared for war

**Charles and his court**

**Religion**
- Arminianism imposed across the country
- The Book of Sports

**Ireland**
- Unhappy but subdued under Wentworth

**Lack of opposition**
- No forum for expressing discontent
- Did not mean acceptance of changes

## ONLINE EXTRAS
AQA **WWW**

Test your understanding of 'the why factor' by completing Worksheet 11 at www.hoddereducation. co.uk/accesstohistory/extras

# CHAPTER SUMMARY

The reign of Charles I began with high hopes on both sides, but these hopes were to be short lived. Undoubtedly, the dominant position of the Duke of Buckingham played a large part in this as it was very difficult for alternative views to obtain a hearing at court. The death of Buckingham did nothing to improve relations but merely showed that Charles was behind many of the unpopular policies. However, the failure of the Commons to give Charles sufficient money to run the country, let alone conduct a war, was also to blame and both sides could feel they had justifiable grievances.

The conduct of foreign policy added hugely to the mistrust which developed in the early years of the reign. The French marriage and Arminian religious reforms, which looked suspiciously like Catholicism, created fears about the intentions of the court and soured relations with Parliament to the point where Charles resolved to rule without it in future.

The Personal Rule saw Laud implementing sweeping religious reforms. Wentworth in Ireland followed similar 'Thorough' policies. Rule without Parliament might have been extended indefinitely, despite the unpopularity of Charles's financial expedients, if he had not embarked on an ill-considered attempt to force the Scots into compliance with his religious changes in England. It was a mistake that was to have momentous consequences.

## Refresher questions

Use these questions to remind yourself of the key material covered in this chapter.

1 Why did the relationship between Charles and Parliament go sour so quickly?

2 Why was the foreign policy of the 1620s so unsuccessful?

3 Who was to blame for the failures in foreign policy?

4 What was the impact of Buckingham on the political life of the country?

5 Why did religion become such a source of conflict in Charles's reign?

6 In what ways did both the Commons and Charles break with tradition in the 1620s?

7 What was the significance of the Petition of Right?

8 Why did Charles resolve to rule without Parliament?

9 How successful was Charles's government in the Personal Rule?

10 Why were Wentworth's actions in Ireland regarded with suspicion in England?

11 How did Laud attempt to change the Church of England?

12 How unpopular were Laud's changes to the Church?

13 Why did the attempt to impose religious uniformity lead to war with Scotland?

14 How far did Charles's actions in the first fourteen years of his reign show him to be trustworthy?

## Question practice: AQA

### Essay questions

**1** 'Financial problems were at the heart of disputes between the Crown and Parliament.' Explain why you agree or disagree with this view of the period 1603–29. [AS level]

**EXAM HINT** You should argue both for and against the proposition by considering financial problems as well as two or so other factors, and reach a clear judgement.

**2** 'The Stuart governments mishandled the religious problems they faced during the years 1603–38.' Assess the validity of this view. [A level]

**EXAM HINT** You should analyse the evidence in favour and against the statement. It is important that your answer should cover the whole period adequately, but beware the danger of writing a narrative.

## Question practice: OCR

### Essay questions

**1** Assess the reasons why Charles I decided to rule without Parliament in 1629. [AS level]

**EXAM HINT** This question requires you to consider a range of reasons as to why Charles I decided to rule without Parliament in 1629. To reach the top levels you would need to weigh up the relative importance of those reasons and explain which was the most important and why others were less important.

**2** To what extent was religion the cause of conflict in the reign of Charles I up to 1638? [A level]

**EXAM HINT** The question requires you to consider a range of reasons for conflict in the period to 1638. You would need to consider the role of religion, but also other issues such as finance and the policy of 'Thorough'. You should reach a judgement on the role of each issue in causing conflict and use these interim judgements to reach an overall judgement as to the relative importance of religion.

# CHAPTER 4

# The collapse of the Personal Rule and the approach of civil war 1638–42

This chapter examines the key period during which Charles and Parliament found their mutual distrust was so great, and the demands made by Parliament were so extreme, that only armed conflict would bring a resolution of their differences. Both sides must take some of the responsibility for these developments. The stages by which the relationship broke down can be traced through the following events:

◆ The end of the Personal Rule

◆ Attacks on Charles's government

◆ The emergence of a royalist party

◆ The move towards civil war

The key debate on page 108 of this chapter asks the question: How have historians interpreted the causes of the English civil war?

## KEY DATES

| | | |
|---|---|---|
| 1638 | Nov. | Scottish general assembly abolished bishops |
| 1639 | June | First Bishops' War, ended by Treaty of Berwick |
| | Sept. | Return of Wentworth, who became the Earl of Strafford |
| 1640 | April | The Short Parliament |
| | May | New canons issued by convocation |
| | Aug. | Second Bishops' War. Scots invaded Northumberland |
| | Oct. | Treaty of Ripon |
| | Nov. | The Long Parliament |
| 1641 | March | The trial of Strafford began |
| 1641 | May | Strafford was executed |
| | | Act preventing the Long Parliament from being dissolved without its own consent |
| | June | Ten Propositions agreed by Parliament |
| | Nov. | News of Irish rebellion reached England |
| 1642 | Jan. | Failed attempt to arrest five MPs; Charles left London |
| | June | Parliament agreed Nineteen Propositions, giving itself executive power |
| | Aug. | Events at Nottingham signalled the start of civil war |

## 1   The end of the Personal Rule

◼ *How misguided was Charles's policy towards the Scots?*

◼ *How was the Short Parliament mishandled?*

The Personal Rule was brought to an end by Charles's need for money to fight the Scots. He hoped to raise sufficient funds without summoning a Parliament but this proved to be impossible.

# The Bishops' War 1639

Charles was resolved to suppress the Scots by force but, to gain time, he agreed to summon a Scottish general assembly to meet in November. At this assembly, **episcopacy** (only in force since 1618) was abolished, which alarmed Charles and made him more determined to take action against the Scots. For many of Charles's subjects, his willingness to take up arms against his Protestant subjects contrasted painfully with his refusal to help Protestants in the Thirty Years' War (see page 37) and confirmed suspicions that the king favoured the Catholics.

For the first time since 1323, the king did not call a Parliament before declaring war. Instead, he summoned the lords to meet him at York in April 1639 with appropriate military assistance to fight the Scots. This brought to a head a number of issues which had been simmering below the surface, including:

- a feeling that people were already contributing excessively to the exchequer – they refused to pay more tax

- deep unease about supporting the king in his attempt to impose Laudianism on the Scots (see page 81), which was closely allied to Roman Catholicism in the popular mind.

Despite this, the lords agreed to the king's demands, with some reluctance. An army was assembled, but it was so poorly equipped and trained that a campaign against the Scots could not be contemplated. Eventually, the two sides reached an agreement in the Treaty of Berwick in June 1639. A Scottish Parliament was to meet and both sides would demobilise.

The relief which this agreement brought was short lived. To Charles's delight, the Parliament was dissolved without achieving anything. Charles remarked: 'They must not imagine that our granting of a free assembly and Parliament obliges us to ratify all their fancies.' But this meant that none of the issues was resolved, especially concerning the future of the Kirk. Wentworth (see page 80) was recalled from Ireland and was finally given the earldom that he craved. As the new **Earl of Strafford**, he urged the king to call an English Parliament, judging from his experience in Ireland that it would be easy to handle. The rest of the Privy Council was not so sure, but Charles agreed to meet another Parliament in April 1640 in the hope that it would grant him sufficient money to crush the Scots.

# The Short Parliament 1640

People were not convinced that the king intended to restore a working relationship with Parliament. By not calling one earlier, Charles had lost the opportunity to unite the country behind him in his campaign against the Scots. It was traditional to summon a Parliament at the outset of a war, not only to get subsidies but also for propaganda purposes so that the nation could join together against the enemy.

One of the functions of Parliament was to give legitimacy to royal acts. But this was not its only role, and in the absence of Parliament for eleven years there were other matters more pressing than supporting the king's war. There were many issues in the 1630s which had promoted division – ship money, changes in religion and the activities of the prerogative courts (see pages 72–7) – and these needed discussion. There was an accumulation of grievances which would require careful handling by the king if he wished Parliament to be generous. For this reason, the elections aroused an unprecedented degree of interest. The concerns of the Lincolnshire electorate were encapsulated in the rhyme:

*Choose no ship sheriff, nor court atheist*
*No fen drainer, nor church papist.*

## Another dissolved Parliament

The king's hope of a quick and profitable session of Parliament was not to be realised. **Lord Keeper Finch** ended his opening speech with the warning that 'the king did not require their advice, but an immediate vote of supplies'. Unmoved, the Commons began to discuss its grievances, which were put by John Pym in a famous speech into three categories (see Source A, page 88):

- infringement of parliamentary liberties
- innovations in religion
- violations of property.

**KEY FIGURE**

**Lord Keeper Finch (1584–1660)**

Speaker in the 1629 Parliament who was held down in his chair. As a judge in the 1630s he presided over the trial of John Hampden and declared ship money to be legal. Charles made him lord keeper of the great seal. He was impeached by the Long Parliament.

# John Pym

| | |
|---|---|
| **1584** | Born into a gentry family in Somerset |
| **1614** | Became an MP through the patronage of the Earl of Bedford |
| **1627** | Began to work for the Earl of Warwick |
| **1630s** | Treasurer of the Providence Island Company |
| **1640** | Made the opening speech of the Short Parliament |
| **1642** | One of the five MPs whom Charles tried to arrest |
| **1643** | Died from cancer |

John Pym came from a conventional gentry background. He was a convinced Puritan and played a leading role in attempts to impeach Buckingham in the 1620s. He came to prominence largely through the patronage of the Earls of Bedford and Warwick. Through the latter, he became treasurer of the Providence Island Company, which brought him into the centre of a close-knit and influential Puritan group.

Pym was an accomplished orator. He articulated the grievances felt about Charles's rule in the 1630s very persuasively in both the Short and Long Parliaments. He acquired the nickname 'King Pym' as a mocking title. He began to behave like a government leader by issuing orders which looked very like royal proclamations but which bore Pym's name.

Pym was a leading member of the Committee of Safety which co-ordinated the military response to the royalists. He established an effective system of parliamentary government with new taxation and committees. He advocated the need for an alliance with the Scots, which came into effect in 1643 with the Solemn League and Covenant. His death robbed the parliamentary side not only of a very able administrator but also of a potentially moderating voice who had promoted negotiations for a treaty with the royalists despite his firm Puritanism.

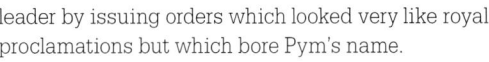

**SOURCE QUESTION**

What does the tone of Source A suggest about the mood of the country?

---

**SOURCE A**

From a speech made by John Pym to the Short Parliament in April 1640, quoted in William Jennings Bryan, editor, *The World's Famous Orations*, volume III, Funk & Wagnalls, 1906.

*Now tonnage and poundage, old and new impositions, are all taken by prerogative, without any grant in Parliament … Men's goods are seized … and justice denied to those that desire to take the benefit of the law …*

*That great and unparalleled grievance of the ship money, which, tho it may seem to have more warrant of law than the rest … the judgment is founded upon the naked opinion of some judges without any written law, without any custom, yea, without any precedent for it …*

*Ambitious and corrupt men of the clergy abuse the truth of God and the bond of conscience; preaching down the laws and liberties of the kingdom, and pretending Divine authority for an absolute power in the king, to do what he would.*

The Commons were not prepared to make any new grant of money until the question of ship money had been settled. Charles offered to relinquish ship money in return for twelve subsidies, but before the Commons had had any real chance to discuss the matter, the king dissolved Parliament after only three weeks. He did so because he had unrealistic expectations of the speed at which an occasional legislative body, with no effective leadership, could be expected to take decisions but his impatience filled the country with foreboding.

Charles had lost an opportunity to swing the country behind him. Now his position was far worse. In Dorset, troops went home when they heard of the dissolution. Parliament had not voted any money; only a small minority of the country was still paying ship money; there were demonstrations of discontent in London and reports of unrest in the country; and some members of Parliament (MPs) were questioned and imprisoned. The Crown seemed to be acting in an increasingly autocratic manner.

# The canons of 1640

**KEY TERM**

**Convocation**
The Church equivalent of Parliament. Traditionally, it met at the same time and was dissolved with Parliament. It dealt with Church affairs including Church taxation.

More worryingly still, **convocation** was not dissolved at the same time as Parliament but continued to sit in defiance of custom. It produced a set of canons intended to show the legitimacy of Charles's religious measures and to show that he opposed both Catholics and 'sectaries' who undermined the Church. All clergy had to swear that they approved 'the doctrine and discipline, or government established in the Church of England, as containing all things necessary for salvation' and that they would not consent to alter 'the government of this church by archbishops, bishops, deans and archdeacons, etc.'

This oath misfired disastrously. Instead of reassuring people that the Church was safe in the king's hands, the 'etc.' was interpreted to mean the pope. The 'etcetera oath', as it became known, was seen as part of a plot to destroy the Protestant Church and convert it to Catholicism. Puritan pamphlets were produced showing Laud setting fire to a cannon which then exploded in his face (see Source B, below). The level of outrage was such that the oath had to be abandoned. Yet again, it seemed that Charles could not be trusted with matters of religion.

# The Second Bishops' War 1640

It proved even harder for Charles to raise an army than in the previous year. Many of the poorly disciplined troops were threatening to mutiny. Two army officers were murdered by their own men on the grounds that they were Catholics. In August 1640, the Scots invaded Northumberland. This came as a relief to the king's opponents because it gave them a lever to put pressure on Charles. There is clear evidence that those who wished to ensure another

**SOURCE B**

A satire against Archbishop Laud by the artist Wenceslaus Hollar, 1640.

**SOURCE QUESTION**

What is the message of Source B?

English Parliament had been in communication with the Covenanters (see page 82) and had pushed for a Scottish invasion. Since there was no royal army capable of defeating the Scots, Charles had to agree to a truce at Ripon in Yorkshire in October.

The Scots were allowed to occupy Northumberland and County Durham, and were paid a subsidy of £850 a day until peace could be made. This effectively tied Charles's hands. He had to summon a Parliament to obtain money to pay the Scots, and he would not be able to dismiss it while the Scots remained in England. This removed the king's principal weapon against a difficult Parliament – that he could dissolve it at will.

The new Parliament would not be like the one in the spring. Lords and Commons were united in their determination to remedy the ills of the past eleven years and to return to the traditional government of England. In particular, they wanted to get rid of the 'evil counsellors' who had led the king astray and to mobilise the widest possible demonstration of public opinion against his policies. This Parliament would break new ground in its dealings with the king.

**ONLINE EXTRAS**
**OCR** **WWW**

Get to grips with ranking factors by completing Worksheets 14 and 15 at **www.hoddereducation. co.uk/accesstohistory/extras**

---

**SUMMARY DIAGRAM**

**THE END OF THE PERSONAL RULE**

| **June 1639** First Bishops' War against Scots. Humiliating failure for England | → | Charles needed money | → | **April 1640** Short Parliament. No grievances heard and no money voted | → | **August 1640** Second Bishops' War. Scots occupy the north of England | → | Desperate need for money to pay Scots £850 a day for the occupation | → | **November 1640** Long Parliament opened. End of Personal Rule |

---

# 2 Attacks on Charles's government

- *What did the opening of the Long Parliament reveal about attitudes to the actions of Charles in the Personal Rule?*
- *How far can the trial and execution of Strafford be seen as illegal?*
- *How far had the unpopular policies of the 1630s been reversed by August 1641?*

## The opening of the Long Parliament, November 1640

The Long Parliament was so-called because it was not officially dissolved until 1660. There were high hopes when it met. A typical sentiment was expressed by Sir Henry Slingsby MP: 'Great expectation there is of a happy Parliament where the subject may have total redress of all grievances.' This, however, proved impossible because Charles wanted to restore his authority, even if he was forced into immediate concessions. His opponents were determined to prevent this, not least as the king would no doubt take revenge on those who had humiliated him.

Right from the start, the Parliament was different in character from its predecessors. Compared with an average of 20–40 **contested elections** in the 1620s, 86 elections were contested. As many of these constituencies returned two MPs, it meant that about a quarter of MPs had won their seats after a contest. It was clear that many people mistrusted Charles's policies, even those who would later be **royalists** in the civil war:

- Puritans saw Parliament as the best defence against popery (see page 30). They feared a popish plot to take over the realm, and they wanted to ensure that Parliament's place in the constitution was safeguarded from the absolutism which seemed to be established in the 1630s. Many also wanted to go further and make the Church protestant in every way.

- Moderates wished to undo the innovations of the 1630s but then to return to the *status quo*. They began to fear that their colleagues were bent on creating 'parliamentary absolutism' and that this was a greater threat than the actions of the king. They also tended to be against further reformation of the Church, especially the removal of bishops, and supported the use of the prayer book. This group can be described as 'constitutional royalists'. They emerged gradually over the first few months of the Long Parliament.

These differences were not obvious at first. Indeed, what is striking is the degree of consensus about what needed to be done: to dismantle the financial and religious innovations of the 1630s and to punish those deemed responsible, especially Strafford and Laud. These concerns were reflected in a flood of petitions sent in from all over the country. The first of these, from Hertfordshire, was typical.

**KEY TERMS**

**Contested election**
An election in which there was more than one candidate, allowing a real choice.

**Royalists** Those who would fight for the king in the civil war.

**SOURCE C**

From the Hertfordshire petition presented to the House of Commons on 7 November 1640, quoted in John Adamson, *The Noble Revolt*, Weidenfeld & Nicolson, 2007.

1 *Not having Parliaments [since 1629] and breaking up [of] the last.*
2 *[The] Canons [of the Church] lately made.*
3 *The insufficient and unmeet [unworthy] Ministry.*
4 *The great abuse of ordinances [ecclesiastical regulations].*
5 *[The prohibition on] services in the afternoon. …*
7 *Unduly raising of military charges.*
8 *The pressing [forcible conscription] of men for military service. …*
11 *The fomenters of [those who stirred up] the calamities of this Kingdom should be identified that they may be punished.*

**SOURCE QUESTION**

According to Source C, what were the main concerns of people in the county?

The Parliament opened with a series of speeches denouncing the actions of the king. Pym repeated his speech to the Short Parliament, but added that there was a plot by papists to alter both law and religion: 'with the one, the other falls'. In the first few weeks, Strafford and Laud were imprisoned; Finch and Secretary of State Windebank fled abroad; and the ship money judges were impeached. The presence of the Scots in Northumberland removed the threat of a premature dissolution. Two subsidies were voted in December to cover immediate needs while discussions were held on how to proceed against the Earl of Strafford. Parliament was dominated at this point by the 'Junto'.

## The Junto

### What was the Junto?

A group of parliamentarians led in the Lords by the Earl of Bedford, Lord Saye and Sele, Lord Mandeville and Lord Brooke, and in the Commons by John Pym, Denzil Holles, Nathaniel Fiennes and Oliver St John. They had petitioned Charles for a Parliament in the summer, and had been in collusion with the Scots. They now wished to be become the king's advisers and change his policies. They favoured a Protestant foreign policy and Puritan reforms to the Church. Many of these had been associated in the 1630s with the Providence Island Company (see page 75).

In contrast to Charles, who had always been notoriously bad at managing Parliament, the members of the Junto were very skilled:

- They made effective speeches which could sway both Houses.
- They dominated the important committees.
- They put additional pressure on the king by promoting petitions and demonstrations in favour of their policies, such as those attacking the bishops, received in late 1640 and early 1641.

The Junto's principal aim was to become part of the government; for example, Bedford would be lord treasurer and Pym chancellor of the exchequer, while others would be part of the Privy Council. Religious reforms would sweep away the Laudian innovations, although bishops would be retained if they acted in consultation with the rest of the clergy and were bound by the law. The Junto understood that part of the problems of the 1630s had been caused by Parliament's reluctance to grant Charles sufficient funds. If Charles took its members into office, they promised to provide adequate parliamentary revenue based on the system of collection of ship money.

These policies might have offered a solution but they were to fail for a number of reasons:

- Charles was not willing to see his freedom of action curtailed.
- MPs were reluctant to countenance vastly increased taxation.
- The Scots were unhappy about the retention of bishops.

The biggest stumbling block was what to do about the Earl of Strafford.

# The trial and execution of Strafford

Strafford was hated and feared in equal measure. Hated because he was associated most closely with the attempt to rule without Parliament, and feared because, as Lord Deputy of Ireland, he had a large army at his disposal with which to take revenge on his enemies. He was also the most formidable of Charles's ministers. On his return to London a few days after the Long Parliament opened, Strafford was preparing to accuse key MPs of treasonable dealings with the Scots. He was impeached and sent to the Tower before he could take action. Parliament then spent much of November debating what to do with him.

## Charges against Strafford

As treason was defined as 'offences against the king', it was difficult to accuse Strafford of this as he had clearly been acting with the king's approval. Pym therefore suggested that although none of Strafford's actions in themselves could be defined as treason, together they amounted to 'constructive treason', which threatened to make a division between the king and his people – a rather loose definition of treason which could be dangerously extended. As Pym put it: 'Other treasons are against the rule of the law. This is against the being of the law. It is the law that unites the king and his people, and the author of this treason hath endeavoured to dissolve that union.'

The most potent charge against Strafford was that in May 1640 he had told the king at a meeting of the Privy Council, 'You have an army in Ireland you may employ here to reduce this kingdom.' As the matter under discussion was what to do about Scotland, it was clear that 'this kingdom' referred to Scotland, but many in Parliament feared that he also meant England. Unfortunately for Parliament, two men were needed to attest for a charge of treason but only one man would confirm Strafford's words. However, the Junto was not going to let Strafford get away with the policies he had promoted in the 1630s.

## The trial, March 1641

Strafford's trial was carefully stage-managed. It was held in public and news of the trial was widely disseminated to build up feeling against the earl. The trial took place not in the Lords, as usual, but in the far larger Westminster Hall. In another departure from tradition, the whole of the Commons was present, arrayed around the Lords. There was still space for an audience of about 1000 and those who could not attend in person could read about proceedings in hastily produced news-sheets. In another act of great significance, Charles was forbidden by the Lords from publicly attending the trial. His throne on a **dais**, complete with **cloth of estate**, was there but was kept empty. Charles was only allowed to watch proceedings from behind a lattice, which he angrily tore down on the first day.

**KEY TERMS**

**Dais** A low platform for a throne.

**Cloth of estate** A canopy that hung above the throne. Together with the dais, it symbolised the concept of royalty even in the absence of the actual king.

**SOURCE QUESTION**

What does Source D suggest about the nature of power in England in 1641?

**SOURCE D**

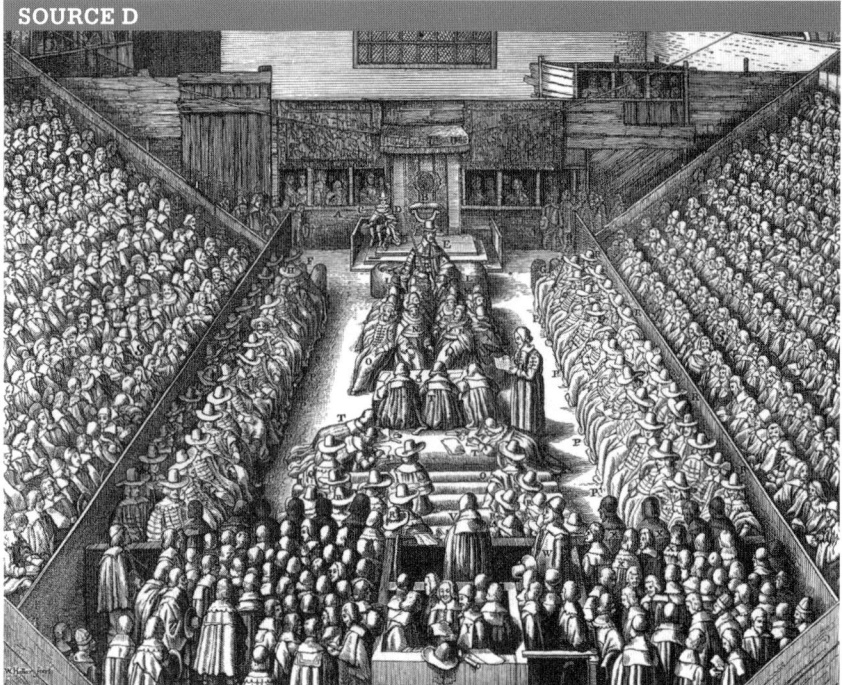

Strafford's impeachment in Westminster Hall, a contemporary engraving by Wenceslaus Hollar. Note the Commons sitting above the Lords' benches and the king's empty throne.

This was the first time that the representatives of the nation had been on public view in such a way. It was an attempt to portray the 'commonwealth' as a body independent of the king. The separation between the person of the king and his role in the State (as represented by the empty throne, to which officers of the court made their bows) was to be repeated only a year later when many parliamentarians claimed to be loyal to the king in his 'politic capacity' while simultaneously preparing to fight his person.

The trial did not go according to plan for Pym and his associates. Strafford defended himself with skill, and the public nature of his trial as it stretched into four weeks, enabled him to attack his accusers. As Strafford pointed out, the whole idea of 'constructive treason' was flawed: 'How can that be treason in the whole which is not in any of the parts?' The flimsy nature of the evidence against him allowed Strafford to persuade many of the Lords that he should not be found guilty – an unthinkable outcome for the Junto.

## The Act of Attainder

Several MPs, growing impatient at the slow progress of the trial and fearing it might not be successful, moved to have Strafford attainted. This was different from impeachment as the guilt of the accused was merely declared and voted on and there was no need for a trial. By giving his assent, Charles would be condemning Strafford to death, as there was no possibility of a pardon. Pym originally opposed the attainder. He still hoped for office but it was unlikely that Charles would forgive him and the Junto for forcing his hand in this way. However, in the absence of any alternative, Pym eventually backed the bill. Many others took the easier way out of absenting themselves from proceedings. Just over 200 voted in favour of the bill with 59 against. There was more resistance in the Lords but the so-called 'army plot' (a bungled attempt to free Strafford from the Tower) created fears that Charles was preparing to attack Parliament. The plan was to infiltrate the garrison of the Tower and take control of it, release Strafford and then bring the army south to dissolve Parliament. It was ill-conceived and helped to persuade waverers in the Lords that Charles was not to be trusted. The bill was passed by 26 to 19.

## Strafford's death

Now everything depended on Charles. He had sworn to Strafford that 'upon the word of a king you shall not suffer in life, honour or fortune'. The presence of a large, hostile mob outside Whitehall Palace, baying for Strafford's blood, and the anguished pleas of Henrietta Maria to do what the crowds wanted, made Charles rethink his promise. These events, coupled with a letter from Strafford sent on 5 May advising him to pass the attainder 'for the prevention of evils which may happen by your refusal', eventually persuaded him to sign the Act of Attainder. Strafford was executed three days later on 12 May in front of a huge crowd that may have numbered 200,000. Charles regretted this decision all his life and never forgave those who had forced him into it. The hopes of the Junto's replacing Strafford were given a final blow by the death on 9 May of Bedford, the peer with whom Charles had the best relationship.

# The dismantling of prerogative government

While action was being taken against Strafford, there were also moves to dismantle the apparatus of prerogative government which Charles had used in the 1630s to rule without Parliament. The first move was to ensure that Charles could not use his weapon of dissolution. Parliament relied on the protection of the Scots army to keep them safe until legislation could be passed. Parliamentary leaders openly admitted this in a meeting with the Scots commissioners, who were in London to arrange a treaty. Progress towards a treaty was therefore very slow.

However, this alliance with the Scots came at a price, namely the abolition of bishops which, as the many petitions supporting bishops demonstrated, was unlikely to be popular in England. There was also the actual price of £850 a day for the Scots army (see page 90). Since much of the popular support for Parliament rested on discontent about taxation, allowing costs to mount in this way undermined this support. A treaty could not be postponed indefinitely.

## The Triennial Act 1641

The first measure to dismantle prerogative government was the Triennial Act. This not only stipulated that there should be a Parliament every three years, but also laid down the mechanism for calling one using sheriffs, should the king fail to do so. This was highly offensive to Charles, who protested he would not sign it. Financial pressure forced him to pass the bill, but it left Parliament convinced that he would ignore it if he could. Thus, he got the worst of both worlds. It was effectively the Petition of Right (see page 66) all over again and suggested that Charles had learned nothing. To drive the message home, in May (at the same time as Strafford's attainder) Charles had to sign a bill which declared that the present Parliament could be dissolved only with its own consent. This was rushed through both Houses amid fears that the king was contemplating resorting to force in the 'army plot'. Charles would have to find some way of accommodating the demands of this Parliament.

## Remedial measures, May to August 1641

A series of acts dealt with the abuses of the 1630s:

- Tonnage and poundage (see page 63) was finally granted to Charles, although only for a few months, and all other customs charges were forbidden 'without common consent in Parliament'. This put Charles's major source of revenue firmly under Parliament's control.

- In July 1641, acts abolished the Star Chamber and the Court of High Commission (see page 75).

- In August 1641, ship money and distraint of knighthood (see pages 72–3) were outlawed. Forest boundaries were restored to their traditional limits.

The effect of these acts made the king dependent on Parliament for the financing of his government, and removed the possibility of his using the law courts to enforce his will. At this stage, it did not seem that Pym or any of the other parliamentary leaders wanted to establish a parliamentary government. They wanted a share in executive power and to have their policies taken note of by the king. Nearly all MPs lived outside London; remaining in the capital was expensive and kept them away from home. Long sessions had always seen a decline in attendance and the sessions of 1640–2 were no exception.

### Pym's effectiveness

Pym had successfully manoeuvred to reduce Charles's power. He achieved this by securing control of key committees, which prepared the legislation, and by using his associates to maintain a high degree of unity. As he had done against Strafford, he was also ready to use his contacts in the City of London and elsewhere to organise petitions and demonstrations in favour of policies he was promoting.

Pym understood that government could not function without adequate revenues. The Commons had increased its original two subsidies to six in June 1641, but this brought in a total of only £300,000 and there would be a delay in collecting it. The Scots army had already cost £230,000 and the amount increased every day. There was also the English army, which needed to be paid before it could be disbanded. It was decided to pay off both armies by means of a **poll tax**, which aroused great opposition and much resentment in the country.

Pym's recognition of the financial realities was not shared by many of his fellow MPs. Pym had become an MP as a client of the Earl of Bedford. Others were more aware of the effect of government decisions on the country, especially of financial grants. As Sir Roger Twysden put it, 'what was it to me whether the Earl of Strafford or Mr Pym sat at the helm of government, if their commands carried equal pressure?'.

## The Ten Propositions, June 1641

Charles announced his intention of visiting Scotland in August. There were fears about whether he would use one of the armies in the north to help him reassert his power. The English army had come to regard Parliament with hostility because it had not received money for wages or board. In alarm, the Commons rushed through the act authorising the poll tax in only two weeks, to ensure the army was disbanded before Charles arrived. They then drew up the Ten Propositions in June 1641, urging the king:

- to postpone his journey until the armies were disbanded

- to dismiss 'evil counsellors' and replace them with 'such officers and counsellors as his people and Parliament may have just cause to confide in'

- to give control of the military forces of the counties to those who were 'faithful and trusty and careful of the peace of the kingdom'

- to exclude Catholics as advisers of the queen and those responsible for the upbringing of the royal children.

The Ten Propositions show how deep Parliament's distrust of Charles was. Parliament was now seeking to control his advisers and to influence the command of the army. These restrictions would have been difficult for any monarch to accept, let alone one as inflexible as Charles. This is the point at which Parliament moved from restoring the ancient constitution to imposing radical new restrictions on the monarch. This stemmed from a fear that Charles would seek to reverse all the gains of the last nine months. It is essential to remember just how frightened most MPs were of a savage royalist reaction.

Considering how innately conservative and resistant to innovation the House of Commons was, it is a tribute both to the skill of Pym and to Charles's failure to understand those who opposed him that it was prepared to move into such unchartered waters. What would prove more difficult to navigate were the troubled waters of religious difference.

**KEY TERM**

**Poll tax** A tax levied on all of the adult inhabitants of England, Scotland and Ireland according to a graduated scale ranging from £100 for a duke to a base rate of 6*d.* per head for anyone aged sixteen or over.

**ATTACKS ON CHARLES'S GOVERNMENT**

| Government actions in 1630s | Measures taken by Long Parliament |
|---|---|
| • 'Evil counsellors' leading king astray<br>• Financial demands of dubious legality<br>• No Parliament for eleven years<br>• Law courts supporting royal actions of dubious legality<br>• Arminian religious practices enforced<br>• Charles's government ruled in an autocratic manner which seemed to favour Catholics | • Laud imprisoned, Strafford executed<br>• Ship money, forest law, knighthood fines and impositions all abolished<br>• Triennial Act passed<br>• Star Chamber and High Commission abolished<br>• Laud imprisoned, attacks on the role of bishops<br>• The Ten Propositions |

# 3 The emergence of a royalist party

■ *Why was the fear of a popish plot so powerful?*

■ *Why did the Irish rebellion have such an impact on events in England?*

## Religious divisions

Religion was the best predictor of who would fight for Parliament and who for the king. Although there was broad agreement in England that Laudianism had gone too far, there was widespread support for the traditional establishment and services of the Church of England. On the other hand, many wanted to seize the opportunity to complete the Reformation, which they felt had been left unfinished. They wanted:

■ to remove the last vestiges of popery as seen in church vestments and the decoration of churches

■ to establish a godly preaching ministry which would put more emphasis on sermons and extempore (spontaneous) prayer

■ to allow some deviation from the form of services laid down in the prayer book.

**KEY TERM**

**Radicals** Those who favoured sweeping changes to Church or State. They contrast with traditionalists who wanted to preserve the *status quo*.

These traditionalists and **radicals** were to diverge greatly through the course of 1641.

### Attacks on Laudianism

Initially, the anti-Laudians created petitions not only to remove the innovations of the 1630s, but also to abolish episcopacy outright 'with all its dependencies, roots and branches'. Before 1640 there had been little opposition to bishops. Yet the enthusiastic support many bishops gave to Laudianism and their justification of the royal prerogative (see page 62) encouraged a more radical approach. Many parishioners took matters into their own hands by tearing down altar rails (see page 77), moving the communion table back to the centre of the church and interrupting prayer book services.

With Laud in prison, ecclesiastical (Church) authority was breaking down. The Lords attempted to maintain control by ordering: 'That the divine service be performed as it is appointed by the acts of Parliament of this realm; and that all such as shall disturb that wholesome order shall be severely punished, according to law.' There was additional pressure for the abolition of episcopacy from the Scots, who had made this one of their conditions for reaching a settlement with the king. However, few in England wanted the imposition of a Presbyterian system on the Scottish model.

The threat to the established order of the Church was met with a petitioning campaign in favour of bishops. These petitions suggest that most of the population would have preferred a middle way between Laudianism and Puritanism. There were fears that the destruction of the ecclesiastical hierarchy would have implications for social order, since it threatened to undermine all forms of authority. A number of riots in the summer of 1641 in places as diverse as the fens of Lincolnshire and the forests of Windsor appeared to support this view. In fact, these had more to do with economic factors, but to conservative-minded gentlemen it looked as if the entire social fabric was coming under attack.

## Fears of a popish plot

With no clear agreement on how to progress, there was stalemate until May, when the botched 'army plot' gave substance to the idea of a popish plot to subvert England's liberties and impose a new Catholic tyranny by force. There was evidence that Charles had made moves to bring the army south to restore his power. He made no secret of his desire to regain his power. In addition, Henrietta Maria was seeking assistance from foreign Catholic powers. Pym claimed there was a threat to 'the true reformed Protestant religion expressed in the doctrine of the Church of England' and proposed an oath to defend it. He set out the situation in the preamble.

> **SOURCE E**
>
> From the preamble to the Protestation Oath, May 1641, quoted in Barry Coward, *The Stuart Age*, Routledge, 2014, p. 178.
>
> *The designs of the priests and other adherents of the see of Rome, have of late been more boldly and frequently put in practice than formerly, to the undermining and danger of ruin of the true Reformed Religion … There are endeavours to subvert the fundamental laws of England and Ireland, and to introduce the exercise of an arbitrary and tyrannical government by most pernicious and wicked counsels … and divers [diverse] innovations and superstitions hath been brought into the*

**SOURCE QUESTION**

How has Pym linked religion and politics in Source E?

> *Church, multitudes driven out of his Majesty's dominions, jealousies raised and fomented [stirred up ] between the King and people, a popish army levied in Ireland and two armies brought into the bowels of this kingdom … and … endeavours have been used to bring the English army into misunderstanding of this Parliament.*

Pym was undoubtedly sincere in his desire to protect the Church and make it more Protestant, although he also saw the opportunity to strengthen his political position by emphasising the threat to liberty and the rule of law. His attempts to bring about more reform were, however, threatened by the growth of extremism. With the abolition of the Court of High Commission (see page 96), there was no effective censorship. Subsequently, there was a flood of pamphlets attacking the established Church, in extreme language that offended many.

As one person said, clergy 'stumble forward … into the new-vomited paganism, of sensual idolatry attributing purity or impurity to things indifferent … [using] the skeleton of a Mass-book'.

At the same time, Charles made two important gestures:

■ He appointed Laud's enemy, John Williams, who had been imprisoned in the 1630s, to be Archbishop of York.

■ He wrote to the Lords to reassure them: 'I am constant to the discipline and doctrine of the Church of England established by Queen Elizabeth … and I resolve … to die in the maintenance of it.'

The forces of moderation might have triumphed were it not for events in Scotland and Ireland that raised new fears about absolutism and popish tyranny.

## Charles in Scotland

The departure of Charles and worries about his intentions led Parliament to extend the scope of its activities into new areas. Two committees were set up: one monitored the king's activities in Scotland and the other managed business in the absence of the king while Parliament was in recess. The lord keeper refused to allow the use of the **great seal** but Simonds D'Ewes, an MP and lawyer, assured Parliament that both Houses acting together had the right to issue ordinances which would have the validity of statutes. This was another step in Parliament's acquiring the powers it needed to run the country.

In Scotland, Charles hoped to capitalise on the discontent of those who felt the Covenanters had moved too far, too fast. Yet, as always with Charles, his concessions were grudging and apparently insincere:

■ For example, he agreed in September 1641 that his choice of key officials should be confirmed by the Scottish Parliament – and then proceeded to appoint the royalist Earl of Morton as his chancellor, thereby suggesting that he had no intention of sticking to this agreement.

■ More damaging was the 'Incident', a shadowy plot to seize and possibly assassinate the Covenanter leaders, Argyll and Lanark and the Duke of Hamilton, Charles's one-time agent in Scotland. He had become the target

**KEY TERM**

**Great seal** Used to show that documents had the king's approval and made them official.

of a hostile whispering campaign at court which had lost him the favour of the king. The plot failed and it is not clear how much Charles knew of it. But his subsequent action of turning up at Parliament to protest his innocence, with a force of several hundred armed men, hardly helped to win over the doubters. Instead, he was forced to appoint the leading Covenanters to key positions.

It was clear that Charles would make no further headway in Scotland, so he returned to London in late November. The new session opened in October with many fearing a possible **coup**. One of the first actions of the Parliament was to appoint 100 men to stand guard in Palace Yard at Westminster. In addition, there was a corresponding fear of Puritan populism and extremism. In time, this might have worked to the king's advantage, but time was not on Charles's side.

At the beginning of November, the news reached London of a rising by Irish Catholics and the slaughter of Protestants.

## The Irish rebellion, November 1641

The Irish rebellion transformed events in England and showed the interrelationship between the three kingdoms most clearly. Strafford's return to England had led to a breakdown of the alliance which had been established against him by the different groups in Ireland (see page 79). Charles had handled the possibility of support with his usual ineptness. In return for financial assistance in May 1641, the 'Old English' had been promised confirmation of the Graces and an end to further plantations. In the summer, Charles went back on his promise and the Irish Parliament was formally subordinated to the English one. Source F reveals how alarming this was to the Catholics.

> **SOURCE F**
>
> From a letter from Lord Gormanston to the Earl of Clanricard (both members of the 'Old English'), November 1641, quoted in Trevor Royle, *Civil War*, Little, Brown, 2004.
>
> *It was not unknown to your lordship how the Puritan faction in England, since by the countenance of the Scottish army they invaded the regal power, have both in their doctrine and practice laid the foundation of slavery in this country. They teach that the laws of England, if they mention Ireland, are without doubt binding here, and the Parliament has wholly assumed the management of the affairs of this kingdom, as a right of pre-eminence due to it. And what might be expected from such zealous and fiery professors of an adverse religion but the ruin and extirpation of ours.*

In protest, a number of prominent Irish leaders rebelled, hoping to force a change of administration more sympathetic to the Catholics. This was typified by the request that the (Protestant but 'Old English') Earl of Ormonde should replace the hated 'New English', who had been taking measures against the

**KEY TERM**

**Coup** An attempt to overthrow a government by force.

**SOURCE QUESTION**

According to Source F, what did the Catholics fear?

Catholics. Many of those who joined the rising felt they were acting in support of the king.

The aims of the rebels at this stage were moderate:

- parliamentary independence under the Crown
- security of title to lands
- freedom of worship without financial or political penalty.

An attempt to seize Dublin Castle failed and the conspirators were arrested. Sir Phelim O'Neill, a Gaelic landowner, had more success, capturing key towns in Ulster. The rising took the Protestants by surprise. Stories of atrocities soon began to circulate as the accumulated grievances of the Irish Catholics led to a wave of killings, and the rebellion began to rage out of control. Gruesome tales were told of children being boiled alive and even of a priest tearing a Protestant minister apart with his bare hands. It was reported that over 200,000 Protestants had been murdered. In fact it was more like 5000, but the numbers were less important than the impact that the rumours had on public opinion.

As indignation mounted in England, O'Neill's revelation that he had a commission from the king confirmed the deepest fears about Charles's intentions. It did no good for Charles to protest (correctly) that the commission was a forgery. It seemed only too credible that he was behind this popish plot and its horrors. Normal parliamentary government collapsed as Parliament debated how best to defend itself and England.

## The Grand Remonstrance, November 1641

Charles, not unnaturally, was keen to raise an army to suppress the Irish rebellion. Many MPs, however, feared he would use it not against the Irish, but instead against themselves. This fear pushed Parliament into much more radical courses of action than they would have been prepared to consider a few months earlier. The Commons quickly decided to send troops from England to deal with the rebellion, but that raised the awkward question of who would control the army. Moderates felt that to challenge the king's right to control of the country's armed forces was a step too far, but the panic in the country enabled Pym to push through a measure by 151 to 110. This measure stated that the king should employ 'only such councillors as should be approved of by Parliament' otherwise, ominously for Charles, it would 'take such a course for the securing of Ireland as might likewise secure ourselves'. The Earl of Essex was appointed to control the **trained bands** south of the River Trent. This was another important step in Parliament's amassing the powers it needed to challenge the king.

Pym then tabled the Grand Remonstrance. This was a document that he and a committee had been working on since August that stated all that they thought was wrong with the royal government.

**ONLINE EXTRAS** WWW
OCR

Practise introducing and concluding arguments by completing Worksheet 16 at **www.hoddereducation. co.uk/accesstohistory/extras**

**KEY TERM**

**Trained bands** Another name for the militia, composed of householders who had an obligation to undertake some military training for the defence of the locality.

SOURCE QUESTION

What does Source G reveal about the concerns of those who would subsequently become royalists?

### SOURCE G

From a description of the Grand Remonstrance by the Earl of Clarendon, quoted in *The History of the Rebellion and Civil Wars in England*, written in the 1660s.

*It contained a very bitter representation of all the illegal things which had been done from the first hour of the King's coming to the Crown to that minute, with all those sharp reflections which could be made upon the King himself, the Queen, and Council; and published all the unreasonable jealousies of the present government, of the introducing Popery, and all other particulars which might disturb the minds of the people, which were enough discomposed.*

*The house seemed generally to dislike it; many saying that it was very unnecessary, and unreasonable: unnecessary, all those grievances being already fully redressed; and the liberty and property of the subject being as well secured for the future as could possibly be done.*

The Remonstrance was vague about specific policies; its purpose was to create the climate for further reform. In its 204 articles, Charles's past and present actions were discredited. Oliver Cromwell stated that 'if the remonstrance had been rejected he would have sold all he had the next morning and never seen England more'. The debates on the Grand Remonstrance were heated. Ultimately, it was passed by a margin of only eleven: by 159 to 148 votes. Charles was slowly acquiring a body of supporters who were coming to see him as the defender of the constitution rather than Parliament, 'the keystone which closeth up the arch of order and government'. They felt that he had agreed to rectify the abuses of the 1630s, and that they had passed sufficient safeguards to prevent him from acting in an autocratic manner in future. Now the threat seemed to come from the radicals (see page 98) who were pushing for ever more reform. This view was heightened by what happened immediately after the Grand Remonstrance had been passed, when it was proposed that it should be printed.

## The impact of the Grand Remonstrance

Appealing directly to the people was a dangerous game and a complete break with precedent. Sir Edward Dering expressed the opinion of the moderates: 'I imagined we should hold up a glass to his Majesty … I did not dream that we would remonstrate downwards, tell tales to the people and talk of the king as a third person.' The situation in London was becoming increasingly unruly. Already there were concerns about the way that ordinary people were making their views known through demonstrations. Charles took advantage of this to pose as the only person who could defend 'fundamental law'. Charles was encouraged by the clear support for the king growing in the Commons, and especially in the Lords and by the positive reception he had received as he journeyed south. Once again, however, the question of bishops caused trouble.

In October 1641, the Commons had passed a bill demanding that bishops be excluded from the House of Lords. The Lords were not prepared to accept this. To put pressure on them, some radicals encouraged angry mobs to keep the bishops from attending debates. When the bishops returned at the end of December, twelve of them protested that all actions in their absence were void. This annoyed the Lords and they accepted Pym's suggestion that the offending bishops should be impeached and they were imprisoned. Charles decided the time had come to act.

## SUMMARY DIAGRAM

### THE EMERGENCE OF A ROYALIST PARTY

| Actions of Parliament | Royalist reaction |
|---|---|
| • Attacks on Laudian innovations extended to proposed abolition of bishops | • Many felt reforms went too far |
| • Fears about Charles's use of the army in Scotland led to Parliament taking much more power for itself | • Not appropriate for Parliament to try to rule in king's absence |
| • Irish rebellion inflamed fears of a popish plot and led to discussion about whether king should be allowed to control the army | • King was the only one who had a right to control the army |
| • Grand Remonstrance detailed all that was wrong with country | • Grand Remonstrance went beyond criticism of abuses of the 1630s to attacking fundamentals of the constitution |
| • Decision to print Grand Remonstrance seen as appealing directly to the people | • Appealing to the public was a dangerous precedent which invited anarchy |
| • Impeachment of bishops | • Bishops were one of the cornerstones of order and stability in country |

**ONLINE EXTRAS**
OCR
**WWW**

Get to grips with turning assertions into arguments by completing Worksheet 17 at **www.hoddereducation. co.uk/accesstohistory/extras**

# 4 The move towards civil war

- How far was Charles to blame for the breakdown in relations with Parliament?
- How did the power of Parliament increase in the months after January 1642?

## The Five Members

It was not only the position of the bishops which prompted Charles into action. He was also concerned about the increasingly open attacks on his wife Henrietta Maria as the source of Catholic influence at court. Charles embarked on a very high-risk strategy. He accused five MPs (Pym, Hampden, Haselrig, Holles and Strode) and one peer (Mandeville) of treason and demanded their arrest. The Lords refused to cooperate and instead appointed a committee to discuss whether the impeachment was according to precedent. Possibly driven on by his wife, who is reported to have said 'Go, coward and pull these rogues out by the ears, or never see my face more', Charles went to the Commons with armed soldiers in an attempt to arrest the five MPs himself. They had already been forewarned and were safely in the City (see page 75), which was now led by Puritans, who refused to hand them over. Charles's attempted coup had failed and with it his chance of uniting the country behind him.

### The aftermath of the Five Members incident

The Commons declared that the arrest attempt was a violation of parliamentary privilege. It was confirmation that Charles could not be trusted and that he had always intended to try to restore his power by force. Demonstrations against the king and queen persuaded Charles to leave London, first for Hampton Court and later for York. He was not to return to the capital until his trial (see page 133). It would, however, be a mistake to see civil war as inevitable even at this late stage. The petitions which came in from all over the country wanted reform of the Church and expressed fears of a popish plot, but they were not directed against the king himself. Parliamentary politics, as it was normally understood, had broken down. Nobody could agree on the way forward and both sides tried to show themselves as the agents of moderation by a war of words, in which each blamed the other for the crisis.

## Preparations for war

The departure of many of the moderates with the king left the radicals in charge of Parliament and they passed a series of measures which transferred many of the Crown's powers to Parliament. Huge demonstrations put pressure on the Lords not to obstruct the reforming programme of the Commons. There is also evidence of an organised petitioning campaign to support the Commons' actions. The remaining bishops were excluded from the House of Lords and

**KEY TERM**

**Militia ordinance** This took military control away from the king and gave it to Parliament.

a **militia ordinance** was passed which gave Parliament the king's military authority. Charles accepted the first measure but, unsurprisingly, he would not give his assent to the latter. Parliament was now usurping the king's military power and legislating without him. In March, it began to raise money for its own purposes as well through the so-called Act of £400,000. This was based on the ship money principle of fixed amounts from each county and it was efficiently collected, much more so than Charles's attempts to raise revenue had been.

As the prospects of a settlement receded, there was also a rush to take control of the country's arsenals. Charles failed to capture Hull, with its store of ammunition amassed to fight the Scots, nor, in July, could his representative take Manchester. In June, some in the royalist camp invited Parliament to state its terms for a settlement. In response it drew up the Nineteen Propositions.

## The Nineteen Propositions

The Nineteen Propositions effectively made Parliament the sovereign power. Parliament would control:

- the king's advisers
- the army
- the reform and government of the Church
- foreign policy
- who was allowed to sit in the House of Lords
- and even the education and marriages of the king's children.

Many in the country were dismayed at how extreme Parliament had become. Charles's reply to the propositions, which was drafted by the moderates Culpepper and Falkland, eloquently set out the royalist case.

**SOURCE QUESTION**

In Source H, what is meant by the 'fundamental laws' and how are the Propositions shown to be destroying them?

**ONLINE EXTRAS**
**AQA**     WWW

Get to grips with counter-arguments by completing Worksheet 13 at **www.hoddereducation.co.uk/accesstohistory/extras**

**SOURCE H**

From Charles I's reply to the Nineteen Propositions, quoted in John P. Kenyon, *The Stuart Constitution*, Cambridge University Press, 1966, p. 21.

*In this kingdom the laws are jointly made by a king, by a house of peers and by a House of Commons chosen by the people … [The Propositions were] a total subversion of the fundamental laws and that excellent constitution of this kingdom which hath made this nation so many years both famous and happy … [The Propositions would encourage the common people] to set up for themselves, call parity and independence liberty, devour that estate which had devoured the rest, destroy all rights and proprieties, all distinctions of families and merit, and by this means this splendid and excellently distinguished form of government end in a dark, equal chaos of confusion, and the long line of our many ancestors in a Jack Cade or Wat Tyler [two notorious leaders of peasant revolts].*

Source H makes it clear why Charles attracted support. The financial measures Parliament had passed were at least as demanding as anything which Charles had attempted. Their actions were seen as destroying many of the customs which people had taken for granted. In particular, the attacks on the Church and appeals to popular sentiment by encouraging mob violence threatened the very fabric of the social order.

There could be no hope of compromise after the Nineteen Propositions. In July, Parliament voted to raise an army, to be commanded by the Earl of Essex. In early August, the Commons stated that Charles had started a war and declared those who assisted him guilty of treason. On 22 August, Charles raised his standard (the traditional way for a leader to summon supporters) at Nottingham and called on all his loyal subjects to help him to fight Essex's rebellion. The English civil war had begun, a conflict which was to kill proportionately more English than the First World War centuries later, and which would change the direction of British politics forever.

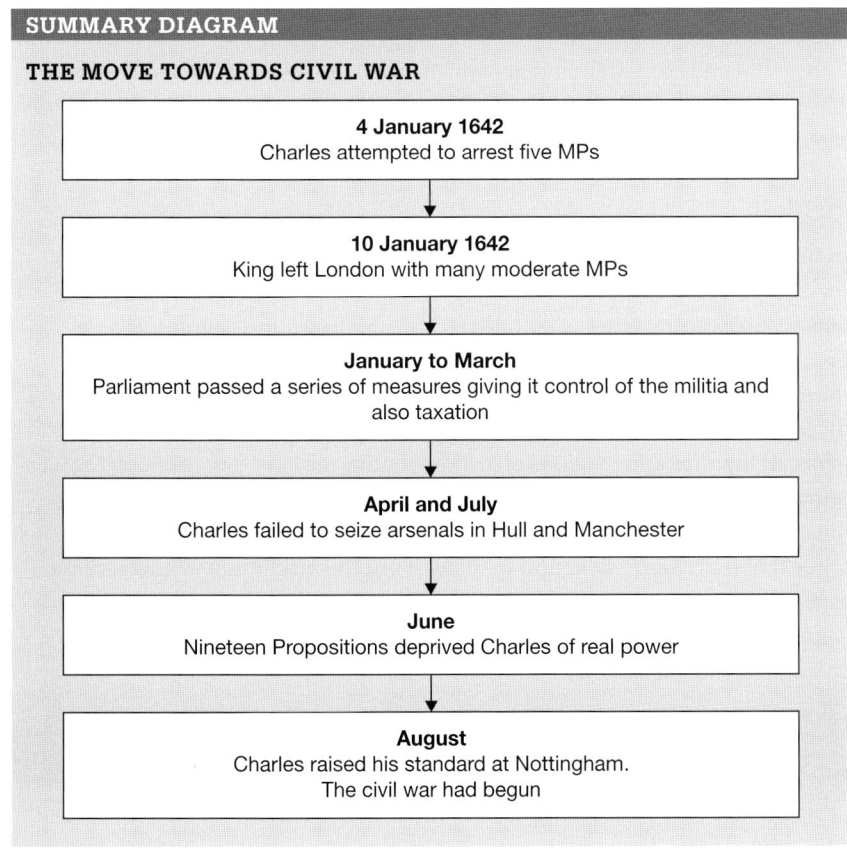

**SUMMARY DIAGRAM**

**THE MOVE TOWARDS CIVIL WAR**

**4 January 1642**
Charles attempted to arrest five MPs

↓

**10 January 1642**
King left London with many moderate MPs

↓

**January to March**
Parliament passed a series of measures giving it control of the militia and also taxation

↓

**April and July**
Charles failed to seize arsenals in Hull and Manchester

↓

**June**
Nineteen Propositions deprived Charles of real power

↓

**August**
Charles raised his standard at Nottingham.
The civil war had begun

**ONLINE EXTRAS**
**AQA** WWW

Practise writing effective conclusions by completing Worksheet 14 at **www. hoddereducation.co.uk/ accesstohistory/extras**

**ONLINE EXTRAS**
**OCR** WWW

Test your understanding of key developments by completing Worksheet 18 at **www.hoddereducation. co.uk/accesstohistory/extras**

**ONLINE EXTRAS**
**OCR** WWW

Get to grips with supporting ideas by completing Worksheets 19 and 20 at **www.hoddereducation. co.uk/accesstohistory/extras**

# 5 | Key debate

■ *How have historians interpreted the causes of the English civil war?*

## Traditional views

The civil war has been a source of fierce controversy since the seventeenth century. Earlier accounts looked at the cataclysmic events of the 1640s and tried to trace their roots back into the sixteenth century. The **Whig** interpretation, dominant in the nineteenth and early twentieth centuries, saw the civil war as part of a long-term process to establish enlightened parliamentary democracy and religious freedom. In this interpretation, Parliament was the defender of law, property rights and individual liberties against the attacks of an autocratic monarchy.

In the mid-twentieth century, a new interpretation was put forward. This was the **Marxist** view, explained most persuasively by Christopher Hill in a series of books written from 1940 onwards. This suggested that at the root of the civil war were social and economic changes which created political divisions. The civil war was the '**bourgeois revolution**' of Marxist theory which opened the way to capitalism and the eventual revolution which would overthrow the State.

## Revisionism

In the 1970s, a new school of thought emerged, that of revisionism. The revisionists sought to get away from the idea that the civil war was inevitable, which was a central tenet of both the Whig and the Marxist interpretations. They stressed the short-term, almost accidental, nature of the war and especially the short-sighted and obstinate behaviour of Charles I, who did not understand the impact of his policies. The monarchy was seen as the innovator attacking personal liberties and religious orthodoxy. Parliament, far from seeking to bring about reform, was merely trying to maintain its ancient privileges and to preserve its view of the relationship between the king and itself. The revisionists argue that there were structural weaknesses in the machinery of government, especially the Crown's inadequate financial resources, but they deny that there were major divisions over political principle, even if the actions of Charles I did provoke considerable resistance.

Conrad Russell was the leading exponent of the revisionist view:

**EXTRACT 1**

From Conrad Russell, *The Crisis of Parliaments*, Oxford University Press, 1971, pp. 339–40.

*Any attempt to analyse the causes of this war must take account of the way it began. Hypotheses which attempt to explain why people might have wanted to fight a civil war are valueless for explaining a situation in which they did not want to fight one.*

> *Attempts to explain a deliberate revolution are inappropriate to a situation in which no deliberate revolution took place. For the political leaders who made the war, there seems to be only one explanation: sheer fear of the intentions of the other side. Behind this fear is a profound depth of misunderstanding of the other side: the misunderstanding is appropriate matter for deep explanations, but they will not be explanations of a war: they will be explanations of personal and ideological distrust, and of the breakdown of a system of government which the parliamentarians desperately wanted to preserve, but which could not keep up with inflation or with divisions in religion.*

## Post–revisionism

The post-revisionists have modified some aspects of the revisionist position. In particular, they have argued that important issues of principle did divide the political nation, especially on the nature of royal power and over theories of resistance to unjust rule. The post-revisionists believe it is important to set the civil war in its British context. Too often, they have argued, it is seen merely as the English civil war when events in Scotland and Ireland – both of which rebelled against their king first – were crucial to what happened in England. Ann Hughes clearly explains the post-revisionist stance:

**EXTRACT 2**

From Ann Hughes, *The Causes of the English Civil War*, Palgrave, 1998, pp. 32, 34 and 46.

> *There were almost unending opportunities, when crises came, for both Charles and his opponents in one kingdom to seek allies in another, and conflicts became ever more serious, longer lasting and harder to untangle. Religious diversity was, of course, a problem for all monarchs given a belief that disunity in religion bred instability and subversion, but Charles's methods and policies were particularly inept and provoked resistance in all his kingdoms. …*
>
> *It would be a mistake to consider the British problem simply in terms of the interrelationships of England and Scotland on the one hand and England and Ireland on the other. There were a multitude of practical, cultural and religious connections between Ireland and Scotland which had independent implications for the British conflicts … As David Stevenson puts it 'The success of the Scots in the Bishops' wars had simultaneously inspired the Irish to revolt, created circumstances in which they could hope revolt could be successful, and made their revolt necessary.'*

## Modifications to the British perspective

Although the importance of events in Scotland and Ireland has now been firmly established, in recent years there has been a move back to emphasising the central role of England. The three kingdoms were very different in nature and although they all experienced upheaval and revolt in the civil war period, events in England can be explained only to a limited extent by what was happening in the rest of Britain. This modification of the post-revisionist stance is explained by Barry Coward:

**INTERPRETATION QUESTION**

How far do the historians quoted in Extracts 1, 2 and 3 differ in their explanations of the importance of the British dimension in interpreting the outbreak of civil war in England?

**ONLINE EXTRAS**
AQA            **WWW**

Practise developing a strong essay answer by completing Worksheet 15 at **www. hoddereducation.co.uk/ accesstohistory/extras**

**EXTRACT 3**

From Barry Coward, *A Companion to Stuart Britain*, Blackwell, 2003, p. xvii.

*Very few people at the time had a vision of creating 'Britain' or thought of themselves as 'British'. Most English people did not often put Scotland or Ireland at the centre of their thoughts. It is highly likely that undue stress on the British context can lead to an exaggeration of the impact of the Scottish and Irish context on England. By the late 1630s and early 1640s, there were enough purely English issues to divide English people and bring about the serious polarization that took place before the outbreak of civil war in England in 1642. Moreover, as John Adamson has argued, to give equal weight to all three kingdoms may be 'politically correct, but it is far from clear that it was also correct historically'. His point is that England was by far and away the most powerful and wealthy of the three kingdoms, and that what was happening there was therefore more important than events in Scotland and Ireland.*

# CHAPTER SUMMARY

The Personal Rule of Charles I from 1628 to 1640 was brought to an end by his determination to bring the Scottish Kirk into conformity with the Church of England, even if this meant going to war. This proved to be a disaster. The Short Parliament was a missed opportunity for the king. The refusal to listen to any grievances and the Parliament's abrupt dissolution meant that opinions hardened against Charles.

The Long Parliament, called following the second disastrous war against the Scots, saw the dismantling of all the measures which had enabled Charles to rule without Parliament and the punishment of those who were held responsible, especially Strafford, who was executed. Up to this point there had been very little support for Charles, but attacks on the Church and the involvement of ordinary people through petitions and demonstrations led some to fear Parliament's novel demands more than the king. The debates over the Grand Remonstrance illustrated the extent of the division.

The Irish rebellion heightened fears about a popish plot and the attempt by Charles to arrest five MPs drove the two sides further apart. Each side began to prepare for war, which broke out in August 1642. The causes of the civil war are the subject of the key debate on page 108.

## Refresher questions

Use these questions to remind yourself of the key material covered in this chapter.

1 Why was Charles so determined to impose his will on the Scots even at the cost of a war?

2 What mistakes did Charles make in his handling of the Bishops' Wars?

3 What do the Short Parliament and the opening of the Long Parliament reveal about public attitudes to Charles's government in the 1630s?

4 Why was the Earl of Strafford considered such a threat by parliamentarians?

5 How far could the execution of Strafford be seen as legal?

6 How important was John Pym in leading the opposition to Charles?

7 Why did conflict with Parliament continue once the abuses of the 1630s had been reversed?

8 What led to the creation of a party in support of the king?

9 How did events in Scotland and Ireland influence what happened in England?

10 Why was there a fear of a popish plot?

11 Why did Charles try to arrest the Five Members?

12 What was the impact of the common people on events of 1640–2?

13 Was Charles or Parliament more to blame for the outbreak of civil war?

## Question practice: AQA

### Essay questions

1 'James I and Charles I followed the same religious policies in their respective reigns between 1603 and 1642.' Explain why you agree or disagree with this view. [AS level]

**EXAM HINT** It is important to cover the whole period, but build this up in a comparative approach, illustrating similarities and differences in policies.

2 'Both James I and Charles I had problems with Parliament in the period 1603–42 because they were kings of both England and Scotland.' Assess the validity of this view. [A level]

**EXAM HINT** This question requires an analysis of whether it was the Dual Monarchy that caused problems with Parliament, or whether it was due to other factors. It is important that both reigns are adequately covered.

### Interpretation questions

1 With reference to Extracts 1 (page 108) and 2 (page 109) and your understanding of the historical context, which of the two extracts provides the more convincing interpretation of the crises that led to the civil war in 1642? [AS level]

**EXAM HINT** Select what you think are the main arguments in each interpretation and use your contextual knowledge to analyse how convincing the arguments are. Reach a clearly argued judgement on which you think is more convincing. Do not bring in theories about the start of the civil war that are not contained in the passages.

2 Using your understanding of the historical context, assess how convincing the arguments in Extracts 1 (page 108), 2 (page 109) and 3 (page 110) are in relation to the reasons for the civil war. [A level]

**EXAM HINT** Analyse the main arguments in each interpretation, and use your contextual knowledge to explain how convincing each one is. There is no need for an overall judgement – just a judgement on each one. Historiography is not relevant here.

## Question practice: OCR

### Essay questions

**1** Assess the impact of John Pym in leading the opposition to Charles I. [AS level]

**EXAM HINT** The question requires you to weigh up the contribution of Pym. In discussing the importance of Pym, answers might include his securing control of the key committees, his role in the dismantling of prerogative government and the use he made of the City of London. Answers should evaluate the importance of his role in each of these issues and reach an overall judgement as to the relative importance of the issues discussed.

**2** To what extent can Charles I be blamed for the breakdown in the relationship between Crown and Parliament by 1642? [A level]

**EXAM HINT** The question requires you to consider a range of reasons for the breakdown in the relationship. You would need to consider the role of Charles I, but also other issues such as the role of Parliament or John Pym. You should reach a judgement on the role of each issue in causing the breakdown and use these interim judgements to reach an overall judgement as to the importance of Charles I in the breakdown.

# CHAPTER 5

# The civil wars and their aftermath 1642–9

The first civil war lasted from 1642 until the defeat of the royalists in 1646. In those years a significant political shift occurred. In order to strengthen its position, Parliament formally entered into a Covenant with the Scots, who joined the war against the royalists on the understanding that Presbyterianism would be introduced as the State religion. This offended the army which, under the growing influence of Oliver Cromwell, became the voice of sectarian independence. Hoping to play on the divisions among his opponents, the king joined with the Scots in 1648 in a second civil war against Parliament. Defeated for a second time, Charles was denounced by the army as 'that man of blood', put on public trial and executed. In the same period, encouraged by the collapse of social norms, a Leveller movement developed which demanded the extension of political rights. These developments are examined under the following themes:

◆ The first civil war 1642–6

◆ Analysing the first civil war

◆ The failure to reach a settlement 1646–9

◆ The trial and execution of the king 1649

◆ The growth of political radicalism: the Levellers

## KEY DATES

| 1642 | Aug. | Outbreak of civil war | 1647 | June | Army's seizure of the king |
| | Oct. | Battle of Edgehill | | Aug. | 'Heads of the Proposals' |
| 1643 | Sept. | Solemn League and Covenant | | Oct. | 'Agreement of the People' |
| 1644 | | Royalist defeat at Marston Moor | | Oct.–Nov. | Putney debates |
| | | | 1648 | April | Second civil war started |
| 1645 | April | Self-denying Ordinance | | Aug. | Royalists and Scots defeated at Preston |
| | | Formation of New Model Army under Cromwell | | Dec. | Pride's purge |
| | June | Royalist defeat at Naseby | 1649 | Jan. | Trial and execution of Charles I |
| 1646 | May | Charles surrendered to the Scots | | May | Cromwell's crushing of the Levellers |
| 1647 | Jan. | Charles's 'Engagement' with the Scots | | | |

# 1 The first civil war 1642–6

■ *Why was Parliament able to defeat the king by 1646?*

It is still common to refer to the civil war as a struggle between king and Parliament, but it has to be remembered that these terms are a form of shorthand. They are useful but imprecise. Approximately one-third of the Commons supported the king in the war and two-thirds supported Parliament. In the House of Lords the proportions were reversed: two-thirds supported the king and one-third supported Parliament. Thus, as a body, Parliament was split in half diagonally. There was a similar division of support in the country at large; a rough line of demarcation ran from the north-east to the south-west, with Parliament stronger to the south of that line and the royalists stronger to the north. This was by no means an exact division; there were pockets of resistance of a royalist or parliamentarian kind dotted throughout enemy territory.

## Edgehill, October 1642

The war may be said to have begun in earnest with Charles's attempt to recover the capital, London. Marching south from Nottingham with an army drawn from supporters from Wales, the Midlands and the north, he found his way blocked by parliamentary forces at Edgehill in south Warwickshire. The battle that followed in October was indecisive but it left open the path to London. However, Charles chose to delay. This proved a fateful decision. Had his forces arrived in London before Parliament had time to organise its defence and turn it into a stronghold, the capital might well have fallen to him, thereby effectively ending the war after it had scarcely begun. In the event, when, three weeks later, the royalists did reach the outskirts of London at Turnham Green, they were confronted by a determined parliamentary force led by the **Earl of Essex** and drawn from the city's trained bands (see page 102). Declining to fight, Charles withdrew to Oxford, his headquarters for the rest of the war. London was in a key strategic position and was England's major port and a centre of finance and trade. Possession of it gave Parliament its greatest asset throughout the war (see page 142). Charles's base at Oxford never afforded the royalists the political and material resources that London provided for the parliamentarians.

## The Solemn League and Covenant 1643

Obliged by circumstances to make Oxford his headquarters, Charles's basic aim continued to be the retaking of London. The royalists' plan in 1643 was for three separate armies in the north, the west and the south-east to secure their areas for the king and then attack London in a pincer movement. The plan had some success; **Prince Rupert** took Bristol and royalist commanders made gains in other areas. But key regions such as Gloucester and Plymouth remained in Parliament's hands, making the planned pincer movement an impossibility. Nevertheless, the successes the royalists had initially achieved intensified

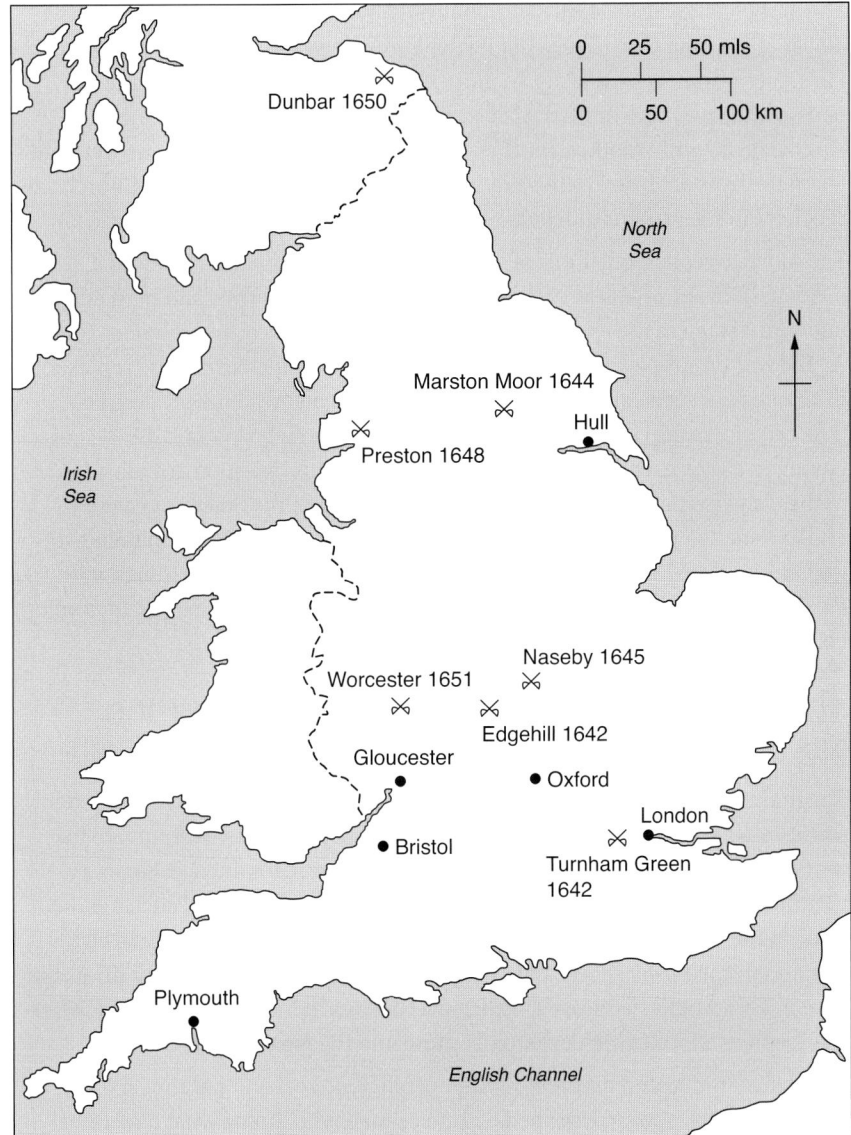

**Figure 5.1** Map showing the main engagements of the civil wars 1642–8.

Parliament's fears that it lacked the manpower to sustain the war. It began to consider ways of supplementing its forces. In his last great contribution to the parliamentary cause, John Pym (see page 87), by now a dying man, urged his colleagues to form an alliance with the Scottish Presbyterians. So it was that in September 1643, the English Parliament entered into the Solemn League and Covenant, a formal agreement whose main terms were:

■ The Scottish Covenanters agreed to bring their forces into England to help defeat the royalist armies.

■ Parliament, in return, agreed to impose Presbyterianism as the State religion in England.

The agreement was militarily and politically momentous. It made the eventual defeat of the king more likely, but it split Parliament and ultimately divided Parliament from its own army. In its anxiety to defeat the king, Parliament had now formally committed itself to replacing one form of State religion, Anglicanism, with another, Presbyterianism. Those parliamentarians who had taken up arms against Charles I in order to be free of an established Church saw the Solemn League and Covenant as a betrayal.

The move to replace one form of state religion with another also caused a major shift in the relations between Parliament and the army, and marked an important stage in the emergence of the latter as a political and religious force. As the war progressed, the parliamentary army came increasingly to represent the Protestant sects (also known as the Independents) who deeply desired freedom of worship for individual congregations and who loathed the idea of having to conform to a centralised State Church. This development ran counter to the trend in the Commons. There, as the signing of the Solemn League and Covenant showed, the upper hand had been gained by those members of Parliament (MPs) who wanted to replace the Laudian Anglican Church with the Presbyterian State model. A critical divergence of attitude had begun to develop between Parliament and its own army.

## The emergence of Oliver Cromwell and the New Model Army

The individual who became the outstanding representative of the Independent sectaries was Oliver Cromwell, the towering figure who was to dominate the years 1642–58. The war had brought him swiftly into prominence. He was a naturally gifted military commander, who did not realise he had such talent until, at the age of 43, he took up arms for Parliament at the start of the civil war and immediately showed his strategic and tactical prowess. From his home base in East Anglia, Cromwell, hitherto a backbench MP, organised the Eastern Association, a force which eventually grew into the **New Model** Army.

Renowned and feared for their discipline, religious zeal and fighting ability, Cromwell's forces were described by him as men who 'know what they fight for and love what they know'. However, a note of caution is appropriate here. Authoritative historian John Morrill (1999) warns against overstating the importance of the religious and idealistic attitudes of the New Model troops. He suggests that the factor that bonded them into such a formidable force was a more materialistic one. 'The reason lies more in the maintenance of regular pay than in any professionalism, nationalism, godliness or political consciousness engendered by the iron will and pure mind of Oliver Cromwell.' Yet, whatever their motivation, the fighting qualities of Cromwell's soldiers came to be regarded by many as the model for all the parliamentary forces to follow.

### KEY TERMS

**New Model** Referred to the unprecedented level of organisation, training and religious fervour that characterised the troops under Cromwell's command.

**A man of blood** A biblical reference well known to Cromwell and his troops from the Book of Samuel 16:7: 'thou art taken in thy mischief, because thou art a man of blood'.

**ONLINE EXTRAS**
**OCR**   **WWW**

Get to grips with assessing impacts by completing Worksheet 21 at www. hoddereducation.co.uk/ accesstohistory/extras

# Oliver Cromwell

| | |
|---|---|
| **1599** | Born in Huntingdon |
| **1616** | Attended Cambridge University |
| **1640** | Became an MP |
| **1643** | Colonel in the Eastern Association |
| **1644** | Victorious in the Battle of Marston Moor |
| **1645** | His New Model Army won the Battle of Naseby |
| **1647** | His army marched into London |
| **1648** | Defeated royalists at Preston |
| **1649** | Signed King Charles's death warrant Crushed Levellers |

One of the most extraordinary persons of his or any other time, Cromwell rose within two decades from an obscure East Anglian, landed-gentry background to become an outstanding soldier and statesman, ending his days as Lord Protector. His distinguishing feature throughout his life was the intensity of his religious faith. He believed sincerely that he was God's instrument for introducing godly rule into England. As a young man, he had considered himself to be steeped in sin. Saved, as he judged it, by divine mercy, he was convinced it was God's will that he should render Him total service in atonement. Convinced that he was divinely directed, Cromwell concluded that the royal government of the 1630s was corrupt and ungodly. Having previously played only a minor part as a backbench MP during the struggle of 1640–2 between king and Parliament, he took up Parliament's cause as a soldier. It was then that Cromwell found he possessed remarkable gifts as a commander.

Although impulsive in many ways, Cromwell, once he had decided on a course of action, rarely questioned that he had done the right thing. His first great achievement was to turn his local Eastern Association into the New Model Army, which swiftly became renowned for its fighting strength and sense of purpose. Cromwell's military gifts soon raised him to high rank, and, working under Thomas Fairfax, he was largely responsible for Parliament's victory over the king by 1646.

Cromwell's intense religious belief led him to regard freedom of conscience as essential if the individual was to come close to God. That was why he favoured independent congregations rather than a State Church. Such views made him a major representative of the Independents.

Cromwell judged that Charles I's dishonesty in the negotiations for a settlement had directly led to a second civil war and marked him as '**a man of blood**'. After much soul searching, Cromwell came to the conviction that it was only by the king's death that the way could be opened to a righteous settlement of the nation's problems. That same sense of certainty was to guide Cromwell through the next decade as he struggled to achieve a godly establishment.

Ironically, it was the New Model's very eagerness to wage war under Cromwell that strained his relations with Parliament. To understand why this was so, it has to be remembered that, despite their occasional military successes, the feeling among many parliamentarians was that the royalists had had the better of the first two years of the war. Critics of Parliament's failure included Cromwell, who believed that the fault lay with the aristocratic leaders of the parliamentary forces, principally the Earl of Essex and the **Earl of Manchester**, who were reluctant to wage all-out war. Unhappy at fighting against their king, these leaders were seeking not victory but some form of compromise settlement. The clash of attitudes was expressed in an exchange between Essex and Cromwell. Essex remarked: 'If we beat the King ninety-nine times, yet he is King still and so will his posterity be after him; but if the King beat us but once, we shall all be hanged and our posterity made slaves.' Cromwell responded: 'If this be so, my lord, why then did we take up arms at first? The Lord of Hosts who gives us victory will show us the way to use it.'

**KEY FIGURE**

**Earl of Manchester (1602–71)**

He had been a companion of Charles I in earlier years, but disapproved of royal policies and helped to lead opposition in the Lords. As with the Earl of Essex, with whom he served, he was reluctant to fight an all-out war against the king.

● ● ● ● ● ● ● ● ● ● ● ● ● ● ● ● ● ● ● ● ● ● ● ● ● ● ● ● ● ● ● ● ● ● ● ● ● ● ● ● ● ● ● ●

## Cromwell and his God

Cromwell wrote the following in a letter of October 1638 (quoted in J.C. Davis, *Cromwell*, Arnold, 2001, p. 81):

> *Oh, I have lived and loved darkness, and hated the light. I was a chief, the chief of sinners. I hated godliness, yet God had mercy on me. O the riches of His mercy! Praise him for me, pray for me, that He hath begun a good work would perfect it to the day of Christ.*

The following verse from Matthew 10:29–30 was Cromwell's favourite biblical quotation (quoted in Paul Lay, *Providence Lost: The Rise and Fall of Cromwell's Protectorate*, Head of Zeus, 2020, p. 121):

> *Are not two sparrows sold for a penny? Yet not one of them will fall to the ground outside your Father's care. And even the very hairs of your head are all numbered.*

● ● ● ● ● ● ● ● ● ● ● ● ● ● ● ● ● ● ● ● ● ● ● ● ● ● ● ● ● ● ● ● ● ● ● ● ● ● ● ● ● ● ● ●

## Marston Moor, July 1644

By the beginning of 1644, the war had gained an added intensity with the entry of Scottish forces into England under the terms of the Solemn League. Charles's response was to bring over some 10,000 Protestant troops from Ireland to swell the royalist ranks. The difference these moves made to the progress of the war became evident at Marston Moor near York in July when the Anglo-Scottish parliamentary forces came face to face with Charles's Anglo-Irish army.

In terms of the number of troops involved, 27,000 parliamentarians outnumbering 18,000 royalists, this was the biggest battle of the war. It was in this engagement that Cromwell showed his extraordinary tactical skill as a cavalry commander in scattering the royalist units when they were on the verge of winning the infantry struggle. It was the determination and resolution of Cromwell's troops that won them the battle and led Prince Rupert to call them 'Ironsides', a nickname that stuck.

Yet instead of seizing the opportunity that Cromwell's victory at Marston Moor had given them to inflict total defeat on the royalists, the parliamentary generals, Essex and Manchester, delayed during the months that followed and eventually moved their armies elsewhere. Their diffidence gave the royalists the chance to recover, thereby, as events were to show, extending the war by another two years.

### The Self-denying Ordinance, April 1645

The failure of Essex and Manchester to follow up Parliament's victory at Marston Moor led directly to their being removed from their commands. This was done by a ruse known as the Self-denying Ordinance. The majority in Parliament now accepted Cromwell's contention that victory over the king could be achieved only if the dedication shown by the New Model was adopted by all their forces. Under the terms of Self-denying Ordinance, the less resolute commanders were required to surrender their commissions and then seek re-appointment. The faint-hearts, including Essex and Manchester, found that their commissions were not renewed. Their places were taken instead by the fully committed generals. Interestingly, Parliament exempted Cromwell from the process. **Thomas Fairfax** became commander-in-chief of Parliament's army with Cromwell appointed as his second in command. Cromwell's New Model Army now became increasingly significant, politically as well as militarily, as the war continued.

## Naseby 1645

In June 1645, two months after the Self-denying Ordinance had been implemented, the quality of the New Model was dramatically illustrated at Naseby in Northamptonshire, the last major battle of the first civil war. Cromwell again showed inspired generalship, but it was two crucial decisions that combined to hand victory to Parliament. The first was the king's decision to fight at Naseby contrary to Rupert's advice to avoid battle since the royalist forces were outnumbered two to one. When the battle was joined, Rupert compounded Charles's original mistake by leaving the field to pursue fleeing parliamentarians, only to discover on his return that Cromwell had seized the initiative and again scattered the royalist ranks. Not only was this a major defeat from which the royalist cause never recovered militarily, but it also resulted in the capture of the royal baggage train containing incriminating documents revealing Charles's attempts to enlist foreign armies to fight for him in England.

Naseby effectively ended the war. Although sporadic fighting continued for another year, any realistic chance of a royalist recovery, let alone victory, had gone. After finally losing Oxford in May 1646, Charles moved to Newark, where he gave himself up to the Scots in the same month.

> **KEY FIGURE**
>
> **Thomas Fairfax (1612–71)**
>
> Although overshadowed by Cromwell, he was a brilliant commander in his own right and contributed greatly to Parliament's ultimate military success. Unlike Cromwell, he was unsuited to politics and declined to become involved in the events leading to the trial of the king.

---

**SUMMARY DIAGRAM**

**THE FIRST CIVIL WAR 1642–6**

```
┌─────────────────────────────────────────────┐
│          Parliament vs royalists            │
│   Edgehill 1642 – lost opportunity for      │
│                 Charles                      │
└─────────────────────────────────────────────┘
                      ↓
┌─────────────────────────────────────────────┐
│     The Solemn League and Covenant 1643     │
│        Royalists now faced two armies        │
└─────────────────────────────────────────────┘
                      ↓
┌─────────────────────────────────────────────┐
│             Marston Moor 1644               │
│      Royalists lost the north of England     │
└─────────────────────────────────────────────┘
                      ↓
┌─────────────────────────────────────────────┐
│ • The emergence of Cromwell's New Model     │
│ • Displacing of Essex and Manchester        │
└─────────────────────────────────────────────┘
                      ↓
┌─────────────────────────────────────────────┐
│                Naseby 1645                  │
│        Proof of Cromwell's methods          │
└─────────────────────────────────────────────┘
```

# 2 Analysing the first civil war

■ *What were the outstanding characteristics of the war?*

■ *What are the explanations for Parliament's victory over the royalists?*

The four-year war placed great demands on both the parliamentary and royalist sides. How they responded gave the war its particular character.

## Recruitment

Parliament and the royalists found raising sufficient troops a constant problem. Initially, both sides relied on volunteers, but, since these were not enough to fight a prolonged war, conscription was soon imposed. Parliament used the terms of the Militia Ordinance (see page 106) to oblige civilians to join its ranks as soldiers, while the king's side resurrected the **Commissions of Array**. As the war lengthened, enforced recruitment became increasingly indiscriminate and harsh; localities dreaded the approach of recruiting squads which were not above using terror tactics, such as burning down houses and barns, in order to force the men of the area to join the ranks. Unsurprisingly, in such circumstances desertions and the expedient changing of sides were common. Given all this, it proved difficult for commanders to maintain discipline and fighting effectiveness among their units. This was why when Oliver Cromwell's forces showed loyalty, cohesion and purpose they became so successful a fighting unit (see page 116).

## Neutralism

The difficulties that both sides experienced in raising forces suggests that enthusiastic commitment to the actual fighting was limited to a minority of the population. Understandably, most people wanted to avoid involvement. The threat to life and limb and the absence from home and family that a soldier's life entailed did not make it attractive. It was significant that desertions increased when men were asked to move with their regiment away from their locality; they were unwilling to leave their family and possessions unprotected. This reluctance to sacrifice personal interests underlay the development of neutralism, the wish not to take sides in the struggle. This was not simple apathy. It arose from resentment at such impositions as billeting (see page 65), the assessment, sequestration and the contribution (see page 124).

### 'Clubmen'

The resentment felt in the localities most affected by the fighting and the presence of foraging armies grew as the war progressed. Groups known as '**Clubmen**' began to form, pledged to prevent both royalists and parliamentarians from disrupting local life. Their basic attitude had been expressed in a declaration by a group of Cheshire neutralists (see Source A).

**KEY TERMS**

**Commissions of Array** A device dating back to medieval times which entitled the monarch to call up civilians to join local militias to fight for him in a time of crisis.

**Clubmen** Taking their name from the wooden clubs with which they were prepared to defend themselves, they called for king and Parliament to make peace.

## SOURCE A

From a set of demands from the county of Cheshire, quoted in John Morrill, editor, *The Revolt of the Provinces*, Longman, 1976.

*… that the commission of array and order or ordinance of Parliament for the Militia be wholly suspended in the county until such time as some course be agreed upon for the ordering of the Militia for the King and Parliament and this without disputing the legality or illegality of either but as finding of neither of them so necessary at this time as for setting them on foot to involve this county in blood …*

*… that no ammunition, [or] forces whatsoever shall be suffered to enter the county in a hostile manner … and whatsoever and they that shall attempt to do it, the whole county shall rise against them as enemies against the peace to be suppressed …*

*… that none shall be arrested in this county as delinquents for either party but [by] a legal peaceable and quiet way, that is by the legal officers and their assistants only, and not by armed men and soldiers who may be an occasion to bring fire amongst us.*

**SOURCE QUESTION**

According to Source A, what fears do the neutralists have about the likely behaviour of both royalist and parliamentary armies?

The significance of the Clubmen in the civil war period can be gauged from the following details:

- By 1645, associations of Clubmen were to be found in 22 counties, being especially prominent in Wales and the West Country.
- At their largest, groups amounted to thousands, big enough to be regarded as a third force competing with the king's and Parliament's armies.
- Their basic demand was that stability and the rule of law be restored by the warring sides' withdrawing from the field.
- They were not, of course, pacifists. Their willingness to defend themselves forcibly put them in the paradoxical position of being prepared to fight against fighting.
- They resisted enforced enlistment by negotiating on occasion directly with royalist and parliamentarian recruiting agents.
- They were particularly concerned not to allow outsiders or upstarts under either a royalist or a parliamentarian banner to disrupt the established flow of community life or interfere with its social and political structure.

How seriously Cromwell regarded the Clubmen was illustrated in August 1645 in an incident at Hambledon Hill near Shaftesbury. A group of 10,000 Clubmen had been bold enough to take prisoner a number of parliamentary troops. Cromwell acted swiftly, breaking up the Clubmen, arresting their ringleaders and sternly admonishing them as a group. A report of the time records that he accepted the Clubmen's right to prevent plundering but warned them that they were 'to refrain in the future from stopping any soldier who went about his business'. A list was drawn up of those who had caused trouble, and 'Any man whose name was in the list deserved to be hanged if he should be taken again opposing Parliament.'

The neutralist movement did not determine the outcome of the war, but what it indicated was the strength of local feeling. At this time, most people thought in local rather than national terms. Their first loyalty was to their immediate region. Modern historian John Morrill (2013) has neatly captured this sense of localism. He accepts that it was fear of social disorder that made some people royalists but adds that this fear 'drove far more into neutralism. Faced by the threat of social disintegration … most counties closed ranks behind county barriers, determined (as they had been in the 1630s) to protect the administrative integrity of their shires as the first line of defence against disorder.'

## Casualties

There are no entirely reliable figures for the civil war period, but modern estimates suggest that, taken together, the three wars, 1642–6, 1648 and 1649–51, resulted in the death toll shown below in Table 5.1. It should be stressed that it is often difficult to distinguish between death in battle, later deaths from wounds sustained earlier, and death from hunger or disease. Indeed, the number of deaths from diseases such as **typhoid** and **malaria** may well have been higher than that from battle injuries. In addition, some 11,000 houses were burned down or razed, leaving some 75,000 people homeless.

**Table 5.1** Civil war deaths

| Region | Deaths |
| --- | --- |
| England | 185,000 (3.7% of the population of 5 million) |
| Scotland | 60,000 (6% of the population of 1 million) |
| Ireland | 600,000 (40% of the population of 1.5 million) |

As the figures in Table 5.1 indicate, the civil wars were a very destructive affair, the death rate being notably high in proportion to the overall population. Yet, while acknowledging that brutalities were perpetrated which went beyond the needs of war, it is important not to exaggerate their occurrence. Blair Worden, an outstanding authority on the period, puts the figures in perspective (see box).

## The human cost

From Blair Worden, *The English Civil Wars 1640–1660*, Weidenfeld & Nicolson, 2009, p. 71:

> [W]ithin England atrocities were at least confined to a numerically small scale. They were newsworthy because they were exceptions. Codes of conduct governing the granting of quarter on surrender, and the treatment of the enemy's wounded or the burial of the dead, were generally observed … The battles were fought for control of the nation, not as civil wars sometimes are, between the centre and movements for independence. The awareness of common nationhood was a restraining bond. Ties of kinship and friendship that crossed the party lines held savagery back.

### KEY TERMS

**Typhoid** A stomach infection contracted from polluted food or water, often causing fatal dehydration.

**Malaria** An enervating condition caused by a mosquito bite. Cromwell was thought to have contracted it while campaigning in the marshlands in Ireland.

ONLINE EXTRAS
AQA   WWW

Test your understanding of academic language by completing Worksheet 16 at www.hoddereducation. co.uk/accesstohistory/extras

# Royalist defeat, Parliamentary victory

In hindsight, the victory of Parliament looks to have been certain, but that was not how contemporaries saw it. While it is true that Parliament's obvious material and strategic advantages grew as the war went on, this did not mean that the decisive military engagements had to go the way they did. Critical decisions were made at pivotal moments which changed the outcome of the war. Three important examples illustrate this: Edgehill (see page 114), Marston Moor (see page 118) and Naseby (see page 119).

## Royalist weaknesses

A number of factors combined to weaken the royalist cause and give eventual victory to Parliament.

### Leadership

- As the war progressed, Charles I was unable to provide the inspired leadership that the situation required.
- Moreover, his army commanders lacked imagination in regard to tactics and strategy. It is true that Rupert brought flair and panache to the battlefield, but he proved too headstrong too often.
- The royalists invariably fought courageously and sometimes effectively, but they never developed the necessary organisation and discipline to sustain a successful war effort.
- In contrast, the leadership of Fairfax and particularly that of Cromwell was inspirational to the parliamentary cause. Cromwell's intense self-belief, allied to his supreme gifts as an organiser and tactician, transferred themselves to his troops and made them an invincible force

### The length of the war

Charles I's best hope lay in a short, victorious war. In the early stages many parliamentarians were conscious that, whatever the justice of their claims, they were rebels against an anointed king. In an intensely religious age, the notion of **sacrilege** was very powerful, which is why the parliamentarians were so eager to stress that, despite appearances, they were fighting for the king, to rid him of the evil advisers who had introduced tyrannical policies. It was also the reason why the traditionalist army leaders such as Essex and Manchester, fought so circumspectly. Had the royalists been able to exploit this diffidence, they might well have gained an overwhelming advantage. However, as the war lengthened and the king's forces were unable to achieve supremacy, attitudes among parliamentarians hardened and they became increasingly willing to distinguish between Charles as a royal personage and Charles as a destructive leader whose forces had to be defeated. The moral advantage swung Parliament's way.

**KEY TERM**

**Sacrilege** Profaning or desecrating a sacred person or institution.

### Cavalry

In the middle of the seventeenth century, firearms, such as the musket, were still cumbrous, short-range and inaccurate. The basic weapon of the foot soldier was the long and heavy pike which, while an effective defence weapon, limited infantry movement. Cavalry, therefore, was the decisive force. At the beginning of the war, this gave the royalists an advantage since the young men who were wealthy enough to own a horse and be skilled riders (cavaliers) tended to be on the king's side. Yet, here again, the longer the war continued the smaller that advantage became. The New Model that Cromwell had formed by 1644 contained ten mounted regiments each with 600 men. Notwithstanding Prince Rupert's brilliance in the field, the New Model cavalry under Cromwell more than outmatched the royalists in number and dependability.

### Finance

Fighting wars is highly expensive. Both sides had to find ways of raising money. Here Parliament's control of London proved pivotal. It was in the capital that the banks and finance houses and chief merchants were to be found, along with the administrative system for collecting taxes, customs duties and fines that Charles had had to leave behind when he fled London in 1642. Initially, Charles had received generous gifts of gold and silver plate from his aristocratic supporters, but welcome though these were, they could be only a short-term source of income. Thereafter, he resorted to such financial expedients as **sequestration** and **'the contribution'**, although royalist methods of raising money were never as effective or productive as Parliament's, particularly its **assessment**. Such impositions were deeply resented by those in the localities and were a major factor in the rise of neutralism (see page 120).

## The importance of London

Parliament's unbroken control of the capital, the nation's largest city and port, gave it the following significant advantages:

- Continued possession of London throughout the war was an important factor in maintaining Parliament's morale and dispiriting the royalists.
- As a source of food, weapons and transport, it was unmatched by any other town or city. There was a common saying of the time: 'He who controls London, controls the nation.'
- To have besieged so large a city as London, as Charles I originally hoped to do, would have required an army of enormous size, something which the royalists were never able to muster.
- From the beginning, London had its own army: the London trained bands. These were a set of local militias who committed themselves wholly to the parliamentary cause. It was from the trained bands that many of Parliament's infantry were drawn. At the start of the war, they were the best organised and drilled troops on either side.

> **KEY TERMS**
>
> **Sequestration**
> A technique used by both sides of confiscating the property and goods of known opponents in the areas they controlled.
>
> **'The contribution'**
> Essentially a tax, usually collected monthly, imposed on a locality whose inhabitants had to raise a decreed amount of money on pain of having their estates and property confiscated.
>
> **Assessment** Very similar to 'the contribution' in that it obliged localities, under threat of severe penalties, to deliver a specific sum of money on a given date to Parliament's collectors, who had calculated what a region was capable of paying.

- London was the main area where radical ideas were developed and broadcast. The mass of pamphlets produced during the propaganda war that accompanied the fighting were printed on London presses.
- London's geographical position made it the centre where all the major routes met, giving Parliament a strategic advantage. Equally significantly, its position on the River Thames allowed Parliament access to supplies from English and Continental ports.
- Parliament's hold over the port of London gave it control of the customs payments levied on transported goods. A connected factor of note was that with London closed to them the royalists found it difficult to receive supplies from the Continent.
- A further advantage was that London also provided Parliament with effective control of the Royal Navy. The irony was that the navy had previously been given scant attention by Parliament, which had declined to grant it adequate funding. It was very much a Royal Navy in the sense that it had been Charles I who had invested in its development. However, at the outbreak of war, the fleet being in port in London, had fallen into Parliament's hands.
- Eighty per cent of the factories and workshops that produced the weapons, uniforms and clothing of war were situated in London.

## Parliament's initial weaknesses

- In the early stages of the conflict, the reluctance of its military leaders, such as Essex and Manchester, to fight an all-out war seriously limited Parliament's chances of victory, and, indeed, suggested that it might even be defeated.
- After the reluctant leaders had been replaced by Fairfax and Cromwell, there was little chance of Parliament's military defeat. The weakening factor was now not military but political. The growing dissension between the Presbyterian Parliament and its Independent army threatened to undermine the parliamentary cause (see page 116). Fortunately for Parliament, military victory over the king was achieved before the divisions became irreparable.

## Parliament's ultimate strengths

- The geographical location of its supporters gave Parliament the advantage of being able to concentrate its forces in key areas.
- Parliament's forces outnumbered those of the royalists.
- Parliament's control of London, the centre of administration, finance and law, was a vital factor throughout the war.
- Its control of the major ports such as London and Hull gave it ready access to supplies.

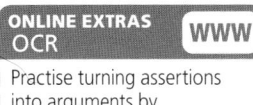

**ONLINE EXTRAS** WWW
OCR

Practise turning assertions into arguments by completing Worksheet 22 at **www.hoddereducation. co.uk/accesstohistory/extras**

- Its control of the navy proved similarly crucial in supply terms.
- After 1643, the presence of the Scottish armies added to Parliament's military strength.
- Between 1642 and 1646, the army remained the loyal servant of Parliament.
- At key moments Parliament's armies maintained their discipline.
- Parliament's recruitment methods proved largely successful.
- Its money-raising methods proved largely successful.
- As strikingly illustrated by Cromwell's New Model Army, parliament was more effective than the royalists in harnessing the religious passions of the time and turning the struggle into a moral cause.
- The genius of Cromwell as a military commander was ultimately the decisive factor in Parliament's victory in the field.

## The royalists' ultimate weaknesses

- The king's supporters were too widespread geographically to be able to concentrate their forces at key moments in key areas.
- Although, initially, there was considerable natural sympathy for Charles as king, this seldom translated into active military support for him, and diminished as the war went on.
- The inability of the royalists to recruit sufficient troops meant their forces were invariably outnumbered, sometimes by as much as two to one.
- The loss of London proved a crippling strategic and economic handicap.
- Oxford, the royalists' administrative base during the war, did not compensate for the loss of London.
- The loss of key ports, such as London and Hull, denied the king the ability to receive and transport vital supplies.
- The seeming ambiguity of Charles's position on religion made him suspect. Fear that he might be prepared to introduce Catholicism deterred many English Protestants from actively supporting him.
- The presence of the Scottish army in England was a constant threat and distraction.
- The royalists were unable to match Parliament in the raising of money, although their tough methods in attempting to do so alienated many of those who might have been their natural supporters.
- Throughout the war the king attempted to bring foreign forces into England. This undermined the royalists' claim that they were fighting to preserve the independence and integrity of the nation.

**ONLINE EXTRAS**
AQA    **WWW**

Practise ranking factors by completing Worksheet 17 at www.hoddereducation. co.uk/accesstohistory/extras

- Despite Rupert's undoubted abilities, his impulsive tactics and his strained relations with fellow commanders weakened the royalists as a fighting force.
- Whatever the successes of the royalists elsewhere, their defeat at the decisive battles of Marston Moor and Naseby meant they were condemned to losing the war.

When listing the relative strengths and weakness of the two sides, the obvious point to stress is that wars are military affairs and are won or lost for military reasons, and that the military advantages lay with Parliament. Cromwell proved the major factor in the defeat of the royalists. Despite the brilliance of individual commanders within it, the king's army could not match Cromwell's New Model Army in ability, organisation and resolve.

**ONLINE EXTRAS**
**AQA**    **WWW**

Get to grips with creating essay titles by completing Worksheet 18 at **www.hoddereducation.co.uk/accesstohistory/extras**

**SUMMARY DIAGRAM**

**ANALYSING THE FIRST CIVIL WAR**

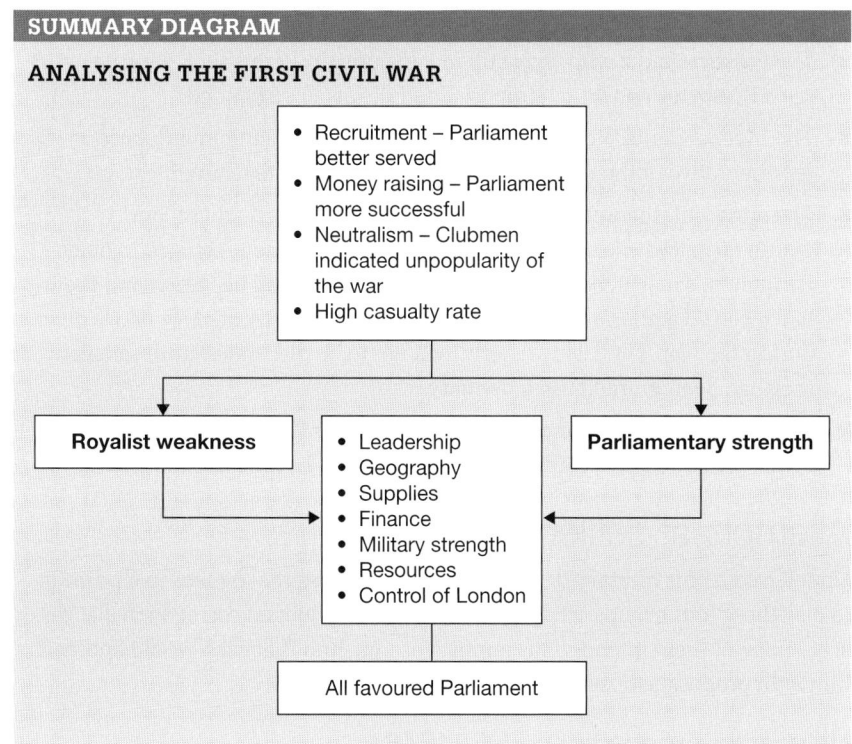

- Recruitment – Parliament better served
- Money raising – Parliament more successful
- Neutralism – Clubmen indicated unpopularity of the war
- High casualty rate

**Royalist weakness**

- Leadership
- Geography
- Supplies
- Finance
- Military strength
- Resources
- Control of London

**Parliamentary strength**

All favoured Parliament

# 3 The failure to reach a settlement 1646–9

■ *Why was there a second civil war in 1648?*

■ *Why did it prove impossible to reach 'an accommodation with his Majesty'?*

In many ways, the defeat of the king in 1646 left the political situation more uncertain than when war had broken out four years earlier.

## The post-war groups

There were now four main competing groups, each with its own agenda:

■ The Presbyterians, who were still in a majority in Parliament, were eager to see a Presbyterian Church imposed and the army disbanded.

■ The Independents, a minority in Parliament but growing in influence as representative of the religious sects resistant to a State Church.

■ The army, still theoretically under the authority of Parliament, but whose rank-and-file soldiers, supported by their officers, refused to obey Parliament's instructions until their arrears of pay had been met and they had received a guarantee that they would not be prosecuted for deeds done during the war. They were determined not to be disbanded until satisfied they had been granted full **indemnity**.

■ The Scots, who were unhappy with Parliament's failure to impose Presbyterianism in accordance with the Solemn League and Covenant.

**KEY TERM**

**Indemnity** Guarantees that soldiers would not be prosecuted later for their earlier actions in the war.

## Attempts at settlement

Undeterred by his military defeat, Charles considered that he was in a position to play these four groups off against each other. He judged correctly that at this stage none of them intended his removal as king and that each would approach him with proposals for settlement.

### Newcastle propositions, July 1646

The first group to make a move towards a settlement after the royalist surrender was Parliament. Its main terms were that in return for making peace, granting the king full honour and guaranteeing his safety, it required that Charles:

■ agree to the establishment of a Presbyterian State Church

■ give up control of his armies to Parliament

■ dismiss those ministers who, Parliament judged, had ill-advised him.

As with nearly all the proposals put to him over the next two years, Charles did not give a straight answer. He deliberately procrastinated, believing that time was on his side. A year later, with the negotiations nowhere near resolution, the army, seeking to outflank the Parliament from which it was becoming increasingly estranged, presented the king with its own terms for a settlement. These were known as the 'Heads of the Proposals'. This followed Charles's abduction by the army in June 1647, a move that had been directly ordered by Cromwell. Angered by rumours that Parliament and the Scots were intriguing with the king, Cromwell decided to take Charles into army custody. A detachment of cavalry was sent to Holmby House in Northamptonshire to seize the king and so remove him from Parliament's control. He was taken first to Newmarket and then to London where he was confined at Hampton Court.

## 'Heads of the Proposals', August 1647

Drafted by **Henry Ireton** and formally presented by the **Council of the Army**, the main terms reflected the army's wish to take things beyond simply the relations of monarch and Parliament. In return for restoring the royal family's 'honour and freedom', the Council required the king's acceptance of the following:

- Parliaments to be called every two years
- control of the army and navy to be in Parliament's hands
- bishops no longer to have authority in civil matters
- the use of the Book of Common Prayer to be no longer mandatory in services
- an Act of Indemnity to be passed absolving the army's troops from any supposed offences committed during the war.

Although Charles did not give a clear response to the 'Heads of the Proposals', any more than he had to the Newcastle propositions, it was evident that he would accept neither since they both required his giving up authority over his own army and ministerial appointments. It was his refusal to accept these key points that had led to the final breakdown of relations with Parliament in 1642 (see page 106). He was unwilling to accept limitations to his authority while he still believed he could restore his royal powers by exploiting the divisions among his opponents.

## The Engagement, December 1647

Having escaped from army custody and fled to the Isle of Wight in November 1647, Charles began negotiations with the Scots. This led in December to an agreement with them, 'the Engagement', which contained the following main terms:

- Charles to be restored to the position he had held before the breakdown of negotiations with Parliament in 1642.
- In return, Charles promised to adopt Presbyterianism as the State religion and to suppress sectarianism.

When the army learned of the Engagement it broke off all negotiations with the king. Although there were still Presbyterians in Parliament who believed a compromise could be reached with Charles, it was the army which was increasingly dictating events. At a 'prayer meeting' at Windsor in May 1648, at

> **KEY FIGURE**
>
> **Henry Ireton (1611–51)**
>
> Cromwell's son-in-law; he committed himself to Parliament at the outbreak of war and proved an able commander. Trained as a lawyer, he was one of the main representatives of the Grandees, drafting many of the key political and constitutional documents produced by the army.

> **KEY TERM**
>
> **Council of the Army**
> Formed in 1647, it was composed of the highest ranking officers ('Grandees'), who were men of good birth, such as Fairfax, or of property, such as Cromwell.

which Cromwell's was the leading voice, the Army Council made a declaration (Source B) that meant a second civil war was unavoidable:

**SOURCE QUESTION**

In Source B, what is the significance of the description of Charles I as 'that man of blood'?

**ONLINE EXTRAS** WWW
OCR

Test your understanding of sources by completing Worksheet 23 at **www. hoddereducation.co.uk/ accesstohistory/extras**

### SOURCE B

An officer in the New Model Army recalls the decisions taken by the army at Windsor in April 1648, just after the second civil war had begun. From William Allen, 'A faithful memorial of that remarkable meeting of many officers of the Army in England at Windsor Castle, in the year 1648', quoted in David L. Smith, *Oliver Cromwell*, Cambridge University Press, 1992, p. 25.

*God did direct our steps, and presently we were led and helped to a clear agreement among ourselves, not any dissenting, that it was the duty of our day, with the forces we had, to go out and fight against those potent enemies with a humble conscience in the name of the Lord only … that it was our duty, if ever the Lord brought us back in peace, to call Charles Stuart, that man of blood, to an account for that blood he had shed and mischief he had done to his utmost, against the Lord's cause and people in these poor nations.*

## The second civil war 1648

It was the attitude of Charles I that had prevented a political settlement being reached between 1646 and 1648. He had no qualms about playing off Parliament, the army and the Scots against each other and making contradictory promises that he did not intend to keep. Charles believed that he was dealing with rebels and, therefore, was not bound by any promises that he made to them. This was why all attempts to find 'an accommodation with his Majesty' eventually broke down. The alignment in the war that followed was almost a complete reversal of 1642. Whereas the war of 1642–6 had been Parliament and Scots against the king, the second civil war was the king and Scots against Parliament.

In the struggle that followed, the Scots and the English royalists failed to co-ordinate their plans effectively. This, and the speed with which the army under Fairfax and Cromwell responded, made Charles I's cause a hopeless one militarily. The royalists experienced crushing defeats in Wales and East Anglia and lost all hope after Cromwell had scattered their combined Anglo-Scottish forces at Preston in August.

## The growth of radicalism in the army

The uneasy relationship between the Presbyterian-dominated Parliament and the Independent-dominated army had broken out into open hostility after the royalists had been defeated in 1646. Fearful of the physical and political threat the army posed, Parliament wanted to disband it. The army refused to consider disbandment until its soldiers had been paid the arrears that they were owed and been given a formal promise of indemnity. In response, Parliament tried to raise a new military force from its sympathisers in London; at the same time, it excluded the Independent MPs from the Commons. Angered by this, Cromwell's New Model Army marched into London in August 1647 and reinstated the dismissed MPs. Clearly, the New Model Army no longer regarded itself as the servant of Parliament.

Up to this point, the army had maintained a united front; the Grandees had supported the troops' demand for payment of arrears. However, cracks now began to appear. Influenced by **Leveller** ideas (see page 138), soldiers' representatives, known as **agitators**, put forward radical demands that went beyond the simple issue of pay. In the 'Agreement of the People', a document drawn up in October 1647, the agitators demanded that:

- the present Parliament be dissolved
- future Parliaments acknowledge that they existed solely by permission of the people
- freedom of worship be recognised
- law be applied to all men equally
- recognition that 'estate, degree, birth or place' did not confer any special privileges beyond those enjoyed by ordinary people.

The last point was a clear challenge to the existing social order, particularly the rights attaching to property, and it was this that formed the main issue discussed between the Grandees and the agitators at a meeting of the army at Putney in October 1647.

## The Putney debates

The Grandees' viewpoint was expressed by Ireton and Cromwell, who declared that they had fought the war not to overthrow society but to preserve it. Their socially conservative position was that it was the possession of property that gave its holders responsibility and 'interests' and entitled them to vote, to sit in Parliament and to make the decisions as to how the nation should be governed. This conservatism was attacked by such people as **Thomas Rainsborough**, who held that rights were natural and universal and did not depend on property. The essence of the disagreement was captured in the following exchange:

> **SOURCE C**
>
> From the Putney debates, October 1647, quoted in John P. Kenyon, *The Stuart Constitution*, Cambridge University Press, 1966, pp. 313–14.
>
> Rainsborough: *I really think that the poorest he that is in England hath a life to live, as the greatest he … I think it's clear that every man that is to live under a government ought first by his own counsel to put himself under that government; and I do think that the poorest man in England is not all bound in a strict sense to that government that he hath not had a voice to put himself under.*
>
> Ireton: *I would have an eye to property … Take away that, I do not know what ground there is of anything you can call any man's right. I would very fain [greatly wish to] know what you gentlemen do account the right you have to anything in*

*England – anything of estate, land or goods that you have, what right you have to it. What right hath any man to anything if you lay not down that principle … If you will resort only to the law of nature you have no more right to this land, or anything else, than I have.*

So considerable were the differences between the Grandees and the Leveller agitators that they would prove impossible to resolve. These differences were contained while the royalists were still a threat, but after the king's defeat in the second civil war and his execution (see page 133), the conflict within the army re-emerged. It was settled ultimately by Cromwell's ruthless crushing of the Leveller regiments (see page 139).

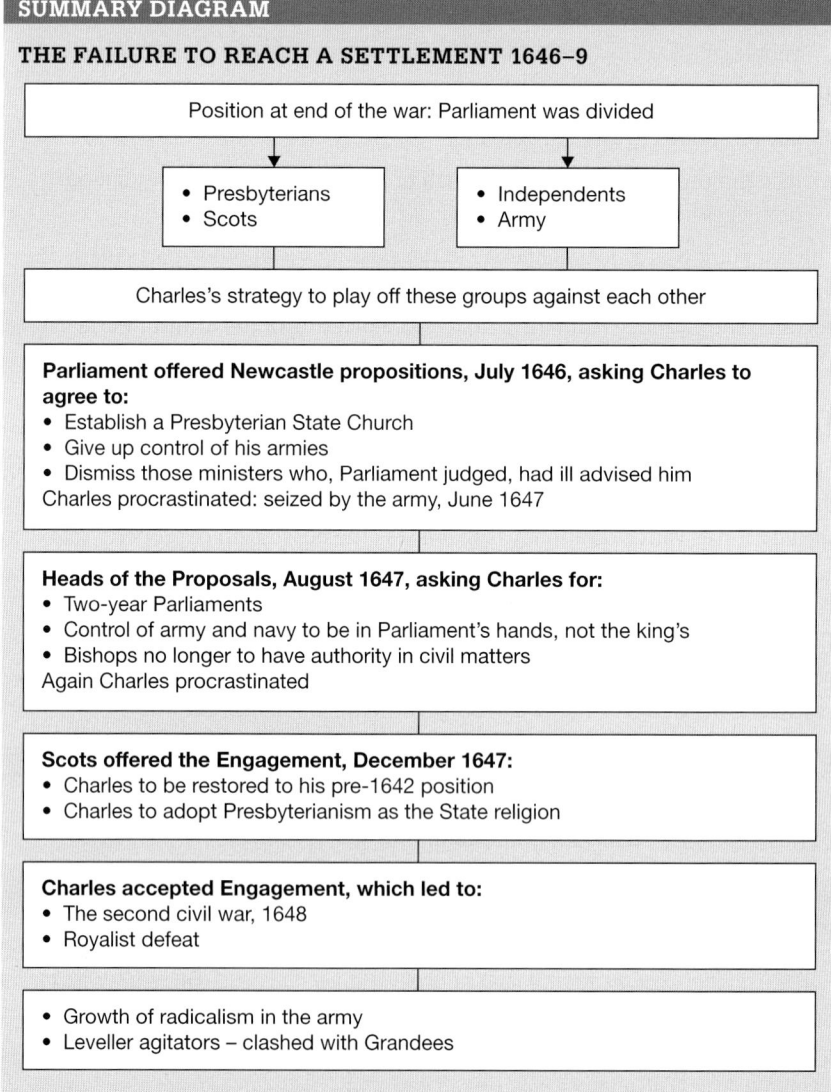

**SUMMARY DIAGRAM**

**THE FAILURE TO REACH A SETTLEMENT 1646–9**

Position at end of the war: Parliament was divided

- Presbyterians
- Scots

- Independents
- Army

Charles's strategy to play off these groups against each other

**Parliament offered Newcastle propositions, July 1646, asking Charles to agree to:**
- Establish a Presbyterian State Church
- Give up control of his armies
- Dismiss those ministers who, Parliament judged, had ill advised him

Charles procrastinated: seized by the army, June 1647

**Heads of the Proposals, August 1647, asking Charles for:**
- Two-year Parliaments
- Control of army and navy to be in Parliament's hands, not the king's
- Bishops no longer to have authority in civil matters

Again Charles procrastinated

**Scots offered the Engagement, December 1647:**
- Charles to be restored to his pre-1642 position
- Charles to adopt Presbyterianism as the State religion

**Charles accepted Engagement, which led to:**
- The second civil war, 1648
- Royalist defeat

- Growth of radicalism in the army
- Leveller agitators – clashed with Grandees

# 4 The trial and execution of the king 1649

■ *Was the trial of Charles I legal?*
■ *Did Parliament have any choice but to execute the king?*

The king's unwillingness to seek a genuine settlement with his opponents reinforced a powerful feeling among the army and some of the MPs that he was personally responsible for all the bloodshed and misery suffered by the kingdom since 1642. The General Council of the Army decided that Charles must be removed. However, they resolved that this would be done not 'in a hole and corner manner', but by putting him on public trial. The army wished to clothe its actions in legal form. Modern historians have stressed how important this is as an illustration of how far the army was from contemplating revolution.

However, there were still MPs who did consider it possible to reach agreement with the king. Indeed, on 5 December 1648, the Commons voted 129 to 83 that the parliamentary commissioners who had been sent to Newport, Isle of Wight, where Charles was held, should continue their talks with him. This was too much for the army leaders who, on the following day, made the move that became known as Pride's purge.

## Pride's purge, December 1648

On the morning of 6 December, Colonel Pride, acting on behalf of the Army Council, stood at the door of the Commons and forcibly turned away those members, mainly Presbyterians, who had voted in favour of continued negotiations with the king. Those MPs who were allowed to remain in the Commons after the purge became known collectively as the Rump.

## The trial

To give themselves the authority to try the king, the Commons asserted early in January 1649 that 'the supreme power in this nation' was now vested solely in them, without the need of king or House of Lords. At the trial, the High Court, specially created by the Rump to prosecute the king, claimed to represent the will of 'the people of England', against whom the king had offended. This claim, which flew in the face of all precedent and law, was the Rump's weakest point. When the charge was read out, impeaching the king in the name 'of the people of England', a woman in the gallery cried out: 'It's a lie, not half, nor a quarter of the people of England! Oliver Cromwell is a rogue and a liar.' The rumour was that she was Lady Fairfax, the wife of the commander of Parliament's army, a sign of how deeply the king's trial had divided the nation.

The trial was in no sense an impartial attempt to establish Charles's guilt or innocence. It was a show trial; his guilt was assumed from the beginning. This had been evident at the outbreak of the second civil war in May 1648 when the

**ONLINE EXTRAS** **WWW**
**AQA**

Develop your analysis of consequences by completing Worksheet 19 at **www. hoddereducation.co.uk/ accesstohistory/extras**

army had declared its intention to call to account 'Charles Stuart, that man of blood'.

## Charles's demeanour

Against expectation, Charles conducted himself impressively at his trial. He behaved with dignity and lost the stammer that had habitually handicapped his public speaking. He refused to recognise the court or to plead, but took the opportunity, when permitted to speak, to ask his accusers by what legal authority he was brought before them. It was the one question to which they had no legitimate answer. He had a case grounded in law and tradition that the hastily created High Court could not match. He rejected the whole proceedings on the grounds that 'a king cannot be tried by any superior jurisdiction on earth'.

**SOURCE QUESTION**

In Source D, on what principles does Charles make his stand?

### SOURCE D

From Charles's address to the court at his trial, January 1649, quoted in Barry Coward, editor, *The English Revolution*, John Murray, 1997, p. 123.

*I am your King. I have a trust committed to me by God. I stand more for the liberty of my people than any here that sitteth to be my judge.*

*It is not my case alone; it is the freedom and liberty of the people. And do you pretend what you will, I must justly stand for their liberties. For if a power without law may make law, may alter the fundamental laws of the kingdom – I do not know what subject he is in England can be assured of his life or anything he can call his own … I do plead for the liberties of the people of England more than any of you do.*

Whatever Charles's personal responsibility may have been for the civil wars, there is no doubt that he had the better of the argument at his trial. As he said to his accusers, if he, a king, could be treated with complete disregard of existing laws of which he was the representative, 'what justice will my people have?'. His fate, however, had been predetermined. He was declared guilty and condemned to death by beheading. On 30 January 1649, the sentence was duly carried out.

## Cromwell's role

After the Restoration (see page 211), it suited the royalists to portray Oliver Cromwell as a black-hearted man who had forced his wavering parliamentary and army colleagues to accept the trial and execution when they had favoured clemency. Modern scholars see this largely as a myth. Cromwell did not speak publicly on the issue until late in December 1648 and did not act as chief instigator of the proceedings against Charles. Indeed, it was his uncertainty that stands out. Addressing the Commons in the final week of December, he declared: 'I cannot but submit to Providence, though I am not yet provided [willing] to give you my advice.' What appears to have happened was that, having given the issue long deliberation, he concluded that the king's execution was both legal and just. Thereafter, he acted with resolution, confident that he had made the right decision. Consistent with his belief that all his actions were ultimately guided by the will of God, Cromwell rarely had doubts after the event. He attended all but two of the trial sessions and his signature appears boldly on Charles's death warrant. Two months after the execution, Cromwell told the Commons that God had guided the decision to exact justice on Charles, 'the prime leader of all this quarrel in the three kingdoms'. In an account composed in the following reign, Bishop Gilbert Burnet, who had meticulously consulted eyewitnesses who had observed the preparations for the trial, wrote the following (Source E):

---

**SOURCE E**

From Bishop Burnet, *History of My Own Time*, quoted in W.C. Abbott, editor, *The Writings and Speeches of Oliver Cromwell*, volume I, Harvard University Press, 1937–47, p. 757.

*Ireton was the person that drove it on, for Cromwell was all the while in some suspense about it. Ireton had the principles and the temper of a Cassius [an assassin of Julius Caesar] in him; he stuck at nothing that might have turned England to a Commonwealth. … Fairfax was much distracted in his mind, and changed purposes often every day. The Presbyterians and the body of the City were much against it, and were everywhere fasting and praying for the King's preservation. There was not above 3,000 of the army about the town; but these were selected out of the whole army as the most engaged in enthusiasm; and they were kept at prayer in their way almost day and night, except when they were upon duty … the King's party was without spirit; and as many of themselves have said to me, they could never believe his death was really intended until it was too late. They thought all was a pageantry to strike a terror, and to force the King to concessions.*

---

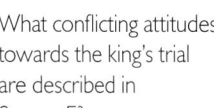

**SOURCE QUESTION**

What conflicting attitudes towards the king's trial are described in Source E?

**SOURCE QUESTION**

Why did the regicides (killers of the king) regard a signed death warrant as shown in Source F (transcription on page 147) as being an essential part of their proceeding against the king?

---

**SOURCE F**

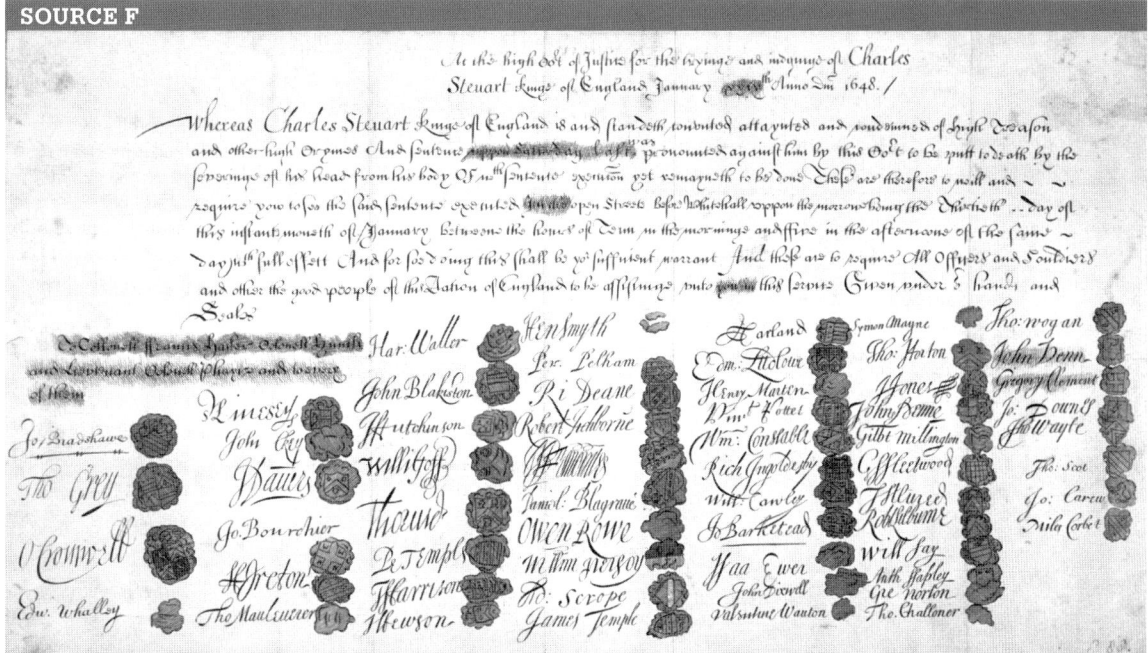

Charles I's death warrant. Cromwell's signature is third down in the first column (see a transcription of this document on page 147).

Writing fifteen years after the trial, Lucy Hutchinson, wife of one of the regicides, Colonel Hutchinson, recalled the attitude of those involved in trying the king (Source G).

**SOURCE QUESTION**

What does the writer of Source G mean by saying that some of the regicides were 'under the awe of the army'?

> **SOURCE G**
>
> From Lucy Hutchinson (writing between 1664 and 1669), *Memoirs of the Life of Colonel Hutchinson*, edited by Julius Hutchinson, Longman, 1808, p. 157.
>
> *Some of the regicides afterwards, for excuse, belied themselves and said they were under the awe of the army, and overpersuaded by Cromwell. But it is certain all men herein were left to their free liberty of acting, neither persuaded nor compelled; and as there were some nominated to the High Court of Justice that sat at first, but dared not hold on, so all the rest might have declined if they could, when it is apparent they would have suffered nothing by so doing. For those who then declined were afterwards, when they offered themselves, received in again. Most of them retreated not for conscience but for fear and worldly prudence, foreseeing that the insolence of the army might grow.*

## Reaction to the execution

The majority of the people in Britain were shocked by the sacrilege that the execution of an anointed monarch represented. The strength of this feeling was shown by the large number of Charles's opponents who, no matter how much they blamed him for the nation's sufferings, could not bring themselves to be involved in his judicial murder. However, for the regicides (those who signed his death warrant) it was a duty they had to fulfil. Charles was a man 'against whom the Lord himself hath witnessed'. Cromwell is reputed to have said at the time that 'we will cut off his head with the crown upon it' and that the execution was a 'cruel necessity'. There is no hard evidence that he said either of these things, but their sentiment accurately expressed the attitude of the regicides in 1649.

**ONLINE EXTRAS**
**AQA**   WWW

Practise assessing individuals by completing Worksheet 20 at **www.hoddereducation. co.uk/accesstohistory/extras**

**ONLINE EXTRAS**
**OCR**   WWW

Test your understanding of sources by completing Worksheet 24 at **www. hoddereducation.co.uk/ accesstohistory/extras**

After Charles I's execution, the next logical step was for the Rump to abolish both the monarchy and the Lords and create a Commonwealth (republic). This was formally done in March 1649, but only after considerable debate about whether it was the right course. The delay and uncertainty suggest how far from being truly revolutionary the Rump actually was. Of course, in one sense there are few things more revolutionary than the beheading of a reigning monarch, but it has to be re-emphasised that Charles's execution was not undertaken primarily in order to bring about a constitutional change. It was foremost a remedy for the insoluble problem of what to do with a defeated king who would not accept his defeat.

Republicanism had never been very strong in England. The civil wars had been fought not to destroy kingship but to limit its powers. The decision to put Charles on trial was made very late in the struggle between king and Parliament. It was an act of desperation that arose from the impossibility of negotiating with him. The members of the purged Parliament and of the army who voted for the king's trial and execution had decided reluctantly that there was no alternative to his permanent removal. Although it was to be dressed in legal forms and justified by arguments of principle, the king's execution marked the culmination of ten years of political failure. The unfolding of events had forced people of influence into making decisions and taking steps that they would not have contemplated earlier.

**ONLINE EXTRAS**
**AQA**   **WWW**

Develop your comparative skills by completing Worksheet 21 at **www. hoddereducation.co.uk/ accesstohistory/extras**

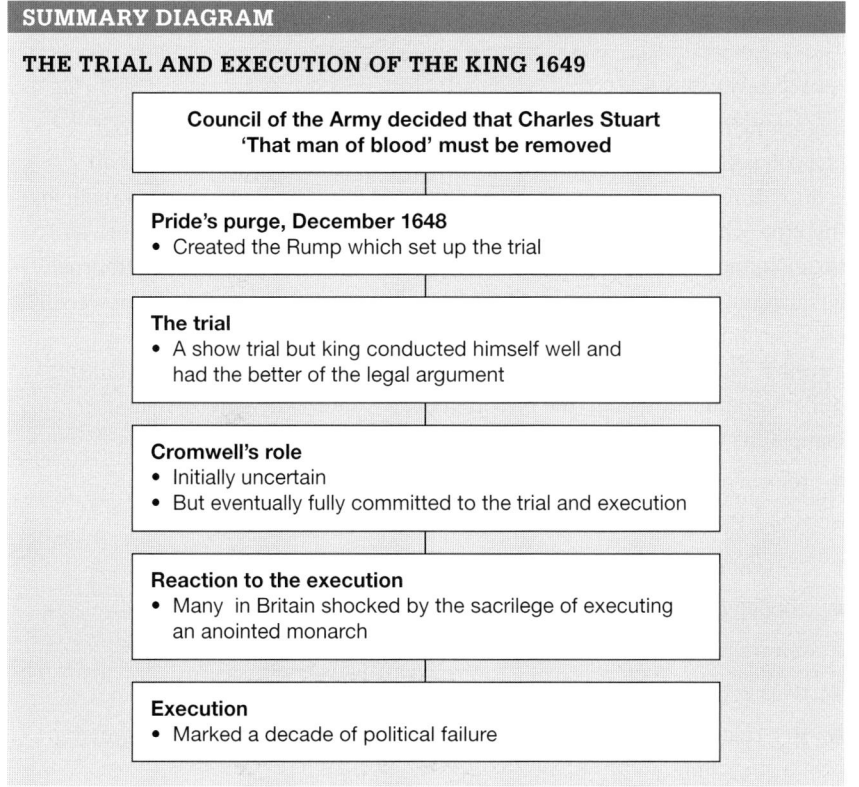

**SUMMARY DIAGRAM**

**THE TRIAL AND EXECUTION OF THE KING 1649**

> **Council of the Army decided that Charles Stuart 'That man of blood' must be removed**

> **Pride's purge, December 1648**
> • Created the Rump which set up the trial

> **The trial**
> • A show trial but king conducted himself well and had the better of the legal argument

> **Cromwell's role**
> • Initially uncertain
> • But eventually fully committed to the trial and execution

> **Reaction to the execution**
> • Many in Britain shocked by the sacrilege of executing an anointed monarch

> **Execution**
> • Marked a decade of political failure

# 5 The growth of political radicalism: the Levellers

■ *How great a threat to the political and social system were the Levellers?*

The challenge to the established order of life caused by the disruption of war encouraged the growth of radical ideas. Most of the popular radical movements were religious (see page 150), but the outstanding example of a radical movement that was predominantly secular and political was the Levellers, its ideas, although largely rejected at the time, could be said to have changed the political landscape in Britain.

## The Levellers

Beginning in London in the mid-1640s, the Leveller movement grew out of a conviction among traders and merchants that the war had created an economic recession which threatened their livelihoods. It was understandable, therefore, that initial Leveller demands were concerned with such things as taxation, monopolies and restriction of trade. However, led by John Lilburne, its outstanding spokesman, the Leveller movement developed into a powerful critique of the nation's social and political system. In September 1648, a Leveller 'Humble Petition' was presented to Parliament, in which the failures of Parliament to attend to the nation's needs were listed. Among the major complaints were that Parliament had failed to introduce measures to:

■ reform and extend the franchise

■ make Parliament answerable to the people

■ prevent enforced enlistment

■ abolish tithes and excise duties

■ reform the law so that it was no longer a tyranny

■ release those imprisoned for debt

■ free trade from restrictions and prevent monopolies from being formed

■ introduce liberty of conscience and freedom of worship

■ take property from the wealthy, thereby 'making all things common'.

The Levellers had hoped that the removal of Charles I would be a prelude to a social and religious reformation. However, the Rump quickly made it clear that it intended making no concessions to Leveller demands. Lilburne responded by publishing a pamphlet, *England's New Chains Discovered*, a withering attack on the Rump in which he denounced it for seizing power from the people. He also condemned the **Council of State** as an unelected clique to whom the people of England owed neither loyalty nor obedience.

**KEY TERM**

**Council of State**
The body appointed by the Rump Parliament after the execution of the king to act as the government under the direction of the Rump.

# John Lilburne

| | |
|---|---|
| *c.***1614** | Born in Sunderland to a Durham landowner |
| **1638–40** | Imprisoned by the Star Chamber for his anti-government pamphlets |
| **1642–5** | Fought as a soldier for Parliament |
| **1646** | Imprisoned for challenging the authority of the Presbyterian-dominated Parliament |
| **1648** | Released |
| **1649** | Opposed Cromwell and the regicides Tried for sedition |
| **1649–51** | Became a prominent figure in the Leveller resistance to the Rump |
| **1652** | Banished from England |
| **1653** | Tried for sedition |
| **1653–5** | Held in prison |
| **1655** | Became a Quaker |
| **1657** | Died |

A natural rebel, John Lilburne was a constant thorn in the side of the authorities. Throughout his life he retained a deep distrust of those who wielded power, no matter whether they were kings, generals, parliaments or protectors. In the late 1630s he suffered a series of severe punishments at the hands of the Star Chamber for his opposition to Charles I's 'tyranny'. His unbreakable spirit earned him the popular title of 'free-born John'. Released from prison by the Long Parliament, he took up arms against the royalists during the first civil war. He was captured in 1643 but later released. As the war developed, he grew alarmed at the growing strength of the Presbyterians and refused to fight for Parliament after 1645. He became equally disturbed by the emergence of the army leaders as a political force. In 1649, he launched a bitter pamphlet war against Cromwell and the Army Council. He denied the Rump's right to try Charles I and was outraged by what he regarded as its usurping of authority after the king's execution. For this, he was tried for sedition but acquitted.

Despite Cromwell's crushing of the Levellers in 1649, Lilburne continued to attack the Rump, directing particular venom at the merchant monopoly companies, whom he accused of profiteering under the new republic. Fierce retaliation from the republicans in the Rump, among whom Arthur Haselrig was the most prominent, resulted in Lilburne being formally banished from England in 1652. However, he returned a year later, was re-arrested and again charged with sedition. Once more he was acquitted to great popular acclaim. It was said that the shouts that went up from the crowd when the jury declared him not guilty could be heard over a mile away. But 'free-born John' was too disruptive a figure to be allowed to go entirely free. Under the pretext that he was still under banishment, he was held in a variety of prisons until 1655, when he was released on becoming a Quaker. In his final years, he devoted himself to writing religious works.

## Cromwell and the Levellers

In another pamphlet, Lilburne accused Cromwell of high treason for his part in the king's execution (see Source I, page 142). Such defiance could not be tolerated; Lilburne was arrested and brought before the Council of State, which committed him to the Tower of London. However, Lilburne's opposition helped to inspire resistance in the ranks of the army. Dislike of the Rump, combined with the soldiers' fear of being sent to Ireland with their arrears unpaid (see page 128), led in May 1649 to a number of units mutinying. Cromwell was instructed by the Rump to crush this rising. He needed little urging. Lilburne, in his account of his interrogation by the Council of State recorded Cromwell as saying the following of the Levellers (Source H, overleaf):

**SOURCE QUESTION**

How is the bitterness expressed by Cromwell in Source H to be explained?

**ONLINE EXTRAS**
OCR | WWW

Test your understanding of tone and language by completing Worksheet 25 at **www.hoddereducation. co.uk/accesstohistory/extras**

**SOURCE H**

From Ivan Roots, editor, *Speeches of Oliver Cromwell*, J.M. Dent, 1989, p. x.

*I tell you, you have no other way to deal with these men but to break them, or they will break you; yea, and bring all the guilt and blood and treasure shed and spent in this kingdom upon your heads and shoulders, and frustrate and make void all that work that, with so many years' industry, toil and pain you have done, and so render you to all rational men in the world as the most contemptiblest generation of silly, low-spirited men in the earth, to be broken and routed by such a despicable, contemptible generation of men as they are.*

## Cromwell's suppression of the Levellers

The speed and severity with which Cromwell moved against the Levellers in 1649 illustrated his determination to win support for the Commonwealth from the traditional governing classes by proving that the new regime would not tolerate social disruption. Having assured the loyal regiments of the Rump's intention to settle their arrears of pay, he appealed for their assistance in subduing 'the army revolters which are now called by the name of Levellers'. Then he and Fairfax pursued the retreating Levellers across two counties before cornering them at Burford in Oxfordshire on 14 May. After a token resistance, the mutineers surrendered; they were court-martialled, and three of their ringleaders were shot. This, together with the scattering of two mutinous troops of cavalry in Northamptonshire two days later, marked the end of the Leveller rising in the army. It also meant, in effect, the end of the Leveller movement as a political force in the country at large.

## The character of the Leveller movement

It should be noted that the word 'Leveller' was in many ways misleading. Indeed, much of the voluminous pamphlet literature that the movement produced was concerned with denying that it intended the levelling of society. Most modern historians now warn against viewing the Levellers as democrats in anything approaching a modern sense. They did not believe in **universal suffrage**. They wanted the vote for the 'middling sort', by which they meant such self-made people as craftsmen, shopkeepers and the smaller property-owners. Their movement never represented the poor and showed no interest in the agricultural labourers. Nor did they advocate votes for women, this despite the significant supportive role played by a number of women as Leveller agitators. These included Lilburne's wife Elizabeth, who in 1649 collected the signatures of 10,000 women demanding that the Rump release her husband from prison.

The Leveller movement was an almost exclusively urban movement. In demanding an extended franchise, it deliberately excluded wage earners and servants. But, since it frightened the propertied classes, it was never able to win support among people of influence. The weight of modern research suggests that the upheavals of the period 1640–60 were essentially political rather than social. The traditional ruling classes remained very much in control and closed

**KEY TERM**

**Universal suffrage** Votes for all adult citizens.

ranks in the face of a challenge to their customary authority. The Levellers could make little headway against this. As modern historian Austin Woolrych put it in 1983: 'The Levellers were in fact a precociously well-organized pressure group rather than a revolutionary movement, and much more interested in principles than in power.'

There was once a widely held view that radicalism was a major force in England between 1640 and 1660. This has largely been abandoned by modern historians, who stress that there was never a single radical movement. There were various radical groups but these did not unite as a serious social or political force. They are interesting as forerunners of the liberals and socialists of a later age, but, in their own time, they were far from being capable of taking power – even had that been their aim. Their influence was minimal.

## The failure of the Levellers

■ The Leveller movement proved weaker than it appeared. By 1649 it was little more than three years old, far too short a time for it to have taken root in English society.

■ The movement's leaders, such as Lilburne, Overton and Walwyn, were effective propagandists, and attracted considerable attention. But attention does not necessarily mean support. The Leveller 'agitators' in the ranks had very limited success. For example, they were never able to persuade more than a small minority of the army units to follow them into open defiance of authority. Out of an army of 40,000, barely 800 soldiers joined the revolt in May 1649.

■ The truth was that although the army rank and file had certainly become politicised since 1647, they had not become radicalised. The troops were primarily concerned with gaining better pay and conditions of service. When Cromwell and Ireton persuaded the Rump in 1649 to provide the back pay owed to the soldiers, unrest in the ranks was greatly reduced.

■ By 1649, the conditions which had given the Levellers such strength as they had possessed had changed. There had been occasions during the previous two years when the turmoil of the times worsened by poor harvests and bread shortages had made Leveller arguments appear attractive as a means of protesting against the grimness of the prevailing conditions. But when better times returned in 1649, in the form of improved harvests, lower prices and higher wages, the Levellers had less fertile ground for sowing dissension.

■ A particular weakness of the Levellers was that they gained few adherents among the army officers. The Grandees were seldom willing to forego their natural conservatism by actively supporting a group of social radicals.

■ The inability of the Leveller movement to make headway among the officers was compounded by its failure to gain substantial support in parliament, either before or after Pride's Purge. This failing denied the Levellers an effective power base. A similar limitation applied geographically. At no time,

**SOURCE QUESTION**

Why, as illustrated in Source I, was Lilburne so bitter towards Oliver Cromwell?

**SOURCE I**

# AN IMPEACHMENT
## OF
# HIGH TREASON
### AGAINST

*Oliver Cromwel*, and his Son in Law *Henry Ireton* Esquires, late Members of the late forcibly diffolved Houfe of Commons, prefented to publique view ; by *Lieutenant Colonel John Lilburn* clofe Prifoner in the Tower of London, for his real, true and zealous affections to the Liberties of his native Country.

In which following Difcourfe or Impeachment, he engageth upon his life, either upon the principles of Law (*by way of indictment, the only and alone legall way of all tryals in England*) or upon the principles of Parliaments ancient proceedings, or upon the principles of reafon (*by pretence of which alone, they lately took away the Kings life*) before a legal Magiftracy, when there fhal be one again in England (*which now in the leaft there is not*) to prove the faid *Oliver Cromwel* guilty of the higheft Treafon that ever was acted in England, and more deferving punifhment and death

Then the 44 Judges hanged for injuftice by *King Alfred* before the Conqueft ; or then the Lord *chief Juftice Wayland* and his affociates tormented by *Edw. 1.* Or, then Judg *Thorpe*, condemned to dye for Bribery in *Edw. 3.* time ; Or, then the *two dif-throned Kings* Edw. 2. and Rich. 2. Or, then the Lord chief Juftice *Trefillian*, (who had His throat cut at Tyburn as a Traitor in Rich. 2. time, for fubverting the Law ) and all his affociates ; Or, then thofe two grand Traytorly fubverters of the Laws and Liberties of England, *Empfon* and *Dudley*, who therefore as Traytors loft their heads upon Tower-hill, in the beginning of Henr. 8. raign ; Or, then trayterous Cardinal *Wolfey*, who after he was arrefted of Treafon, poyfoned himfelf ; Or, then the late trayterous *Ship-Money Judges*, who with one Verdict or Judgment deftroyed all our propertie ; Or, then the late trayterous Bifhop of *Canterbury*, Earl of *Strafford*, Lord-Keeper *Finch*, Secretary *Windebanck*, or then Sir *George Ratcliff*, or all his Affociates ; Or, then the two *Hothams*, who loft their heads for correfponding with the Queen, &c. Or, then the late King *Charls* whom themfelves have beheaded for a *Tyrant* and *traytor*

In which are alfo fome Hints of Cautions to the Lord **FAIRFAX**, for abfolutely *breaking his folemn Engagement with his fouldiers, &c.* to take head and to regain his loft Credit in acting honeftly in time to come; in helping to fettle the Peace and Liberties of the Nation, which truly, really, and laftingly can never be done, but *by eftablifhing the principles of the Agreement of the Free. People;* that being really the peoples intereft, and all the reft that went before, but particular and felvifh. &c,

In which is alfo the Authors late Propofition fent to Mr *Holland*, June 26. 1649. to juftifie and make good at his utmeft hazard (upon the principles of *Scripture, Law, Reafon*, and the *Parliaments and Armies ancient Declarations*) his late actions or writings in any or all his *Books.*

Ier. 5. 26, 27, 28, 29. *For among my people are found wicked men : they lye in wait as he that fetteth fnares; they fet a trap, they catch men. As a cage is full of Birds, fo are their houfes full of deceit ; therefore they are become great, and waxen rich. They are waxen fat, they fhine; yea, they overpafs the deeds of the wicked; they judge not the caufe, the caufe of th Fatherlefs, yet they profper; and the right of the needy doe they not judge. Shall I not vifit for thefe things, faith the Lord ? Shall not my foul be avenged of fuch a Nation as this ?*

Imprinted at LONDON, Anno Dom. 1649.

An impeachment of high treason against Oliver Cromwell, drafted by the Leveller leader, John Lilburne.

outside London and parts of the south-east, did the movement command regular support. It never had the numbers to offer a serious threat.

■ A further factor was that the Levellers never really produced a co-ordinated plan of action for changing society. They had striking political ideas, but these did not amount to a practical alternative constitution. They were essentially outbursts of frustration at the political and social imbalance which allowed, first a royal tyranny and then a parliamentary one, to operate in England.

■ Although the Levellers were capable of exciting considerable fear, they were never fully committed to the use of force. In any case, as long as the great body of the army remained loyal to their commanders, chief among whom was the formidable Oliver Cromwell, there was never a realistic chance that the Levellers could impose themselves by force of arms.

How far the Levellers were from being a truly revolutionary force is evident from a comparison of them with a movement that made a brief but remarkable appearance in the late 1640s.

## The True Levellers (the Diggers)

In 1649, a group of some 50 people, calling themselves the **True Levellers (the Diggers)**, took over a patch of wasteland on St George's Hill in Surrey, which they began to cultivate. This was the practical expression of their belief that land and property belonged not to individuals but to the community. They called for an end of private property; in an exact sense, they were communists. Their inspiration was in large part biblical, they sought a godly society, but they also looked back to a time before the Norman Conquest when, in their belief, Englishmen had been free because the land had been held in common.

Such a movement was too visionary for its time. Harmless and, indeed, attractive though it now appears, it was regarded at the time as an intolerable affront to the established rights of property. The inevitable reaction occurred. The Council of State ordered Fairfax to interrogate Gerard Winstanley and William Everard, the two leading 'diggers', as they were mockingly called. An army unit then supervised the destruction by a local mob of the crops sown on the wasteland. The diggers attempted to carry on with their plan of making 'the earth a common treasury', but local hostility and interference proved too much and the movement collapsed. A similar fate befell the digger colonies that had been set up in ten other southern and midlands counties. At no point did active diggers number more than a few hundred.

> **KEY TERM**
>
> **True Levellers (the Diggers)** A group that tried to put into practice their belief that land belonged to the community and not to individuals.

> **ONLINE EXTRAS**
> **AQA** **WWW**
>
> Develop your analysis of continuity and change by completing Worksheet 22 at **www.hoddereducation. co.uk/accesstohistory/extras**

**SUMMARY DIAGRAM**

## THE GROWTH OF POLITICAL RADICALISM: THE LEVELLERS

**The growth of political radicalism – the Levellers**
- Army Levellers
- Crushed by Cromwell
- Lilburne imprisoned

**Character of Leveller movement**
- Not a democratic movement
- Represented the 'middling sort'

**Reasons for Levellers' failure**
- Never a single united movement
- Unable to win over influential interests
- Frightened the propertied classes

**The Diggers' experiment suppressed**
- The Commonwealth consolidated

# CHAPTER SUMMARY

The royalists failed to exploit their initial advantages effectively and, the longer the war lasted, the poorer their prospects became. Their failure to take London proved critical.

Parliament also started diffidently but once it had replaced its half-hearted commanders with Fairfax and Cromwell it gained the upper hand. Cromwell's New Model Army proved an unstoppable force, never losing a major engagement. Although victorious in 1646, the Presbyterian Parliament found itself increasingly at loggerheads with its Independent-dominated army.

Hoping to take advantage of the divisions among his enemies, the king deliberately procrastinated before lining up with the Scots in a second civil war.

In the meantime a serious split had occurred within the army between the Grandees and the Leveller agitators from the ranks. However, this did not weaken the army as a fighting force and it again triumphed over the royalists in the second civil war in 1648. Having purged Parliament of the faint-hearts, the Army Council put the king on trial 'as a man of blood'. His conviction and execution were predetermined.

The Levellers, a radical political movement produced by the disturbed times, briefly threatened social disruption before being crushed by Cromwell.

## Refresher questions

Use these questions to remind yourself of the key material covered in this chapter.

1  What was the significance of the Battle of Edgehill?

2  How did the signing of the Solemn League and Covenant alter the political situation in England?

3  What impact did the New Model Army have on the course of the war?

4  How much did the military victory of Parliament depend on Oliver Cromwell?

5  What underlay the tensions between Parliament and its army?

6  What factors explain the defeat of the royalists in the first civil war?

7  What role did London play in Parliament's victory?

8  What was at issue in the Putney debates?

9  Why was there a second civil war in 1648?

10  Was there an alternative to the execution of Charles I?

11  How dependent on Lilburne was the Leveller movement?

12  How serious a threat to the Rump were the Levellers?

13  Why did the Leveller movement fail to achieve its main objectives?

14  Why was Cromwell so ruthless in suppressing the Leveller mutinies?

15  In what sense were the Diggers true levellers?

## Question practice: AQA

### Essay questions

1  'It was Charles I's own mistakes that led to the difficulties he faced as king in the period 1625–49.' Explain why you agree or disagree with this view. [AS level]

**EXAM HINT** This question requires an analysis of why Charles I faced difficulties – looking at how far it was his own mistakes or how far problems were caused by other factors. It is important that your answer is illustrated by examples that cover the whole reign. The best answers might argue that factors were very much interlinked.

2  'Of the major problems that confronted the early Stuarts in the period 1603–49, it was finance that proved the most troublesome.' Assess the validity of this view. [A level]

**EXAM HINT** The answer must focus on the troubles faced by James and Charles, and assess how much they were due to finance. Other factors will need to be considered as well, and the answer must include examples of evidence that are scattered across the reigns.

# Question practice: OCR

## Essay questions

**1** How far was the victory of Parliament in the first civil war (1642–6) due to the weakness of the royalists? [AS level]

**EXAM HINT** Responses should consider a range of reasons for the victory of Parliament, including the weakness of royalists. Other issues, such as geographical control, finance, the support of the Scots and the creation of the New Model Army might also be considered. A judgement should be reached as to the importance of each issue and these interim judgements should be used to reach an overall judgement as to the relative importance of the weakness of the royalists in their defeat.

**2** To what extent was Parliament's success in the first civil war, 1642–6, due to Oliver Cromwell? [A level]

**EXAM HINT** Responses should consider a range of reasons for Parliament's success. Candidates will need to write a good paragraph on the named factor even if they argue that Cromwell was not the most important factor. Having considered a range of factors, responses will need to weigh up the importance of Cromwell against other factors and reach a judgement as to his relative importance in Parliament's victory.

## Source questions

**1** Study Sources B (page 130), C (page 131) and D (page 134) and then answer both questions. [AS level]

   **a)** Use your knowledge of the events after the end of the first civil war to assess how useful Source B is as evidence of the attitude of the army towards Charles I.

**EXAM HINT** Explain in what ways Source B provides evidence of his attitude. Also consider the provenance of the source and link this to contextual knowledge to test the view of the source. Finally, reach a judgement as to the usefulness of the source.

   **b)** Use your knowledge of the events of 1648–9 and the three sources to assess the view that the second civil war was the main reason for the execution of Charles I.

**EXAM HINT** Group the sources according to whether they support the view given in the question. Each source should be explained in relation to the question, its provenance evaluated and contextual knowledge used to test the validity of the view in the source. A judgement about each source in relation to the question should be reached allowing an overall judgement about whether the sources support the view that the second civil war was the main reason for the execution of Charles I.

**2** Using Sources D (page 134), E (page 135), F (transcription provided opposite) and G (page 136) in their historical context, assess how far they support the view that the trial and execution of the king were illegal acts forced through by the army. [A level]

**EXAM HINT** Group the sources according to whether they support the view given in the question. Each source should be explained in relation to the question, its provenance evaluated and contextual knowledge used to test the validity of the view in the source. A judgement about each source in relation to the question should be reached allowing an overall judgement about whether the sources support the view that the trial and execution were illegal acts forced through by the army.

### SOURCE F

Charles I is sentenced to death. Charles I's death warrant, 1649.

*At the high Court of Justice for the trying and judging of Charles Stuart King of England, January 29th AD 1648*

*Whereas Charles Stuart King of England is and standeth convicted attainted and condemned of High Treason and other high Crimes, And sentence upon Saturday last was pronounced against him by this Court to be put to death by the severing of his head from his body Of which sentence execution yet remaineth to be done, These are therefore to will and require you to see the said sentence executed In the open Street before Whitehall upon the morrow being the Thirtieth day of this instant month of January between the hours of Ten in the morning and Five in the afternoon of the same day with full effect. And for so doing this shall be your sufficient warrant And these are to require All Officers and Soldiers and other the good people of this Nation of England to be assisting unto you in this Service*

# CHAPTER 6

# The Commonwealth 1649–53: an experiment in republicanism

The execution of Charles I led to the eleven-year Interregnum (a period between reigns) during which England faced a series of demanding questions. How would it govern itself without a king? How would it tackle the political, religious and social issues that the civil wars had left unresolved? The major developments of the period between the king's death and the end of the Rump are the subjects of this chapter, whose key themes are:

◆ The Rump and the establishment of the Commonwealth

◆ The radical sects

◆ The third civil war 1649–52: Cromwell in Ireland and Scotland

◆ The achievements of the Rump

◆ The dissolution of the Rump, April 1653

The key debate on page 167 of this chapter asks the question: How repressive was Cromwell's military policy in Ireland?

## KEY DATES

| | | |
|---|---|---|
| **1649** | **Jan.** | Republic established |
| | | Commons claimed 'supreme power' |
| | **Feb.** | Charles II proclaimed king in Scotland |
| | | Council of State appointed |
| | **March** | Abolition of monarchy and House of Lords |
| | | Cromwell appointed Lord Lieutenant of Parliament's army |
| | **April** | Digger commune set up in Surrey |
| | **May** | Leveller uprising crushed by Cromwell |
| | **Aug.** | Cromwell landed in Ireland |
| | **Sept.** | Siege of Drogheda |
| | **Oct.** | Siege of Wexford |
| **1650** | **May** | Rump recalled Cromwell to England |
| | **June** | Cromwell replaced Fairfax as commander-in-chief |
| | **Aug.** | Blasphemy Act |
| | | Cromwell entered Scotland |
| | **Sept.** | Cromwell's victory over Scots at Dunbar |
| **1651** | **Sept.** | Cromwell defeated Charles II at Worcester |
| | **Oct.** | Navigation Act introduced |
| | | Charles II escaped to France |
| **1652** | | Irish land confiscation began |
| **1653** | **April** | Rump forcibly dispersed by Cromwell |

# 1 | The Rump and the establishment of the Commonwealth

■ *How dependent on the army was the Rump between 1649 and 1653?*

## Relations between Parliament and army

Pride's purge in December 1648 had reduced the House of Commons from 470 members of Parliament (MPs) to 211 (see page 133). But this remnant was not a united body. Only 70 of them had been involved in the setting up of the High Court that tried the king, and of that number only 43 members had signed his death warrant. It claimed to be the legitimate continuation of the Long Parliament, elected in 1640, and therefore entitled to the loyalty and obedience of the whole nation, including the army. It was a hollow claim. The truth was that the Rump existed as the result of a military purge ordered by the Council of the Army. Thereafter, the Rump depended on the willingness of the army to support it, a fact that compromised its authority throughout its four years of government.

The army had clearly become a formidable political force by 1649. It was well represented in Parliament since a large number of the army officers were also MPs, Oliver Cromwell being the most notable example. If the army chose to insist on a certain policy, it would be difficult for the Rump to resist it, let alone ignore it. Thus, although in theory the army after 1649 continued as the servant of Parliament, in reality the relationship had been reversed.

### Cromwell's position

By 1649, Oliver Cromwell's great military successes and his involvement in the removal of the king had made him a powerful figure. But it is important to emphasise that at this stage he held no formal position that conferred authority on him. As a soldier, he was technically still subordinate to Lord Fairfax. However, since Fairfax had chosen, by 1649, to withdraw from public affairs, Cromwell became increasingly important politically. As the effective leader of the army, he became the dominant figure in the nation. Although this did not mean he was all-powerful – he never became that – it did mean that his actions were critical in determining how the political situation developed.

## The establishment of the republic

In a series of statutes of February and March 1649 the Rump passed the following measures:

■ abolition of monarchy
■ abolition of the House of Lords

- creation of a Council of State to act as the government
- a declaration that England was now a Commonwealth (see page 3).

These measures were not intended as a prelude to revolution. They were meant to consolidate what had been achieved by the defeat of the royalists in the civil wars. The Rump's purpose was to preserve rather than to undermine the constitution. Charles I, it was claimed, had tried to subvert the fundamental laws of the kingdom and impose a tyranny. That was why it had been necessary to remove him. As for the House of Lords, the argument was that, by making no effort to prevent royal oppression, it had ceased to play its proper constitutional role. It had, therefore, to be removed.

The first Council of State was composed of 41 members, 34 of whom were MPs. Its composition reflected the conservatism of the Rump. It was successful in preventing a number of influential officers, including Henry Ireton and Thomas Harrison, the leader of the Fifth Monarchists (see page 153), from being voted onto the Council.

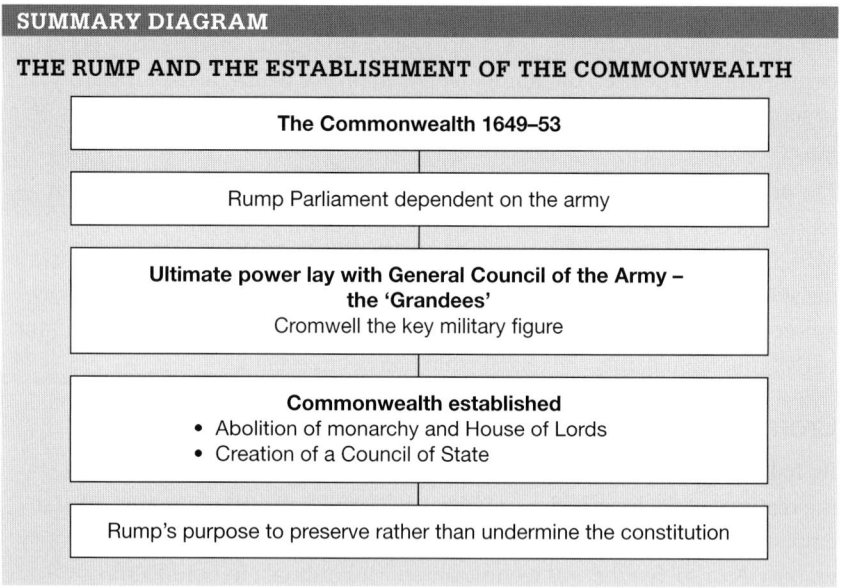

**SUMMARY DIAGRAM**

**THE RUMP AND THE ESTABLISHMENT OF THE COMMONWEALTH**

The Commonwealth 1649–53

Rump Parliament dependent on the army

Ultimate power lay with General Council of the Army –
the 'Grandees'
Cromwell the key military figure

Commonwealth established
- Abolition of monarchy and House of Lords
- Creation of a Council of State

Rump's purpose to preserve rather than undermine the constitution

# 2 The radical sects

- *Why was religion such a demanding issue during the Interregnum?*

Judged by the amount of attention paid to it, the most pressing concern of the Interregnum was religion. What made it so was the religious splintering that had followed in the wake of the civil wars. The challenges to the established Anglican Church and its difficulty in imposing effective censorship in wartime had encouraged the growth of separatist denominations which rejected the idea of a central State Church. Ten years had seen a great change. In 1640, there had been two main Protestant Churches: in England, the Anglican with its Arminian and Puritan wings; in Scotland, the Presbyterian with its strongly Calvinist beliefs (see page 31). In contrast, by the early 1650s, there were scores of separatist sects in existence, none of them willing to conform to the dictates of an established Church, Anglican or Presbyterian.

## Providence and millenarianism

The upheavals of the 1640s, climaxing with the abolition of the monarchy, had created a ferment of ideas, and had convinced many that they were living in a unique period. This conviction was expressed in the 1650s in a widespread belief in '**providence**'. Cromwell himself had declared: 'The Lord hath done things amongst us as have not been known these thousand years.' For the radical sectaries it was a short step from a belief in providence to an utter conviction that the extraordinary events which had occurred were portents of some great cataclysm. This thought process is often described as **millenarianism** and the term is often extended to include all those who believed that a great and revolutionary change in the order of things was about to take place in England.

The extreme forms of millenarianism were deeply disturbing to the civil authorities. It is not difficult to understand why. Those who believed that the end of the world was at hand were very ready to dispense with existing laws and practices. The wilder millenarians asked why they should bother with man-made laws and regulations when God himself was about to sweep all these away.

Since the sectaries played such a prominent role in the period, it is necessary to understand the beliefs of the main sects that came into being or into prominence during the English Revolution:

■ Baptists

■ Congregationalists

■ Fifth Monarchists

■ Muggletonians

■ Quakers

■ Seekers

■ Ranters

■ Shakers.

The numbers belonging to each group are difficult to assess, but they cannot have been large. For example, the Baptist movement in the 1650s represented barely one in 400 of the population. However, it was not their numbers that gave the sects significance, but their disruptive ideas. It was these that frightened the authorities into believing that they were faced by forces intent on destroying existing society.

**KEY TERMS**

**Providence** The concept that events are never random and isolated but are part of a larger divine plan.

**Millenarianism** The belief in the imminence of the millennium, the thousand-year period during which Jesus Christ would return to reclaim the earth and govern it with his saints.

**KEY TERM**

**Theology** A structured set of definitions of, and justifications for, a particular religious belief.

Care should be taken not to give sectarian ideas more precision than they actually had. Many of the sectaries were inspired as much by emotional impulse as by rational **theology**. That is why they were so impatient with the traditional type of Church organisation and worship which had been based on prescribed doctrine. It also explains why many of them did not restrict themselves exclusively to membership of one sect. For instance, Laurence Clarkson, who ended up as a Muggletonian, had begun his religious life as an Anglican; in between, he had been variously a Presbyterian, an Independent, a Particular Baptist, a Ranter and a Seeker.

## Baptists

The Baptist movement, which had begun earlier in the century, became particularly prominent during the 1640s. Its central belief was that faith was a matter of personal experience and acceptance; it could not be taught or learned. Infant baptism was, therefore, meaningless. Great importance was placed on the act of adult baptism, usually by total immersion in water, as an expression of the individual's choosing to become one with Christ. Such a practice and belief involved a direct denial of the need for an organised Church led by priests or ministers with authority to teach and to administer sacraments.

The movement became divided between 'General' Baptists, those who were willing to cooperate with other sects, and 'Particular' Baptists, those who believed in remaining exclusive. In the 1650s, the Baptists became detested by religious and political conservatives. This was because the movement was thought to be associated with the German Anabaptists of sixteenth-century Münster, a group who had been notorious for their defiance of the law and social convention. In truth, there was little connection between the English and German forms apart from the similarity in name, but in the religious controversies of the mid-seventeenth century such distinctions easily became blurred. Baptists tended to look to Cromwell to protect them, and he did intervene on a number of occasions to prevent their persecution by Parliament.

## Congregationalists (Independents)

It would be misleading to think of congregationalism as a particular denomination. The term refers broadly to the separatist or independent Protestant congregations who rejected the idea of a national centrally administered Church. It is often used to describe the 'gathered churches', those congregations of godly persons who came together to worship in the spirit of the Lord. This activity often covered a wide range of viewpoints. Since congregationalism did not seek to impose a rigid theology, many former Anglican priests found themselves able to make the transition into congregational pastors.

That Oliver Cromwell was regarded as an Independent is instructive. He was not opposed to Church organisation as such, but he believed it must be a voluntary association; it ought not to be imposed on believers. In this respect, Cromwell may be viewed as an interesting representative of congregationalism, one of the more moderate religious movements of its time. On a number of occasions, when the extreme sectaries threatened to create religious chaos, the Congregationalists closed ranks with the Presbyterians and Anglicans.

## Fifth Monarchists

The clearest expression of millenarianism was to be found among the Fifth Monarchists. This sect, which never numbered above 10,000, drew the majority of its members from the army and included officers, chaplains and troopers. Colonel **Thomas Harrison** became their leading spokesman. They derived their central belief from the Book of Revelations in the New Testament and the Book of Daniel in the Old. They interpreted these as prophesying that five great monarchies would rule the earth in sequence. They believed that the Assyrian, the Persian, the Greek and Roman had been the first four, and that the execution of Charles I had ushered in the fifth and greatest monarchy, the reign of King Jesus. It followed that the government of England must be given over to the rule of the saints. As one of their pamphlets declared: 'All earthly governments, and worldly administrations may be broken and removed by the first administration of the Kingdom of Christ, appointed unto him by the decree of the Father.'

The Fifth Monarchists' great opportunity seemed to have arrived with the convening of the Nominated Assembly in 1653 (see page 172). However, the subsequent failure of this 'Parliament of Saints', which they had hoped would be the dawn of the rule of godliness, left them embittered. They turned their anger against Cromwell, whom they had hailed earlier as a second Moses, the great prophet who had led the Israelites out of Egyptian bondage. They remained a constant nuisance throughout the Protectorate, challenging Cromwell's authority and accusing him of thwarting God's purpose on earth.

The more fanatical Fifth Monarchists posed a real threat to Cromwell's life. They were behind the majority of assassination attempts against him, the most notorious being the plot in 1657 to murder him as a prelude to the enforced establishment of the rule of the saints in England. Neither the foiling of this attempt nor the death of Cromwell in 1658 marked the end of their efforts. They made further unsuccessful challenges to the government in 1659 and 1661 (see page 205).

## Muggletonians

This sect took its name from Lodowick Muggleton, a London tailor, who had developed strong **predestinarian** ideas. He believed that Christ had visited him in person and given him the power to save or damn all other men. The small sect he formed in 1652, made up unsurprisingly of those whom he had declared to be saved (the 'elect'), saw no need to seek converts among the damned (the 'ungodly'). Assured of their own unique virtue, his followers felt free to reject any State or Church laws that impinged on them. The Muggletonians were far too small a group to represent a serious challenge to the social or political order. Nevertheless, their extreme views made them useful bogeymen to be used by the authorities as a warning against the dangers of permitting too much religious freedom.

**KEY FIGURE**

**Thomas Harrison (1606–60)**

A major-general on the parliamentary side in the civil wars, he was one of the signatories of Charles I's death warrant; after the Restoration, he was condemned and executed for regicide.

**KEY TERM**

**Predestinarian** Believing that whether an individual person is saved or damned has been predetermined by God's unchangeable will.

## Seekers and Ranters

These two groups may be logically taken together since there was considerable overlap between them. They are both interesting examples of the type of religion that is based on feelings rather than theology. Their basic conviction was that God manifested Himself not as an external power but as a spiritual force within the individual. Believers should, therefore, 'seek' the divine spirit not in an organised Church or even in the Bible but within themselves, by responding to their own promptings. The Ranters gained their name from the practice of loudly declaiming their thoughts whenever the inspiration took them. What made such groups dangerous in the eyes of the authorities was their flouting of social convention. Ranters tended to live communally with wives and property held in common, which gave opportunity for opponents to condemn them as sexually depraved. It was largely in order to check the activities of the Seekers and Ranters that the Rump introduced the Blasphemy Act of 1650, which declared that 'all persons who shall profess that acts of uncleanness and profane swearing are not things in themselves detestable shall be committed to prison for the space of six months'.

The importance of these two sects historically is that their idea of an inner light or spirit became the essential tenet of the Quakers, the most politically and socially disruptive of the religious movements of the 1650s.

## Quakers (Society of Friends)

The most clearly defined rejection of the authority of Church and State was to be found in the Quaker movement, which began in the early 1650s under the leadership of **George Fox** and grew by 1660 to be over 50,000 strong. The prayer meetings of the 'Society of Friends' (the Quakers' formal title) took the form of individual believers calling out their thoughts as the Lord inspired them. This invariably involved much physical rocking or quaking, hence their nickname. Among key Quaker beliefs were the following:

- The Lord's message came to individuals directly through the 'inner light' of their own personal inspiration, 'God within them'.
- Since there was no intermediary between God and man, only the Lord Himself was entitled to obedience.
- It followed that all earthly authority and the Church and State officials who represented it were undeserving of respect or obedience.

Quakers often expressed their beliefs with a vigorous disregard of propriety. They frequently disrupted Church services by abusing and shouting down the preacher. They were also resolute, as were many other sects, in refusing to pay tithes. It is easy to see why contemporaries regarded the Quakers as among the most socially dangerous of the radical groups.

It is interesting that the modern Quaker movement is now strongly identified with pacifism. In the 1650s, it was seen as an aggressive organisation quite prepared to use force when it felt threatened. The Quakers' distinctive style of

**KEY FIGURE**

**George Fox (1624–91)**

Convinced by the troubled times that all man-made laws were corrupt, he travelled throughout England appealing to the people to follow their inner light to salvation. Although persecuted by the authorities, by the time of his death his movement claimed to have 65,000 followers.

**SOURCE A**

# THE QVAKERS DREAM: 14
### OR,
### The Devil's Pilgrimage in England:
### BEING
## An infallible Relation of their several Meetings,
Shreekings, Shakings, Quakings, Roarings, Yellings, Howlings, Tremblings in the Bodies, and Risings in the Bellies: With a Narrative of their several Arguments, Tenets, Principles, and strange Doctrine: The strange and wonderful Satanical Apparitions, and the appearing of the Devil unto them in the likeness of a black Boar, a Dog with flaming eyes, and a black man without a head, causing the Dogs to bark, the Swine to cry, and the Cattel to run, to the great admiration of all that shall read the same.

London, Printed for G. Horton, and are to be sold at the Royal Exchange in Cornhil, 1655. *April. 26.*

'The Quakers Dream'. The cover of an anti-Quaker pamphlet, published in April 1655. The balloons read (from left to right): 'Free-will'; 'walk answerable to the light within you'; 'be thou merry'; and 'Above ordinances'.

**SOURCE QUESTION**

What aspects of Quaker meetings are being mocked in the pamphlet? Who would have been likely to have produced the pamphlet shown in Source A?

speech, their sombre black clothing and their disregard of laws and conventions aroused opposition in the localities. This may well be the reason why the court lists of the time show so many prosecutions of Quakers and why the magistrates frequently imposed severe sentences on them. Over 2000 Quakers were brought to trial during the Interregnum.

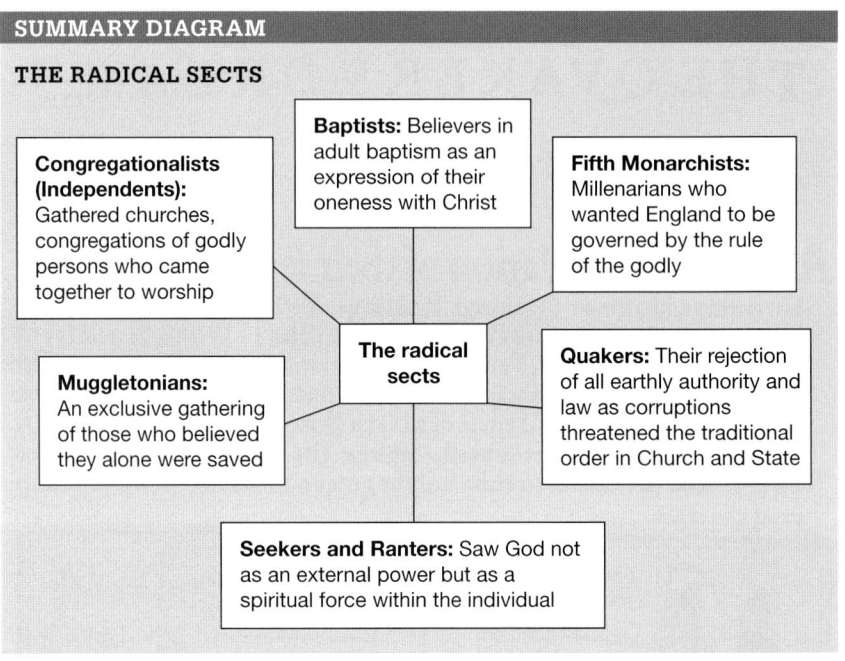

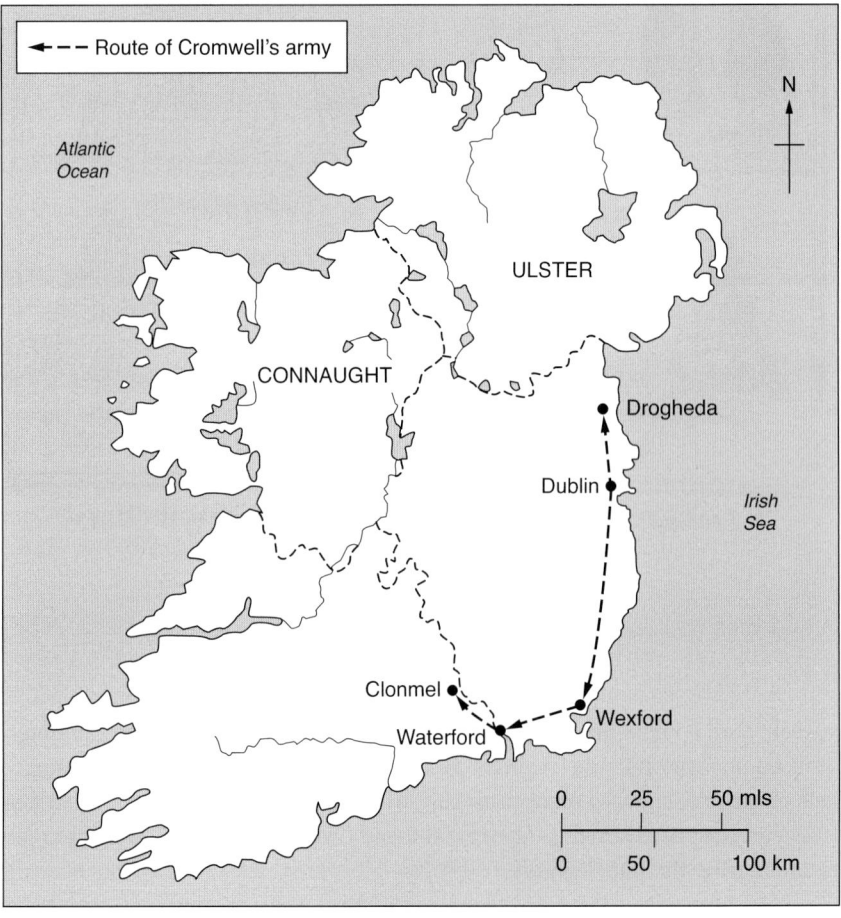

**Figure 6.1** Map of Ireland in the 1650s.

# 3 The third civil war 1649–52: Cromwell in Ireland and Scotland

■ *What methods did Cromwell use to subdue Ireland and Scotland?*

When the English Commonwealth was established in 1649, its most pressing task was to subdue rebellion in Ireland. Active opposition to the imposition of English authority had been continuous in Ireland since 1641, when the Irish Catholics had risen in a fierce attack on the Protestant settlers in **Ulster** (see page 12). Following the execution of Charles I, the Stuarts' chief Irish supporter, the **Earl of Ormonde**, had persuaded the Protestant royalists in southern Ireland to join with the Catholics in a league against the English Parliament. In March 1649, the Rump appointed Oliver Cromwell Lord Lieutenant and commissioned him to crush this Irish combination.

## Cromwell's Irish campaign 1649–50

Having landed south of Dublin with 12,000 men in August 1649, Cromwell began a nine-month campaign in Ireland. Although Ormonde's forces outnumbered the English army, they were no match for it in artillery or discipline. In addition, Parliament's control of the Irish Sea meant that Cromwell's army was kept regularly supplied, a resource which Ormonde's troops never enjoyed. It had been Ormonde's hope that the forces of **Owen Roe O'Neill**, the leader of the Irish peasantry, would help to form a combined royalist army against Cromwell. However, O'Neill's death in November put an end to such plans. It was, nonetheless, the fear that an alliance between Ormonde and O'Neill might be formed that had led Cromwell to begin his campaign with an advance on Drogheda, a town to the north of Dublin that commanded the main north–south route.

### Drogheda and Wexford

The inhabitants of Drogheda put up a stout resistance before the town was taken in a welter of blood. Its fall effectively secured the English army's control of the north of Ireland. With this achieved, Cromwell turned back south and began a long advance that within six months brought the whole of the country under his army's domination. It was during the southern march that the town of Wexford was captured, again after fierce resistance and bloodletting.

The horror of the Drogheda and Wexford sieges has become part of Irish folklore. It is certainly the case that there was a chilling similarity about the fate that befell both places. Each was a fortified stronghold in which civilians had gathered as well as troops. Since the towns were judged to be strategically

**KEY TERM**

**Ulster** The area of Ireland where, since Tudor times, the English government had pursued a 'plantation' policy of dispossessing Catholic peasants of their lands and giving them to Protestant settlers.

**KEY FIGURES**

**Earl of Ormonde (1610–88)**

Commanded the royalist forces in Ireland from 1641 to 1650, fled into exile with Charles II in the 1650s; he returned following the Restoration in 1660 to take up a number of government offices.

**Owen Roe O'Neill (1585–1649)**

A member of the influential O'Neill family in Ulster, he served as a mercenary in Europe and led the Catholic Irish Confederates forces from 1641 to 1649.

important, military considerations required that they both be taken. The occupants were first offered quarter if they surrendered. They refused. Cromwell thereupon, in accordance with the **rules of war** of the time, instructed his troops that once they had stormed the town they were to kill those who had resisted.

No matter how Cromwell's actions and motives are judged, it remains undeniable that the engagements at Drogheda and Wexford were appalling affairs. In his lengthy reports to Parliament, Cromwell described how desperate the fighting had been on both sides. Detailing the storming of Drogheda, he wrote (see Source B):

**SOURCE QUESTION**

In Source B, on what grounds does Cromwell justify the Drogheda massacre?

**KEY TERMS**

**Rules of war** There were no such rules in a formal sense, but there was a broad understanding in Europe around this time that if troops and non-combatants refused to surrender when offered quarter they thereby sacrificed their right to be treated mercifully.

**Anti-Christ** Satanic forces opposed to God; Cromwell applied the term to those he regarded as ungodly Irish papists (Catholics) who had been in arms against the English Protestants since 1641.

### SOURCE B

From Cromwell's letter to the Speaker of the Commons, September 1649, quoted in W.C. Abbott, editor, *The Writings and Speeches of Oliver Cromwell*, volume II, Harvard University Press, 1937–47, p. 127.

*The enemy retreated into the Mill-Mount … Our men getting up to them were ordered by me to put them all to the sword. And indeed, being in the heat of action, I forbade them to spare any that were in arms … About one hundred of them possessed St. Peter's church-steeple … These being summoned to yield, refused, whereupon I ordered St. Peter's Church to be fired [set on fire]. When they submitted, their officers were knocked on the head and every tenth man of the soldiers killed … this is a righteous judgement of God upon these barbarous wretches, who have imbrued their hands in so much innocent blood; and that it will tend to prevent the effusion of blood for the future.*

Wexford was a repeat of the horrors of Drogheda, with even greater casualties. In his account to Parliament, Cromwell gave the death toll as 2000 and admitted that he and his soldiers had been 'crazed' by the excitement of battle. He again ascribed the massacre to the will of God: it was His fitting punishment on the **'Anti-Christ'**.

One of the most persistent myths about Cromwell was that he went to Ireland intent on creating a reign of terror over the Irish people. This has been shown to be quite contrary to the evidence. Modern Irish writers such as Tom Reilly and Jason McElligott have stressed that, from the time he landed in Ireland to the time he left nine months later, Cromwell insisted that the person and property of civilians be fully respected. On first arriving in Ireland he issued this stern order to his troops (Source C):

**SOURCE QUESTION**

According to Source C, how does Cromwell intend to prevent 'cruelties upon the Country people'?

### SOURCE C

From Cromwell's instructions to his troops, August 1649, quoted in W.C. Abbott, editor, *The Writings and Speeches of Oliver Cromwell*, volume II, Harvard University Press, 1937–47, pp. 111–12.

*Whereas I am informed that a liberty hath been taken by the Soldiery to abuse and pillage, and too often to execute cruelties upon the Country people: being resolved, by the grace of God, diligently to restrain such wickedness.*

*Hereof I require all under my command to take notice and observe the same: as they shall answer to the contrary at their utmost perils. Strictly commanding all Officers and others, to see to it that no wrong be done to any such persons as aforesaid. Being resolved, through the grace of God to punish all that shall offend hereunto, very severely, to displace and punish, all such Officers as shall be found negligent, and not see the due observance hereof.*

These were not mere words. Cromwell was quick to punish any of his troops who disobeyed these orders. In his dealings with the Irish people, he was tough and resolute, but he was not gratuitously cruel or vindictive. It is true that in the heat of battle his measured instructions may have been ignored. Excesses undoubtedly occurred, as at Drogheda and Wexford, but they were not part of a deliberate policy. Yet this has to be measured against the intensity of Cromwell's belief that the Irish rebels deserved severe treatment. As shown in Source D, he asserted that the rebels had brought retribution on themselves by the savagery of their behaviour in the rising of 1641.

### SOURCE D

From Cromwell's declaration to the Irish Catholic clergy, January 1650, quoted in Barry Coward, editor, *The English Revolution*, John Murray, 1997, p. 173.

*You unprovoked put the English to the most unheard-of and most barbarous massacre (without respect of age or sex) that ever the sun beheld. And at a time when Ireland was in perfect peace … You are part of Antichrist whose kingdom the Scripture so expressly speaks, should be laid in blood ... You have shed great store of it already, and ere it be long you must have blood to drink; even the dregs of the cup of fury and the wrath of God, which will be poured into you. For those who persist in arms they must expect what the providence of God (in that which is falsely called the chance of war) will cast upon them.*

### SOURCE QUESTION

In Source D, in what ways does Cromwell seek to justify his harsh methods in Ireland?

### ONLINE EXTRAS OCR **WWW**

Get to grips with evaluating sources by completing Worksheet 26 at **www.hoddereducation.co.uk/accesstohistory/extras**

### Land confiscation

By the time of his recall to England, in May 1650, Cromwell's principal aim had been achieved. The royalist cause in Ireland was a lost one. Cromwell left Ireton in command of the English forces to complete the subjugation of Ireland. The previous plantation policies (see page 79) were continued. To prevent further Irish risings, the lands of the defeated royalist leaders were confiscated and given to Protestant settlers. By 1660, Catholic ownership of land was a bare twenty per cent, compared with 60 per cent in 1641. This had the additional effect of further reducing the condition of the mass of the Catholic peasantry, whose only possible future was as despised labourers under the new Protestant landed ascendancy.

This policy was not simply a matter of retribution against the Irish rebels. The expropriation of land provided a way for the Rump to meet some of its heavy financial commitments. Soldiers were encouraged to accept land in Ireland in lieu of their arrears of pay. Land was also offered to the many creditors that

Parliament had acquired since 1642. All this suggests that it was finance as much as religious or political principle that dictated the Commonwealth's policy towards Ireland.

# Cromwell's Scottish campaign 1650–1

Soon after the execution of Charles I in January 1649, the king's eldest son proclaimed himself Charles II. His hope was that this would lead to a full-scale Scottish uprising on his behalf, but the division within Scotland between Presbyterians, Episcopalians (see page 86) and Catholics prevented a united front being formed. Nonetheless, Charles persevered. In April 1650, he declared his willingness to enter into agreement with the Scots. Two months later, he returned to Scotland and formally swore to the Covenant on terms very similar to those his father had accepted in 1647 (see page 129). Charles II's willingness to take the Covenant and form an alliance with the **Marquess of Argyll**, the leading Covenanter, prompted the Rump into recalling Cromwell from Ireland. Having formally replaced Fairfax as lord general and commander-in-chief in June 1650, Cromwell was redirected to deal with the growing Scottish danger.

Cromwell declared that he felt no personal animosity towards the majority of the Scots, whom he regarded as his Protestant brothers. He spoke of his 'longing to have avoided blood in this business'. Nonetheless, when his army met the Scottish forces at Dunbar in September 1650 his victory was overwhelming. The Covenanters were left broken and dispirited, many of them interpreting their defeat as a sign of God's anger at their having dared to fight on Charles II's side. Cromwell remained in Scotland until well into 1651, but then, as he had in Ireland, he left subordinate generals to complete the subjugation. John Lambert and George Monck (see pages 208 and 206) carried out the task ruthlessly and successfully.

Yet Charles II did not allow the crushing of the Covenanters to destroy his own hopes. In a bold attempt to achieve in England what he had failed to do in Scotland, he marched south into England with a force of 12,000. His hope was that his personal presence would inspire a royalist uprising. It was not to be. The response was small scale and disorganised, and it was a despondent royalist army that was routed by Cromwell's forces at Worcester on 3 September 1651, the anniversary of Dunbar. Charles II accepted defeat and, narrowly avoiding capture, fled abroad into an exile that was to last nine years.

The Rump proceeded to declare that Scotland was now totally under its authority:

- The separate Scottish Parliament was dissolved.
- The power of the Presbyterian Church was greatly reduced; it was ordered to tolerate the existence of the individual Protestant sects in Scotland.
- The Scots were required to pay for the upkeep of the English army of occupation.

It was the Rump's belief that these measures would extinguish for good the embers of royalism in Scotland.

**KEY FIGURE**

**Marquess of Argyll (1607–61)**

Chief of the Campbell clan and a major figure in the Covenanter movement in the 1640s and during the Interregnum.

**SUMMARY DIAGRAM**

**THE THIRD CIVIL WAR 1649–52: CROMWELL IN IRELAND AND SCOTLAND**

---

**Ireland**
- Cromwell regularly maintained supplies from England
- His swift marches prevented Ormonde's attempt to unite Irish resisters
- Cromwell's concept of the Irish as a 'deluded and seduced people'
- Ruthless methods at Drogheda and Wexford

---

**But**
Cromwell's dark reputation can be disputed

---

**Legacy**
English policy of confiscating peasant land continued

---

**Scotland**
- Cromwell's regret at having to suppress Scottish Protestants
- Cromwell's brilliant victories at Dunbar broke the Covenanters and at Worcester forced Charles into exile

---

# 4  The achievements of the Rump

■ *How successfully did the Rump deal with the problems it faced?*

Until relatively recently, the Rump Parliament had a very poor reputation. It tended to be regarded as an incompetent oligarchy, which clung to power for four years, until it was forcibly dissolved. However, modern research, most prominently that of David Underdown and Blair Worden, has led to an adjustment of this dismissive view. What now tends to be emphasised is the severity of the problems that preoccupied the Rump.

## Religious policy

The civil wars had left the Anglican Church in a very uncertain position. In 1645, Parliament had recommended the adoption of Presbyterianism, but had made no real effort to implement this. The Rump was divided on the issue. The Presbyterians, with their desire for a centrally controlled State Church, were roughly equal in number to the Independents, who stood for the principle of permitting the local congregations to pursue their own form of worship. So evenly split was the Rump that it required the casting vote of the speaker to defeat a proposal in August 1649 that Presbyterianism should be confirmed as the State religion of England. In addition to the two main groups, there were a number of MPs who cannot be easily labelled, except by such confusing terms as 'independent Presbyterians', who favoured some form of compromise such as maintaining a central Church while denying it a controlling authority over the local congregations.

Whatever the religious differences within the Rump, few MPs wished society to be left completely free in matters of morality. The majority of members were more concerned to enforce '**godliness**' on the nation than to allow '**liberty of conscience**'. Acts were introduced that imposed penalties on adultery, fornication and profane language. 'An Act against Blasphemy' was passed in August 1650 with the aim of curbing the more extreme sectarians (see page 154).

The absence of more sweeping measures indicated that the Rump had no real intention of reforming the Church along the lines hoped for by the religious radicals. It was not until late in 1650, and then with some reluctance, that the Rump finally repealed the statues passed in Elizabeth's reign that had required Sunday worship in the Anglican Church. On the contentious question of tithes (see page 154), the Rump did nothing; the clergy continued to be paid in the old way.

Since the days of Archbishop Laud, it had been very clear that control of the pulpit was the key factor in deciding what form of worship was followed in the localities (see page 60). 'A Committee for the Propagation of the Gospel' was appointed by the Rump in 1652, with the intention of creating a system for the strict supervision of clerical appointments. But the wide divisions within Parliament over religion meant that there was no final agreement over how the suitability of individual clerics was to be judged.

There is no doubt that in the country at large, the shock of the king's defeat and execution had encouraged the growth of millenarianism. Some believed that since the end of the world was nigh, the old forms of Church and government no longer mattered and, therefore, should be abandoned (see page 151). As a body, the Rump was far from representing this attitude. In matters of religion, as in politics, its basic conservatism meant that it resisted the radicals' calls for a complete break with the past. In an attempt to counter the flood of radical broadsheets and pamphlets that appeared in London, the Rump published its own government journal, *Mercurius Politicus*, which presented an official version of public affairs.

## Legal reform

Demands for reform of the law were heard from those who wanted the Rump to curb the lawyers' powers and open the law to all by simplifying its procedures. The main objections to the current operation of the law were that it was:

- the preserve of the privileged
- highly expensive
- scandalously slow in operation
- in the hands of corrupt lawyers.

## KEY TERMS

**Godliness** Living by a code of moral conduct in keeping with biblical precepts.

**Liberty of conscience** Freedom to think and act according to one's own judgement rather than conforming to an imposed set of beliefs laid down by a Church.

Among the Rump's responses were the adoption of more lenient methods for punishing debtors and the authorisation of the use of English in the courts instead of Latin and French. But it did nothing to ensure lower legal fees or to provide easier access to the courts for the ordinary person. The Rump's reluctance to consider major changes in the law is largely explained by the composition of the Commons:

- Of the 211 MPs who attended the House during the Commonwealth period, nearly 50 were from the legal profession.
- The largest single group among the average of 60–70 members who attended the daily sessions of Parliament were lawyers.

Such men were naturally reluctant to undertake changes that would weaken their privileges. The same was true of another interest group strongly represented in the Commons, the merchant traders. They used their influence to prevent interference with current commercial practices, such as monopolies, and were instrumental in the Rump's passing of the **Navigation Act** of 1651.

What was true of the legal and commercial interests applied to the Rump overall. It contained few dedicated republicans intent on sweeping change. Its primary aim was to gain the support of the established classes in society. A policy of moderation and regard for existing structures was far more likely to win over men of influence and authority in the localities. It was the provincial gentry, the traditional ruling order, whom the Rump was trying to impress.

## Social policies

The Rump did give some attention to proposals for social reform, which included schemes for the extension of education and for some form of poor relief. How genuine its interest was in this area cannot be easily assessed, since, in practice, the demands of war and the maintenance of national security deprived it of both the time and the resources to turn such proposals into reality. Such pressures gave the Rump limited opportunity to engage in reform.

## Financial policies

Judged by the amount of revenue it gathered, the Rump was a highly successful body. It raised finance through:

- the taxation of goods
- assessment (taxes on land)
- excise levies at the ports
- the sale of Crown lands and Church property
- the proceeds of confiscated royalist estates.

In spite of its successful financial policies, the Rump still remained short of money. Its revenue could not keep up with the cost of the campaigns in Ireland and Scotland and the **Dutch War**. It is important to stress again that the Rump

> **KEY TERMS**
>
> **Navigation Act** Required that all goods imported into Britain from outside Europe were to be carried in British vessels, and that exports from Europe were to be admitted only in British ships or those of the exporting country.
>
> **Dutch War** Anglo-Dutch commercial rivalry (1652–4) resulted in a series of naval engagements, fought mainly in the Channel and the North Sea; after initial success, the Dutch, subjected to a blockade of their ports, made peace on English terms.

had to spend so much time and revenue in running the various wars in which it became engaged that it was restricted in what it could do on the domestic front. The Rump cannot be said to have failed through want of trying. If anything, it tried too hard. As its legislative record indicates, there were clear signs that its energies had begun to flag by 1653. For four years it had been in almost constant session, sitting on four or five days a week throughout the year.

In view of the pressures on it from outside, doubts about its legitimacy, its own internal divisions and the military burdens it carried, the Rump could claim to have provided four and a half years of relatively stable government. This was a considerable achievement given the troubled times in which it operated.

## The Rump Parliament in action

- Total number of MPs who attended the House, 1649–53: 211.
- Active members: 60–70.
- Average attendance: 50–60.
- Number of committees established:
  - 152 in 1649
  - 98 in 1650
  - 12 in 1653.
  - 51 in 1652
  - 61 in 1651
- Number of Acts passed
  - 125 in 1649
  - 78 in 1650
  - 10 in 1653.
  - 54 in 1651
  - 44 in 1652
- Percentage of legislation devoted to particular issues:
  - security and finance: 51%
  - social problems: 9%
  - religion: 3%
  - local government and the army: 30%
  - economic and social reform: 4%
  - law reform: 3%

SUMMARY DIAGRAM

**THE ACHIEVEMENTS OF THE RUMP**

---

**Religion**
- Rump divided between Presbyterians and Independents
- Rump narrowly failed to vote for Presbyterian Church system
- Rump resisted calls from sectarians for sweeping change

---

**But**
Passed repressive Blasphemy Act, denying 'liberty of conscience' and seeking to impose 'godliness'

---

**Finance**
- Revenue raised through taxation, assessment, excise levies, sale of Crown lands and seizure of royalists' property
- Navigation Act 1651 led to war with Dutch

---

**Social**
Limited attempts to provide poor relief but financial constraints prevented wider reforms

---

**Law**
Minor changes but no sweeping reforms

---

- Rump policies reflected dominating influence of lawyers and merchants
- Four years of Rump government had created relative stability

---

# 5 The dissolution of the Rump, April 1653

◼ *What led Cromwell to dissolve the Rump in 1653?*

The Rump was never expected to be a permanent body. Indeed, in September 1651 it had made provision for its own dissolution by voting to disband itself by the end of 1654. It had also produced plans for a 'new representative' Parliament. However, this failed to impress the Army Council, which believed that the Rump was simply manoeuvring to prevent a genuinely new Parliament from being elected. The two main groups offended by the Rump were the republicans, whose main spokesman was Colonel John Lambert, and the Fifth Monarchists, whose leader was Colonel Thomas Harrison (see page 153).

# Cromwell's motives

In the event, it was Oliver Cromwell who forcibly ended the life of the Rump. Considerable research has been conducted into his motives. Not all historians who have studied the question are in agreement. Nevertheless, the broad lines of the story can be established. In April 1653, the Rump, rather than carry on indefinitely, had actually begun to consider a bill that would have brought forward its dissolution by over a year. However, the army's fear was that this was simply a ruse to disguise the fact that the qualifications being written into the bill would result in any new Parliament being composed of substantially the same members.

It is impossible to judge how justified the army's suspicions were, since the only copy of the bill was torn up by Cromwell at the time of the dissolution. His anger seems to have been aroused not so much by the bill itself but by the Rump's members going back on a promise they had previously given him that they would suspend their consideration of it. On 20 April, he marched to Westminster at the head of a column of troopers, entered the Commons, and told the startled members that their sitting was at an end. Edmund Ludlow, an eyewitness, recorded the scene (see Source E). Though modern research has raised doubts about the authenticity of the *Memoirs*, what they describe is still held by historians to be substantially true.

After a token protest by a few individuals, the members did as Cromwell commanded. The next day a wag nailed a notice to the door of the Commons that read: 'This House is to be let, now unfurnished'.

The ending of the Rump was also accompanied by a forcible dispersal of the Council of State. Cromwell's role in all this was obviously the critical one, but it is important not to anticipate events by assuming that his eventual move had always been part of his plans. For the whole of the period 1649–53, he had remained loyal to Parliament, as shown by the letters and reports that throughout the Irish and Scottish campaigns he regularly sent to the speaker. Moreover, the evidence suggests that, despite the firmness with which he acted

 **SOURCE QUESTION**

What insight does Source E offer into the character and temperament of Cromwell?

**ONLINE EXTRAS**
OCR **WWW**

Test your analysis of the reliability of a source by completing Worksheet 27 at **www.hoddereducation. co.uk/accesstohistory/extras**

**SOURCE E**

From S.H. Firth, editor, *The Memoirs of Edmund Ludlow*, volume I, *written 1625–72*, Oxford University Press, 1894, pp. 341–5.

*[Cromwell] sat still for about a quarter of an hour, and then, suddenly standing up, he made a speech, wherein he loaded the Parliament with the vilest reproaches, accusing them of an intention to perpetuate themselves in power. This he spoke with such passion and discomposure of mind, as if he had been distracted ... [He] stepped into the midst of the House, where continuing his distracted language, he said 'Come, come, I will put an end to your prating [prattling]'; then walking up and down the House like a mad-man, and kicking the ground, he cried out, 'You are no Parliament, I say you are no Parliament; I will put an end to your sitting; call them in'; whereupon two files of musketeers entered the House.*

in April 1653, he had genuinely agonised over the decision to use force to end the Rump. It is true that after Pride's purge in 1648 the Rump depended on the goodwill of the army, but it would be wrong to think of the military as a constant threat to Parliament. Indeed, although the army often urged MPs to pursue certain courses of action, it rarely tried to impose its will directly on the Commons.

One reason for the army's restraint was its preoccupation between 1649 and 1652 with the Scottish and Irish wars. Another is the attitude of its commander-in-chief. Right up to the time he dissolved the Rump, Cromwell appears to have wanted it to succeed. His religious ideas may have been radical, but his social and political views were conservative. As his later rule as Lord Protector was to show, he never lost his belief in Parliament as an essential part of any constitutional settlement. He held his army in check until he became outraged by the Rump's failure to live up to his expectations.

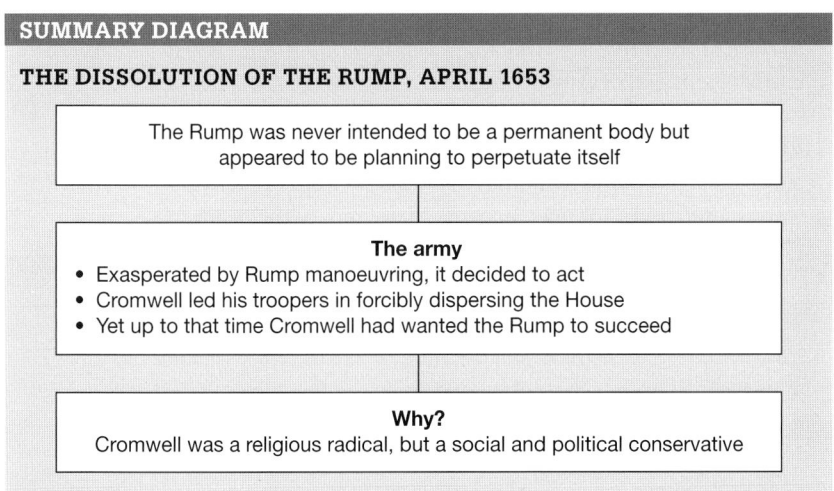

**SUMMARY DIAGRAM**

**THE DISSOLUTION OF THE RUMP, APRIL 1653**

The Rump was never intended to be a permanent body but appeared to be planning to perpetuate itself

**The army**
- Exasperated by Rump manoeuvring, it decided to act
- Cromwell led his troopers in forcibly dispersing the House
- Yet up to that time Cromwell had wanted the Rump to succeed

**Why?**
Cromwell was a religious radical, but a social and political conservative

# 6 Key debate

■ *How repressive was Cromwell's military policy in Ireland?*

A question that continues to divide historical opinion is whether Cromwell was unnecessarily repressive in the methods he used to break Irish resistance in his 1649–50 campaigns. Historians are not moralists but it is difficult to avoid the moral aspects of the question. In his letters from Ireland to the English Parliament, Cromwell repeatedly claimed that, despite their apparent severity, his methods were intended to prevent a greater 'effusion of blood'.

Historian Ronald Hutton has accepted Cromwell's contention that his harsh measures cowed the Irish into a quicker submission, thereby shortening the struggle and saving lives. Hutton has further suggested that judged by the standards of his day Cromwell was not notably severe; he argues that Cromwell's actions have to be understood in their context.

**? INTERPRETATION QUESTION**

How far do Extracts 1–5 provide a conclusive verdict on Cromwell's policy in Ireland?

### EXTRACT 1

From Ronald Hutton, *The British Republic 1649–1660*, Macmillan, 2000, pp. 47–8.

*Oliver's instructions were quite specific: to strike terror into other garrisons, he forbade his men 'to spare any that were in arms' within Drogheda. But nobody at the time claimed that a single woman or child died, and most of the male population, being unarmed, also survived. At Wexford the same instructions obtained, but some women and children did perish, not at the hands of Cromwell's soldiers but because the boats in which they were trying to escape capsized.*

*Such behaviour was certainly more brutal than* **most** *of that during the English Civil Wars, but how did it compare with the practice in Ireland? The Catholic uprising of 1641 began with the greatest massacre of civilians recorded in the history of the British Isles … I am not attempting to dismiss the suffering of those who died at Drogheda and Wexford … But the fact that it suited both nations to magnify the actions of Cromwell remains a glaring example of bad history.*

A different emphasis has been given by Barry Coward, a major biographer of Cromwell. He has pointed out that the massacres did not terrorise the other garrisons into rapid surrender, and so did not reduce the death toll.

### EXTRACT 2

From Barry Coward, *Oliver Cromwell*, Longman, 2000, pp. 74–5.

*After the capture of Drogheda and Wexford Cromwell's troops did not carry all before them … As the Cromwellian army marched south from Dublin after the capture of Drogheda and Wexford the garrisons at Duncannon and Waterford successfully held out in November and December. His army was ravaged by dysentery: 'our foot [soldiers] falling sick near ten of a company every night', he wrote on 19 December, and he too was 'crazy in his health'. Later in the spring, on 27 April 1650, about 2000 Cromwellian troops were killed attempting to take Clonmel in south-west Ireland. Ireton called that disaster 'the heaviest we ever endured, either in England or here'.*

Gerald Aylmer, another major authority, shares Coward's view, pointing out that the Drogheda and Wexford massacres 'did not – as Cromwell hoped – succeed in terrorizing by example. Waterford, Clonmel, and Limerick were all defended with stubborn courage, and the massacres were not in fact repeated.'

The contribution of Irish historian Tom Reilly to the debate caused considerable controversy. Reilly produced a revisionist work in 1999 in which he suggested that Cromwell's reputation was the consequence of later writers, who deliberately distorted the record in order to blacken Cromwell's name. Reilly claimed that his research found no firm evidence that there were any civilian casualties at all at Drogheda. His findings further showed that Cromwell, at no time during his Irish campaigns, ordered an attack on unarmed civilians.

### EXTRACT 3

From Tom Reilly, *Cromwell: An Honourable Enemy*, Phoenix, 1999, p. 171.

*To summarise the events at Drogheda, it seems that not only was there no outright slaughter of the defenceless inhabitants, but we now find that there is absolutely no evidence to substantiate the stories of the massacre of even one unarmed person on the streets of Drogheda. It is the words of the actual participants that we have used and not those transcribed years later which Nationalist historians have so far relied upon. Cromwell may well have had no moral right to take the lives of the defending garrison of Drogheda, but he certainly had the law firmly on his side.*

Such revisionism has not received full acceptance from fellow historians. Their critical view is represented in the comment of John Morrill, arguably the most authoritative voice in modern Cromwellian studies, that certainly 'a major attempt at rehabilitation was attempted by Tom Reilly … but this has been largely rejected by other scholars'. The broadly accepted view remains that expressed by David Loades:

### EXTRACT 4

From David Loades, *Politics and the Nation 1450–1660*, Fontana, 1986, pp. 454–5.

*[Cromwell] set off for Ireland, and in a series of ferocious battles and sieges reduced that intractable country to obedience. Never had the New Model Army fought better, or more savagely, than against the confederate Irish, whom the soldiers genuinely regarded as children of Satan. Not only did this bloodthirsty campaign give great encouragement to the apocalyptic orators in the ranks, it also strengthened Cromwell's own sense of mission in a manner which the modern mind is bound to find barbarous. The Protector's policy in Ireland … has left a permanent blot on his reputation. The answer must lie partly in religious fanaticism, but it seems that he was also ill in the course of the campaign and this may have impaired his judgement.*

Notwithstanding the leniency Cromwell occasionally showed and his firm instruction to his troops to show restraint, the fact remains that Cromwell went to Ireland intent on crushing the Irish rebels beyond recovery. In that sense, he was typical of his time, seeing the Irish as reprobate. Modern historian Derek Hirst provides an appropriate conclusion: 'Cromwell, like so many English Protestants, had been swept up in the apocalyptic ferment of 1641, and saw the Irish in arms not only a troublesome enemy but Antichrist.'

Paul Lay, a prominent modern authority sums up the effect that the policies followed by Cromwell's in Ireland continue have on his reputation.

**EXTRACT 5**

From Paul Lay, *Providence Lost: The Rise and Fall of Cromwell's Protectorate*, Head of Zeus, 2020, p. 280.

*The Cromwellian conquest of Ireland created conditions that would prove permanent: the Irish Catholic elite lost all in the permanent transfer of power and land to Protestant newcomers. The hostility to Cromwell, which has marked Irish political mythology for generations and sees no sign of receding, has parallels in Britain, too, where Cromwell remains at the least a divisive figure. This despite his well-documented personal tolerance [and] genuine desire for religious liberty.*

# CHAPTER SUMMARY

The Rump Parliament, which established the Commonwealth by abolishing the monarchy and the House of Lords and setting up a Council of State as government, was ultimately dependent on the Army Council for its survival. It was the army under Cromwell that suppressed the Leveller challenge and then broke royalist resistance in Ireland and Scotland. The reputation that Cromwell gained by the brilliance of his generalship in these campaigns of 1650–1 was somewhat overshadowed by the arguably unnecessary violence with which he crushed the Irish and by the severity of the land confiscation policy which he and his successors set in place there. The claims of the many sects that flourished in this period presented the Rump and Cromwell with difficult questions to resolve.

Although the Rump introduced important religious, financial, social and economic reforms, these were not enough to make it genuinely popular with republicans and Independents. The army, too, grew increasingly frustrated when it appeared that, although the Rump had never been intended as a permanent body, the majority of its members were planning to perpetuate their sittings. Cromwell, who had genuinely hoped that the Rump would be the means of creating the settled nation that he desired, was technically the servant of Parliament but he showed where true authority resided when, in 1653, he marched his troopers into the House and forcibly dispersed its members.

# Refresher questions

Use these questions to remind yourself of the key material covered in this chapter.

1 What principles underlay the creation of the Commonwealth?

2 Why did so many radical sects appear during the English Revolution?

3 Why did the Rump regard the Fifth Monarchists as dangerous?

4 What was the attitude of the Quakers towards government and society?

5 What was Cromwell aiming to achieve by his campaigns in Ireland?

6 Why have Cromwell's Irish campaigns traditionally received such a bad press?

7 What was the legacy of Cromwell's Irish campaigns?

8 Why were the Scots unable to mount an effective resistance to the Rump?

9 How successful was the Rump Parliament of 1649–53?

10 What was Cromwell's motive for dissolving the Rump in 1653?

# Question practice: OCR

## Source questions

1 Study Sources B (page 158), C (page 158) and D (page 159) and then answer both questions. [AS level]

**a)** Use your knowledge of the events during Oliver Cromwell's campaigns in Ireland to assess how useful Source B is as evidence of his attitude towards the Irish rebels.

> **EXAM HINT** Explain in what ways Source B provides evidence of his attitude. Also consider the provenance of the source and link this to contextual knowledge to test the view of the source, then reach a judgement as to the usefulness of the source.

**b)** Using the three sources in their historical context, assess how far they support the view that Cromwell was motivated by religious hatred in his dealings with Irish people.

> **EXAM HINT** Group the sources according to whether they support the view in the question. Each source should be explained in relation to the question, its provenance evaluated and contextual knowledge used to test the view of the source. A judgement about each source should be reached allowing an overall judgement about whether Cromwell was motivated by religious hatred.

2 Using Sources B (page 158), C (page 158), D (page 159) and E (page 166) in their historical context, assess how far they support the view that Cromwell's way of dealing with problems was to resort to military force. [A level]

> **EXAM HINT** Group the sources according to whether they support the view in the question. Each source should be explained in relation to the question, its provenance evaluated and contextual knowledge used to test the view of the source. A judgement about each source should be reached allowing an overall judgement about whether Cromwell's way of dealing with problems was to resort to military force.

# CHAPTER 7

# The search for a settlement 1653–8

Between 1653 and 1658, England experimented with various forms of government in a series of attempts to establish a stable constitution. The dominant figure in all this was Oliver Cromwell. It was he who initiated the experiments and it was his frustrations that largely determined the unfolding of events; these included his suppression of royalist resistance and his relations with the radical sects. This chapter examines the following themes:

◆ The Nominated Assembly 1653

◆ The early Protectorate 1654–5

◆ Cromwell and the sects

◆ Royalist resistance 1652–9

◆ The Major-Generals 1655–7

◆ The later Protectorate 1656–8

## KEY DATES

| | | | | | |
|---|---|---|---|---|---|
| **1653** | **July** | Nominated Assembly convened | **1656** | **Sept.** | Second Protectorate Parliament |
| | **Dec.** | Nominated Assembly dissolved; *Instrument of Government* adopted | **1657** | **Jan.** | Rule of Major-Generals ended |
| | | Cromwell became Lord Protector | | **April** | Cromwell declined the kingship |
| | | | | **May** | *Humble Petition and Advice* |
| **1654** | **Sept.** | First Protectorate Parliament | | **July** | First session of Parliament |
| **1655** | **Jan.** | Cromwell dissolved first Protectorate Parliament | **1658** | **Jan.–Feb.** | Second session of Parliament |
| | | | | **Feb.** | Cromwell dissolved Parliament |
| | **March** | Penruddock's rising | | | |
| | **Oct.** | Beginning of rule of Major-Generals | | **Sept.** | Death of Oliver Cromwell |

## 1 The Nominated Assembly 1653

■ *What did Cromwell hope to achieve by convening the Nominated Assembly?*

■ *Why was the Assembly so short lived?*

Cromwell's forcible dissolution of the Rump and the Council of State left the Commonwealth under direct military rule. Yet, although the Army Council now held power, it immediately took steps to try to restore constitutional forms.

# Cromwell's summons

On behalf of the Army Council, Cromwell announced that a new assembly was to be established, not by election but by nomination. After his officers had vetted lists of reliable persons in the localities, he issued a summons, shown in Source A, to 140 selected individuals:

From Cromwell's summons, July 1653, in S.R. Gardiner, editor, *The Constitutional Documents of the Puritan Revolution 1625–1660*, Oxford University Press, 1906, p. 405.

*Forasmuch as, upon the dissolution of the late Parliament, it became necessary that the peace, safety, and good government of this Commonwealth should be provided for; and in order thereunto, divers [diverse] persons fearing God and of approved integrity and honesty are, by myself, with the advice of my Council of Officers, nominated; to whom the great charge and trust of so weighty affairs is to be committed; and having good assurance of your love to, and courage for, God and the interest of his cause and of the good people of the Commonwealth; I, Oliver Cromwell, Captain General and Commander-in-Chief of all the armies and forces raised and to be raised within this Commonwealth, do hereby summon you … to be and appear at the Council Chamber at Whitehall upon the 4th day of July next, then and there to take upon you the said trust; unto which you are hereby called and appointed.*

**SOURCE QUESTION**

According to Source A, what are the characteristics of the members summoned to the Nominated Assembly?

Cromwell's summons to 'persons fearing God' led to the Assembly's being referred to as the 'Parliament of the Saints'. Alternative names by which it became known include:

■ Nominated Assembly

■ Little Parliament

■ Barebone's Parliament.

The last title came from the attempt by royalists and republicans to ridicule the Assembly, by giving it a mocking nickname after one of the backbench members, Praise-God Barebone, a London leather-seller.

As the wording of the summons shows, the Nominated Assembly represented Cromwell's attempt to achieve stable rule in England by entrusting government to the godly. This used to be interpreted by historians as a concession to the ideas of Harrison and the Fifth Monarchists (see page 153), who had urged that a ruling body like the **Sanhedrin** should be established. However, modern writers see it more as a compromise between the ideas of Harrison and those of **John Lambert**, the leading republican, who had wanted government to be carried on, in the interim before a full republic could be established, by a council nominated by the army. In its final form, the 140-member Assembly was exactly twice the size of the Sanhedrin model, which enabled it to appear more representative than a smaller body would have been.

**KEY TERM**

**Sanhedrin** The presiding council of the ancient Israelites.

**KEY FIGURE**

**John Lambert (1619–84)**

A friend of Oliver Cromwell, he fought for parliament in the first civil war and in Scotland 1650–1. Entering politics in the 1650s, he drafted the *Instrument of Government*, but declined to take the oath of allegiance to Cromwell as Protector. He made unavailing efforts to prevent the Restoration.

## Character of the Nominated Assembly

After the Restoration in 1660, it became customary to dismiss this Assembly as if it had been composed simply of inexperienced social upstarts. This was a false picture as the following details indicate:

- 116 of the members ranked as gentry (substantial landowners)
- 119 members were justices of the peace in their local communities
- 40 members had attended university, while another 40 had trained as lawyers
- 24 members had sat in a previous Parliament, and 67 would be elected to later Parliaments.

As with the Rump earlier, the Assembly was not intended to be permanent. This is clear from its decision to fix a date, November 1654, for its dissolution. At the time of its first gathering in July 1653, the Assembly appointed a new Council of State of 31 members. This contained a number of officers, including Cromwell, but the majority were civilians. Soon after it first gathered, the Assembly declared itself to be a Parliament. This did not please Cromwell and was the first sign that the Assembly would disappoint his expectations.

By selecting men of 'approved integrity', the Army Council had hoped that the Assembly would prove easy to manage. But, from the beginning, there was a sizeable minority of members who refused to be overawed by the military. These were largely Fifth Monarchists and extreme sectarians who believed that Christ's Second Coming was imminent. To prepare for this, they demanded the sweeping away of all man-made laws. This was a rejection of the social order and the rights of property. Although the fanatics were a minority, their extremism overshadowed proceedings and tended to be taken as characterising the Assembly as a whole during its five-month existence.

## The Assembly's dissolution

The moderates and conservative members eventually grew exasperated with the sectarians and concluded that the only way to stop them was to dissolve the Assembly. Accordingly, in December, the moderates met in a special session, from which the wildest of the sectarians were excluded, and voted to end the Parliament. In doing this, they gave back to Cromwell the authority he had granted them.

The tame ending of the Nominated Assembly should not be taken to mean that it had been a total failure. It is true that it disappointed the hopes of reformers. Cromwell later referred to his calling of the Assembly as 'a story of my own weakness and folly' and admitted that 'these 140 honest men could not govern'. But scholars now recognise that the work of the Assembly marked a key period in the development of public administration in England. Among the measures considered by the fifteen committees into which it divided were the following:

- reform of the law on debt
- humane treatment of the insane
- civil registration of births, deaths and marriages
- protection for travellers on the highways.

In many respects, these proposed measures were ahead of their time. There are good grounds, therefore, for speculating that had the Nominated Assembly not been riven by the religious issue it would have been able to implement the proposals and thus perform as effectively as any of the other Parliaments of the period. Like them, it was weakened by its failure to reconcile social conservatism with religious fanaticism.

Cromwell claimed to have known 'not one tittle' about the manoeuvre by which the moderates had outwitted the extremists and ended the life of the Nominated Assembly. Yet the evidence suggests that he had already lost faith in the Assembly. He had been particularly annoyed by its proposal to end the monthly assessment, a move which he interpreted as an attack on the army, since it was the assessment which paid for the army's upkeep. What is certain is that he was fully aware that the *Instrument of Government*, the alternative constitution creating him Lord Protector, had been drawn up even before the Assembly dissolved itself.

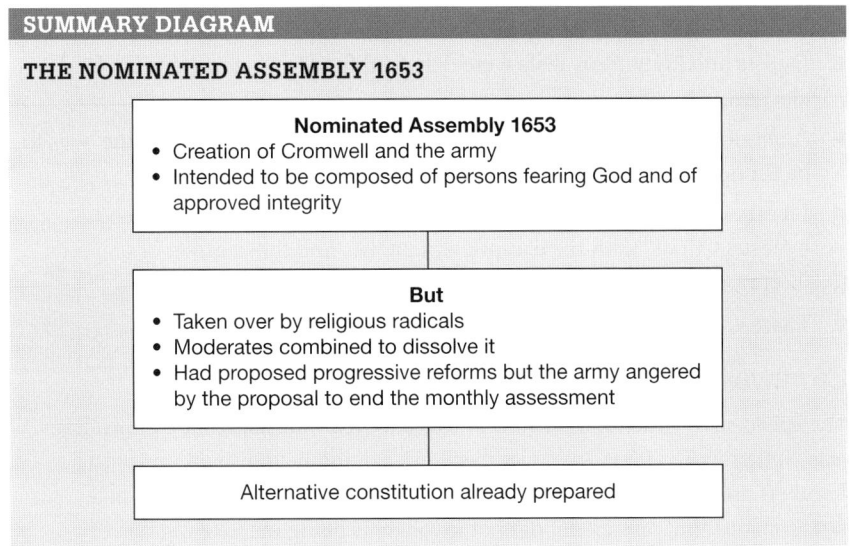

**SUMMARY DIAGRAM**

**THE NOMINATED ASSEMBLY 1653**

**Nominated Assembly 1653**
- Creation of Cromwell and the army
- Intended to be composed of persons fearing God and of approved integrity

**But**
- Taken over by religious radicals
- Moderates combined to dissolve it
- Had proposed progressive reforms but the army angered by the proposal to end the monthly assessment

Alternative constitution already prepared

# 2 The early Protectorate 1654–5

■ *What powers did Cromwell have as Protector?*

The new constitution was the work of John Lambert, one of the brightest of the younger officers, who for some time had been pressing for a written constitution that would give the republic stability.

## The *Instrument of Government*

The main features of the constitution that the *Instrument of Government* established were as follows:

- A Lord Protector with governmental powers, aided by a Council of State.
- A single-chamber Parliament of 400 members from England and Wales, which was to meet at least once every three years.
- Ireland and Scotland were to be represented in the House by 30 members of Parliament (MPs) apiece, thus making it the first-ever truly British Parliament.
- In a direct rejection of Leveller ideas, the *Instrument* stipulated that the right to vote was to be restricted to men of substance, those who had property or income of at least £200 in value.
- Papists and known royalists were debarred from voting or standing for election.
- A national church, loosely defined as one professing 'sound doctrine' was to be set up.
- Liberty of worship was to be the right of 'such as profess faith in God by Jesus Christ', with the exception of papists and those guilty of 'licentiousness', a reference to the extreme sectarians.
- There was to be a standing (permanent) army of 30,000 soldiers.

## Cromwell and the *Instrument*

The speed with which the *Instrument* was adopted indicates that Cromwell was well prepared for it. In November 1653, having held discussions with Lambert and the army officers, he had keenly supported the drafting of a new constitution, provided it did not involve his being made 'King Oliver'. Cromwell's objection was meant to quash rumours that had been circulating for some months that he contemplated being made emperor or king. Cromwell preferred the renewal of the title of 'Lord Protector' since this office had a number of precedents in English history going back to the fifteenth century. It was his way of maintaining links with the ancient constitution, while at the same time distancing himself from the recently overthrown monarchy. An illuminating detail is that, at the ceremony formally installing him as Protector, Cromwell insisted on wearing a simple black coat rather than military uniform, his way of showing that he regarded himself primarily as a civilian ruler.

## Cromwell's ordinances

Within four days of the ending of the Nominated Assembly, Cromwell had been installed as Lord Protector. During the following nine months, before the meeting of the first Parliament of the Protectorate in September 1654, Cromwell worked with his Council of State in drafting a large number of ordinances which he intended to present to Parliament for ratification. Among the key measures were the following:

- financial reform and the regularising of the two main types of taxation, the 'assessment' and the 'excise', a centrally imposed tax on goods and commodities

- religious reorganisation

- the legal and administrative reforms first proposed by the Rump.

Although the Protectorate had now become the effective constitution, its legitimacy remained in question throughout its six-year existence (1653–9). The *Instrument of Government* from which the Protectorate derived its authority was solely the product of the Council of Officers; it never received full civilian backing and was never formally ratified by any of the Parliaments called during these years. It was a governmental system imposed by the military, something which Cromwell remained very conscious of throughout his time as Lord Protector. This is worth stressing, for it corrects the notion that the Protectorate Parliaments were merely obstructive bodies standing in the way of reform and progress. The MPs who challenged the *Instrument* and Cromwell's authority under it had as much right to do so as the Army Council had in imposing it originally. After all, Parliament could claim that it was an elected body, whereas the Army Council represented nobody but themselves.

# The first Protectorate Parliament, September to January 1654–5

Under the terms of the *Instrument*, a Parliament was scheduled to meet in September 1654. The elections, in which the army did not interfere, took place during the preceding summer months. Interestingly, the results did not return a House submissive to Cromwell and the army. The 460 members included Presbyterians, republicans, and even some royalist sympathisers.

In his opening address, Cromwell reminded the MPs that their first duty was to provide the people of England with 'good and wholesome laws'. However, the new Parliament gave priority not to reform but to attacking the *Instrument*. The assault was led by the **Commonwealthsmen**, who challenged the right of the Protector to exercise the civil and military authority granted him by the *Instrument*. They also complained that the Council of State contained too many army officers. In addition, they objected to the high cost of maintaining the standing army that had been sanctioned by the *Instrument*. They demanded that it be reduced from 50,000 to 30,000, as laid down in the new constitution.

**KEY TERM**

**Commonwealthsmen**
Republican MPs who claimed that Cromwell's dissolution of the Rump in 1653 had been unlawful; they argued for limited government and religious freedom.

## SOURCE B

**SOURCE QUESTION**

How does the illustration in Source B suggest that Cromwell was king in all but name?

A contemporary engraving of Cromwell as Lord Protector. The ceremony which accompanied his installation in December 1653 gave credence to the idea that he was king in all but name. Cromwell, however, was not carried away by it all. When the size of the crowd lining the streets of the procession was pointed out to him, he remarked, 'There would have been an even greater throng to see me hanged.'

It had been Cromwell's declared wish that this Parliament would begin 'healing and settling' the religious differences that divided the nation. However, far from taking a conciliatory line, Parliament voiced its concern at the tolerance that had already been shown under the Protectorate. Cromwell tried to lessen the growing opposition by obliging the MPs to take an oath of loyalty to the Protectorate. This resulted in the exclusion of 100 members who refused to swear allegiance, but it did not greatly diminish the criticism of his regime. None of the 84 ordinances which Cromwell had previously prepared was passed by Parliament. Not content simply with obstructing his proposals, the Parliament sought to restrict his powers as Protector by introducing a new bill, which would have effectively undermined the authority granted him under the *Instrument*. This proved the final straw for Cromwell; in January 1655, he dissolved Parliament after just five months' sitting.

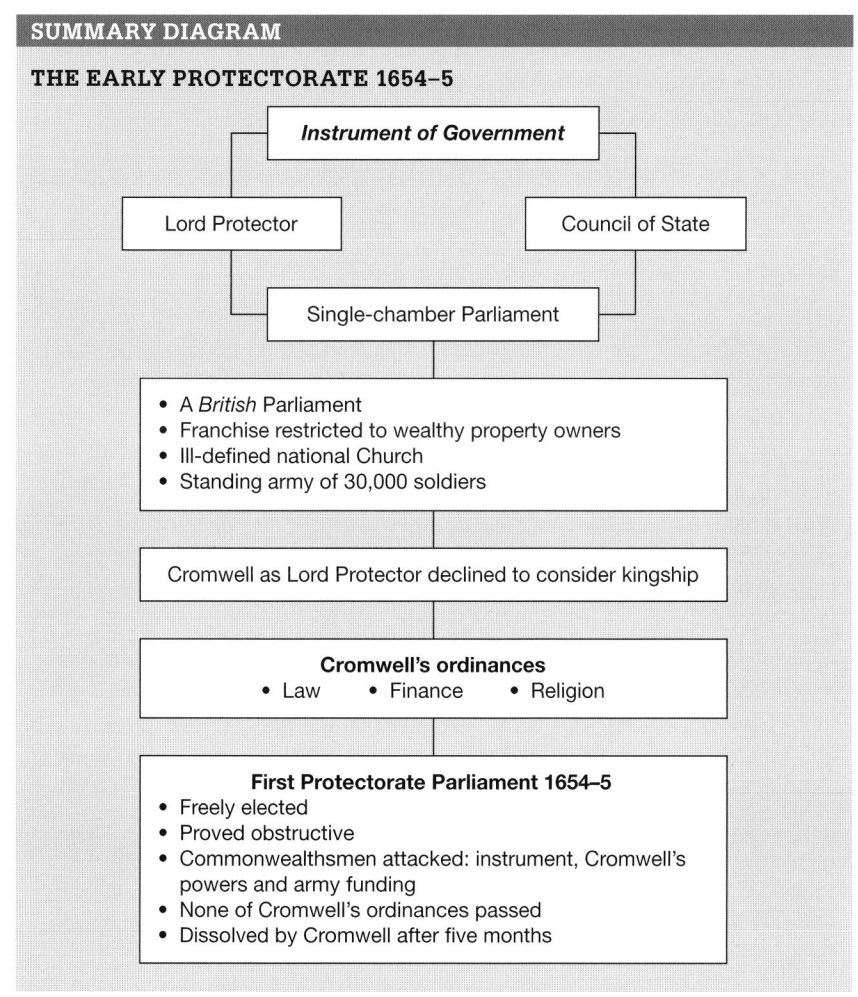

**SUMMARY DIAGRAM**

**THE EARLY PROTECTORATE 1654–5**

*Instrument of Government*

Lord Protector

Council of State

Single-chamber Parliament

- A *British* Parliament
- Franchise restricted to wealthy property owners
- Ill-defined national Church
- Standing army of 30,000 soldiers

Cromwell as Lord Protector declined to consider kingship

**Cromwell's ordinances**
- Law • Finance • Religion

**First Protectorate Parliament 1654–5**
- Freely elected
- Proved obstructive
- Commonwealthsmen attacked: instrument, Cromwell's powers and army funding
- None of Cromwell's ordinances passed
- Dissolved by Cromwell after five months

# 3 Cromwell and the sects

■ *How tolerant was Cromwell in his dealings with the sects?*

Religious considerations weighed heavily with Cromwell, both because of the intensity of his own faith, and because he held that the root cause of the civil wars had been religious division. When, as Protector, he spoke of 'healing and settling', he was referring to the need to establish religious harmony in England. His conviction was that the turmoil of the civil wars had been God's way of preparing England for 'godliness' and religious peace, which it was now the duty of those in government to implement.

## Cromwell's religious toleration

Cromwell condemned those religious fanatics who 'press their finger upon their brethren's conscience'. His view was typically expressed in his words to Major-General Crawford, a Presbyterian, who had wanted to take action against one his officers suspected of being an Anabaptist (see page 152):

**SOURCE QUESTION**

What point is Cromwell making in Source C when he says 'the State, in choosing men to serve it, takes no notice of their opinions'?

### SOURCE C

Cromwell to General Crawford, 10 March 1643, quoted in Thomas Carlyle, editor, *Oliver Cromwell's Letters and Speeches with Elucidations*, volume 1, Chapman & Hall, 1857, p. 278.

*'[The man] is an Anabaptist' … shall that render him incapable to serve the Public? 'He is indiscreet.' … In some things: we have all human infirmities. … If you had none but such 'indiscreet men' about you, and would be pleased to use them kindly, you would find [them] as good a fence to you as any you have yet chosen.*

*Sir, the State, in choosing men to serve it, takes no notice of their opinions. … I advised you formerly to bear with men of different minds from yourself. … Take heed of being sharp, or too easily sharpened by others, against those to whom you can object little but that they square not with you in every opinion concerning matters of religion.*

Cromwell believed that 'liberty of conscience' was a natural right, but he was very conscious of the difficulty in bringing the various sects to recognise each other's freedoms. 'Every sect saith: "Oh, give me liberty!" but give him it, and he will not yield it to anybody else.' Cromwell held that unless a particular religious belief led to subversive public behaviour it should be tolerated:

**SOURCE QUESTION**

In what sense is Source D a plea for religious toleration?

### SOURCE D

From Cromwell's speech in the Commons, 1656, quoted in S.C. Lomas, editor, *The Letters and Speeches of Oliver Cromwell*, volume II, Methuen & Co., 1904, p. 535.

*Our practice hath been, to let all this Nation see that whatever pretensions to religion would continue quiet, peaceable, they should enjoy conscience and liberty.*

*If a man of one form will be trampling upon the heels of another man; if an Independent, for example, will despise him who is under Baptism, I will not suffer it in him. If those of the Baptists shall be censuring the godly ministers that profess Independency; or those that profess under Presbytery shall be reproaching or speaking ill of them – as I would not be willing to see England in the power of Presbytery to impose upon the consciences of others that profess faith in Christ – so I will not endure to reproach them.*

Cromwell's appeal for toleration was not simply a matter of words. He backed it with action. Among the ordinances of 1653 (see page 177) were two notable measures which aimed to bring order to the disputed question of Church appointments. The title of the ordinances gave a clear indication of their purpose: 'An Ordinance for Appointing Commissioners for Approbation of Public Preachers' and 'An Ordinance for Ejecting Scandalous, Ignorant and Insufficient Ministers and Schoolmasters'. Between them, the two Ordinances set up a body of Commissioners, subsequently known as '**Triers and Ejectors**'.

Significantly, the ordinances made no attempt to prescribe what doctrines were acceptable. Cromwell's aim was not to persecute particular beliefs but, on the contary, to provide greater toleration by removing or debarring those clerics whose extreme views or behaviour disturbed the religious peace for which he longed. He was anxious that the Commissioners should be drawn from as many denominations as possible: Baptists, Independents and Presbyterians appeared in the lists of appointees. The evidence suggests that his policy was largely successful. Even some of the strongest critics of Cromwell's religious toleration admitted that the work of the 'Triers and Ejectors' had improved the quality of the Church ministry. Moreover, in practice, relatively few of the incumbent ministers needed to be removed, since the greater majority showed themselves ready to reform and improve their behaviour.

In the interests of historical balance, it should be noted that there were many who thought that Cromwell used religion and toleration as a cover for his political aims. One such was the Venetian ambassador (Source E):

### KEY TERM

**Triers and Ejectors**
Officials responsible for the selection and the supervision of those appointed as ministers in the Church.

---

#### SOURCE E

From Giovanni Sagredo, 'Relation in England', 1656, quoted in David L. Smith, *Oliver Cromwell*, Cambridge University Press, 1992, p. 66.

*While in general he displays a most exemplary exterior, yet it cannot be known what rite he follows. In the late troubles he professed himself an Anabaptist. This cult denies sovereignty and claims obedience to God alone, and to these Independents belonged the majority of the parliament that passed judgement on the King. The moment Cromwell was elevated to power, he not only broke off from the Independents, but condemned and persecuted them. Thus he has changed his creed in accordance with the interests of the state ... it suits his policy that 246 religions should be professed in London ... the division into so many makes them all weak, so that no one is strong enough to cause him apprehension.*

### SOURCE QUESTION

According to Source E, what motive lies behind Cromwell's toleration of the sects?

### ONLINE EXTRAS
OCR    **WWW**

Develop your analysis of the view of a group of sources by completing Worksheet 28 at **www.hoddereducation. co.uk/accesstohistory/extras**

## Cromwell and the Quakers

Cromwell was not opposed to the Quakers over their form of worship; his worry was not their private beliefs but their public behaviour. If they were involved in disruption or scandal, this could only delay the process of healing and settling. He was on good personal terms with George Fox (see page 154), and interceded on occasion to prevent Quakers from being prosecuted. The notable example of this was his reaction to the notorious case of James Nayler in 1656. In October of that year, Nayler had ridden into Bristol on a donkey, surrounded by adoring women, in apparent imitation of Christ's entry into Jerusalem on the first Palm Sunday. He was arrested for blasphemy by the local magistrates. Fears of widespread Quaker disturbances led to what was in itself a minor local affair being taken up by the second Protectorate Parliament, which ordered Nayler to be brought to Westminster. In self-righteous zeal, Parliament denounced Nayler and sentenced him to a series of brutal punishments, which included branding and the boring through of his tongue.

Cromwell was deeply disturbed, not simply by the severity of Nayler's treatment, but because he believed Parliament had exceeded its authority. In December, he wrote sharply to the speaker to inform Parliament that nothing in the *Instrument of Government* conferred on them the legal powers they had claimed. His chief anxiety was that Parliament had gone beyond its constitutional rights by denying 'liberty of conscience'.

## Cromwell's balancing act

Throughout the Protectorate, Cromwell was engaged in a balancing act, trying to satisfy the army, whose natural sympathies were with the sects, without alienating Parliament, which became increasingly dominated by conservative Presbyterians as the 1650s wore on. At the same time, he still had hopes of achieving a religious settlement that would establish godliness and toleration without permitting extremism. During his Protectorate, Cromwell made considerable efforts to ensure that the parish system was maintained and improved. This was because he judged that in the conditions of the 1650s the traditional Church structure in the localities had to be preserved if the ordinary people were to have access to the means of worship. This also meant the continuation of tithes for the support of the clergy.

Cromwell's attempt at religious balance created strains between him and his Parliaments. His dilemma was that he was invariably more tolerant than they were. As the Nayler case showed, his efforts to hold Parliament's repressive tendencies in check were not always successful, but he took pride in how far he had advanced the principle of toleration: 'I have through God's mercy not been unhappy in preventing any one religion impose upon another.'

His apparent sympathy towards the sects worried the more conservative elements in society. He was referred to mockingly as 'the darling of the sectaries'. One of the most insistent themes in the huge volume of pamphlets published in the 1650s was the need to guard against the threat posed by the religious sectaries. The growing readiness in the late 1650s of the Presbyterians to consider making common cause with the royalists (see page 205) arose not from any great love for Charles II but from a fear of what uncontrolled sectarianism might do. A return to some form of centrally controlled Church authority seemed to offer the best means of uniting against the religious extremists.

## Cromwell and Jewish people

It is arguable that, judged against the religious intensity and bigotry of his times, Cromwell was the most tolerant of rulers. He was the first English statesman to make religious toleration the basis of government policy. An interesting example is his giving serious thought in the 1650s to the suggestions that Jewish people be granted full freedom in England. All this needs to be put in its mid-seventeenth-century context. He was not a modern liberal. His toleration was selective and conditional. It did not extend, for example, to Catholicism or what he called 'blasphemy', by which he meant the behaviour of the extreme sectaries. Nevertheless, it was during his Protectorate that England experienced an unprecedented degree of religious freedom.

---

**SUMMARY DIAGRAM**

**CROMWELL AND THE SECTS**

> **Cromwell possessed a deep religious faith**

- An independent in religion
- Involved in a balancing act
- Wished to establish godliness without encouraging extremism
- Cromwell's ordinances aimed at improving public Church ministry

Cromwell's fundamental belief in liberty of conscience:
- Hence troubled relations with Parliament
- Prepared to extend toleration to Jewish people

---

# 4 Royalist resistance 1652–9

> ◼ *Why were the royalists unable to mount an effective challenge to the rule of Cromwell as Protector?*

---

One of Cromwell's constant fears as Protector was that the unsettled situation might encourage a royalist uprising in England. His anxieties are understandable, but with hindsight it can be seen that they were exaggerated. The royalists themselves represented only a minor threat to the Protectorate. It was only when the other conservative forces in England allied with them, something which did not happen until after Cromwell's death, that the restoration of the Stuart monarchy became a possibility.

## Royalist problems

Following his defeat at the Battle of Worcester in 1651, Charles II had fled to the Continent, where he remained for the next nine years. His enforced absence left the royalists leaderless and made it very difficult for them to organise themselves into an effective opposition to the republican regimes of the Interregnum. Until 1658, the strength and reputation of Cromwell's army made thoughts of a royalist rising unrealistic. Moreover, there was little backing in the localities for the royalist cause; while few people were enthusiastic supporters of the Protectorate, they were not willing to put themselves at risk by openly challenging those in power. Most royalists were inhibited by the restrictions that branded them as '**delinquents**', imposed heavy fines on them and, in some cases, made their estates forfeit. The introduction by the Major-Generals of a further '**decimation tax**' on royalists was largely successful in its aim of convincing them that open support for the Stuarts carried too high a price. The **Sealed Knot**, the royalist organisation supposedly concerned with planning a Stuart restoration, spent most of its time discouraging uprisings because it feared that their almost inevitable failure would discredit the royalist cause.

## Penruddock's rising 1655

The one exception to the pattern was the rising led by John Penruddock in Wiltshire in March 1655. It began as an attempt by the Sealed Knot to prove that their cause was still alive. Believing that there were potential centres of resistance throughout the country just waiting to be given a lead, they encouraged Penruddock, a former colonel in Charles I's army, to seize Salisbury, an important administrative centre in Wiltshire. Penruddock duly led a contingent of royalist troops, variously estimated at between 200 and 400, in an attack on the gaol in Salisbury. The information on which the exiles had based their plans proved woefully inaccurate. After only two days, his force was scattered and defeated. Penruddock and the leading conspirators were tried and executed, while a number of the lesser rebels were transported to the **Barbadoes**.

### Reasons for the rising's failure

- The speed with which Cromwell's government moved to put it down.
- The readiness and ability of the authorities in the localities to raise 4000 local militia troops to suppress the rising.
- Penruddock's attack aroused practically no support either locally or nationally.
- Although there might well have been considerable latent sympathy for the idea of a return to monarchy, there were few people in 1655 willing to put their lives or livelihoods at risk by openly siding with the royalists. This illustrates a characteristic of the period 1640–60 on which modern historians

### KEY TERMS

**Delinquents** The name given by Parliament to those who had actively supported the Stuarts in the civil wars and afterwards.

**Decimation tax** A ten per cent levy imposed on known royalists with annual incomes of more than £100.

**Sealed Knot** An organisation founded by a group of aristocratic royalists in 1652 with the aim of organising the overthrow of the Republic.

**Barbadoes** An archaic spelling of Barbados. An island in the Caribbean colonised by the English in 1625.

lay great stress: the tendency of the great majority of the population towards neutrality. Their natural inclination was to avoid trouble.

■ The quality of the intelligence service on which the government could rely. This contrasted sharply with the inadequate royalist network of communication. Credit for this lies with **John Thurloe**, Cromwell's secretary of state. Thurloe operated an elaborate espionage system that enabled him to be always one step ahead of those plotting against the Protectorate. Thurloe's prior knowledge of the royalists' plans helps to explain why Penruddock's rising was overcome so easily.

## Other risings

Besides Penruddock's, there were seven other attempted royalist risings between 1652 and 1659, but none of these posed more than a minor difficulty for the Protectorate. A genuine challenge to the regimes of the Protectorate required an organised coalition of all the forces opposed to it. Given the strength of the army, there was little chance of this happening until after Cromwell's death.

The key to the survival of the Commonwealth and Protectorate was the loyalty of the army. Although, on occasion, groups within the armed forces expressed hostility towards the governments and Parliaments of the 1650s, Cromwell never seriously looked like losing the loyalty of his troops. His unmatchable reputation as a commander and his readiness to take up the grievances of his troops had endeared him to them. Affection for him and respect for his reputation survived throughout the 1650s. However, the situation changed once his strong hand was removed. The precarious stability that Cromwell had been able to preserve broke down. Factions returned and the struggle over who controlled the executive was renewed (see page 202).

**KEY FIGURE**

**John Thurloe (1616–68)**

Trained as a lawyer, became Cromwell's secretary of state in 1653, used his diplomatic contacts to developed an effective and widespread spy network to infiltrate and expose royalist plots.

**SUMMARY DIAGRAM**

**ROYALIST RESISTANCE 1652–9**

**Sealed Knot** — Largely ineffective

**Royalist resistance:**
- Too scattered
- Lacked real resolve
- With Charles II in exile no natural focus of resistance
- Delinquents cowed by Protectorate restrictions

**Penruddock's rising 1655**
- The only notable challenge of the period
- Gathered little support and failed

**Factors in royalist failure**
- Local militia remained loyal to Protectorate
- Army's strength
- Cromwell's reputation
- Thurloe's spies exposed plots

Other risings equally unsuccessful

# 5 The Major-Generals 1655–7

■ *What powers did the Major-Generals have?*

■ *How successful was the rule of the Major-Generals?*

The year 1655 was a critical one for the Protectorate. In addition to the failure of Parliament to fulfil Cromwell's hopes, royalist and republican opposition threatened in the country at large. Rumours of Leveller or republican plots to assassinate the Lord Protector circulated widely. These dangers encouraged Cromwell to look to his natural allies, the army commanders, to ensure not simply military security, but administrative efficiency as well. This led to the introduction of a system of direct military government, known as the rule of the Major-Generals.

## The Major-Generals and the counties they controlled

- John Barkstead – Middlesex
- James Berry – Wales and Worcestershire
- William Butler – Northants, Huntingdonshire, Bedfordshire
- John Desborough – Gloucs, Wiltshire, Dorset, Somerset, Devon, Cornwall
- Charles Fleetwood – Norfolk, Suffolk, Essex
- William Gough – Berkshire, Hampshire, Sussex
- Thomas Kelsey – Surrey and Kent
- John Lambert – Yorks, Cumberland, Westmorland, Northumberland
- William Packer – Oxfordshire and Buckinghamshire
- Philip Skippon – London
- Edward Whalley – Derby, Notts, Lincoln, Warwickshire, Leicestershire
- Charles Worsley – Lancashire, Cheshire, Staffordshire

## The rule of the Major–Generals

The decision to adopt this experiment was not Cromwell's alone; it was taken after lengthy consultation with the Army Council. John Lambert, who was himself to be one of the Major-Generals, was a leading proponent of the scheme. In the late summer of 1655, England was divided into groups of counties each with a major-general appointed to exercise military control and oversee the operation of local government within them. For example, John Lambert had responsibility for Yorkshire, Cumberland, Westmorland and Northumberland. In their official 'Instructions', the Major-Generals were granted unprecedentedly wide powers and duties, as illustrated in the selections in Source F:

**SOURCE F**

From Cromwell's Instructions to the Major-Generals, October 1655, quoted in John P. Kenyon, *The Stuart Constitution*, Cambridge University Press, 1989, pp. 322–4.

*1 They are to endeavour the suppressing [of] all tumults or other unlawful assemblies which shall be within the said counties respectively …*

*6 They shall in their constant carriage and conversation promote godliness, and discourage all ungodliness; and shall endeavour with the other justices of the peace that the laws against drunkenness, blaspheming and taking of the name of God in vain, by swearing and cursing, plays and interludes, and profaning the Lord's Day, and such-like abominations, be put in more effectual execution …*

*19 All gaming houses and houses of evil fame [brothels] be sought out and suppressed …*

*21 All alehouses, taverns and victualling houses towards the outskirts of the said cities be suppressed.*

**SOURCE QUESTION**

What impression do the Instructions in Source F give of Cromwell's expectations of the rule of the Major-Generals?

**ONLINE EXTRAS** **WWW**
**OCR**

Test your understanding of source utility by completing Worksheet 29 at **www. hoddereducation.co.uk/ accesstohistory/extras**

The most striking aspect of the work of the Major-Generals was the introduction of the decimation tax. The measure was intended both to prevent further risings, such as Penruddock's (see page 184), and to provide finance for the Major-Generals, who had the authority to raise local troops in order to maintain the army's strength. It was hoped that the new tax would thus be the means of both preserving a powerful standing army and avoiding a heavy charge on central government funds.

Although, for the sake of convenience, historians have tended to treat the rule of the Major-Generals as if it were a single system, the type of administration in each of the twelve districts depended very much on how the individual Major-General chose to carry out his instructions. For example, while Kelsey, Whalley and Worsley (who is reputed to have closed down over 200 alehouses) were renowned for their sense of duty, Gough frankly acknowledged that he was not up to the task.

## Unpopularity of the Major-Generals

What appears to have made the Major-Generals especially unpopular was their interference with everyday life in the localities, especially their attempt, in accordance with Instruction 6, to impose moral behaviour on the inhabitants. Moreover, their military rank could not disguise the fact that they were of a lower social status than the local gentry over whom they had been placed. For magistrates and officials who functioned in what was very much a traditional hierarchical order, the intrusion of social upstarts into the conduct of affairs was particularly distasteful.

An additional irritant was that few of the Major-Generals were local to the area they controlled. This created a strong feeling among the people in the communities that they were now subject to outside rule. One of the features of mid-seventeenth-century England was that local loyalties predominated over national ones. People's first thoughts were for their own local concerns. Consequently, when intrusive government was imposed from outside, no matter how well intentioned or efficient it might be, it offended local feelings. It was this that made it so difficult for the rule of the Major-Generals to gain acceptance.

## The limited power of the Major-Generals

The strictness of their rule and the resentment it aroused have been customarily taken as proof of the Major-Generals' effectiveness as centralising administrators. However, the evidence suggests that, during the 1650s, local institutions continued to function in the traditional way, regardless of the political changes that took place at the centre. Magistrates' courts operated as they had done before the civil wars. In any case, Cromwell had no wish to undermine the authority of the leaders in the communities; it would have suited him far better if the Major-Generals could have established harmonious relations with the local gentry. However, if that was the intention, it failed since the system had begun to founder on the rock of local resistance long before Cromwell lost faith in it.

## Failure of the Major-Generals as a system of rule

Given that Cromwell had at his disposal a large and godly army, it made sense for him to use it as an instrument for the creation of a godly nation. He claimed in a speech to Parliament in September 1656 that the Major-Generals had been 'very effectual towards the discountenancing of vice and settling religion, than anything else these fifty years'. This was wishful thinking; religion had not been settled. Furthermore, the unpopularity that the regime had aroused outweighed whatever individual successes might have been achieved. Although it had not been Cromwell's intention, the rule of the Major-Generals had challenged the independence of the local gentry; it had imposed taxes and raised local militia with little reference to the opinion of the leaders in the community. In the parliamentary elections, held in the summer of 1656, the protest slogan 'no swordsmen, no decimators' was widely voiced, an indication of how unpopular the Major-Generals had become.

As a system of control, the Major-Generals were not part of the *Instrument of Government*. They were intended to fill the gap before the next Parliament. They did not, therefore, take Cromwell any nearer to solving the problem of how to achieve stable, non-military rule. Indeed, it seemed even clearer that stability and order depended wholly on his military authority.

## Financial problems

It was also the case that the Major-Generals had not eased the Protectorate's financial burdens. As with the Stuarts before him, Cromwell found it difficult to run the government on the income he was granted by his various Parliaments. It was not that he was unduly extravagant. Although his wife and daughters lived in some style, Cromwell's Protectorate court at Whitehall was certainly not lavish by royal standards. He himself lived relatively frugally. Nonetheless, the administrative and military costs of the Protectorate were high. A parliamentary report in 1655 revealed that the government's annual revenue, made up from such sources as customs and excise, assessments and fines on royalists, amounted to £2,250,000, whereas expenditure was £2,611,532. The deficit was increased by the added costs of the **Spanish War** that began in 1654. It was the necessity of raising extra finance that led Cromwell to call another Parliament.

**KEY TERM**

**Spanish War** Fought between England and Spain, 1654–8, principally over colonial possessions in the Caribbean, but climaxing with the English victory at the Battle of the Dunes (Dunkirk) in 1658.

---

**SUMMARY DIAGRAM**

**THE MAJOR-GENERALS 1655–7**

**The role of the Major-Generals**
- Appointed in 11 regions to exercise military control and run local government
- To promote 'godliness and virtue' in public life
- Key role in imposing decimation tax to fund the army
- Quality of administration depended on ability and commitment of individual Major-Generals

**Causes of unpopularity of the Major-Generals**
- Interference with everyday life in the localities
- Upstart status
- Challenge to traditional hierarchical order
- Affront to localism
- Slogan 'no swordsmen, no decimators' expressed local resentment

**Limited power of the Major-Generals**
- Local institutions continued to function in the traditional way
- Unpopularity of their regime outweighed successes achieved
- Major-Generals had challenged the independence of the local gentry

**Without**
- Providing answers to Protectorate's political and religious problems
- Only ever intended to fill the gap between Parliaments

The Protectorate's financial burdens were not eased by the Major-Generals

---

# 6 The later Protectorate 1656–8

■ *Why did Cromwell decline the offer of kingship?*

Cromwell's decision to summon a new Parliament, a year earlier than was required under the *Instrument*, had been prompted by the need to raise money and by the guarantee he received from the Major-Generals they would make sure the elections returned only cooperative members.

# The second Protectorate Parliament 1656–7

It was certainly true that greater efforts were made to shape the composition of the House than at the time of the first Protectorate Parliament. When the new Parliament met in September 1656, 100 members were declared ineligible and prevented from taking their seats. The early signs were that this purge had produced the desired result, since the first months of the session were relatively quiet. Cromwell congratulated the members on their ready attention to business and their willingness to provide money for the Spanish War. However, it was not long before friction developed.

The first major difficulty arose over the House's prosecution of the Quaker James Nayler for blasphemy. This was a matter in which Parliament, in Cromwell's judgement, had exceeded its powers (see page 182). It was against this background of strained relations between Protector and Parliament that the second crisis of the session occurred. In January 1657, John Desborough, the main spokesman for the Major-Generals, introduced a bill to renew the decimation tax for the maintenance of the militia in the counties. Since the upkeep of the Major-Generals depended on this tax, to vote against the bill was to vote against their regime. This is precisely what Parliament proceeded to do.

## The end of the Major-Generals

The defeat of Desborough's militia bill marked the effective end of the Major-Generals as a system of government. Cromwell's reaction was angry, but his anger was directed as much against the Major-Generals for advising him to call Parliament in the first place as against the MPs who had opposed the bill. He did not formally abandon the system of Major-Generals; it was simply allowed to lapse.

That Cromwell did nothing to save the system pointed to the ambiguous position in which he now found himself. Support for him at this point came from two main sources. One obvious group was the army leaders, such as the Major-Generals, who saw him as their representative, the guarantor of national security and strong government. Their experience ever since the civil wars had made them suspicious of all Parliaments, which they regarded as self-seeking oligarchies rather than as guardians of liberty and the constitution. The second group has been identified by modern historians as the 'new Cromwellians', defined as those in public life who wished to see the Protectorate become an essentially civilian government, independent of the military.

# The new Cromwellians

This group included important military figures such as General Monck, Cromwell's commander in Scotland (see page 207), and Lord Broghill, a one-time royalist but now a staunch friend and confidant of the Protector. However, it was largely composed of civilian politicians; leading lawyers such as Bulstrode Whitelock and William Lenthall were prominent among them. These men were traditionalists in that they believed in the virtues of the old constitution and the social order, but they were sufficiently flexible to accept that the Protectorate could be reshaped so as to incorporate the social and political values that they prized. They held that the more Cromwell was able to distance himself from the military, the closer the Protectorate would move towards being an acceptable system of government.

## The offer of kingship 1657

The new Cromwellians formalised their views in a document which eventually became known as the *Humble Petition and Advice*. This was an alternative written constitution to the *Instrument of Government* and was offered to Cromwell in March 1657. It proposed that Cromwell:

- become king
- be granted adequate finance
- rule with a restored Privy Council
- govern with regular Parliaments that would include an upper House.

This proposed renewal of kingship was meant not to extend Cromwell's authority but to limit it. What was envisaged was not the absolute monarchy which the Stuarts had tried to exercise before 1640, but a constitutional monarchy in which Parliament would be an equal and permanent partner.

One aspect of the *Humble Petition and Advice* certainly attracted Cromwell. Since the offer of the new constitution had come from Parliament, it would have a validity and legality that the *Instrument*, the creation of the Army Council, had lacked. He certainly gave the offer much thought. This is evident from a number of contemporary accounts. As early as 1652, Cromwell, in private conversation, had spoken of the attractions of monarchy, whose traditional power could be used 'to curb the insolences of those whom the present powers cannot control'.

During the spring of 1657, rumours that Cromwell was seriously considering becoming king led to a series of petitions from the army officers urging him to reject such a course. They appealed to him to remain faithful to 'the good old cause'. After weeks of discussion and soul-searching, which he described as causing him great 'consternation of spirit', Cromwell finally informed Parliament in April that he had decided not to accept the title of king. He offered the following reason:

**ONLINE EXTRAS**
**OCR**

Test your understanding of sources by completing Worksheet 30 at **www. hoddereducation.co.uk/ accesstohistory/extras**

---

**SOURCE G**

From Cromwell's response to Parliament's offer of kingship, April 1657, quoted in John Towill Rutt, editor, *Diary of Thomas Burton Esq: Volume 2, April 1657–February 1658*, H. Colburn, 1828, p. 493.

*It was said that kingship is not a title, but an office; so interwoven with the fundamental laws of the nation that they cannot, or cannot well, be executed and exercised without it. I cannot take upon me to repel these grounds; for they are strong and rational. Truly the providences of God hath laid aside this title of king providentially and this not by sudden humour or passion; but it hath been by issue*

---

**SOURCE QUESTION** ❓

For what reasons, as stated in Source G, does Cromwell decline the offer of kingship?

> *of as great deliberation as ever was in a nation. It hath been the issue of ten or twelve years civil war wherein much blood hath been shed I will not seek to set up that that Providence hath destroyed and laid in the dust.*

Cromwell had chosen to stay loyal to what the army leaders called 'the good old cause'. Yet Cromwell's rejection of kingship was not a rejection of the proposed new constitution itself. In May, he duly accepted the *Humble Petition* in a modified form. He was to remain 'His Highness, the Lord Protector Oliver' and was empowered to name his successor and to appoint the members of the 'Other' (upper) House. For some, this was kingship by another name. Edmund Ludlow, an ardent republican and representative of those Commonwealthsmen who had been suspicious of Cromwell's aims ever since his dissolution of the Rump in 1653, regarded the revised version of the *Humble Petition* as merely the climax of a Cromwellian plot to extend the Protector's powers still further.

This now seems a harsh verdict. Cromwell's acceptance of the new constitution suggests his anxiety to arrive at a settlement that would unite the whole nation. It is striking how often the word 'settlement' figured in his letters and speeches around this time. For example, addressing a parliamentary committee in April 1657, he said: 'I would rather I were in my grave than hinder you on anything that may be for settlement. I am hugely taken with the word Settlement. A nation is like a house, it cannot stand without settlement.'

## Cromwell's position as Protector

Cromwell's acceptance of the new constitution in 1657 represented a compromise. He had strengthened the civilian base of the Protectorate, but the army still remained the major force within it. This was clear in the way Cromwell used his authority as Protector to appoint a large number of his officer colleagues to seats in the Other House. Since this upper chamber of 40 members had the right to veto legislation, this gave it considerable power. Republicans were swift to condemn an arrangement which subordinated the will of Parliament to the whim of the army. They complained that the *Humble Petition and Advice* was no more than a tinkering with the existing system. It left Cromwell and the army in control.

At the end of July 1657, a month after Cromwell's second formal installation as Protector, Parliament went into recess. Already there were signs that the adoption of the *Humble Petition* had not solved Cromwell's problems. He was obliged to dismiss John Lambert, his long-standing colleague and the creator of the *Instrument of Government*, from the Privy Council for refusing to take the oath of loyalty to the new constitution. It may well be that Lambert acted out of career aims, hoping that by detaching himself from the new constitutional arrangements he would be in a strong position should they prove unworkable. But whatever Lambert's personal motives, the incident indicated that Cromwell had failed in his aim of establishing a government sufficiently representative to be widely acceptable.

**SOURCE H**

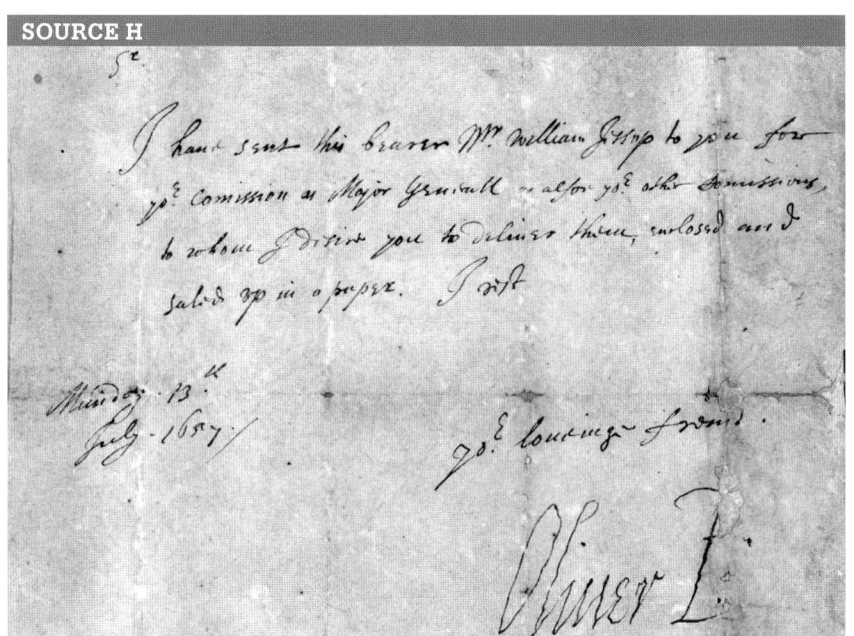

Cromwell's letter dismissing John Lambert, 13 July 1657. The text reads: 'Sir, I have sent this bearer Mr William Jessop to you for your commission as Major General as also your other commissions to whom I desire you to deliver them enclosed and sealed within a paper. Your loving friend, Oliver P[rotector].'

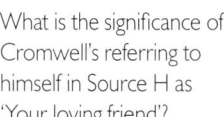

**SOURCE QUESTION**

What is the significance of Cromwell's referring to himself in Source H as 'Your loving friend'?

## Second session of Parliament, January to February 1658

The House of Commons that reassembled in January 1658 was markedly different from the one that had gone into recess six months earlier. The members who had been excluded at the beginning of the first session in September 1656 had returned. Most of these were republicans. They had been debarred originally on the grounds that they were 'unfit' persons as defined by the *Instrument of Government*. But now that a new constitution had been adopted that technicality could no longer be invoked by the government to keep them out. Their return was an important victory for the republicans. Led by Arthur Haselrig, who believed that all government had been illegitimate since the dissolution of the Rump, they launched into an attack on the new constitution. Among their targets were the authority of the Protector, the power of the army and high taxation.

Cromwell's difficulties were increased by the depletion of his supporters in the lower House, the most able of whom he had transferred to the Other House. Fearing that the parliamentary onslaught might lead to his political and religious enemies combining, he decided to end the sitting. His particular reason for dissolving Parliament after a session of less than a month was to prevent it from considering a republican petition that called for the abandonment of the

Protectorate and the restoration of the Rump. Cromwell's deepest worry was that the petition was rumoured to have found favour with some of the troops.

# Cromwell's record as Lord Protector

Cromwell was in a paradoxical position as Protector. He was heir to a revolution but he was not a revolutionary:

- In all that he did as Protector, he favoured traditional forms. His basic political approach was one of caution. This is well illustrated by his rejection of the offer of the crown, even though he believed that the best system for England was one that 'had something monarchical in it'.

- He always sought to work within the constitution as he understood it. He accepted the *Instrument of Government* and the *Humble Petition and Advice*, which placed him under certain constraints.

- He depended on military power, but was reluctant to use it to impose himself on the nation as a dictator.

- He occupied a halfway position. Having been instrumental in removing the Stuart monarchy, he was then unwilling to go further and create an entirely new system.

- Although he was prepared to use force, as in his dissolution of the Rump, it was always as a last resort. When faced by the widespread unpopularity created by the rule of the Major-Generals, he abandoned the experiment.

Cromwell's greatest problem as Protector remained one of finance. The annual income of £1,300,000 that he had been granted under the *Humble Petition* fell short of his governmental costs by £500,000. As had Charles I before him, he found it increasingly difficult to raise loans from the City. That was no doubt why he drew up plans for the calling of another Parliament later in 1658, plans that were never implemented since he died on 3 September.

## His ambiguous position

Cromwell's position as Protector meant that he got the worst of both worlds. On the one hand, he lacked the authority and public acceptance associated with traditional monarchy; on the other, he never pushed his authority to the point where he had absolute power. What added to the ambiguity of his position was that as Protector he was the hope of many who had supported the parliamentary cause since 1640 to create a new order in Church and State. Cromwell's disinclination to follow a radical path when in office deeply disappointed them. He was accused of being both a hypocrite and a turncoat.

'He doth smile and smile even while he smites thee under the fifth rib.' So said a Leveller pamphlet in 1649 by way of illustrating Cromwell's treachery. To those, such as the Levellers and republicans, who found Cromwell's government to be a tyranny both in concept and in practice, his hypocrisy was self-evident. However, for those who understood the difficulties in which Cromwell found himself as Lord Protector, the charge of hypocrisy did not stand. They saw him as being faced with insuperable problems in a time of uncertainty and discord.

## His opportunism

What has to be remembered is that Cromwell was so involved with the everyday running of government that he had little time to develop an overall policy. It is doubtful whether Cromwell really knew his own intentions very far ahead. He was essentially an opportunist, who justified his actions after the event by reference to the Lord's will. He is recorded as saying that, 'he climbs not so high as he who knows not wither he goeth'. Historian Gerald Aylmer, writing in the 1990s, sums him up neatly as 'a pragmatist who waited on providence'.

This did not mean that Cromwell was without broad aims. He wanted a godly commonwealth and a 'reformation of manners', by which he meant that in public affairs moral considerations should determine policy. In social terms, he was very much a conservative. He wanted the traditional strata of society to remain: 'a nobility, a gentry and a yeomanry – that is a good estate', he observed. In religion, he appealed for what he called 'liberty for tender consciences', the right of individuals, provided they were not papists or blasphemers, to worship God freely as they saw fit without having to conform to the dictates of an organised Church.

## Cromwell: a tyrant?

It is the broadness of these aims that is most notable. He seldom translated them into clear and specific programmes. Most of his time as Protector was spent trying to control the excessive demands of others. His dissolutions of Parliament were usually on the grounds that it had exceeded its authority or was making demands that threatened the balance on which order depended. However, he could not escape the reality of his position. He was Protector because he was head of the army. Try as he might to restore effective civilian government, his authority was basically military. Yet, given the power he held, he was very sparing in its use. In a number of remarkable respects Oliver Cromwell's personal rule was the opposite of tyranny. He tried to make Parliament representative, and to give it a genuine role in the constitution. This is an aspect that impresses modern scholars. Aylmer observes: 'Cromwell had both commanded sufficient following and respect to enable the processes of government … to continue, and had successfully set about giving his rule a civilian base.'

However, no matter how genuinely fair-minded and tolerant Cromwell's policies were, he was in a position to introduce them only because of his military strength. He may have been reluctant to use force, but this could not disguise the fact that he retained the power to do so. As Derek Hirst, writing in the 1990s, has pointed out: 'He [Cromwell] craved a parliamentary settlement which would secure the liberty of "men as men"; yet he had also fought for liberty for the Christian conscience, and only the army could guarantee the latter'.

## Cromwell's legacy

When Cromwell became Protector in 1653, he had faced a number of demanding questions:

- How was a stable executive government to be created to replace traditional monarchy?
- What was to be the place of Parliament?
- Was the army to continue to play a political role?
- How was government to be effectively financed?
- How were the religious differences in the nation to be settled?

At his death on 3 September 1658, these issues remained largely unresolved. Some sceptics have suggested that it was never his intention to resolve them, that his essential aim was to wield power, not to reach settlements. Many contemporaries held that view and it has been restated periodically ever since. However, most modern historians incline to the view that to regard Cromwell simply as a military leader exercising authority for its own sake is to ignore the strength of his religious and political motivation. Even though he did not achieve his aims, there is no reason to doubt the sincerity of his desire to reach a just and godly settlement of the nation's problems.

There will obviously never be a final verdict on Oliver Cromwell, but it would be appropriate to end a study of him by quoting the words of two distinguished historians, one a royalist contemporary of his, the other a modern authority (see Sources I and J, below).

**SOURCE QUESTION**

In Source I, how does Clarendon balance Cromwell's virtues and failings?

### SOURCE I

From the Earl of Clarendon, *The History of the Rebellion and Civil Wars*, 1702.

*As he had all the wickedness against which damnation is denounced, and for which hell-fire is prepared, so he had some virtues which have caused the memory of some men in all ages to be celebrated; and he will be looked upon by posterity as a brave bad man.*

**SOURCE QUESTION**

In Source J, what does the writer mean by saying that Cromwell was 'preoccupied with ends and not with means'?

### SOURCE J

From John Morrill, *Revolution and Restoration*, Collins & Brown, 1992, p. 13.

*He sought to justify himself and the Revolution he led by appeals to a glorious future. It was this that made him so preoccupied with ends and not with means, and this in turn justified his disregard for civil rights whenever anyone or anything stood in the way of what he took to be God's purpose.*

**SUMMARY DIAGRAM**

## THE LATER PROTECTORATE 1656–8

---

**Second Protectorate Parliament 1656–8**
**First session 1656**

- Criticised Cromwell and Major-Generals
- The Nayler case showed basic difference between Cromwell and Parliament
- Cromwell allowed rule of Major-Generals to lapse
- New Cromwellians pressed for return to independent civilian rule

---

**Second session 1658**

- *Humble Petition and Advice*
- Offered Cromwell the crown

**But**

- Although tempted Cromwell declined it
- Remained loyal to 'good old cause'
- Protectorate permanently short of money
- Republicans and sectaries attacked new constitution
- Cromwell died with constitutional issue unsettled
- Cromwell's record as Protector
- His legacy

---

# CHAPTER SUMMARY

Believing that a Parliament still offered the best form of government, Oliver Cromwell summoned a Nominated Assembly in 1653, selecting the MPs on the grounds of their supposed godliness. However, within a short time, the obstructiveness of the extreme sectaries led to its dissolution. The next experiment involved Cromwell's becoming Lord Protector under the terms of a written constitution, the *Instrument of Government*. But the republican MPs in the Protectorate Parliament, challenging the legitimacy of his position and of the constitution itself, declined to pass any of the ordinances by which he tried to govern. Parliament was dissolved early in 1655, after just five months' sitting.

Prompted by his dealings with the sectaries, Cromwell persisted with the idea of establishing godly rule. He turned to the expedient of governing through Major-Generals but these ran up against the resentment of the local establishments and Cromwell allowed the system to lapse. After much deliberation, he rejected the offer of kingship but continued as Lord Protector under a new constitution, the *Humble Petition and Advice*. At his death, the problems he had confronted remained unresolved, but he left a record of an extraordinary leader guided by a burning conviction that he was God's instrument.

## Refresher questions

Use these questions to remind yourself of the key material covered in this chapter.

1 Why was the Nominated Assembly of 1653 known as the Parliament of the saints?

2 What powers did the *Instrument of Government* confer on Oliver Cromwell?

3 What disputes did Cromwell have with the first Protectorate Parliament?

4 What were the main duties and functions of the Major-Generals in 1655–7?

5 Why did Cromwell allow the rule of the Major-Generals to lapse?

6 What difficulties did Oliver Cromwell encounter in his dealings with the second Protectorate Parliament 1656–8?

7 Why was the Nayler case such a contentious issue between Oliver Cromwell and the second Protectorate Parliament?

8 Who were the new Cromwellians?

9 What differences were there between the *Instrument of Government* and the *Humble Petition and Advice*?

10 Why, despite its attractions, did Oliver Cromwell decline the offer of kingship in 1657?

11 Why did Cromwell dissolve the second Protectorate Parliament in 1658?

12 What political problems were left unresolved at the time of Oliver Cromwell's death in 1658?

# Question practice: OCR

## Source questions

**1** Study Sources A (page 173), C (page 180) and D (page 180) and then answer both questions. [AS level]

  **a)** Use your knowledge of the religious issues during the civil wars and the Protectorate to assess how useful Source C is as evidence of Oliver Cromwell's attitude towards the religious sects.

**EXAM HINT** Explain in what ways Source C provides evidence of his attitude. Also consider the provenance of the source and link this to contextual knowledge to test the view of the source and then reach a judgement as to the usefulness of the source.

  **b)** Using the three sources in their historical context, assess how far they support the view that Oliver Cromwell in religious matters believed in liberty of conscience.

**EXAM HINT** Group the sources according to whether they support the view in the question. Each source should be explained in relation to the question, its provenance evaluated and contextual knowledge used to test the view of the source. A judgement about each source should be reached allowing an overall judgement about whether Cromwell believed in liberty of conscience.

**2** Using Sources A (page 173), C (page 180), D (page 180) and F (page 187) in their historical context, assess how far they support the view that Oliver Cromwell was seeking to establish godly rule in England. [A level]

**EXAM HINT** Group the sources according to whether they support the view in the question. Each source should be explained in relation to the question, its provenance evaluated and contextual knowledge used to test the view of the source. A judgement about each source should be reached allowing an overall judgement about whether Cromwell was seeking to establish godly rule in England.

**3** Using Sources 1–4 (below) in their historical context, assess how far they support the view that Cromwell's aim during the Interregnum was to enforce his own authoritarian rule. [A level]

**EXAM HINT** Group the sources according to whether they support the view in the question. Each source should be explained in relation to the question, its provenance evaluated and contextual knowledge used to test the view of the source. A judgement about each source should be reached allowing an overall judgement about whether Cromwell's aim was to enforce his own authoritarian rule.

### SOURCE 1

**Cromwell is impeached by Lilburne for high treason. From John Lilburne, June 1649.**

*An Impeachment of HIGH TREASON against Oliver Cromwell, and his Son in Law Henry Ireton Esquires, late members of the forcibly dissolved House of Commons, presented by Lieutenant Colonel John Lilburne.*

*In which the following Impeachment [is based] either upon the principles of Law (by way of indictment, the only legal way of all trials in England) or upon the principles of Parliaments ancient proceedings (by pretence of which they lately took away the King's life).*

*… the said Oliver Cromwell [is] guilty of the highest Treason that ever was acted in England, and more deserving punishment and death.*

---

**SOURCE 2**

Cromwell dissolves the Rump Parliament, April 1653. The Memoirs of Edmund Ludlow

*[Cromwell] sat still for about a quarter of an hour, and then, suddenly standing up, he made a speech, wherein he loaded the Parliament with the vilest reproaches, accusing them of an intention to perpetuate themselves in power. This he spoke with such passion and discomposure of mind, as if he had been distracted … [He] stepped into the midst of the House, where continuing his distracted language, he said 'Come, come, I will put an end to your prating'; then walking up and down the House like a mad-man, and kicking the ground, he cried out, 'You are no Parliament, I say you are no Parliament; I will put an end to your sitting; call them in; whereupon two files of musketeers entered the House.*

---

**SOURCE 3**

The Venetian Ambassador doubts Cromwell's sincerity. From a report by Giovanni Sagredo, 1656.

*While in general he displays a most exemplary exterior, yet it cannot be known what rite he follows. In the late troubles he professed himself an Anabaptist. This cult denies sovereignty and claims obedience to God alone, and to these Independents belonged the majority of the parliament that passed judgement on the King. The moment Cromwell was elevated to power, he not only broke off from the Independents, but condemned and persecuted them. Thus he has changed his creed in accordance with the interests of the state. It suits his policy that 246 religions should be professed in London. The division into so many makes them all weak, so that no one is strong enough to cause him apprehension.*

---

**SOURCE 4**

Cromwell's response to Parliament's offer of kingship in a letter of April 1657.

*It was said that kingship is not a title, but an office, so interwoven with the fundamental laws of the nation that they cannot, or cannot well, be executed and exercised without it. I cannot take upon me to repel these grounds; for they are strong and rational. But if I shall be able to make any answer to them, I must not grant that they are necessarily conclusive: Truly the providences of God hath laid aside this title of king providentially and this not by sudden humour or passion; but it hath been by issue of as great deliberation as ever was in a nation. It hath been the issue of ten or twelve years civil war wherein much blood hath been shed I will not seek to set up that that Providence hath destroyed and laid in the dust.*

# CHAPTER 8

# From Protectorate to Restoration 1658–60

Great uncertainty followed Oliver Cromwell's death. Much as the civilian and religious groups may have disliked the dominance of the Protectorate by the military, even Cromwell's opponents acknowledged that as long as he was Lord Protector, disorder had been contained. But with his passing nothing was certain any more. The ensuing twists and turns that led to the Restoration twenty months later are examined under the following headings:

◆ Richard Cromwell's Protectorate, September 1658 to April 1659

◆ The restored Commonwealth, May to December 1659

◆ The path to the Restoration, December 1659 to May 1660

◆ Reasons for the failure of the republic by 1660

The key debate on page 219 asks the question: What was the legacy of the English Revolution of 1640–60?

## KEY DATES

| | | | | | |
|---|---|---|---|---|---|
| **1658** | **Sept.** | Death of Oliver Cromwell | **1660** | **Feb.** | Monck's troops reached London |
| | | Richard Cromwell became Protector | | | Rump dissolved |
| **1659** | **Jan.–April** | Third Protectorate Parliament | | | Long Parliament restored |
| | | | | **April–May** | Convention Parliament |
| | **April** | Richard Cromwell resigned – end of the Protectorate | | **April** | House of Lords reconvened |
| | **May** | Rump reassembled | | | Charles II issued Declaration of Breda |
| | **Aug.** | Booth's rising | | | Both Houses voted to accept Declaration of Breda |
| | **Oct.** | The army expelled the Rump | | **May 8** | Charles II proclaimed king |
| | **Oct.–Dec.** | Government by Committee of Safety | | **May 29** | Charles II entered London |
| | **Dec.** | Rump reassembled | | | |

# 1 | Richard Cromwell's Protectorate, September 1658 to April 1659

■ *Why was there a political vacuum after the death of Oliver Cromwell?*

■ *Why was Richard Cromwell's Protectorship so short lived?*

In September 1658, under the terms of the *Humble Petition and Advice*, Richard Cromwell duly succeeded his father as Lord Protector and commander-in-chief. Richard's besetting weakness was that he was not a genuine solider. Hitherto, he had lived as a country squire, showing little aptitude for either military or political affairs. As Protector, he now found himself thrust deeply into both. Unlike his father, he could not call on the natural loyalty of the army. This left him only one recourse, to turn towards the civilian elements in government.

## The political vacuum following Oliver Cromwell's death

Great as Oliver Cromwell's difficulties had been, he had managed to preserve an uneasy balance between the demands of army, the religious radicals and the traditionalists. But he had been able to do this only through his personal authority and power. The permanence he had sought had eluded him. He had not created the new form of self-sustaining civilian government that he so much desired. Consequently, Richard Cromwell inherited a power vacuum in which four main political groupings vied for authority:

■ the army

■ the republicans

■ the Presbyterians

■ the radical sectaries.

To these could be added a fifth element, the royalists. Although they had been subdued during the rule of Oliver Cromwell, his death and the inexperience of the new Protector encouraged them into action again. What gave the royalists hope was that the Presbyterians, who had been disturbed by the disruptive notions among the sectaries, had become more reactionary in their attitude. The Presbyterians had never been wholly reconciled to the republic, largely because the religious settlement they had hoped for had not materialised. They were quite prepared, therefore, to consider alliance with the royalists, not out of love for monarchy, but because the alternative was social disorder and religious factionalism.

Another important political factor was the lack of unity in the army:

- **Charles Fleetwood** and a number of the senior officers wished to maintain the Protectorate, since, with a diffident Protector, they felt they would be able to control the situation.

- The lower ranks tended to side with the sectaries, who were unhappy with a Protector who seemed to have distinct Presbyterian sympathies. This grouping of soldiers and sectaries called for a return to the pre-Protectorate days of 1653 and a reinstating of the Rump Parliament.

## Richard Cromwell as Protector

How sincere Richard Cromwell's Presbyterianism was is difficult to judge, but his uneasy relationship with the army certainly led him to rely increasingly on civilian advisers of a conservative outlook. The difficulty of Richard's relations with the military soon showed itself when they urged him to give up his position as commander-in-chief. At first he refused, which brought fierce criticism from the leading generals, **John Desborough** and Charles Fleetwood. Richard tried to counterbalance this by cultivating the more sympathetic officers. He had some success; Edward Whalley and William Gough, who had ruled as Major-Generals in 1655, and George Monck (see page 207) were some of the more notable officers who sided with Richard.

However, the bulk of the army was not to be won over. There was still deep resentment over the perennial problem of arrears; the total owed to the troops was £900,000. The problem was the Protectorate could not pay; it was in debt to the tune of £2,500,000. Its expenditure ran far ahead of its revenue, a problem made worse by the widespread economic depression that England experienced in the late 1650s. Richard's only recourse was to call Parliament in order to raise money.

## The third Protectorate Parliament, January to April 1659

Given the conflicting opinions it represented, Parliament was unlikely to prove cooperative towards Richard:

- In a House of 549 members, pro-Protectorate conservatives were in a majority.

- Unfortunately for Richard, the republican minority proved much more active and vocal; it launched a series of attacks on the legitimacy of the Protectorate. The republicans' main aim was to arouse support among the army.

- Fearing that such tactics would increase the military's influence, the Presbyterian members of Parliament (MPs) attempted to undermine the army's power. They introduced a resolution that the Council of Officers should sit only with the permission of Parliament. They also voted to take the command of the local militia out of the hands of the army and bring it under direct parliamentary control. Officers and ranks united in the face of this and demanded that the Protector dissolve Parliament.

**KEY FIGURES**

**Charles Fleetwood (1618–92)**

Fought for Parliament at Naseby; married Oliver Cromwell's daughter in 1652; Lord Lieutenant in Ireland 1652–5, one of Oliver Cromwell's Major-Generals; a member of the Committee of Safety in 1659; debarred from public office after the Restoration.

**John Desborough (1608–80)**

Related by marriage to the Cromwell family; fought against the royalists but avoided any involvement in the king's trial and execution; one of Oliver Cromwell's Major-Generals; imprisoned after the Restoration, but later exonerated.

■ Richard resisted, but when he learned that England was on the verge of an army insurrection, he eventually gave way and did as he was told.

Little was now left of his authority. It was clear that he wanted to move towards a predominantly civilian administration by reducing the influence of the army, but it was equally clear that the military would not allow this. With Parliament dissolved against Richard's wishes, power was effectively back in the hands of the Army Council, which was prepared to allow the Protectorate to continue, provided it left the army in charge. However, in order to make their power appear somewhat less stark, the Council recommended the recalling of the Rump, a move that was highly pleasing to the republicans, who felt that their agitation was having an effect.

# End of the Protectorate

The Rump reassembled in May 1659. The end of the Protectorate was not long delayed. Richard Cromwell, having tried unavailingly to summon loyal troops from Ireland and Scotland, resigned and withdrew from public life. Three factors explain his failure as Protector:

■ his inability to fashion a government free of army control

■ the strength of the republican campaign against the Protectorate

■ the financial bankruptcy of his government.

Richard Cromwell was not especially incompetent, but effective government in the political vacuum created by his father's death required a leader of extraordinary talent. Richard Cromwell was not extraordinary; he was a stolid, honest, squire, who lacked the political skills that the times demanded.

---

**SUMMARY DIAGRAM**

**RICHARD CROMWELL'S PROTECTORATE, SEPTEMBER 1658 TO APRIL 1659**

**Cromwell's legacy**
- Richard dependent on the army
- Faced by five main political groups:

| • Army | • Republicans | • Presbyterians | • Radical sectaries | • Royalists |

**Army split**
- Senior officers sided with Presbyterians          • Lower ranks pro-sectaries

Richard short of money and was unable to manage army, so was obliged to call:

**Third Protectorate Parliament 1659**
- Clash between Presbyterians and army
- Army pressured Richard into dissolving Parliament
- Rump recalled in May 1659

Marked end of Richard's Protectorate

# 2 The restored Commonwealth, May to December 1659

■ *Why were neither the royalists nor the religious and political radicals able to exploit the situation to their advantage?*

■ *What role did General George Monck play?*

The resurrected Rump soon showed itself to be the same in character and attitude as when it had been dispersed six years earlier.

## The restored Rump, May to October 1659

Declaring that its restoration marked the return of a 'Commonwealth without a king, single person, or house of lords', the Rump proceeded to act as if the events of the intervening six years had never taken place. It claimed legitimacy as the only authority representing constitutional continuity. The army was told that its duty was to obey the Parliament it had restored. The faint possibility of this happening disappeared when the army leaders learned that the Rump had no intention of considering their requests for reform. A particular point of contention was the Rump's refusal to vote funds for the troops' arrears of pay. The truth was that Rump and army regarded each other as no more than a regrettable necessity. The Rump knew that to preserve itself in troubled times an army was necessary to maintain the peace. For its part, the army appreciated that the Rump served to clothe what would otherwise be recognised as naked military rule.

### Resurgent radicalism

The irony was that in the country at large the Rump was thought to be too radical. What encouraged this idea was that in a number of counties the restored Rump had tried to curb the influence of the army by deliberately putting the local militia into the hands of the extreme sectaries, including Fifth Monarchists, Quakers and Baptists. This strange development excited fears of a takeover by the religious fanatics. There were even rumours that the Levellers were reorganising (see page 138). The outpouring of pamphlets in 1659 gave the superficial impression that the radical forces were much stronger than they were. It was this that frightened the conservatives into retreating further towards a restoration of the old constitution.

Something approaching national panic occurred. There was talk of Church and State being under threat from radical forces. It was in this disturbed atmosphere that a series of scattered Presbyterian–royalist risings took place in the summer of 1659. These were less a genuine attempt to restore the Stuart monarchy than an outburst of irritation at what the Rump was allowing to happen. The government acted quickly. Forewarned of the conspiracies, it was able to break them with a series of military strikes.

**KEY FIGURE**

**George Booth
(1622–84)**

Fought for Parliament in the civil wars; MP in the Long Parliament and the Nominated Assembly; his Presbyterian sympathies drew him towards the royalists; arrested after his failed rising in 1659, he was soon released and helped to prepare the way for Charles II's return in 1660.

### Booth's rising

The one serious challenge was in Cheshire, where, in August 1659, Sir **George Booth** held large parts of the county in defiance of the Rump. Booth did not actually call for a return of Charles II, but for a 'free Parliament'. This amounted to much the same thing, since it was now widely held that a freely elected Parliament would be the prelude to a royal restoration. However, that Booth did not openly advocate Charles II's return shows how relatively weak the monarchists still were at this point. It was the disgruntled Presbyterians rather than the royalist supporters of Charles who were making the challenge, thus suggesting that it was more an expression of anti-Rump sentiment than a genuinely pro-Stuart movement. Booth held on for a number of weeks, but his expectation that Spanish troops would arrive to assist him proved unfounded and he eventually surrendered.

## Divisions among the radicals

There now seemed to be an opportunity for the radicals to establish a hold on England. The Presbyterians and their conservative allies had been broken, and the army had again shown itself able to overcome any royalist challenge. However, the following factors seriously weakened the radicals:

- They were too ill-defined a group to constitute a single source of opinion, let alone power.

- The divisions between the religious sectaries, who still hankered after the rule of the saints, and the republicans, who wanted a single-chamber secular Parliament, prevented a unified radical approach.

- There was something very unreal, therefore, about the long debates over possible constitutional change that occupied so much of the Rump's time in the summer and autumn of 1659.

- The truth was that no settlement could satisfy the wide range of political and religious opinions among the radicals. Still more important, no settlement stood a chance of being adopted unless it first met the approval of the army.

## Role of John Lambert

The crushing of Booth's rising had been directed by John Lambert. His success put him back in the political limelight. He became the hero of the rank and file in the army's growing dispute with the Rump. Lambert gave his support to an army petition which demanded that the Rump's authority be reduced by the creation of a Senate (upper House) and that all the army leaders be promoted to the rank of general and confirmed in their command. The petition also insisted that the army be granted authority to purge all those local corporations that had not actively opposed the recent royalist risings.

The Rump interpreted this as a direct attempt by the army to usurp political authority. Arthur Haselrig moved that Lambert and his fellow petitioners be removed and imprisoned. The animosity between Lambert and Haselrig, who were respectively the leading military and civilian republicans, was an indication of how far republicanism was from being a cohesive movement. Haselrig hoped that there were still enough troops faithful to Parliament to prevent an army coup. But he had miscalculated. Retaliation came quickly. In October, regiments loyal to Lambert occupied London and forcibly dissolved the Rump.

## Committee of Safety, October to December 1659

There was now nothing to hide the reality of military rule. The army had previously brought down the Protectorate; it had now broken the remaining link with the old constitution. England was again without a legitimate government. Authority lay with the Council of the Army. In an attempt to give its power the semblance of legality, the Council appointed a 'Committee of Safety', composed of the officers and a few token civilians, to act as an interim government until a more permanent body could be established.

# The role of Monck

The Army Council's dispersal of the Rump had been swift and effective, but it had not won the unanimous support of all the army. This was soon evident in the reaction of General George Monck, destined to become the critical figure in the events leading to the Restoration. Monck protested at the dissolution of the Rump. He negotiated with the members of the expelled House, who offered him the post of commander-in-chief and invited him to bring his army south to London. Monck prepared to do so and issued a justification for his action; he claimed to have received a call from God to march south from Scotland into England 'to assist and maintain the liberty and being of Parliaments, our ancient constitution, and therein the freedom and rights of the people from arbitrary and tyrannical usurpation'.

The Army Council first tried to dissuade Monck from continuing his march. When this failed they despatched Lambert north to intercept him. But Lambert's forces were no match for Monck's in either morale or discipline. They scattered with scarcely a fight.

## Growing disturbances

Monck's protest at the Rump's dissolution and his easy victory over Lambert gave a considerable lift to the forces opposed to army rule. The internal divisions within the army encouraged serious challenges. Widespread disturbances occurred between October and December, notably in Bristol and London. Portsmouth, an important garrison town, declared against the government. So, too, did the navy. It was as if all those unhappy with the prevailing system were now prepared to risk openly challenging it.

The Committee of Safety was taken aback by the sheer scale of the pent-up anger that expressed itself. The seriousness of the disorders in London may be gauged from the following description in Source A (see overleaf).

# George Monck

| | |
|---|---|
| **1608** | Born to a landed Devonshire family |
| **1625–37** | Fought as a mercenary in Europe |
| **1637–41** | Fought for Charles I against rebels in Scotland and Ireland |
| **1642–4** | Fought as a royalist |
| **1644** | Imprisoned by Parliament |
| **1646** | Joined the parliamentary side |
| **1650** | Fought alongside Cromwell in Scotland |
| **1653** | MP in the Nominated Assembly |
| **1654–8** | Commander-in-chief of Parliament's army in Scotland |
| **1659** | Scattered Lambert's forces |
| **1660** | Marched into England to defeat Lambert's republicans |
| | Negotiated with Charles II |
| | Escorted the king to London for his coronation |
| | Became Duke of Albemarle |
| **1670** | Died |

George Monck's colourful public life began in 1625 when he joined the army in order to avoid being arrested for assaulting a county sheriff. He developed his military skills as a mercenary soldier on the Continent. During the English civil wars he fought first for the royalists before changing sides and joining Parliament's forces. In Ireland and Scotland, he fought alongside Cromwell, whom he greatly admired. Left by Cromwell to carry out the settlement of both these countries, Monck proved to be as able an administrator as he was a soldier. On the death of Oliver Cromwell in 1658, Monck supported Richard, believing that a continuation of the Protectorate offered the best chance of stability. But he was never committed to any particular form of settlement purely on grounds of theory. What he wanted was a return of order.

Monck's greatest achievement came in the disturbed period between the end of the Protectorate and the Restoration. His mixture of firmness and political discretion enabled him to keep the republican and religious extremists at bay and to play the role of go-between in the negotiations between Parliament and Charles Stuart. It is difficult to think of any other contemporary who could have matched Monck's achievements. His combination of military strength and political judgement made him an indispensable figure. It is a fascinating irony that it was Monck, a soldier and a Cromwellian, who was chiefly responsible for the restoration of civilian government and monarchy in 1660.

 **SOURCE QUESTION**

According to the description in Source A, who was to blame for the disturbances?

**ONLINE EXTRAS OCR** WWW

Test your understanding of the reliability of a source by completing Worksheet 31 at **www.hoddereducation. co.uk/accesstohistory/extras**

**SOURCE A**

From a London newsletter published in December 1659, quoted in C.H. Firth, editor, *The Clarke Papers*, Longman, 1901, p. 229.

*A petition was on foot by the apprentices to be delivered to the Council, which, coming to the knowledge of the Committee of Safety, they made a Proclamation against it, which was proclaimed yesterday morning in Cheapside by some troopers, who were beaten back by the apprentices, which occasioned the bringing in of all the horse and foot of the army into the City, who came with their swords drawn and pistols cocked against a multitude of naked [unarmed] men, and killed 6 or 7, and wounded more; but that did not quieten them, till about 5 o'clock the Lord Mayor made proclamation that they should all depart, the soldiers being withdrawn, some of them being killed and wounded.*

Protest petitions poured into the Committee of Safety and to the City of London. Monck was also inundated with petitions as he made his way south. The three commonest themes in all of these were:

- the grim economic circumstances of the day
- the tyranny of army rule
- the need for the restoration of ancient liberties through a free Parliament or monarchy.

Source B is an example of how many of the petitions voiced the sense of disillusion among those who found that the defeat of Charles I had brought not harmony but chaos.

### SOURCE B

From a 'Petition of the Gentlemen of Devon to the Committee of Public Safety, December 1659', quoted in Mary Ann Everett Green, editor, *Calendar of State Papers, Domestic Series 1659–60*, Longmans & Co., 1886, p. 331.

*Since the death of the King, we have been governed by tumult; bandied from one faction to the other; this party up today, that tomorrow – but still the nation under, and a prey to, the strongest. So long as this violence continues over us, no other government can settle the nation than that which pleases the universality of it. You speak of the necessity of a republic. We say it is not necessary, not even effectual, but if it were both, a free parliament ought to introduce it. The consent of the people must settle the nation, the public debt must be secured out of the public stock, and interests of opinion and property must be secured by a free parliament.*

**SOURCE QUESTION**

In Source B what is the significance of the petitioners' reference to the 'consent of the people'?

Since the capital was the source of authority and power it mattered hugely what Londoners felt about the condition of England. After all, it had been Parliament's retention of London that had been a key factor in the defeat of the king in the civil wars (see page 124). As indicated in Source C, the clear signs were that London had grown fearful of army rule and wanted a return to genuinely free parliamentary government.

### SOURCE C

From a 'Petition of the Apprentices and Young Men of London', December 1659, quoted in Mary Ann Everett Green, editor, *Calendar of State Papers, Domestic Series 1659–60*, Longmans & Co., 1886, pp. 344–5.

*Our glory and comfort consist in our privileges and liberties, the inheritance of all the free people of England, the grand privilege being free representation in Parliament.*

*This dear privilege has been assaulted by violence and heavy taxes are imposed on men's estates, and new laws without consent of the people in a free Parliament. Trade is decayed and we are like to suffer much.*

*We therefore beseech you … by your zeal to our liberties, by the great renown you have lately gained in opposing the cruel raging of the sword, to use the great advantages God has put into your hands to secure your country from dangerous usurpation and preserve us in the liberties to which we were born.*

**SOURCE QUESTION**

Why are the London petitioners, as stated in Source C, particularly concerned that 'trade is decayed'?

**ONLINE EXTRAS**
**OCR**

Test your understanding of tone and language by completing Worksheet 32 at www.hoddereducation. co.uk/accesstohistory/extras

Rather than face a renewal of civil war, Fleetwood and the army officers bowed before this flood of opposition. They allowed the Rump to reassemble in December 1659. This fulfilled Monck's immediate objective, but he continued his march south.

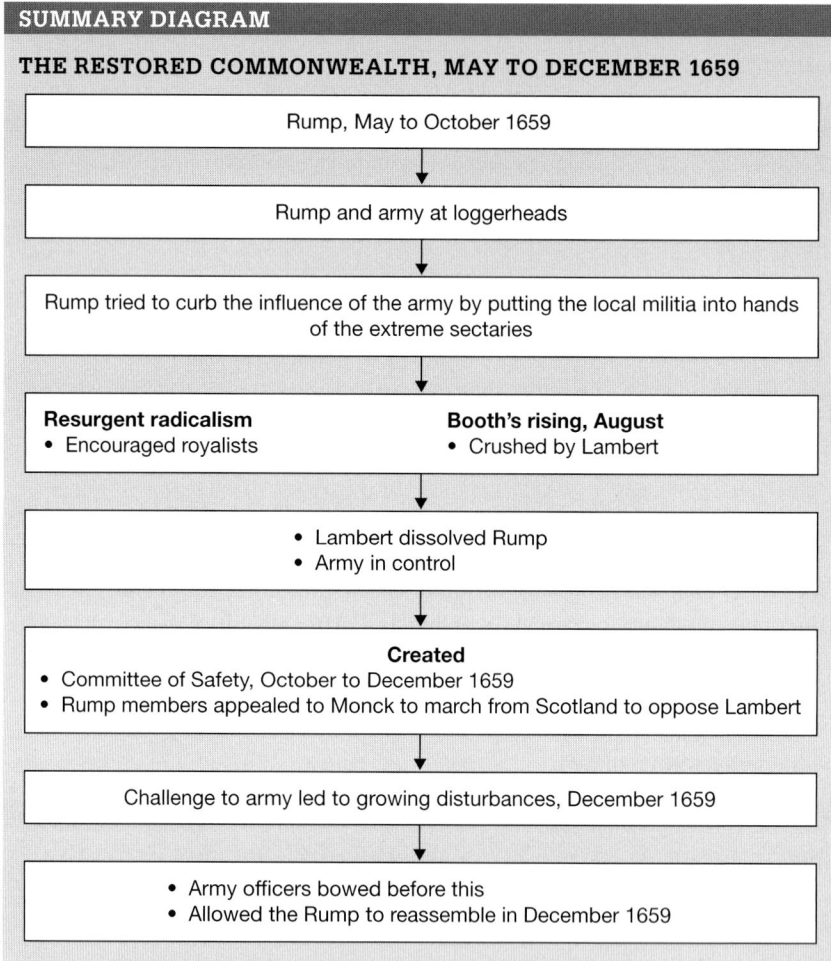

**SUMMARY DIAGRAM**

**THE RESTORED COMMONWEALTH, MAY TO DECEMBER 1659**

> Rump, May to October 1659

> Rump and army at loggerheads

> Rump tried to curb the influence of the army by putting the local militia into hands of the extreme sectaries

> **Resurgent radicalism**
> • Encouraged royalists
>
> **Booth's rising, August**
> • Crushed by Lambert

> • Lambert dissolved Rump
> • Army in control

> **Created**
> • Committee of Safety, October to December 1659
> • Rump members appealed to Monck to march from Scotland to oppose Lambert

> Challenge to army led to growing disturbances, December 1659

> • Army officers bowed before this
> • Allowed the Rump to reassemble in December 1659

# 3 The path to the Restoration, December 1659 to May 1660

■ *Why were neither the republicans nor the religious radicals able to prevent the movement towards Restoration?*

■ *What role did George Monck play in bringing about the Restoration?*

The second recalling of the Rump showed the deep unpopularity of the army's rule up to that point. The paradox was that army authority could be removed only by the exercise of further military power. None of the civil institutions was capable in itself of resisting the army. The reinstalling of the Rump in December could not have been achieved without the intervention of Monck. It was his action that had forced the Committee of Safety to dissolve itself and permit the Rump's reassembly.

## The recalled Rump, December 1659 to February 1660

The climbdown of the army leaders caused a major political shift; the conservative forces began to recover. Desborough, Lambert and Fleetwood were dismissed by the Rump, and Monck was invited to become commander-in-chief. The Rump now appeared to be in a strong position. It had removed the army leaders, re-established itself as a Parliament and government, and had the backing of Monck, the most powerful general in the land, who had crossed into England by the beginning of January 1660. However, it then proceeded to throw away its advantage by a series of avoidable mistakes. Instead of tackling the nation's most pressing grievances, the Rump seemed intent on settling old scores. It undertook a purge of the army. Half the serving officers were removed. The vindictive spirit in which the purge was carried out and the corruption and nepotism that accompanied the appointment of new officers and officials did not speak well for the integrity of the Rump. Its growing unpopularity was evident in a widespread refusal by traders and merchants to pay parliamentary taxes.

The Rump further revealed its ineptitude in the way it treated Monck after his arrival in London in February. Rather than honouring him as its saviour, it sought to restrict his influence politically by burdening him with the policing of London, which was still in a highly volatile mood. However, Monck refused to be overawed; he did use his troops to bring order to the City, but he declined to withdraw from the politics that had brought him south in the first place. He insisted that the Rump confirm the promise given to him that it would not sit beyond May 1660. More significantly still, he outmanoeuvred those MPs who claimed that the Rump was now the sovereign power by forcing the House to readmit the 'secluded' members – those who had been debarred at the time of Pride's purge in December 1648 (see page 133).

## The restored Long Parliament, February to March 1660

Monck's insistence that the secluded MPs be permitted to retake their seats had striking results:

- The return of a substantial number of members of the pre-1649 Long Parliament altered the political balance. Although their ranks had been thinned by death over the intervening ten years, they were still a large enough group to tilt the scales against Haselrig's republican faction.

- Since they had not been implicated in the trial of Charles I or the creation of the Commonwealth, they represented a direct constitutional link with 1642. The claim of the Rump and of the Army Council to direct events had rested ultimately on the legitimacy of Pride's purge. Allowing the secluded members to return amounted to a denial of that legitimacy and made a restoration of the Stuart monarchy much more likely.

- The first steps towards this were soon taken when Parliament turned the tables by excluding the most committed republicans from its ranks. Lambert was a prominent victim of this purge.

## Moves towards a royal restoration

Monck was careful at the recalling of the Long Parliament not to declare openly that he was working for an eventual royal restoration. He wanted to avoid pressing the issue too early. He presented himself very much as the moderate, who, while being resolute against extremists, was prepared to tolerate all forms of responsible opinion. He persuaded Parliament to keep its promise to make him commander-in-chief, to appoint a new Council of State, and then, having made preparations for elections for a new Parliament, to vote for its own dissolution. Another push towards a royal restoration was given by the Long Parliament's reappointment of Edward Montague, a former Cromwellian general but now a royalist sympathiser, as commander of the fleet. This meant that the two leading military commanders, on land and at sea, now favoured Charles II's return.

The tide was running strongly towards a Stuart restoration. Whether this had been Monck's intention all along remains uncertain, but it is significant that as early as the previous July he had entered into a very cordial correspondence with the exiled Charles II. The favourable impression that Monck had made on Charles was expressed in a letter by the king-in-waiting to a confidant. 'I am confident that George Monck can have no malice in his heart against me; nor hath he done anything against me which I cannot easily pardon. I will very liberally reward him with such honour as himself shall desire, if he will declare for me, and adhere to my interest.'

Lambert made one last bid to save the republican cause. He attempted to halt the movement towards a royal restoration by a show of force. A number of regiments supported him, but the bulk of the army declined to challenge Monck. Fleetwood and Desborough made no move; neither did Haselrig, the leading civilian republican. In a final engagement at Edgehill, the site in 1642 of the first of the civil war battles (see page 114), Lambert's army was defeated and he was captured.

## Convention Parliament, April to May 1660

Monck had overcome the republicans militarily. The election results now showed that his mixture of tact and firmness had undermined them politically. Although the writs for the election had specified that no known royalists were to stand, this was widely ignored; over 60 monarchists took seats in the new House. In contrast, republicans and supporters of the Commonwealth did badly. This was not unexpected. What it proved was that the holding of genuinely free elections encouraged the return of members with royalist sympathies. The new Parliament, known as the Convention Parliament, gathered on 25 April. The House of Lords was reconvened and the joint Houses then considered the terms for restoration which Charles had previously offered in his Declaration of Breda issued on 4 April (see Source D, below).

## Negotiations for the return of the monarchy under Charles II

In a sense, all Charles II needed to do after Monck's dramatic entry into English politics six months earlier was to wait and do nothing. He had shown himself adept at this. His inaction proved decisive for it carried the impression that he was not seeking to impose himself on the nation but was awaiting their invitation. His Declaration of Breda showed the same shrewd political judgement. Said to have been drafted by Clarendon, Charles's chief adviser in exile, it was a skilful act of conciliation, based on an astute perception of the outstanding grievances of the time and how they could be resolved. Charles promised a general pardon and religious toleration, and accepted the right of Parliament to decide the disputed questions of property entitlements and the army's arrears of pay. The key passages read as follows (see Source D, below):

> **ONLINE EXTRAS OCR** WWW
>
> Test your understanding of source utility by completing Worksheet 34 at **www. hoddereducation.co.uk/ accesstohistory/extras**

---

**SOURCE D**

From Charles II's Declaration of Breda, 4 April 1660, quoted in John P. Kenyon, *The Stuart Constitution*, Cambridge University Press, 1986, pp. 331–2.

*We do grant a free and general pardon to all our subjects … No crime whatsoever, committed against us or our royal father before the publication of this, shall ever rise in judgement, or be brought in question, against any of them …*

---

> **SOURCE QUESTION**
>
> What technique does Charles II use in his Declaration in Source D to lessen possible opposition to his return as king?

*And because the passion and uncharitableness of the times have produced several opinions in religion … we do declare a liberty to tender consciences …*

*And because so many grants and purchases of estates have been made … we are likewise willing that all such differences, and all things relating to such grants, sales and purchases, shall be determined in parliament …*

*We will be ready to consent to any Act or Acts of Parliament to the purposes aforesaid, and for the full satisfaction of all arrears due to the officers and soldiers of the army under the command of General Monck.*

Both Houses voted to accept the Declaration as the constitutional basis for the restoration of the monarchy. On 8 May 1660, England was formally declared to be no longer a republic; government again resided in Crown, Lords and Commons. On 14 May, a parliamentary deputation visited Charles to invite him to retake the throne. On 29 May, King Charles II, escorted by George Monck, made a ceremonial entry into London.

Royalist contemporaries described the occasion as being accompanied by universal jubilation. In one sense, this was an obvious exaggeration; for die-hard republicans and the extreme radical sectaries, Charles's triumphant return marked the failure of their hopes and dreams. However, most historians acknowledge that in 1660 there was a widespread feeling of relief that twenty years of turmoil had come to an end. This reaction was captured by the diarist John Evelyn: 'This day his Majesty Charles II came to London after a sad and long exile. All this was done without one drop of blood shed, and by that very army which rebelled against him.'

The Restoration settlement that followed the accession of Charles II in 1660 attempted to obliterate all that had happened since 1649. The execution of the surviving regicides and the grisly disinterring and public hanging of Oliver Cromwell's body were intended to symbolise the expunging of an unworthy period of history. The Interregnum was to be regarded as an aberration. This was how the royalist chroniclers wished it to be. But too much had happened during the Interregnum for it simply to be dismissed as an unhappy memory.

## THE PATH TO THE RESTORATION, DECEMBER 1659 TO MAY 1660

**The Recalled Rump, December to February 1659–60**
- Recalling of the Rump showed unpopularity of the army but could not have been achieved without Monck, who continued his march south

**Rump errors**
- Intent on settling old scores rather than reform
- Attempted to purge the army
- Guilty of corruption
- Offended tax-paying classes

**Role of Monck**
- Refused to be overawed by Rump
- Insisted on readmission of the 'secluded' members

**The restored Long Parliament, February to March 1660**
- Republican faction outflanked and excluded
- Key military figures: Monck (army commander-in-chief) and Montague (navy chief) both favoured restoration

**Convention Parliament, April to May 1660**
- Lambert attempted to interfere with elections
- But bulk of the army declined to challenge Monck
- Lambert's army defeated
- 60 monarchists took seats in the new House
- Republicans did badly in election
- Charles issued Declaration of Breda, 4 April
- Convention Parliament, gathered on 25 April
- The House of Lords was reconvened
- Joint Houses voted to accept Declaration of Breda restoration as basis for Restoration

**Results**
- 8 May 1660, Republic ended
- Government of Crown, Lords and Commons re-established
- 14 May, Parliament invited Charles to retake the throne
- 29 May, King Charles II made a ceremonial entry into London

# 4 Reasons for the failure of the republic by 1660

◼ *Why had the republic been unable to establish itself as a permanent system of government?*

Within two years of Oliver Cromwell's death in September 1658, the Stuart monarchy had been restored in the person of Charles II. However, it would be wrong to assume that it was simply royalist strength that brought it about. The reasons for the Restoration are to be found less in royalist pressure than in the failure of the republic to resolve the difficulties and contradictions that had dogged it since its inception in 1649, and which became particularly pronounced after Oliver Cromwell's death. In the words of modern historian Austin Woolrych, writing in 1983: 'The fast rising flood of enthusiasm for the monarchy and the ancient constitution expressed a hankering for security and the rule of law … the Commonwealth had collapsed inwards, destroyed by its own internal strife.'

## The political weakness of the republic

Paradoxically, Oliver Cromwell's problem as Protector was that, despite the military power on which he could rely, he had not been prepared to use force to impose a settlement to his liking. He had maintained his belief that godly rule could be achieved by relying on the goodwill of honest men. Similarly, after 1658, although the army frequently intervened in affairs, it never did so with sufficient sense of purpose to achieve a lasting settlement. The army leaders remained the final arbiter since no solution would work that was not acceptable to them, but this was a negative power; it did not guarantee that a solution could be found. The army could destroy, but it could not create.

The monarchy was restored because the republic had discredited itself. The Protectorate created in 1653 had attempted to establish a workable system of government based on a written constitution. With the abandonment of the Protectorate in 1659, there was a power vacuum, which the successive regimes were unable to fill. Lacking constitutional credibility, and sustained only by the authority of an increasingly divided army, the republic had no claim on the nation's loyalty. In the end, the forces of conservatism proved stronger than those of radicalism.

### The unpopularity of army rule

What the period 1658–60 showed was that military rule was unwelcome to the majority of those in positions of social and political influence. The cost of maintaining the army and navy meant the retention of heavy taxation, one of the grievances that had previously done so much to poison the relations between Charles I and Parliament. No political settlement that involved the maintenance of high taxation would be acceptable to the established classes.

## Disunity within the army

A dominant characteristic of the army in the period after Oliver Cromwell's death was its lack of unity. There was rivalry among its leaders and unrest among its troops. The outstanding example of this was the disintegration of Lambert's forces when they tried to prevent Monck's march southwards. Their condition typified that of many of the regiments: unpaid, badly provisioned and reluctant to obey the orders of squabbling commanders. The chief complaint of the lower ranks was that the generals had yet to meet the two demands that the troops had been making since the civil wars began: full settlement of arrears of pay and indemnity against prosecution for deeds done in the wars. It was ironic that, in the end, it was the return of Charles II that resolved these grievances. His promise of pay and indemnity, guarantees which the generals had not been able to deliver to their men in nearly twenty years of fighting, made monarchy appealing even to the rank and file.

# Importance of London

London is a striking illustration of the financial issue. Ever since 1640, the capital had been one of the most dependable sources of parliamentary strength; throughout the 1650s it had backed the various governments of the Commonwealth and Protectorate. However, in 1659, large numbers of Londoners had become so embittered by the costs of military rule that they were willing to contemplate a return to monarchy. It was no mere coincidence that the first serious civilian challenge to the army came with a protest of the London apprentices against the Committee of Safety, and an organised tax boycott by the London merchants, in the autumn of 1659.

# The contribution of Monck

George Monck's particular skill was in being able to play the role of a moderate throughout the period leading up to the Restoration. This made him acceptable to the growing body of opinion that wanted peace and social stability. He could have made a bid for personal power but chose not to; he seems to have genuinely wanted a civilian government. This is very reminiscent of Oliver Cromwell; as with Cromwell, Monck's ability to influence events rested on his command of a reliable army. It was again the paradox of an army leader using his military authority to impose a civilian settlement. It could not have been achieved any other way. Without Monck, the royalists would not have been able to recover in the manner that they did.

# The attraction of monarchy

Few people are wedded to constitutional forms on grounds of pure principle. Self-interest largely determines whether or not a particular system is acceptable. A republic that appeared to increase rather than lessen the financial burdens on the nation and to have no answer to the great social, political and religious questions of the day was finally judged to be not worth preserving.

In contrast, by 1660, a restored monarchy offered the hope of a return to political and religious stability, the end of the army's intrusion into civil affairs, and the re-establishment of the authority of the traditional ruling classes in central and local government. These were sufficiently powerful incentives to convince all but the most extreme religious or political radicals that the republic had outlived its usefulness and that 'the old order was the natural order'.

## The legacy of the English Revolution 1640–60

- Parliament had been established as a permanent part of government.
- Although monarchy, the House of Lords and the established Anglican Church were all restored after 1660, they would never again wield the power or influence they had before 1640.
- The idea of the divine right of monarchy had been effectively destroyed. All subsequent monarchs had to come to terms with Parliament if they were to survive successfully. In the words of historian Christopher Hill (1967), 'after 1649, all kings remembered that they had a crick in their neck'.
- Radical political and religious ideas had been aired, which, while not successful in their time, transformed the character of public debate.
- Concepts of democracy and social and legal equality had been advanced and debated. Although rejected by the powerful, that they had been discussed at all had created a political precedent.
- Britain was left with a strong suspicion of standing armies. Never again would the military act as a direct political force in public affairs.
- Religious toleration had been introduced as a basic principle. It would take time for this to become legally and socially enforced but the groundwork had been laid.

## SUMMARY DIAGRAM

### REASONS FOR THE FAILURE OF THE REPUBLIC BY 1660

**The political weakness of the Republic**
- Its authority rested ultimately on Oliver Cromwell and the army

**Yet**
- Army rule was unpopular
- Disunity within the army after Cromwell's death
- Dissension with the army destroyed stability

**Importance of London**
- Londoners were embittered by the cost of military rule and were willing to contemplate a return to monarchy

**The contribution of Monck**
- Monck's ability to influence events rested on his command of a reliable army
- Without Monck, the royalists would have been unable to recover

**The attraction of monarchy**
- After 1658 a restored monarchy offered the best hope of a return to political and religious stability

Key debate on the revolution

# 5  Key debate

■ *What was the legacy of the English Revolution of 1640–60?*

There has long been a major historiographical debate over the impact of the revolution that occupied the years 1640–60. A leading contributor to that debate, Gerald Aylmer, made the following observation:

### EXTRACT 1

From G.E. Aylmer, *Rebellion or Revolution?*, Oxford University Press, 1986, pp. 204–5.

*[I]f a revolution is taken to entail a new, or radically different economic order and social structure, then mid-seventeenth-century England did not experience one. A rebellion, on the other hand, is normally taken to mean an armed uprising against an established order, without its being replaced by anything fundamentally new … In 1660 the traditional upper classes regained control of the country, and they were not to lose it again until the twentieth century and then so far without bloodshed. There had indeed been a 'great rebellion'. There had also, if only temporarily and partially, been a middle-class as well as a Puritan revolution.*

**INTERPRETATION QUESTION**

In the light of the discussion above, and with particular reference to the Extracts 1–4, how convincing is the suggestion that the mid-century 'English Revolution' was not a revolution?

Accepting that the events from 1640 to 1649 were a revolution, since they led to the execution of the reigning king and the abolition of monarchy, the following eleven years did not necessarily consolidate that revolution. Despite the excitement and fears created by the religious sectaries and political radicals, the predominant feature of the Interregnum was the strength and persistence of conservative attitudes. Few of those in positions of real influence after 1649 wanted to challenge the existing social order. There is little doubt that the political and religious radicalism of the times frightened the nobility and the gentry and made them determined to resist the extension of rights to those they regarded as the lower orders. Thus, the events of the Interregnum, far from encouraging social revolution, made the conservative classes more conservative still. John Morrill summarises the impact in these terms:

**EXTRACT 2**

From John Morrill, editor, *Revolution and Restoration*, Collins & Brown, 1992, p. 200.

*The English Revolution consolidated the elite when it might have destroyed it; consolidated order by giving everyone a taste of, and distaste for, disorder; prepared the way for the collapse of the confessional State while discrediting the Puritan dream of a godly commonwealth.*

However, this reversion to conservatism does not in itself prove that the Restoration was inevitable. Monarchy was not necessarily seen as the guarantee of order; the image of Charles I as 'that man of blood', responsible for bringing about the civil wars, was still a potent one. Had the Protectorate been able to offer genuine hope of a satisfactory and lasting civil settlement, the established classes might well have found it acceptable. But the truth was that Oliver Cromwell was never able to transform his military authority into a genuinely civilian one. After his death, the struggle for power within the army and among the political factions convinced all those with a vested interest in preserving stability that there really was no alternative to a return to the pre-1649 condition of things, this time with a king who would respect the limits of his power.

Austin Woolrych is eager to emphasise that the attempt at revolution had collapsed from within.

**EXTRACT 3**

From Austin Woolrych, *England Without a King*, Methuen, 1983, p. 44.

*Monarchism [in 1660] was triumphant, yet when the Protectorate had perished a year earlier it had fallen not to the royalists, but to its own radical opponents: the commonwealthmen, the disaffected elements in the army and the sectarian extremists. The Rump whose agents had exploited their discontents, had been quite unable … to satisfy their aspirations, and had proved even more politically bankrupt and nationally unpopular than in 1653. The fast rising flood of enthusiasm for the monarchy and the ancient constitution expressed a hankering for security and the rule of law.*

It is true that the developments during the Interregnum, which led eventually to the restoration of monarchy, appeared thereby to undo the revolution that had occurred between 1640 and 1649. Yet it is still possible to look at the twenty years after 1640 as a revolutionary period overall. Its impact was powerful and long lasting. Blair Worden suggests (2009) that the struggles of the period gave a permanent adversarial character to British politics. 'The conflict of 1640–60, by polarizing the nation, bequeathed habits of polarized thinking.' Ronald Hutton (1990) sees the true significance of 1640–60 as residing in the influence it had on the development of the three British realms. 'In 1660 they divided once more into three kingdoms, theoretically linked only by a crown, but there is little doubt that the balance between them had been determined by the events of the previous decade.'

There will obviously never be total agreement among experts regarding the character of the period, but the observation of a prominent modern scholar, Paul Lay, is worth quoting since it offers a carefully balanced evaluation of how Cromwell and his times are regarded in current historical thinking.

---

**EXTRACT 4**

Paul Lay, *Providence Lost: The Rise and Fall of Cromwell's Protectorate*, Head of Zeus, 2020, pp. 280–1.

*Perhaps what is least understood about Cromwell is his conservatism, which often dragged him into conflict with his more radical supporters. Above all, it was Charles I, his head turned by the new ideology of European absolutism, who was the innovator. Cromwell preferred to hold to some form of the Ancient Constitution – though he bowed to 'cruel necessity', for none of his parliaments came close to his ideal on more than one occasion. Nor, ultimately, did his nation, which he had hoped was rather more saintly than it actually was.*

*Consider this: an East Anglian, nonconformist, philosemite [admirer of Jewish people], suspicious of, though not fundamentally opposed to, monarchy; a unionist uncomprehending of Ireland, a courageous advocate of military action, who left considerable problems of succession to those who came after.*

# CHAPTER SUMMARY

Lacking his father's powerful personality and military strength, Richard Cromwell was unable to maintain harmonious relations with the army or with the two Parliaments he called. His failure effectively marked the end of the Protectorate and he withdrew from politics. Presbyterian members soon fell out with the army, which itself divided into pro-Presbyterian and pro-sectarian wings. The constitutional impasse encouraged the growth of political and religious radicalism; serious social unrest occurred in London and elsewhere.

A royalist rising in August 1659 was broken by a leading republican, General Lambert, who then tried to reassert army control by dissolving the recalled Rump, some of whose members appealed to General Monck to march from Scotland to assist them. Monck did as requested, scattering Lambert's forces in the process. Monck, already on good personal terms with Charles, was now the key in the move towards Restoration. His influence ensured that the elections to the Convention Parliament were conducted fairly, with the result that it returned a House in which royalists were strongly represented. It was the Convention Parliament that then invited Charles to become king on the terms he had stated in his astutely diplomatic Declaration of Breda. Charles II's entry into London to take up the crown was met with genuine popular enthusiasm.

## Refresher questions

Use these questions to remind yourself of the key material covered in this chapter.

1 Why was Richard Cromwell unable to overcome the problems he inherited as Protector?

2 Why were neither the radicals nor the royalists able to exploit the situation after the death of Oliver Cromwell to their advantage?

3 Why were the restored Rump's relations with the army so strained?

4 How far did the army lose control of events after September 1658?

5 Why were the disturbances in London in late 1659 so important?

6 Was the Restoration inevitable after February 1660?

7 Why did John Lambert gain so little support in April 1660?

8 How crucial was the role of Monck in the Restoration?

9 What steps did Charles II take to ease the path to his restoration in 1660?

10 Why was the Republic unable to meet the challenges facing it between 1649 and 1660?

# Question practice: OCR

## Source questions

**1** Study Sources A (page 173), B (page 178) and C (page 180) and then answer both questions. [AS level]

   **a)** Use your knowledge of the situation between the end of Oliver Cromwell's Protectorate and the Restoration to assess how useful Source A is as evidence of the disorder that overtook London in that period.

> **EXAM HINT** Explain in what ways Source A provides evidence of the disorder. Also consider the provenance of the source and link this to contextual knowledge to test the view of the source. Finally, reach a judgement as to the usefulness of the source.

   **b)** Using the three sources in their historical context, assess how far they support the view that the end of Oliver Cromwell's Protectorate ushered in a period of unrest and uncertainty.

> **EXAM HINT** Group the sources according to whether they support the view in the question. Each source should be explained in relation to the question, its provenance evaluated and contextual knowledge used to test the view of the source. A judgement about each source should be reached allowing an overall judgement about whether the Protectorate was a period of unrest and uncertainty.

**2** Using Sources A (page 173), B (page 178), C (page 180) and D (page 180) in their historical context, assess how far they support the view that the political confusion and social unrest of the period 1658–60 made a restoration of the monarchy unavoidable. [A level]

> **EXAM HINT** Group the sources according to whether they support the view in the question. Each source should be explained in relation to the question, its provenance evaluated and contextual knowledge used to test the view of the source. A judgement about each source should be reached allowing an overall judgement about whether it made a restoration of the monarchy unavoidable.

# Exam focus: AQA

## Essay guidance

At both AS and A level for AQA Component 1: Breadth Study: The Early Stuarts you will need to answer an essay question in the exam. Each essay question is marked out of 25:

- for the AS exam, Section B: answer **one** essay question from a choice of two
- for the A level exam, Section B: answer **two** essay questions from a choice of three.

All questions at both levels have the same basic requirement: to analyse and reach a conclusion, based on the evidence you provide.

This book only covers the AS/Part 1 content of the AQA specification, but the following advice is for AS and A level (Parts 1 and 2) as it will be helpful regardless. The AS questions give a quotation and then ask whether you agree or disagree with this view. Almost inevitably, your answer will be a mixture of both. The task for A level has the same basic requirement for analysis, but the demands are more extensive. Detailed essays with accurate deployment of dates and own knowledge are more likely to do well than vague or generalised essays.

Both mark schemes for AS and A level emphasise the need to analyse and evaluate the key features related to the periods studied. The key feature of the highest level is sustained analysis: analysis that unites the whole of the essay.

Opposite is a summary of the A level mark scheme but it is always worth checking the full version on the AQA website.

| Level | AS level | A level |
|-------|----------|---------|
| 1 | Extremely limited or irrelevant information. Unsupported, vague or generalist comments (1–5) | Extremely limited or irrelevant information. Unsupported, vague or generalist comments (1–5) |
| 2 | Descriptive or partial, failing to grasp full demands of question. Limited in scope (6–10) | Descriptive or partial, failing to grasp full demands of question. Limited in scope (6–10) |
| 3 | Some understanding and the answer is adequately organised. Information showing understanding of some key features (11–15) | Understanding of question and a range of largely accurate information showing an awareness of key issues and features, but lacking in precise detail. Some balance established (11–15) |
| 4 | Understanding shown, with range of largely accurate information showing an awareness of some of the key issues and features (16–20) | Good understanding of question. Well-organised and effectively communicated, with a range of clear and specific supporting information showing a good understanding of key features and issues, with some conceptual awareness (16–20) |
| 5 | Good understanding. Well-organised and effectively communicated. A range of clear information showing a good understanding and some conceptual awareness leading to a substantiated judgement (21–25) | Very good understanding of the full demands of question. Well-organised and effectively delivered, with well-selected, precise supporting information. Fully analytical, with a balanced argument and well-substantiated judgement (21–25) |

Essay questions for Paper 1 (Breadth Studies) will relate directly or indirectly to one of the six key issues listed at the beginning of the syllabus:

- How far did the monarchy change?
- To what extent and why was power more widely shared during this period?
- Why and with what results were there disputes over religion?
- How effective was opposition?
- How important were ideas and ideology?
- How important was the role of key individuals and groups and how were they affected by developments?

# Writing an essay: tips from examiners' reports

## Focus and structure

- Be sure what the question is asking and plan what the paragraphs should be about.
- On Paper 1 breadth essay questions it is especially important that the whole of the time period in the question is considered. Essay titles in Breadth essay questions will cover at least twenty years. Do not just focus on the beginning or the end of the period. A response that fails to cover the full date range set in the question will struggle to reach the higher levels.
- Your introduction to the essay should be focused and outline the overall argument of the essay. It is not the place to talk about different definitions of what is meant by ideology, for example. Make sure you clearly state what your opinion is and why you think that.
- Be sure that each paragraph highlights the structure of the answer, for example, the opening sentence should be analytical and not descriptive.
- Make sure that the introductory sentence of each paragraph relates directly to the focus of the question.
- Avoid writing a narrative (an account of what happened). Simply listing events and telling the story will result in a low-level mark.

## Use detail

- Make sure that you show detailed knowledge – but only as part of an explanation being made in relation to the question. No knowledge should be stand alone; it should be used in context.
- For every piece of detailed knowledge think 'so what?' Why have you added this piece of information? What role is it playing in advancing your argument?

## Explanatory analysis and evaluation

Consider what words and phrases to use in an answer to strengthen the explanation. A good place to start is to use adjective qualifiers (words that precede a noun to increase or decrease the quality it signifies). For example: *relative* strength, *convincing* argument, *overwhelming* odds.

## Use of primary sources and references to historians

- Primary sources can be referred to in your answer in order to add substance to an explanation.
- The views of historians can also be used *but* do not parade knowledge about several historians who do not always agree with each other unless you are actively using their views to augment your own argument. Extensive historiography is not wanted. Indeed, an answer can be in the top level and make no mention of historians whatsoever.

## Balance

Your answer must be a balanced response. This does not mean giving two alternative viewpoints and sitting on the fence or in the middle – you will need to consider a variety of factors and make a judgement. You will need to explain why the alternative view or factors are not as important or valid as the one you are advancing.

## Argument and counter-argument

- Think of how arguments can be juxtaposed as part of a balancing act to give contrasting views.
- Think how best to 'resolve' contradictory arguments.

## Relative significance and evaluation

- Think how best to reach a judgement when trying to assess the relative importance of various factors, and their possible interrelationship.

# Planning an essay

## Practice question 1

**'James I's difficulties with Parliament during his reign, 1603–25, were caused by his reliance on favourites.'**

**Explain why you agree or disagree with this view. [AS level]**

**Assess the validity of this view. [A level]**

This question requires you to analyse why James had difficulties with his Parliaments. You must discuss:

- How James's reliance on favourites made Parliament more wary of the king (your primary focus).
- The other factors that damaged the relationship (your secondary focus).

A clear structure makes for a much more effective essay and is crucial for achieving the highest marks. In addition to an introduction and conclusion, you need three or four paragraphs to structure this question effectively. In each paragraph you will deal with one factor. One of these *must* be the factor in the question. If you don't address the factor (in this case, James's difficulties with Parliament) you aren't answering the question and will only score a low level.

A very basic plan for this question might look like this:

- Paragraph 1: the impact of James's reliance on favourites, especially Buckingham.
- Paragraph 2: the importance of finance and James's plans for a union with Scotland in causing distrust from early in the reign.
- Paragraph 3: the effect of foreign policy linked to religion, which caused trouble as the reign progressed.

It is a good idea to cover the factor named in the question first, so that you don't run out of time and forget to do it. Then cover the others in what you think is their order of importance, or in the order that appears logical in terms of the sequence of paragraphs.

## The introduction

Maintaining focus is vital. One way to do this from the beginning of your essay is to use the words in the question to help write your argument. The first sentence of question 1, for example, could look like this:

> James faced considerable difficulties with his Parliaments. One reason for this was his reliance on favourites but there were other factors as well to explain this.

This opening sentence provides a clear focus on the demands of the question, although it could, of course, be written in a more exciting style. Then go on to outline the argument of the essay, anticipating the conclusion. The rest of the essay should flow from these opening statements because you have indicated a clear sense of direction.

## Focus throughout the essay

Structuring your essay well will help with keeping the focus of your essay on the question. To maintain a focus on the wording in question 1, you could begin your first main paragraph with 'favourites'.

> James had a number of favourites and his devotion to them was one very important factor in causing difficulties with his Parliaments.

- This sentence begins with a clear point that refers to the primary focus of the question (James's difficulties with his Parliaments) while linking it to a factor (his reliance on favourites).
- You could then have a paragraph for each of your other factors.
- It will be important to make sure that each paragraph focuses on analysis and includes relevant details that are used as part of the argument.

■ You may wish to number your factors. This helps to make your structure clear and helps you to maintain focus. However, this can make the essay appear to be concerned with a list, and may not encourage links between paragraphs.

## Deploying detail

As well as focus and structure, your essay will be judged on the extent to which it includes accurate detail. There are several different kinds of evidence you could use that might be described as detailed. These include correct dates, names of relevant people, statistics and events. You can also make your essays more detailed by using the correct technical vocabulary. For example, for practice question 1 (page 226) you could use terms such as the Privy Chamber and the Protestation.

You might also be able to use specific primary sources, including brief quotations, and also references to the views of particular historians who support your arguments. However, the quotations and arguments of historians must be relevant. There is no point in learning historians' quotes and squeezing them in somewhere just because you learnt them. This will not gain you marks – they need to relate to your argument.

## Analysis and explanation

'Analysis' covers a variety of high-level skills including explanation and evaluation; in essence, it means breaking down something complex into smaller parts. A clear structure that breaks down a complex question into a series of paragraphs is the first step towards writing an analytical essay.

The purpose of explanation is to account for why something happened, or why something is true or false. An explanatory statement requires two parts: a *claim* and a *justification*.

For question 1 (page 226), for example, you might want to argue that one important reason was the king's foreign policy in the 1620s. Once you have

made your point, and supported it with relevant detail, you can then explain how this answers the question. For example, you could conclude your paragraph like this:

> James's policy of trying to persuade the Spanish to restore the Palatinate through a marriage treaty rather than a war was important[1] because[2] it meant that Parliament did not trust the king's commitment to Protestantism. It was less willing to grant him money and there was a loss of trust on both sides[3].

**1** The first part of this sentence is the claim while the second part justifies the claim.

**2** 'Because' is a very important word to use when writing an explanation, as it shows the relationship between the claim and the justification.

**3** The justification.

## Evaluation

Evaluation means considering the importance of two or more different factors, weighing them against each other, and reaching a judgement. This is a good skill to use at the end of an essay because the conclusion should reach a judgement that answers the question. Ideally, this will have been anticipated in the introductory paragraph, thereby ensuring that the essay has a clear sense of direction from beginning to end.

For example, your conclusion to question 1 might read:

> Clearly[1], James's reliance on favourites damaged his relationship with Parliament. However[2], more significant were the policies he followed in finance and foreign policy which left Parliament feeling bewildered and uneasy. Therefore[3], James's favourites only provide part of the explanation for the difficulties which the king experienced with Parliament.

**1** Clearly.    **2** However.    **3** Therefore.

Words like 'however' and 'therefore' are helpful to contrast the importance of the different factors.

# Complex essay writing: argument and counterargument

Essays that develop a good argument are more likely to reach the highest levels. This is because argumentative essays are much more likely to develop sustained analysis. As you know, your essays are judged on the extent to which they analyse.

After setting up an argument in your introduction, you should develop it throughout the essay. One way of doing this is to adopt an argument–counterargument structure. A counterargument is one that disagrees with the main argument of the essay. This is a good way of evaluating the importance of the different factors that you discuss. Essays of this type will develop an argument in one paragraph and then set out an opposing argument in another paragraph. Sometimes this will include juxtaposing the differing views of historians on a topic.

Good essays will analyse the key issues. They will probably have a clear piece of analysis at the end of each paragraph. While this analysis might be good, it will generally relate only to the issue discussed in that paragraph.

Excellent essays will be analytical throughout. As well as the analysis of each factor discussed above, there will be an overall analysis. This will run throughout the essay and can be achieved through developing a clear, relevant and coherent argument.

A good way of achieving sustained analysis is to consider which factor is most important.

Here is an example of an introduction that sets out an argument for practice question 1:

James I experienced difficulties with his Parliaments almost from the start, which intensified as the reign progressed to the point where Parliament was not providing sufficient money for the king to follow his policies[1]. One reason for this is that James placed a great deal of reliance on favourites, particularly Buckingham, and this angered many. However, there were other reasons why James had problems with Parliament[2]. One of these was his failure to give a decisive lead in the fight to protect Protestants on the Continent. But the most important reason was financial. The system for raising money was no longer adequate[3].

1 The introduction begins with a claim.

2 The introduction continues with another reason.

3 Concludes with outline of argument of the most important reason

- This introduction focuses on the question and sets out the key factors that the essay will develop.

- It introduces an argument about which factor was most significant.

- However, it also sets out an argument that can then be developed throughout each paragraph, and is rounded off with an overall judgement in the conclusion.

# Complex essay writing: resolution and relative significance

Having written an essay that explains argument and counterarguments, you should then resolve the tension between the argument and the counterargument in your conclusion. It is important that the writing is precise and summarises the arguments made in the main body of the essay. You need to reach a supported overall judgement. One very appropriate way to do this is by evaluating the relative significance of different factors, in the light of valid criteria. Relative significance means how important one factor is compared to another.

The best essays will always make a judgement about which was most important based on valid criteria. These can be very simple – and will depend on the topic and the exact question.

The following criteria are often useful:

- Duration: which factor was important for the longest amount of time?

- Scope: which factor affected the most people?

- Effectiveness: which factor achieved most?

- Impact: which factor led to the most fundamental change?

For example, you could compare the factors in terms of their duration and their impact.

A conclusion that follows this advice should be capable of reaching a high level (if written, in full, with appropriate details) because it reaches an overall judgement that is supported through evaluating the relative significance of different factors in the light of valid criteria.

Having written an introduction and the main body of an essay for question 1, a concluding paragraph that aims to meet the exacting criteria for reaching a complex judgement could look like this:

There were several reasons for James's difficulties with his Parliaments, and his reliance on favourites was one of these. Undoubtedly, the favours showered on Carr and Buckingham made Parliament unhappy. MPs thought James would need less money if he were not so generous. James's foreign policy and his apparent reluctance to support fellow Protestants, including his own son-in-law, caused dismay and distrust of Crown intentions. But the most important factor in creating a rift between the two sides was finance. The traditional means of raising money no longer produced sufficient for the Crown's needs. James's need for money led to the use of impositions which Parliament felt undermined its tax-raising role. Both sides had reason to feel aggrieved.

# Interpretations guidance

Section A of the examination for AQA Component 1: 1D Stuart Britain and the Crisis of Monarchy, 1603–1702 contains extracts (of approximately 120–150 words) from the work of historians. This section tests your ability to analyse and evaluate different historical interpretations. Therefore, you must focus on the interpretations outlined in the extracts. The advice given here is for both the AS and the A level exams.

| AS exam | A level exam |
|---|---|
| You will be given two extracts and asked which is the more convincing interpretation (25 marks) | You will be given three extracts and will be asked how convincing each of the arguments in the extracts is in relation to a specified topic (30 marks) |

An interpretation is a particular view on a topic of history held by a particular author or authors. Interpretations of an event can vary, for example, depending on how much weight a historian gives to a particular factor and largely ignores another one. For example, there is an on-going debate among historians as to how influential Scottish and Irish affairs were in creating the crisis which led to the outbreak of civil war between king and Parliament in 1642. Some scholars regard developments in Scotland and Ireland as the decisive factors in causing the war. This view is challenged by Barry Coward, a major authority on the period, who argues that 'England was by far and away the most powerful and wealthy of the three kingdoms, and that what was happening there was therefore more important than events in Scotland and Ireland.'

Interpretations can also be heavily conditioned by events and situations that influence the writer. For example, judging the merits or otherwise of the Grand Remonstrance will tend to produce different responses – a contemporary royalist writing of the document would regard the Remonstrance an unacceptable challenge to legitimate royal authority while historians writing in later periods might well value it as a highly valuable catalogue of the issues that divided king and Parliament.

The interpretations that you will be given will be largely from recent or fairly recent historians, and they may, of course, have been influenced by events in the period in which they were writing.

When looking at a historian's argument you will need to consider the following questions:

- What is the main argument/interpretation that the historian is putting across?
- How good is the argument?
- What factors does the historian consider?
- What evidence does the historian use?
- What subsidiary arguments does the historian make?

## Interpretations and evidence

The extracts will contain a mixture of interpretations and evidence. The mark scheme rewards answers that focus on the *interpretations* offered by the extracts much more highly than answers that focus on the *information or evidence* mentioned in the extracts. Therefore, it is important to identify the interpretations. The main interpretation might not be the first line that you read. It could be towards the end of the extract or just an overall feeling.

- *Interpretations* are a specific kind of argument. They tend to make claims such as 'Cromwell's military skills were the most important reason why Parliament won the civil war'.

- *Information or evidence* tends to consist of specific details. For example: 'Pride's purge was important in preparing the way for the king's trial.'

- *Arguments and counterarguments*: sometimes in an extract you will find an interpretation which is then balanced in the same paragraph with a counterargument. You will need to decide with which your knowledge is most in sympathy.

## Fact and opinion

It's important to be able to identify the difference between a fact and an opinion. For example, a weak candidate will write 'the historian says Charles I was put on trial in January 1649. I know this to be true.' However, the task is to assess not how accurate the historian is but how convincing the argument is.

## The importance of planning

At AS level you are allowed 45 minutes for this question. At A level you are allowed one hour. It is the planning stage that is vital in order to write a good answer. You should allow at least one-quarter of that time to read the extracts and plan an answer. If you start writing too soon, it is likely that you will waste time trying to summarise the *content* of each extract. Do this in your planning stage – and then think how you will *use* the content to answer the question.

# Analysing interpretations: AS (two extracts)

The same skills are needed for AS and A level for this question. The advice starts with AS simply because it involves only two extracts rather than three.

**With reference to these extracts and your understanding of the historical context, which of these two extracts provides the more convincing interpretation of James I's performance as king? (25 marks)**

Extracts A and B are used for the AS question. Extracts A, B and C are used for the A level question.

---

**EXTRACT A**

From D.H. Willson, *King James VI and I*, Jonathan Cape, 1956, p. 174.

*To the problems of [England] James gave no serious study. No doubt in any case he would have lacked the patience and humility to do so, but in his present exalted state of mind application became superfluous. Hence, he arrived at his decisions far too quickly and in too offhand a manner. They were based upon preconceived ideas and principles forged in the melee of Scottish politics and now applied uncritically to England. They were founded upon emotion and self-interest. His approach to government was personal, and much of his policy was a mere projection of plans for his own advantage.*

---

**EXTRACT B**

From Barry Coward, *The Stuart Age*, Routledge, 1980, pp. 98–9.

*The political tensions of the reign were not caused solely, or indeed mainly, by James I. Elizabeth's legacy to the new king in 1603 was not a good one: a country at war, dissatisfaction in many quarters with the condition of the Church [and] a royal revenue system in need of radical reform. … It is now clear that James carried out the daunting task of governing Britain with much more success than he has often been given credit for, using the political skills of flexibility and compromise that he had long deployed in Scotland to defuse some of the fears of his new English subjects. James saw himself as a peacemaker king in foreign affairs. He also displayed the same qualities in domestic affairs. James's experience in coping with the factional jungle of Scottish politics made him adept at balancing faction in the English court; and also at defusing the factional tensions within the English Church.*

From Tim Harris, *Rebellion: Britain's First Stuart Kings*, Oxford University Press, 2014, pp. 501–2.

*Certainly, in terms of the goals James set himself one could argue that James failed on virtually all accounts: he failed to achieve his much-desired union between England and Scotland, he failed to put the monarchy on a firmer financial footing, he failed to heal his kingdoms' religious divisions, and he failed in his foreign policy ambition to be the peacemaker of Europe. We should also question the assumption that there was a fundamental discontinuity between the reigns of James and Charles. In many respects, Charles saw himself as continuing policies which had been begun by his father. In continuing and bringing to fruition what he thought were his father's policies, Charles inevitably went further than his father had done and did things James might never have done. We have noted already James's tactical acumen. It has also been said that although the early James was not a particularly good politician, he improved with time. He learned from his mistakes.*

## Analysing Extract A

From the extract:

- James gave little real attention to the problems he faced in England.
- His lofty view of his status meant he was unwilling to give problems proper time and attention.
- Experienced only in Scottish affairs, his policies were based on an unrealistic assessment of what was needed.

Assessing the extent to which the arguments are convincing:

- Deploying knowledge to create a strong picture of James's failings.
- Using knowledge to stress James's lack of realism.
- Suggesting that James's approach to government was based on self-interest.
- The extract is highly critical and pays no attention to James I's possible merits.
- The extract omits any reference to the problems confronting James mentioned in Extract B.

## Analysing Extract B

From the extract:

- The political tensions of James's reign were not primarily his fault.
- James achieved considerable success in the face of daunting problems.
- Drawing on his Scottish experience, James skilfully balanced opposing factions.

Assessing the extent to which the arguments are convincing:

- Deploying knowledge to illustrate James's positive qualities as king (and disagreeing with Extract A).
- Deploying knowledge to highlight the phrase 'James carried out the daunting task of governing Britain with much more success than he has often been given credit for'; for example, his use of the techniques of flexibility and compromise.
- Juxtaposing the success of James's policies against the daunting problems he faced by providing more knowledge to substantiate the argument in the source.

Comparing the analysis of each extract should give the direction of an overall conclusion and judgement about which of the extracts is more convincing. In this case it may be that Extract B is more convincing because it does try to present a more balanced view.

## The mark scheme for AS

The mark scheme builds up from Level 1 to Level 5, in the same way as it does for essays:

- Do not waste time simply describing or paraphrasing the content of each extract. Simply copying out long quotations of an interpretation doesn't demonstrate a high level of understanding and won't gain you any marks.
- Make sure that when you include your knowledge that it is being used to advance the analysis of the extracts, not as knowledge in its own right. Always think 'so what?' What job is

the addition of your knowledge doing? How is that knowledge advancing your answer? When deploying information always think how it helps in evaluating the interpretation.

- The top two levels of the mark scheme refer to 'supported conclusion' (Level 4) and 'well-substantiated conclusion' (Level 5).

- For Level 4, 'supported conclusion' means finishing your answer with a judgement that is backed up with some accurate evidence drawn from the source or sources and your knowledge.

- For Level 5, 'well-substantiated conclusion' means finishing your answer with a judgement which is very well supported with evidence, and, where relevant, reaches a complex conclusion that reflects a wide variety of evidence.

## Writing the answer for AS

There is no one correct way. However, the principles are clear. In particular, contextual knowledge should be used *only* to back up an argument. None of your knowledge should be standalone – all your knowledge should be used in context.

For each extract in turn:

- Explain the evidence in the extract, backed up with your own contextual knowledge, for James's failings as king.

- Explain the points in the extract where you have evidence that contradicts the idea of James's being a failure.

Then write a conclusion that reaches a judgement on which is more convincing as an interpretation. You might build in some element of comparison during the answer, or it might be developed in the last paragraph only.

## Analysing interpretations: A level (three extracts)

For the AQA A level exam, Section A gives you three extracts (see pages 231–2), followed by a single question.

**Using your understanding of the historical context, assess how convincing the arguments in each of these three extracts are in relation to James I's performance as king. (30 marks)**

An analysis of Extracts A and B has already been provided for the AS question (see page 232).

## Analysing Extract C

From the extract (see page 232):

- It is arguable that James I failed to achieve all the major aims he set himself.

- There was an essential continuity between the policies pursued by James I and Charles I.

- James improved his political skills as his reign progressed.

Assessing the extent to which the arguments are convincing:

- Deploying knowledge to point to James's failures in financial, religious and foreign affairs.

- Deploying knowledge to explain the continuity between the policies followed by James and Charles.

- The extract hints at the political acumen James developed despite the failures of his earlier reign.

## Writing the answer for A level

First, make sure that you have the focus of the question clear. In this case, the focus is on James I's performance as king and how convincing the extracts are on that subject. Then you can investigate the three extracts to see how convincing they are.

You need to analyse each of the three extracts in turn. A suggestion is to have a large page divided into nine blocks.

| Extract's main arguments | Knowledge to corroborate | Knowledge to contradict or modify |
|---|---|---|
| A | | |
| B | | |
| C | | |

- In the first column, list the main argument and any subsidiary arguments each uses.

- In the second column, list points that corroborate the arguments.

- In the third column, list what might contradict or modify the arguments (you might find that you partly agree, but with reservations).
- You may find, of course, that some of your knowledge is relevant more than once.

## Hints from examiners' reports: how to write a good answer

There is no one correct way to organise an answer. It is the overall argument or arguments that you are being judged on.

- Briefly refer to the focus of the question.
- For each extract in turn set out the main argument and any subsidiary ones, with corroborating and contradictory evidence.
- Do this by treating each argument (or group of arguments) in turn.
- Refer to the content of an extract directly – perhaps by a brief quotation – but do not copy out whole sections.
- The argument that has been summarised should be related to the focus of the question, not simply a summary of the extract.
- Your own knowledge must only be used to support or refute an argument in the extract, not presented as a separate entity.
- Do not wander into provenance or value. You are concerned only with the content of each extract. You do not need to know anything about the historian or schools of history (for example Marxist, post-revisionist, and so on). Evaluate the extract, not the historian!
- Do not attempt to analyse the extract by focusing on what is not there. Focus on what you are given to analyse.
- Make comparisons between the extracts if this is helpful. The mark scheme does not explicitly give credit for doing this, but a successful cross-reference may well show the extent of your understanding of each extract and add to the weight of your argument. Bear in mind, this is a high-level skill so only do this if you feel particularly confident with this approach.

- Write a brief judgement at the end of the analysis on each extract. Do not write an introduction or an overall conclusion saying which was most convincing.
- This is not an exercise in English literature so do not stray into focusing on tone or particular use of emotive language. If the historian comes across as angry, for example, this doesn't make the argument any less or more convincing.

### The mark scheme for A level

For each of the three extracts, the mark scheme makes it clear that a good answer will:

- Identify the arguments presented in each extract.
- Assess the extent to which the arguments are convincing, using own knowledge.
- Take every opportunity to make a balanced answer wherever this is appropriate, by corroborating and contradicting the arguments in each extract. An unbalanced answer will be that the interpretation is completely convincing or conversely completely unconvincing.

The mark scheme progresses upwards like this:

- Level 1: general comments about the three extracts or accurate understanding of one extract.
- Level 2: some accurate comments on the interpretations in at least two of the three extracts, but with limited comments or with description.
- Level 3: some supported comments on the interpretations, putting them in their historical context. Some analysis of the content of the extracts, but little attempt to evaluate them.
- Level 4: good understanding of the interpretations provided in the extracts, with knowledge to give a good analysis and some evaluation.
- Level 5: very good understanding and strong historical awareness to analyse and evaluate.

Notice that there is no reference in the A level mark scheme to *comparing* the extracts or reaching a judgement about the most convincing.

# Exam focus: OCR

## Essay guidance

The assessment of Units Y108 and Y138: The Early Stuarts and the Origins of the Civil War 1603–1660 depends on whether you are studying it for AS or A level.

| AS level | A level |
|---|---|
| You will answer one essay question and one two-part source question | You will answer one essay question and one source question |

The guidance below is for answering both AS and A level essay questions.

For both OCR AS and A level History, the types of essay questions set and the skills required to achieve a high grade for Unit Group 1 are the same. The skills are made very clear by both mark schemes, which emphasise that the answer must:

- focus on the demands of the question
- be supported by accurate and relevant factual knowledge
- be analytical and logical
- reach a developed and supported judgement about the issue in the question.

There are a number of skills that you will need to develop to reach the higher levels in the marking bands:

- understand the wording of the question
- plan an answer to the question set
- write a focused opening paragraph
- avoid irrelevance and description
- write analytically
- write a conclusion which reaches a supported judgement based on the argument in the main body of the essay.

These skills will be developed in the section below, but are further developed in the 'Period Study' chapters of the *OCR A level History* series (British Period Studies and Enquiries).

## Understanding the wording of the question

To stay focused on the question set, it is important to read the question carefully and focus on the key words and phrases. Unless you directly address the demands of the question you will not score highly. Remember that in questions where there is a named factor you must write a good analytical paragraph about the given factor, even if you argue that it was not the most important.

| Types of AS and A level questions you might find in the exams | The factors and issues you would need to consider in answering them |
|---|---|
| **1** Assess the reasons for Parliament's victory in the first civil war 1642–6 | Weigh up the importance of a range of factors and reach a judgement as to their relative importance in explaining why Parliament won the civil war |
| **2** How important was royalist weakness as a cause of Parliament's victory in the first civil war, 1642–6? | Weigh up the relative importance of a range of factors, including comparing the importance of royalist weakness with other factors |
| **3** 'The strength of the New Model Army was the main reason for the defeat of the royalists in the first civil war (1642–6).' How far do you agree? | Weigh up the relative importance of a range of factors, including comparing the strength of the New Model Army with other issues, to reach a balanced judgement |

## Planning an answer

Many plans simply list dates and events – this should be avoided as it encourages a descriptive or narrative answer, rather than an analytical answer. The plan should be an outline of your argument; this means you need to think carefully about the issues you intend to discuss and their relative importance before you start writing your answer. It should therefore be a list of the factors or issues you are going to discuss and a comment on their relative importance.

For question 1 in the table above, your plan might look something like this:

- Parliament's strengths:
  - ☐ Most important was the military genius of Oliver Cromwell.
  - ☐ After initial diffidence, Parliament developed a sustained sense of purpose.
  - ☐ Held key geographical strategic areas – London the most significant of these.
  - ☐ Maintained regular supplies.
  - ☐ Developed more successful recruitment methods than the royalists.
  - ☐ Raised more money than the royalists.
- Royalist weaknesses:
  - ☐ Seldom able to match Parliament in strategy or tactics.
  - ☐ Difficulty in maintaining supply lines.
  - ☐ No leader to match Cromwell.
  - ☐ Entry of Scots meant royalists had to fight two armies.
  - ☐ Morale weakened over four years of fighting.

## The opening paragraph

Many students spend time 'setting the scene'; the opening paragraph becomes little more than an introduction to the topic – this should be avoided. Instead, make it clear what your argument is going to be. Offer your view about the issue in the question – what was the most important reason for the victory of Parliament? – and then introduce the other issues you intend to discuss. In the plan it is suggested that Cromwell's military genius was the most important factor. This should be made clear in the opening paragraph, with a brief comment as to why – perhaps that Cromwell's skill as a strategist and commander in battle was unmatched. This will give the examiner a clear overview of your essay, rather than it being a 'mystery tour' where the argument becomes clear only at the end. You should also refer to any important issues that the question raises.

For example:

There are a number of reasons why Parliament won the civil war, including military strength, resources and morale[1]. However, the most important reason was the military leadership and determination of Cromwell[2]. This proved particularly important as in the early stages of the war Parliament had been diffident and half-hearted in its struggle against Charles I[3]. The length of the war proved a greater drain on the royalists than on Parliament, which was able to exploit its control of key geographical and administrative areas, especially London, from which it drew its greater supply of finance and war materials. In this respect, Parliament's control of the navy and through it control of the ports was another crucial advantage, as was the presence of the Scottish forces after 1643, since this meant that the royalists were facing two armies[4].

1 The student is aware that there were a number of important reasons.

2 The answer offers a clear view as to what the student considers to be the most important reason – a thesis is offered.

3 There is a brief justification to support the thesis.

4 Some of the other factors and their relative importance are briefly stated.

### Avoid irrelevance and description

Hopefully, the plan will help to stop you from simply writing all you know about why Parliament won and force you to weigh up the role of a range of factors. Similarly, it should help prevent you from simply writing about the military events of the civil war. You will not lose marks if you do that, but neither will you gain any credit, and you will waste valuable time.

Look at the paragraph below written in answer to question 2: How important was royalist weakness as a cause of Parliament's victory in the first civil war, 1642–6?

Royalist weakness became an important factor once the war developed into a long struggle[1]. But at the start of the war it was not an important factor since the royalists had greater resources. However, Parliament grew stronger financially and economically as the war progressed[2]. The military leadership of Cromwell and Fairfax was also important as was the presence of the Scottish army in England following the Solemn League and Covenant in

1643**[3]**. These developments damaged the royalists and made their weaknesses the major reason for their defeat**[4]**.

1 The answer acknowledges that royalist weakness was a key issue.

2 The answer describes what happened but does not explain directly how this contributed to Parliament's victory.

3 The descriptive approach continues with some useful hints, but these are not developed.

4 The response asserts that the issue of royalist weakness was a major cause, but this has not been clearly shown.

There is no real explanation as to how the royalists' weakness led to their defeat, something which would be needed to reach Level 3, and certainly no evidence of either evaluation or judgement that would be needed for the higher levels.

## Write analytically

This is perhaps the hardest, but most important skill you need to develop. An analytical approach can be helped by ensuring that the opening sentence of each paragraph introduces an idea, which directly answers the question and is not just a piece of factual information. In a very strong answer it should be possible simply to read the opening sentences of all the paragraphs and know what argument is being put forward.

If we look at the third question on the strength of the New Model Army as the main reason for the defeat of the royalists (see page 235), the following are possible sentences with which to start paragraphs:

- The New Model Army brought a new form of warfare.

- The New Model was made up of soldiers wholly committed to their tasks and duty.

- Taking their lead from their commander, Oliver Cromwell, who was inspired by religious zeal, the New Model fought with ruthless tenacity and efficiency.

- As creator of the New Model, Cromwell's organisational skills were unmatched by any other commander on either side.

- Cromwell's brilliant deployment of infantry and cavalry made the New Model invincible.

- Cromwell and the New Model provided Parliament with the military leadership that it had lacked in the early years of the war.

You would then go on to discuss both sides of the argument raised by the opening sentence, using relevant knowledge about the issue to support each side of the argument. The final sentence of the paragraph would reach a judgement on the role played by the factor you are discussing regarding the New Model. This approach would ensure that the final sentence of each paragraph links back to the actual question you are answering. If you can do this for each paragraph you will have a series of mini essays, which discuss a factor and reach a conclusion or judgement about the importance of that factor or issue. For example:

The strength of the New Model Army, built on Cromwell's unmatched military skills and leadership, was a highly important factor in securing parliamentary victory, particularly after 1645 when Cromwell and Fairfax provided Parliament with the drive and purpose it had lacked hitherto**[1]**. It was with the Self-denying Ordinance in 1645 that Parliament's weak military leaders were finally removed and free rein given to Cromwell to adopt a purposeful strategy, with his already successful New Model Army at its centre, for the complete defeat of Charles's armies. The impact of this was evident in the New Model's routing of the royalists in 1645 at the decisive Battle of Naseby. Important as other factors were, such as royalist military and economic deficiencies, it remains the case that the strength of the New Model, a product of Cromwell's inspiring leadership and peerless military talent, was the main reason for Parliament's achieving victory in the first civil war**[2]**.

1 The sentence puts forward a clear view that New Model strength was a highly important factor.

2 The claim that is developed and some evidence is provided to support the argument.

The paragraph above explains the importance of the New Model in the royalists' defeat but explaining that role will take you only to Level 3 or 4 depending on how well developed and how well supported your explanation is. At this level, answers will produce a list of reasons as to why the New Model was victorious. Answers that are not developed or are poorly explained will be placed in Level 3, while those that are well developed will reach Level 4. The answer above, if the same standard were repeated in other paragraphs, would certainly reach Level 4.

In order to reach Levels 5 and 6 there needs to be clear evidence of the evaluation of factors – how important were the other factors in Parliament's success. The paragraph above does start to move towards that by arguing that royalist weaknesses were a central factor but it does not give a full coverage to the other factors. The paragraph also provides some support for that claim and it is this that turns an assertion that they were important into a judgement and takes the response to the higher levels.

At Level 5, the judgement is likely to be present only in the conclusion, as shown in the example below. However, responses that reach Level 6 will make a judgement about the importance of each factor as they explain their role so that there will be a series of interim judgements which are then pulled together in an overall conclusion.

**Questions for practice**

Write six opening sentences for the following questions:

- 'There was never a realistic chance of the royalists' winning the first Civil War, 1642–6.' How far do you agree?

- Assess the reasons why the first civil war lasted so long.

- How effective a wartime leader was Charles I?

- 'Parliament was more successful at arousing popular support than the royalists.' How far do you agree?

## The conclusion

The conclusion provides the opportunity to bring together all the interim judgements to reach an overall judgement about the question. Using the interim judgements will ensure that your conclusion is based on the argument in the main body of the essay and does not offer a different view. For the essay answering question 1 (see page 235), you can decide what was the most important factor in Parliament's victory but for questions 2 and 3 you will need to comment on the importance of the named factor – the weaknesses of the royalists and the strength of the New Model – as well as explain why you think a different factor is more important, if that has been your line of argument. Or, if you think the named factor is the most important, you would need to explain why that was more important than the other factors or issues you have discussed.

Consider the following conclusion to question 2: How important was royalist weakness as a cause of Parliament's victory in the first civil war, 1642–6?

> Although the royalists certainly had numerous weaknesses, such as poor supply lines, economic and logistical difficulties, the waywardness of Prince Rupert, their best leader, and the inadequacy of their other generals, weakness was not the most important factor in their defeat[1]. After all, in the early years of the war the royalists had had the better of the military exchanges. However, the emergence of the New Model Army led by Cromwell, working under Fairfax, provided Parliament with the essential resolve and military leadership. It was this, therefore, that proved the most important factor in determining Parliament's victory. Without Cromwell's ability to defeat the king's armies militarily, the weaknesses of the royalists would not have been sufficient to cause their defeat by the parliamentary armies[2].

1 This is a strong conclusion because it considers the importance of the named factor – royalist weakness – but weighs that against a range of other factors to reach an overall judgement.

2 It is also able to show links between the other factors to reach a balanced judgement, which brings in a range of issues, showing the interplay between them.

# Sources guidance

OCR Units Y108 and Y138: The Early Stuarts and the Origins of the Civil War 1603–60 are assessed through an essay and a source-based or enquiry question. There is no choice for the enquiry question. At AS level you will have to answer two source questions using three sources and for the A level you will answer one question using four sources.

## AS question 1

The skills needed to answer this question are made very clear by the mark scheme, which emphasises that the answer must:

- focus on the question
- evaluate the source using *both* provenance and relevant contextual knowledge
- reach a supported analysis of its utility in relation to the issue in the question.

## AS question 2 and A level question 1

The skills needed to answer this question are made very clear by the mark scheme, which emphasises that the answer must:

- focus on the question
- evaluate the sources using *both* provenance and relevant contextual knowledge
- uses detailed and accurate knowledge
- reach a supported analysis of the sources in relation to the question.

There are a number of skills that you need to develop if you are to reach the higher levels in the marking bands for both the AS and A level questions:

- You have to *interpret* the evidence. You need to link it to the issue in the question and decide what the evidence is saying about that issue.
- You need to consider *how useful* the evidence is. This involves thinking carefully about a range of issues concerning the provenance of the source, you might think about who wrote it, why it was written, would the person who wrote it be in a position to know and how typical it might be.
- You need to apply relevant contextual knowledge to the source to judge the validity of the source and its view, you therefore need a good knowledge of the topic in the question.
- You need to link your material to the issue in the question and not write a general essay about the topic.

These skills are illustrated in the guidance to answering the questions below, but are further developed in the 'Enquiry Study' chapters of the *OCR A level History* series (British Period Studies and Enquiries).

## Practice questions

### AS level

- Use your knowledge of the events of 1659–60 to assess how useful Source A is as evidence of the disturbances in London in this period.
- Using Sources A, B and C in their historical context, assess how far they support the view that the unrest of the period 1659–60 prepared the way for the Restoration.

### A level

- Using all the sources in their historical context, assess how far they support the view that the disturbances of 1659 prepared the way for the Restoration.

## SOURCE A

An account of the troubles in London from a newspaper critical of the Committee of Public Safety, *London Newsletter*, December, 1659.

*A petition was on foot by the apprentices to be delivered to the Council, which, coming to the knowledge of the Committee of Safety, they made a Proclamation against it, which was proclaimed yesterday morning in Cheapside by some troopers, who were beaten back by the apprentices, which occasioned the bringing in of all the horse and foot of the army into the City, who came with their swords drawn and pistols cocked against a multitude of naked [unarmed] men, and killed 6 or 7, and wounded more; but that did not quieten them, till about 5 o'clock the Lord Mayor made proclamation that they should all depart, the soldiers being withdrawn, some of them being killed and wounded.*

## SOURCE B

An appeal to the authorities to restore order from 'Petition of the Apprentices and Young men of London', December 1659.

*Our glory and comfort consist in our privileges and liberties, the inheritance of all the free people of England, the grand privilege being free representation in Parliament.*

*This dear privilege has been assaulted by violence and heavy taxes are imposed on men's estates, and new laws without consent of the people in a free Parliament. Trade is decayed and we are like to suffer much.*

*We therefore beseech you … by your zeal to our liberties, by the great renown you have lately gained in opposing the cruel raging of the sword, to use the great advantages God has put into your hands to secure your country from dangerous usurpation and preserve us in the liberties to which we were born.*

## SOURCE C

Complaint to the Committee of Public Safety over the spread of disorder in the nation from the 'Petition of the Gentlemen of Devon', December 1659.

*Since the death of the King, we have been governed by tumult; bandied from one faction to the other; this party up today, that tomorrow – but still the nation under, and a prey to, the strongest. So long as this violence continues over us, no other government can settle the nation than that which pleases the universality of it. You speak of the necessity of a republic. We say it is not necessary, not even effectual, but if it were both, a free parliament ought to introduce it. The consent of the people must settle the nation, the public debt must be secured out of the public stock, and interests of opinion and property must be secured by a free parliament.*

## SOURCE D

Charles II lays the basis for the Restoration in the Declaration of Breda, 4 April 1660.

*We do grant a free and general pardon to all our subjects … No crime whatsoever, committed against us or our royal father before the publication of this, shall ever rise in judgement, or be brought in question, against any of them …*

*And because the passion of the times have produced several opinions in religion we do declare a liberty to tender consciences . . .*

*And because so many grants and purchases of estates have been made we are likewise willing that all such differences, and all things relating to such grants, sales and purchases, shall be determined in parliament*

*We will be ready to consent to any Act or Acts of Parliament to the purposes aforesaid, and for the full satisfaction of all arrears due to the officers and soldiers of the army under the command of General Monck.*

The guidance for AS question 2 and A level question 1 (page 239) is the same. The only difference is that for the A level question you have to use four sources, whereas for the AS question, you must use three.

# Answering AS question 1

The first question is worth ten marks and will ask you to:

**Use your knowledge of a particular topic or issue to assess how useful Source X is as evidence of …**

In order to do well answering this type of question you should evaluate the source, using *both* its provenance (see page 239) and your own relevant knowledge of the historical context (see page 239) that is specified in the question. This will allow you to engage with the source and reach a supported analysis of its usefulness as evidence for the issue in the question. If you use just one – either provenance or your own knowledge – you will be unable to reach the higher levels. You should reach a judgment about its value. Remember it might be useful for some issues but not others.

First, it is important that you use the right source, it will not always be Source A, therefore double check before you start writing! To stay focused on the question set, it is important that you read the question carefully and remain focused on the key phrase 'as evidence for'. Unless you directly address the issue in the question you will not score highly. You can write separate paragraphs on the provenance of the source and the historical context, but the strongest answers will integrate them, often using the context to explain the provenance. Remember both to consider the provenance and to use contextual knowledge if you want to reach the higher levels. The failure to use both is the most common reason answers do not reach the higher levels.

You should use short and appropriate quotations from the source to support the points you are making.

Although the mark scheme does not require you to reach a judgement about the value of the source

in relation to the question, it would be helpful to summarise the strengths and weaknesses of the source as evidence for the issue in the question.

In answering the question 1, an answer might start as follows:

> Source A is a newspaper account detailing the violent disturbances occurring in London following the presentation of a petition of complaint by the London apprentices, a petition which the Committee of Public Safety had forbidden to be presented. Faced with the petitioners' defiance, the Committee had brought in the army to suppress them, a move that had led to violent confrontation between the apprentices and the troops[1]. As a description of events that had been recently and publicly witnessed it is likely to be an accurate account, but it must also be remembered that the events are seen through the eyes of a newspaper that was basically hostile to the Committee of Safety and, therefore, may reflect its critical views. This is clear in the graphic description of the degree of force used by the army against the 'naked', that is, unarmed apprentices[2].
>
> The source is useful in explaining that the unrest afflicting London was a consequence of the frustration and anger towards the authorities felt by the apprentices, who represented the shopkeepers, tradespeople and employees whose businesses and working lives were being disrupted by the breakdown of effective government. The source is also useful in describing the contribution of the London mayor and the governing role of the Committee of Public Safety at this point, but it does not mention that the Committee would not be strong enough to survive beyond the end of December 1659[3].

1 The opening sentence explains the origin of the source and summarises it.

2 The answer considers the origin of the source and discusses the strengths and weaknesses of this in terms of its usefulness.

3 The answer considers the content of the source and whether it is useful in explaining the disturbances of 1659.

The answer should be further developed and might discuss issues such as the role of the London mayor and the growing dissatisfaction with the situation among the various army leaders and their often conflicting attitudes towards the troubles. There might be some comment about the fact that the Committee of Public Safety was the army's own creation and that the newsletter's unfavourable account of the army's violent suppression of the petition was, therefore, most likely to have been by civilians unhappy with the continuation of army rule.

## Answering AS question 2 and A level question 1

The question will be worded as follows:

**Using these three sources/four sources in their historical context, assess how far they support the view that ...**

- Keep a good focus on the question and don't drift off into describing everything the sources say.
- Evaluate the sources – that is say how valid the evidence they give is. You can do this by looking at their *provenance*: what they are, who wrote them, under what circumstances and why. You can also do this by looking at what they say about the issue and testing it against your own knowledge.
- You have to keep a balance. You should not write an essay on the topic in the question just by using knowledge, but you should not just explain what the sources say about the issue either. You need to apply some knowledge to all the sources to answer the question.

In planning your answer to this question it might be helpful to construct a chart similar to the one below (this can be modified to A, B and C for AS):

- In the second column you decide whether the source supports or challenges the view in the question and in third column you should enter evidence from the source which supports your view.
- The next column considers the provenance, which may affect the reliability of the source.
- The next two columns bring in your knowledge to support or challenge the view in the source.
- The final column brings all this together to make a judgement about the source in terms of supporting or challenging the view in the question.

If you complete this chart it should provide you with the material you need to answer the question. Although the mark scheme does not require you to group the sources, it might be more sensible to deal with all the sources that support the view in the question together and those that challenge the view together before reaching an overall judgement. However, remember some sources may have parts that both support and challenge the view in the question!

An opening paragraph to the question using all the sources could start as follows:

*Sources A and B both suggest that the disturbances are a consequence of the restrictions on liberty, Source A regarding the suppression of the London petitioners as an example of oppressive government and perhaps implying that a Restoration was more likely because of the unrest. Complementing this, Source B speaks of 'our privileges and liberties' being blighted*

| Source | View about the issue in the question | Evidence from the source | Provenance | Knowledge that supports the source | Knowledge that challenges the source | Judgement |
|---|---|---|---|---|---|---|
| A | | | | | | |
| B | | | | | | |
| C | | | | | | |
| D | | | | | | |

by heavy taxation and 'the cruel raging of the sword', but B argues strongly that a free Parliament was the main concern[1]. Sources C and D also rue the disturbed times that have produced such public distress, and both relate it to the absence of kingship, C directly claiming that the present troubles can be traced back to the 'tumult' that has afflicted the nation since the death of Charles I. In Source D, Charles II acknowledges 'the passion of the times' that currently divide the people, and offers a workable solution, a restoration of the old order based on a 'general pardon' that will satisfy a whole range of social, religious, political and military interests, and might therefore suggest a Restoration was more likely[2].

1 The answer deals with the two sources that support the view in the question that a major step towards restoration of order and stability is required.

2 The answer now considers the view of the other two sources which suggest, in Source C's case by strong implication and allusion, and in Source D's case by formally stated intention, that such a return to the desired stability is best achieved by the restoration of monarchy. This view is also supported by a brief quotation from Source D.

The opening paragraph could be developed by providing further quotations from Sources A and B.

Answers can deal with each source separately and, in considering Source D, an answer might take the following approach:

Source D supports the view that the disturbances prepared the way for the Restoration. Charles II had observed the conflicts and disagreements that marred the Interregnum and, in response, made a cleverly worded offer of conciliation. Informed by the perceptive ideas of such wily advisers as the Earl of Clarendon, the king lists the outstanding grievances that troubled the various vested interests among the people and provides a set of promises intended to quell doubts and make his Restoration not merely reasonable but desirable[1]. However, the Declaration was an attempt to win support for his cause, hence his offer of a general amnesty for all those who fought against 'us or our royal father'. Aware of how divisive an issue religion had become, Charles pledges to grant freedom of worship 'to tender consciences'. Similarly conscious of how complex

property rights have become as a result of the wartime appropriations and forced sales 'so many grants and purchases of estates have been made', Charles declares his readiness to allow Parliament to resolve disputes[2].

In Source D, Charles endeavoured to appease and satisfy as many vested interests as possible, however it could be argued it did not necessarily mean he was responding directly to the troubles. There are grounds for suggesting that Charles's essential aim was to restore his personal power and that the Declaration may have been a matter of expediency and prudence directed at overcoming possible political challenges. He and his advisers well knew that a return to monarchy was not a universal wish in the nation. As is evident in Source B, there were those who were prepared to continue with a republic so long as their liberties were preserved in a free Parliament. It is noteworthy also that the promise in Source D to pay arrears referred specifically to 'the army under the command of General Monck'. It was his reliance on Monck that made Charles II's restoration possible. The army was the key to power throughout the Interregnum and it was the army that was instrumental in restoring Charles in 1660[3].

Yet, whatever the motivation behind the Breda Declaration there is no doubting its authenticity or that it achieved its immediate objective of preventing significant opposition. Whatever qualifications might be applied to it, Source D helps make the case that it was the troubles that created the situation to which Monck and Charles reacted and followed a path that led to the Restoration[4].

1 The opening sentence outlines the view of Source D about the issue in the question and there is a brief explanation as to why it takes that view.

2 The answer considers the purpose of the source and this raises questions as to its reliability.

3 Although the purpose of the source raises questions about its reliability, own knowledge is applied to confirm the view in the source.

4 The answer concludes by linking the source back to the question and although it acknowledges that queries remain regarding the connection between the unrest and the Restoration, it argues that there was a direct causal link

between the return of Charles II as king in 1660 and the disturbances of the preceding year. Having considered the provenance and used contextual knowledge the response reaches a judgement about the source in relation to the question. This is vital for the higher levels and should be done for each source.

Answers should treat each source in a similar way and then use the judgements reached about each source individually to reach an overall judgement in a concluding paragraph. The conclusion should be based on the evaluation of the sources and not simply own knowledge, as is seen in the example below.

> Although Sources C and D support the view that the disturbances of 1659 prepared the way for the Restoration, the purpose of both these sources raises some questions about their reliability, as both were attempts by monarchists to justify the case for a return of monarchy, attempts that did not depend on the disturbances for their motivation[1]. However, Sources A and B suggest strongly that what motivated particular groups in society was not primarily a wish for a royal restoration but the desire for the re-establishment of stability and order, preferably free of army control. But in the context of the times the only force capable of guaranteeing order was the army. That was why in the event there was a general willingness by all those seeking peace and stability to accept the return of Charles in a manoeuvre organised by Monck, the moderate army leader[2]. Collectively, the four sources A–D explain the paradox of an army leader exploiting the disturbances of the time to mastermind a civilian royalist settlement[3].

1 The opening sentences relates to the issue in the question, namely that the disturbances of 1659 prepared the way for the Restoration, and summarises the extent to which the sources support it.

2 The second sentence offers the counter view.

3 The concluding sentence reaches an overall judgement based on an evaluation of the sources and a very brief reference to own knowledge to support the argument.

If a judgement has been reached about each source based on its provenance and using contextual knowledge then the conclusion above will ensure that the response reaches the top level.

## Common mistakes

- Forgetting that this is the source element of the paper. Your answer needs to be driven by the sources.

- Responses that consider *only* the provenance of each source or use *only* contextual knowledge to evaluate. You must use *both* to reach Level 4 and above.

- Avoid stock comments about provenance such as 'he was there and would therefore know' or 'it is written in private diary so can be trusted'.

- Knowledge is simply deployed rather than used to evaluate the source. You need to make sure that you link your contextual knowledge to the source to show how the view of the source is either valid or invalid.

- Judgements are made about the issue rather than the source. In light of the provenance of the source and your contextual knowledge does the source support the view in the question?

# Timeline

| Year | Government/Parliament | Political events | Foreign/military affairs |
|------|----------------------|------------------|--------------------------|
| 1603 | James VI of Scotland became James I of England | Millenary Petition | |
| 1604 | First Parliament | The Form of Apology and Satisfaction | Treaty of London signed with Spain |
| 1605 | | Gunpowder Plot | |
| 1606 | | Bate's case | |
| 1610 | | The Great Contract | |
| 1612 | | Death of Prince Henry | |
| 1613 | | | Marriage of Elizabeth to Frederick of the Palatinate |
| 1614 | The Addled Parliament | Cockayne's scheme | |
| 1615 | | Overbury affair | |
| 1618 | | Buckingham became the chief minister | Thirty Years' War |
| 1619 | | | Elector Frederick becomes King of Bohemia |
| 1620 | | | Battle of the White Mountain |
| 1621 | Third Parliament | The Protestation | |
| 1623 | | | Charles and Buckingham's trip to Madrid |
| 1624 | Fourth Parliament | Impeachment of Cranfield | French marriage alliance |
| 1625 | Death of James I, Charles I becomes king<br>First Parliament | Marriage of Charles to Henrietta Maria<br>Refusal to grant tonnage and poundage | Mansfeld's expedition<br>War with Spain<br>Trip to Cádiz |
| 1626 | Second Parliament | | War with France |
| 1627 | | Five Knights' Case | Expedition to Rhé |
| 1628 | Third Parliament | Petition of Right<br>Buckingham assassinated | Expedition to La Rochelle |
| 1629 | Personal rule | | Treaty of Souza |
| 1630 | | | Treaty of Madrid |
| 1635 | | Ship money levied on whole country | |
| 1637 | | Hampden's case | |
| 1638 | | Covenant in Scotland against religious changes | |
| 1639 | | | First Bishops' War |
| 1640 | The Short Parliament<br>The Long Parliament | | Second Bishops' War |
| 1641 | | Trial and execution of Strafford<br>Legislation passed to limit the prerogative<br>The Grand Remonstrance | The Irish rebellion |
| 1642 | Monarchy – Charles I | The attempted arrest of five MPs<br>The Nineteen Propositions<br>Outbreak of civil war | Battle of Edgehill |

| Year | Government/Parliament | Political events | Foreign/military affairs |
|------|----------------------|-----------------|--------------------------|
| 1643 | | Solemn League and Covenant | |
| 1644 | | | Battle of Marston Moor |
| 1645 | | Self-denying Ordinance | Battle of Naseby |
| 1646 | | | Charles's surrender to the Scots |
| 1647 | | Charles's 'Engagement' with the Scots<br>Army seizure of the king<br>Heads of the Proposals<br>Agreement of the People<br>Putney debates | |
| 1648 | | Pride's purge | Second civil war started<br>Scots defeated at Preston |
| 1649 | Republic replaces monarchy | King's trial and execution<br>Charles II proclaimed King in Scotland | Cromwell's crushing of the Levellers<br>Cromwell landed in Ireland<br>Sieges of Drogheda and Wexford |
| 1650 | | Blasphemy Act | Cromwell became commander-in-chief<br>Cromwell entered Scotland<br>Cromwell's victory over Scots at Dunbar |
| 1651 | | Navigation Act<br>Charles II escaped to France | Cromwell defeated Charles II at Worcester |
| 1652 | | Irish land confiscation begun | |
| 1653 | Instrument of Government adopted<br>Cromwell became Lord Protector | Rump forcibly dispersed by Cromwell<br>Nominated Assembly convened<br>Nominated Assembly dissolved | |
| 1654 | | First Protectorate Parliament | |
| 1655 | | Cromwell dissolved first Protectorate Parliament<br>Beginning of rule of Major-Generals | Penruddock's rising |
| 1656 | | Second Protectorate Parliament | |
| 1657 | Cromwell declined the kingship | Rule of Major-Generals ended<br>*Humble Petition and Advice*<br>First session of Parliament | |
| 1658 | Richard Cromwell became Protector | Second session of Parliament<br>Cromwell dissolved Parliament<br>Death of Oliver Cromwell | |
| 1659 | Richard Cromwell resigned<br>End of the Protectorate | Third Protectorate Parliament<br>The army expelled the Rump<br>Rump reassembled | Booth's Rising |
| 1660 | Charles II proclaimed king | Rump dissolved<br>Long Parliament restored<br>Convention Parliament<br>Charles II issued Declaration of Breda<br>Charles II entered London | Monck's troops reached London |

# Glossary of terms

**Absolutism**   A system of government where power is concentrated in the hands of one ruler.

**Agitators**   Spokesmen for the soldiers' grievances.

**A man of blood**   A biblical reference well known to Cromwell and his troops from the Book of Samuel 16:7: 'thou art taken in thy mischief, because thou art a man of blood'.

**Anti-Christ**   Satanic forces opposed to God; Cromwell applied the term to those he regarded as ungodly Irish papists (Catholics) who had been in arms against the English Protestants since 1641.

**Arminians**   Protestants who believed in free will and a ceremonial form of religion which resembled Catholic practices.

**Assessment**   Very similar to 'the contribution' in that it obliged localities, under threat of severe penalties, to deliver a specific sum of money on a given date to Parliament's collectors, who had calculated what a region was capable of paying.

**Baptism**   The service by which babies became members of the Church, as symbolised by being sprinkled with water.

**Barbadoes**   An archaic spelling of Barbados. An island in the Caribbean colonised by the English in 1625.

**Battle of the White Mountain**
Destroyed the Bohemian army and left Frederick and Elizabeth with no option but to flee.

**Billeting**   Compelling householders to provide soldiers with shelter and food.

**Black Rod**   A senior official in Parliament who would convey the king's command for the ending of sessions.

**Bohemia**   A region in the modern-day Czech Republic.

**Book of Rates**   Listed the customs duty payable on specific items. It was periodically revised. The last

revision had been in 1558, carried out by officials in Mary I's reign.

**Book of Sports**   A list of activities which were pronounced to be lawful on Sundays, including archery and dancing. The declaration had originally been issued in 1618 but James I had pulled back from insisting that it was read out in churches because Puritans were offended by it. Laud insisted that the declaration be read out.

**Bourgeois revolution**   The stage in Marxist theory which followed feudalism leading to capitalism.

**Broadcloth**   A type of heavy, dense cloth which was shrunk after weaving to make it thicker.

**Calvinist**   Follower of the teachings of John Calvin, who set up a strict Church in Geneva which was non-hierarchical. Calvin believed that preaching was the most important part of the service and he emphasised predestination.

**Catholic interpretation**   Catholics believed that in the communion service or mass, the bread and wine were transformed by a miracle at the moment of consecration into the actual body and blood of Jesus, although their outward form remained the same. This is known as transubstantiation.

**City of London**   The major centre for banking, international trade and commerce and an important source of loans to the king.

**Cloth of estate**   A canopy that hung above the throne. Together with the dais, it symbolised the concept of royalty even in the absence of the actual king.

**Clubmen**   Taking their name from the wooden clubs with which they were prepared to defend themselves, they called for king and Parliament to make peace.

**Commissions of Array**   A device dating back to medieval times which entitled the monarch to call up civilians to join local militias to fight for him in a time of crisis.

**Common law**   Law established by long custom through the decisions of courts.

**Commonwealth**   Often used to describe England and its people. It links back to the idea of the 'common weal' or public good.

**Commonwealthsmen**
Republican MPs who claimed that Cromwell's dissolution of the Rump in 1653 had been unlawful; they argued for limited government and religious freedom.

**Communion**   Service of the Church at which members received bread and wine to represent Christ's body and blood. For Catholics, this was the most important service because of their belief in transubstantiation. Protestants, especially Puritans, gave it less importance.

**Contested election**   An election in which there was more than one candidate, allowing a real choice.

**Convocation**   The Church equivalent of Parliament. Traditionally, it met at the same time and was dissolved with Parliament. It dealt with Church affairs including Church taxation.

**Council of State**   The body appointed by the Rump Parliament after the execution of the king to act as the government under the direction of the Rump.

**Council of the Army**   Formed in 1647, it was composed of the highest ranking officers ('Grandees'), who were men of good birth, such as Fairfax, or of property, such as Cromwell.

**Coup**   An attempt to overthrow a government by force.

**Court of High Commission**
A court created by Henry VIII to exercise control over the Church and enforce ecclesiastical decrees.

**Covenant**   A document to which men subscribed, swearing to resist to the death the innovations in religion. They were known as 'Covenanters'.

**Crown jewels**   The formal, very precious objects used in the coronation and at other state occasions. They included the crowns and symbols of state such as the orb and mace. These were not the personal property of the king.

**Crown**   Used throughout the book as another term for monarch.

**Customs farmers**   Merchants who would pay the Crown for the right to collect customs revenue.

**Dais**   A low platform for a throne.

**Decimation tax**   A ten per cent levy imposed on known royalists with annual incomes of more than £100.

**Delinquents**   The name given by Parliament to those who had actively supported the Stuarts in the civil wars and afterwards.

**Dowry**   Payment in money, goods or land made by the family of a bride to her new husband and his family.

**Dutch War**   Anglo-Dutch commercial rivalry (1652–4) resulted in a series of naval engagements, fought mainly in the Channel and the North Sea; after initial success, the Dutch, subjected to a blockade of their ports, made peace on English terms.

**Early modern age**   The period between the medieval and modern ages, approximately 1485–1789.

**Elector Palatine**   The prince of a Rhineland province in the Holy Roman Empire.

**Embezzlement**   Fraudulently taking money entrusted to an individual because of his position.

**Episcopacy**   Government of the Church by bishops.

**Exchequer**   The government office responsible for collecting revenue and making payments. It was run by the chancellor of the exchequer.

**Excommunication**   Being excluded from the services and membership of the Church. Catholics believed that excommunicants would go to hell, if they did not reconcile themselves to the Church first.

**Farming out**   Leasing out the administration of customs in return for an annual rent.

**Favourite**   A young man with a close relationship to the king who received many gifts of land, titles or money.

**Feoffees for impropriations**   The feoffees were a group of Puritans who appointed their nominees to ministerial and lecturing positions. An impropriation was the right of a layman to collect tithes and to appoint a deputy (or vicar) to take the actual services.

**Forty-shilling freeholders**   The right to vote in the counties was based on owning land worth forty shillings (£2) a year.

**Gentlemen of the chamber**   (Or bedchamber), the personal attendants on the king who performed apparently menial tasks, such as helping the king to dress, yet had great influence.

**Gentry**   The class of landowners ranking just below the nobility.

**Godliness**   Living by a code of moral conduct in keeping with biblical precepts.

**Great seal**   Used to show that documents had the king's approval and made them official.

**Habeas corpus**   Fundamental right in English law whereby if due cause cannot be shown for imprisonment, a prisoner has to be released after 24 hours.

**Habsburg**   The family that ruled both in the Holy Roman Empire and in Spain.

**Hampton Court**   One of the most important royal palaces, just outside London.

**Heterodoxy**   Heretical opinions.

**High church**   Those who favoured beautiful churches, the use of vestments and formal services which followed the pattern of worship in the prayer book.

**Holy Roman Emperor**   Ruled over the Holy Roman Empire, which covered a large area of central Europe centred on Germany. It was an elective title, although in

practice the position was held by the Habsburg family for centuries.

**Huguenot**   The name given to Protestants in France.

**Iberia**   Spain and Portugal.

**Impositions**   Customs duties on specific goods.

**Indemnity**   Guarantees that soldiers would not be prosecuted later for their earlier actions in the war.

**Inflation**   A sustained price increase with a fall in the value of money.

**Justices of the peace (JPs)**   Unpaid members of the gentry who enforced government decisions and acted as judges to lesser crimes.

**King James Bible**   The accepted (or Authorised) version of the Bible used in all English churches for the next 300 years. It is recognised as one of the finest pieces of English prose ever written and many of its phrases have become part of the language.

**Kirk**   The Scottish Church.

**Leveller**   A movement that began among civilians in London around 1645 and challenged the existing social order.

**Liberty of conscience**   Freedom to think and act according to one's own judgement rather than conforming to an imposed set of beliefs laid down by a Church.

**Liturgy**   The form of services laid down in the prayer book which all churches were required to follow.

**Living**   The post of parish priest.

**Lord Lieutenant**   The monarch's representative and head of the government.

**Low church**   Those who wanted simple unadorned churches and services with a minimum of ritual.

**Malaria**   An enervating condition caused by a mosquito bite. Cromwell was thought to have contracted it while campaigning in the marshlands in Ireland.

**Martial law**   The suspension of civil law and its replacement by army rules. This would often include restrictions on movement such as night-time curfews.

**Marxist**   An interpretation of history following the ideas of Karl Marx who believed that changes were caused primarily by economic factors.

**Masques**   Elaborate plays full of symbolism, which were performed at court at enormous cost.

**Master of the wardrobe**
The official in charge of a department in the royal household.

**Merchant Adventurers**   A group of merchants who were the only people allowed to export cloth.

**Militia ordinance**   This took military control away from the king and gave it to Parliament.

**Millenarianism**   The belief in the imminence of the millennium, the thousand-year period during which Jesus Christ would return to reclaim the earth and govern it with his saints.

**Millenary Petition**   Supposedly signed by 1000 clergy asking for moderate Puritan reforms.

**Monopolies**   These gave groups or individuals the right to be the sole supplier of a product or service.

**Navigation Act**   Required that all goods imported into Britain from outside Europe were to be carried in British vessels, and that exports from Europe were to be admitted only in British ships or those of the exporting country.

**Netherlands**   England's biggest trading partner. In the late sixteenth century, the northern Netherlands had waged a protracted campaign to win their freedom from Spain. Elizabeth I had assisted this struggle and had been given the right to hold some towns in return.

**New Model**   Referred to the unprecedented level of organisation, training and religious fervour that characterised the troops under Cromwell's command.

**Palladian**   A style of architecture popularised by the Italian architect Palladio which imitated the classical features of Greek and Roman temples.

**Papal bull**   A formal proclamation issued by the pope.

**Papist**   An uncomplimentary name given to Catholics.

**Pillory**   A device with holes for securing the head and hands used for punishment and public humiliation.

**Plantation**   Government-backed settlement of Protestant emigrants from England or Scotland.

**Pluralism**   Simultaneously holding more than one office in the Church.

**Poll tax**   A tax levied on all of the adult inhabitants of England, Scotland and Ireland according to a graduated scale ranging from £100 for a duke to a base rate of 6*d.* per head for anyone aged sixteen or over.

**Popery**   The derogatory term given to Catholicism. It suggested that Catholics were not merely following a private religion but were part of an international conspiracy led by the pope against 'true' religion or Protestantism.

**Popish**   Anything which appeared to be Catholic or inspired by the pope. This was always used as a term of abuse.

**Post-revisionists**   Historians who modify the stance of revisionist historians without totally discrediting it.

**Predestinarian**   Believing that whether an individual person is saved or damned has been predetermined by God's unchangeable will.

**Predestination**   The belief that God had already decided who would go to heaven and who to hell.

**Presbyterianism**   A system of Church government without bishops, which gave considerable responsibility to individual congregations who chose their own ministers and elders. It was a strict form of Protestantism which placed great emphasis on the Bible and less on tradition.

**Privy councillors**   Members of the Privy Council who were both advisers and administrators.

**Proclamation**   A public statement of the king's wishes, which had less force than a statute.

**Protestant**   The Churches that had broken away from the Catholic Church in the sixteenth century.

**Providence Island Company**
Set up in 1630s to establish godly commonwealths in the Caribbean which would make money from tobacco and cotton. It provided an opportunity for like-minded Puritans to meet legitimately.

**Providence**   The concept that events are never random and isolated but are part of a larger divine plan.

**Puritans**   Members of the Anglican Church who wished to 'purify' it of the last vestiges of Catholic worship. These included an end to the ring in marriage, signing with the cross at baptism, bowing at the name of Jesus and wearing vestments (clergymen's robes).

**Radicals**   Those who favoured sweeping changes to Church or State. They contrast with traditionalists who wanted to preserve the *status quo.*

**Recusancy fines**   Payable by people who did not regularly attend the Sunday services in their local parish church. In practice this was a fine for being Catholic.

**Regent**   A person appointed to run the State when the monarch cannot do so because of either youth or illness.

**Remonstrance**   A formal statement of grievances.

**Revisionists**   Historians who challenge the prevailing historical interpretations.

**Roman Catholic**   The only accepted form of Christianity in western Europe for the 1000 years before the Reformation of the early sixteenth century which brought in Protestantism. Catholics and Protestants tended to regard each other with deep suspicion or even hatred.

**Royal prerogative**   The king's power to act on his own authority without reference to others. It included control of foreign policy, war and peace, the regulation of overseas trade and of the coinage, and the pardoning of criminals.

**Royalists**   Those who would fight for the king in the civil war.

**Rules of war**   There were no such rules in a formal sense, but there was a broad understanding in Europe around this time that if troops and non-combatants refused to surrender when offered quarter they thereby sacrificed their right to be treated mercifully.

**Sabbath**   Another word for Sunday used by Puritans who believed that the instruction in the Ten Commandments to 'keep the Sabbath day holy' prohibited any form of recreational activity.

**Sacrilege**   Profaning or desecrating a sacred person or institution.

**Sanhedrin**   The presiding council of the ancient Israelites.

**Sealed Knot**   An organisation founded by a group of aristocratic royalists in 1652 with the aim of organising the overthrow of the Republic.

**Sequestration**   A technique used by both sides of confiscating the property and goods of known opponents in the areas they controlled.

**Sheriff**   The chief agent of royal authority in each of the shires, responsible for overseeing elections and later ship money.

**Spanish War**   Fought between England and Spain, 1654–8, principally over colonial possessions in the Caribbean, but climaxing with the English victory at the Battle of the Dunes (Dunkirk) in 1658.

**Star Chamber**   A body made up of members of the Privy Council, formed as needed. It was used to attack those who disagreed with government policy. It was particularly useful as a means of raising revenue because it was

speedy and efficient in its dealings and it was able to impose huge fines.

**Statute**   A law passed by Parliament.

**Stipend**   The income received from a parish, the area served by a church.

**Stuart Age**   The period 1603–49 and 1660–1714 when the Stuart monarchs were on the throne.

**Subsidy rolls**   Records of taxation which were used to determine how much each area should pay.

**Subsidy**   The main form of taxation, based on a fixed system of assessments. Over time, the value of the subsidy decreased.

**Supply**   Taxation granted on an occasional basis to supply the monarch's needs.

**Surplice**   A long white tunic worn by a minister when taking a service.

**'The contribution'**   Essentially a tax, usually collected monthly, imposed on a locality whose inhabitants had to raise a decreed amount of money on pain of having their estates and property confiscated.

**The Form of Apology and Satisfaction**   A method for the Commons to show its feelings about royal action or its own privileges in a way that was not confrontational was to write it in a journal, which was a record of all that happened in the Commons.

**The Graces**   Allowed Catholics to take a full part in political life in Ireland and confirmed their titles to land.

**Theology**   A structured set of definitions of, and justifications for, a particular religious belief.

**Tithe**   One-tenth of a farmer's produce which was due to the Church to pay the priest and so he could give assistance to people in need. The produce was stored in a tithe barn.

**Tonnage and poundage**   Taxes on imports and exports.

**Tower of London**   A royal residence, but increasingly it was used more as a secure place to keep influential wrongdoers in relative comfort.

**Trained bands**   Another name for the militia, composed of householders who had an obligation to undertake some military training for the defence of the locality.

**Triers and Ejectors**   Officials responsible for the selection and the supervision of those appointed as ministers in the Church.

**True Levellers (the Diggers)**   A group that tried to put into practice their belief that land belonged to the community and not to individuals.

**Typhoid**   A stomach infection contracted from polluted food or water, often causing fatal dehydration.

**Ulster**   The area of Ireland where, since Tudor times, the English government had pursued a 'plantation' policy of dispossessing Catholic peasants of their lands and giving them to Protestant settlers.

**Ulster**   The area of Ireland where, since Tudor times, the English government had pursued a 'plantation' policy of dispossessing Catholic peasants of their lands and giving them to Protestant settlers.

**United Provinces**   The seven northern provinces of the Netherlands that won their independence from Spain.

**Universal suffrage**   Votes for all adult citizens.

**Whig**   This strand in historiography derives its name from the Whig Party of the eighteenth and nineteenth centuries.

# Further reading

## General texts

**Toby Barnard, *The English Republic* (Longman, 1986)**
A short yet comprehensive account with a helpful selection of documents

**Barry Coward, editor, *A Companion to Stuart Britain* (Blackwell, 2009)**
The essays in Part III have useful insights into politics, religion and the functioning of the State

**Barry Coward, *The Stuart Age* (Routledge, 2012)**
An excellent overview of the period and summarises the ideas of historians. It also has a comprehensive bibliographical section for further reading

**Frances Dow, *Radicalism in the English Revolution* (Blackwell, 1985)**
Traces the growth of radicalism across the whole period

**Derek Hirst, *England in Conflict 1603–1660: Kingdom, Community, Commonwealth* (Hodder Arnold, 1999)**
A good survey of the period which is also accessible

**Ronald Hutton, *The British Republic 1649–60* (Macmillan, 1990)**
A stimulating survey which examines the Interregnum as a British, not simply an English phenomenon

**Mark Kishlansky, *The Penguin History of Britain: A Monarchy Transformed, Britain 1630–1714* (Penguin, 1997)**
Regarded by the author's fellow scholars as an outstanding work

**Allan I. Macinnes, *The British Revolution, 1629–1660* (Palgrave Macmillan, 2005)**
Concerned with the three kingdoms and particularly informative on the period 1644–60

**John Morrill, editor, *Revolution and Restoration: England in the 1650s* (Collins & Brown, 1992)**
A set of informed essays on a range of important themes, edited by an outstanding authority

**John Morrill, *Stuart Britain: A Very Short Introduction* (Oxford University Press, 2020)**
A scintillating and concise analysis of the key issues and interpretations relating to the period

**Conrad Russell, *The Crisis of Parliaments* (Oxford University Press, 1971)**
A very readable account of the breakdown of the relationship between king and Parliament, by a key revisionist historian. Still worth reading even though some of his insights have subsequently been challenged

**Howard Tomlinson, editor, *Before the English Civil War* (Macmillan, 1983)**
A selection of essays which all are worth careful reading. They explore some of the key ideas about the background to the civil war

## Chapter 2

**Thomas Cogswell, *James I* (Allen Lane, 2017)**
A short and sympathetic account of James's life

**Pauline Croft, *King James* (Palgrave, 2003)**
A good summary of James's reign

**Antonia Fraser, *The Gunpowder Plot: Terror and Faith in 1605* (Weidenfeld & Nicolson, 1996)**
An in-depth look at the events of 1605 for those who wish to explore these events further

**Tim Harris, *Rebellion: Britain's First Stuart Kings* (Oxford University Press, 2014)**
Looks at events from the perspective of all three kingdoms and gives contemporary views on what happened as well as a clear analysis. Relevant also for Chapters 3 and 4

**Roger Lockyer, *James VI and I* (Longman, 1998)**
Another reliable account

**Alan Stewart, *The Cradle King: A Life of James VI & I* (St Martin's Press, 2003)**
This sets James in his Scottish context and makes it easier to understand some of his actions

## Chapter 3

**Richard Cust, *Charles I: A Political Life* (Routledge, 2007)**
A more substantial look at the politics of Charles's reign and the actions of the king

**Leanda de Lisle, *White King: The Tragedy of Charles I* (Chatto & Windus, 2018)**
A very sympathetic and readable consideration of Charles which also brings out the role of others, especially Henrietta Maria

**Christopher Durston, *Charles I* (Routledge, 1998)**
A good account of Charles's reign

**Mark Kishlansky, *Charles I* (Allen Lane, 2014)**
A short account of Charles's life which explains his actions from his own viewpoint

Roger Lockyer, *Buckingham: The Life and Political Career of George Villiers, First Duke of Buckingham* (Longman, 1981)
This is a sympathetic biography of a man who is often criticised by historians

Kevin Sharpe, *The Personal Rule of Charles I* (Yale University Press, 1992)
A long and detailed look at the Personal Rule that is well worth dipping into, especially for the summary of the first years of the reign and the sections on the Church and foreign policy

## Chapter 4

John Adamson, *The Noble Revolt* (Weidenfeld & Nicolson, 2007)
Long and detailed but gives an interesting, alternative perspective on the events of 1640–2, focusing particularly on the role of the Junto

Michael Braddick, *God's Fury, England's Fire* (Penguin, 2008)
Looks particularly at the impact of popular protest, in a gripping narrative

R. Cust and A. Hughes, editors, *Conflict in Early Stuart England, Studies in Religion and Politics 1603–42* (Longman, 1989)
A very useful collection of post-revisionist essays

Ann Hughes, *The Causes of the English Civil War* (Palgrave, 1998)
Gives an excellent summary of the period leading up to the civil war

## Chapter 5

Ian Gentles, *The English Revolution and the Wars in the Three Kingdoms 1638–1652* (Pearson, 2007)
A balanced picture of radicalism within the army

Clive Holmes, *Why Was Charles I Executed?* (Continuum, 2007)
Poses and answers eight key questions relating to the trial and execution

Jason McElligott and David L. Smith, editors, *Royalists and Royalism during the English Civil Wars* (Cambridge University Press, 2011)
The informed reflections of a number of leading authorities on the fate of the royalist cause in the 1640s

Diane Purkiss, *The English Civil War: A People's History* (Harper Perennial, 2006)
As its sub-title suggests, a vivid portrait gallery of the ordinary and not so ordinary men and women who experienced the turbulent times

John Rees, *The Levellers' Revolution: Radical Political Organisation in England, 1640–1650* (Verso, 2017)
A sympathetic study which seeks to understand the movement in its own contemporary terms

David Underdown, *Pride's Purge: Politics in the Puritan Revolution* (Oxford University Press, 1971)
Remains the definitive study of a key event and its repercussions

Austin Woolrych, *Soldiers and Statesmen: The General Council of the Army and its Debates, 1647–48* (Oxford University Press, 1987)
Masterly study of the relations between Parliament, the king, the New Model Army and the Levellers

Blair Worden, *The English Civil Wars 1640–60* (Weidenfeld & Nicolson, 2009)
A brilliantly concise study of the causes and course of the civil wars

## Chapter 6

Micheál Ó Siochrú, *God's Executioner: Oliver Cromwell and the Conquest of Ireland* (Faber & Faber, 2009)
While being a strongly critical account of Cromwell in Ireland, the book endeavours to explain his campaigns against the backdrop of the politics and religion of the times

Henry Reece, *The Army in Cromwellian England, 1649–1660* (Oxford University Press, 2014)
Provides valuable insights into the structure and character of the Cromwellian army during the Interregnum

Tom Reilly, *Cromwell was Framed: Cromwell and the Conquest of Ireland 1649* (Chronos Books, 2014)
As its striking title suggests, a revisionist treatment offering a sympathetic study of Cromwell in Ireland

Trevor Royle, *Civil War: The Wars of the Three Kingdoms* (Abacus, 2005)
A detailed narrative account of the three civil wars

Blair Worden, *The Rump Parliament* (Cambridge, 1974)
Acknowledged as still the most authoritative account of the Rump and its significance

## Chapter 7

Christopher Durston, *Cromwell's Major Generals: Godly Government During the English Revolution* (Manchester University Press, 2001)
A sympathetic study of a group who have often had a bad press

Peter Gaunt, *Oliver Cromwell* (Blackwell, 1999)
An accessible biography, written with students in mind

Christopher Hill, *God's Englishman: Oliver Cromwell and the English Revolution* (Penguin, 1990)
A classic Marxist interpretation of Cromwell as religious zealot and bourgeois revolutionary

Patrick Little, editor, *Oliver Cromwell, New Perspectives* (Palgrave Macmillan, 2009)
As its title suggests, a set of revisionist essays covering major aspects of Cromwell's career

David L. Smith, editor, *Cromwell and the Interregnum* (Blackwell, 2003)
A highly important set of essays by eight leading authorities in the field

Blair Worden, *God's Instruments: Political Conduct in the England of Oliver Cromwell* (Oxford University Press, 2012)
Examines the interplay of politics and religion during the civil war and Interregnum

# Chapter 8

Gerald Aylmer, *Rebellion or Revolution?* (Oxford University Press, 1990)
A discussion of the character of the English Revolution by one of the outstanding analysts of the period

Ronald Hutton, *The Restoration: A Political and Religious History of England and Wales, 1658–1667* (Oxford University Press, 1985)
An important work, whose early chapters cover the period between Oliver Cromwell's death and the return of Charles II

Paul Lay, *Providence Lost: The Rise and Fall of Cromwell's Protectorate* (Head of Zeus, 2020)
Entertainingly written analysis of the Protectorate offering new insights into the characters and issues of the time with Oliver Cromwell obviously figuring largely

R.C. Richardson, *The Debate on the English Revolution* (Methuen, 1977)
The book's later chapters cover many of the conflicting interpretations among modern historians

David Underdown, *Royalist Conspiracy in England* (Oxford University Press, 1960)
Details the attempts of the royalists to challenge the Protectorate

# Index